Utilitarianism and beyond

Utilitarianism and beyond

Edited by

Amartya Sen and Bernard Williams

CAMBRIDGE UNIVERSITY PRESS

Cambridge

London   New York   New Rochelle   Melbourne   Sydney

EDITIONS DE
LA MAISON DES SCIENCES DE L'HOMME
Paris

Published by the Press Syndicate of the University of Cambridge
The Pitt Building, Trumpington Street, Cambridge CB2 1RP
32 East 57th Street, New York, NY 10022, USA
296 Beaconsfield Parade, Middle Park, Melbourne 3206, Australia

and Editions de la Maison des Sciences de l'Homme, 54 Boulevard Raspail, 75270
Paris Cedex 06

First published 1982

Printed in Great Britain at the University Press, Cambridge

Library of Congress catalogue card number: 81–17981

British Library Cataloguing in Publication Data

Utilitarianism and beyond.
1. Utilitarianism–Addresses, essays, lectures
I. Sen, Amartya   II. Williams, Bernard
171'.5   B843

ISBN 0 521 24296 7 hard covers
ISBN 0 521 28771 5 paperback

Contents

Preface   vii

Introduction   1

1 R. M. HARE
   Ethical theory and utilitarianism   23

2 JOHN C. HARSANYI
   Morality and the theory of rational behaviour   39

3 J. A. MIRRLEES
   The economic uses of utilitarianism   63

4 PETER J. HAMMOND
   Utilitarianism, uncertainty and information   85

5 T. M. SCANLON
   Contractualism and utilitarianism   103

6 CHARLES TAYLOR
   The diversity of goods   129

7 STUART HAMPSHIRE
   Morality and convention   145

8 JOHN RAWLS
   Social unity and primary goods   159

9 FRANK HAHN
   On some difficulties of the utilitarian economist   187

10 PARTHA DASGUPTA
   Utilitarianism, information and rights   199

11 JON ELSTER
   Sour grapes – utilitarianism and the genesis of wants   219

12 ISAAC LEVI
    Liberty and welfare   239

13 FREDERIC SCHICK
    Under which descriptions?   251

14 AMY GUTMANN
    What's the use of going to school?   261

    Bibliography   279

Preface

These papers discuss utilitarianism, criticisms of it, and possible alternatives to it, and so raise issues which concern not only moral and political philosophy, but also economics and the theory of social choice. Some contributors to this collection are primarily philosophers, while others are primarily economists, and we hope that comparison of their various outlooks and argumentative styles will itself contribute to understanding of these issues.

The papers, with two exceptions, have been specially written for this volume and appear here for the first time. The exceptions are the papers of Hare and Harsanyi, which we have included because we thought it useful to offer, as a background to a collection which is largely, but not exclusively, critical of utilitarianism, two well-known and distinguished modern statements which offer arguments for the utilitarian outlook. We are grateful to these authors for permission to reprint, and to all our contributors for their papers.

Our own contribution takes the form of an Introduction, in which we do not try to summarise the papers, but rather to argue for our own opinions. A good deal of our discussion is explicitly directed to points raised in the papers, but we have also chosen to pursue one or two considerations which seem to us interesting but which happen not to be discussed elsewhere in the volume.

References to the literature which are given in the course of the Introduction and the papers are presented in the standard abbreviated form of an author's name and a date: full details will be found in the consolidated bibliography at the end of the book. We are grateful to Mark Sacks for assistance in preparing it.

A.K.S.
B.A.O.W.

Introduction

Arguments for and against utilitarianism are both forcefully presented in the papers in this volume. Not all the authors represented here would want to go 'beyond' utilitarianism at all, while those (the majority) who are critical of utilitarianism differ about the direction in which they would like to proceed. Some – such as Hahn and Dasgupta – have pointed to specific difficulties with utilitarianism and these would require relaxing the uncompromising narrowness of the utilitarian vision, but possibly not a rejection of the entire approach. Others – such as Hampshire and Taylor – have argued for a totally different route – less ambitious in scope, not tied to consequential analysis, nor to utility itself, and without the insistence on impersonality which characterises utilitarianism (along with some other outlooks).

The title of this collection, *Utilitarianism and beyond,* perhaps most naturally implies an attempt to solve in some more refined, comprehensive or otherwise satisfactory way problems to which utilitarianism has offered only partial or unsatisfactory solutions. But this implication is to some extent misleading, since critics such as Hampshire and Taylor would insist that the questions which utilitarianism tries to answer are not proper questions, or not questions which require that kind of answer. For such critics, the appropriate slogan might rather be 'Utilitarianism and not so far'. They will feel that utilitarianism represents an attempt to do too much, to give too comprehensive and extensive an answer to problems of personal or public choice, and that it is not simply utilitarianism that is at fault, but any theory which displays that degree of ambition.

Personal morality and a unique criterion

Utilitarianism has always been discussed, and is discussed in this collection, in two different roles: on the one hand as a theory of personal morality, and on the other as a theory of public choice,[1] or of the criteria

[1] The modern form of which owes much to the pioneering work of Arrow: see Arrow 1951.

1

applicable to public policy. Many writings on utilitarian theory are neutral between these two applications, and the questions that they raise certainly overlap. However, there are also some significant differences between them, and these affect the question that has just been raised, whether a theory of similar scope to utilitarianism is even needed.

In the theory of personal morality or rationality no large question is being begged if one merely assumes the individual agent to be deciding, quite often, what is the right thing to do, and deciding it, at least sometimes, in the light of moral considerations. A large question is being begged, however, if one assumes that the agent is required in rationality to subject all those decisions to one criterion of decision, and it is still being begged if one assumes that rationality requires that any other criteria of decision must themselves be justified by one over-riding principle. Argument is needed to show why a rational agent should not make his decisions in an 'intuitionist' way (where that is taken in the sense recently made current by Rawls, in which it carries a methodological and not an epistemological implication). He or she may have a number of values or principles, which may, to various degrees and in various ways, be incommensurable with one another: this possibility is discussed by Taylor in his article. It remains to be shown why, for an individual, utilitarianism or any other ethical theory of similar generality, is even necessary.

Public choice and unique sovereignty

In the public case, however, there is a question which can be begged even one stage further back than in the individual case. The individual agent can be allowed without much controversy to be deciding within a certain time span what it is right for him to do – though we do not, in saying that, have to commit ourselves to the view that rationality requires him to deliberate indefinitely into his future. But in the public case, it is already to make some substantive political assumptions to suppose that there is or should be one sovereign decision centre to determine what is right, even within a limited time span, for the society as a whole.

Utilitarianism is more than what has been called 'welfarism',[2] and offers not merely a way of answering questions of the form 'how is society going?', but also a criterion of public action. It therefore must assume a public agent, some supreme body which chooses general states of affairs for the society as a whole. In this public connexion, the same question will anyway arise as in the private connexion: granted such an agency, does it have to use some one criterion of action? That question, indeed, may

[2] See Sen 1979b. The distinctions involved here are considered further below, pp. 3–4.

collect answers in the public case more favourable to general theory than in the private case, because the notion of *public rationality,* as applied to a complex, modern, and open society, plausibly demands general and explicable rules in a way that personal rationality, in itself, need not. (The notions of 'rationality' with which utilitarians, in particular, support their demands for general theory, should be seen, in fact, not as purely abstract requirements, but as expressing the forms of public justification appropriate to a certain kind of social order.)

In the public case, however, there is a different, and prior, question – whether there should be any one supreme agent at all. Only the most primitive theories of sovereignty will suppose that it is a conceptual necessity of the state that there should be such a centre of decision; the existence of a state is compatible with a degree of decentralisation which means that no agency occupies the role that the self occupies in personal decision. In opposition to the monism of utilitarianism and of its similarly shaped alternatives, there can be a pluralism, in the social case, not only of values but also of agency. (Issues involved in the utilitarian conception of the sovereign chooser get some attention from Dasgupta in his paper.)

Some utilitarians will suggest that there is no need to assume a public agency of this kind. It may rather be that the utilitarian criterion will itself justify pluralist, decentralised, perhaps even traditionalist, social arrangements. In particular, the resources of *indirect* utilitarianism, familiar in connexion with personal morality, can be used in the public case. At this point the questions raised by the two different applications of utilitarianism, public and personal, tend to come together again, since one question that presses heavily on indirect utilitarianism as applied to personal morality, namely the question of the *location* of the ultimately utilitarian justification of non-utilitarian moral rules or dispositions, is already a question about society. We shall come back later in this Introduction to problems faced in this connexion by indirect utilitarianism.

Welfarism and consequentialism

Let it be assumed that a theory of this very ambitious scope is needed. What, in particular, is utilitarianism? We have already implicitly referred to the point that it can be regarded as the intersection between two different kinds of theory. One is a theory of the correct way to assess or assign value to states of affairs, and it claims that the correct basis of assessment is welfare, satisfaction, or people getting what they prefer. This theory, one component of utilitarianism, has been called *welfarism.* The other component is a theory of correct action, which claims that actions are to be chosen on the basis of the states of affairs which are their consequences: this has been called *consequentialism*.[3] Utilitarianism, in its central forms, recommends a choice of actions on the basis of consequences, and an assessment of consequences in terms of welfare. Utilitarianism is thus a species of *welfarist consequentalism* – that particular form of it which requires simply *adding up* individual welfares or utilities to assess the consequences, a property that is sometimes called *sum-ranking*.[4] This, at least, is an account of its *direct* forms; it would need some slight modification to accommodate the indirect forms to which we referred in the last paragraph.

Information and persons

A moral principle can be viewed as a requirement to exclude the use of certain types of information in making moral judgements, and utilitarianism imposes, by implication, severe informational constraints.[5] These constraints rule out a great deal of information from being taken into consideration in arriving at moral judgements. This amount to taking, in the context of moral evaluation, a remarkably narrow view of being a *person*.

Essentially, utilitarianism sees persons as locations of their respective utilities – as the sites at which such activities as desiring and having pleasure and pain take place. Once note has been taken of the person's utility, utilitarianism has no further direct interest in any information about him.[6] This view of man is a common feature of different variants of utilitarianism, including the indirect forms such as rule utilitarianism, disposition utilitarianism, etc., since no matter what is taken to be the relevant choice variable, the judgements of states of affairs, conduct, institutions, etc., are all ultimately based exclusively on the amounts of utility and disutility generated. Persons do not count as individuals in this any more than individual petrol tanks do in the analysis of the national consumption of petroleum.

Utilitarianism is the combination, as has just been said, of welfarism, sum-ranking and consequentialism, and each of these components contributes to this narrow view of a person. By virtue of welfarism, a state of

---

[3] This useful term seems to have been introduced by G. E. M. Anscombe: see Anscombe 1958.

[4] A case of welfarist consequentialism that does not use sum-ranking is given by the utility-based interpretation of the Rawlsian Difference Principle, commonly used in economics, in which actions are judged entirely in terms of consequences, and consequences entirely in terms of the welfare level of the worst-off person (see, for example, Phelps 1973). For different axiomisations of sum-ranking, see: d'Aspremont and Gevers 1977; Deschamps and Gevers 1978; Maskin 1978; Roberts 1980b.

[5] For investigation of the informational aspect, see Sen 1977a.

[6] Rawls' paper in this volume goes into this question in some depth.

affairs is judged exclusively on the basis of utility information related to that state. This reduces the collection of diverse information about the n persons in that state into n bits of utility, with the totality of relevant information being given by an n-vector of utilities.

Next, sum-ranking merges the utility bits together as one total lump, losing in the process both the identity of the individuals as well as their separateness. The distributional characteristics of the utility vector are also consequently lost. By now persons as persons have dropped fully out of the assessment of states of affairs.[7]

Next, consequentialism carries this informational constraint from judgements of states to moral assessment of all variables – actions, rules, institutions, etc. – since everything is judged ultimately by the goodness of states of affairs. For example, in judging an action there is no intrinsic interest at all in the non-utility characteristics either of those who take the action, or of those who are affected by it. In judging an action there is no need to know who is doing what to whom so long as the impact of these actions – direct and indirect – on the impersonal sum of utilities is known.

This drastic obliteration of usable information causes some casualties. Not all of them are peculiar to utilitarianism. The neglect of a person's attachments and ties is shared by utilitarianism with Kantianism,[8] and this informational lacuna raises questions a good deal deeper than questioning just utilitarianism. Hampshire's paper in this volume bears on this wider issue.

More specific to utilitarianism, and closely related to its consequentialist structure, is the neglect of a person's *autonomy*. So – to a great extent – is the lack of interest in a person's integrity. These questions have been discussed elsewhere.[9] The indifference to the separateness and identity of individuals, and consequently to their aims, plans and ambitions, and to the importance of their agency and actions, contributes to this neglect.

Utility and moral importance

The difficulty does not arise from a person's utility being independent of his attachment, ties, aims, plans, agency, etc., and indeed it typically will not be independent of these things. The issue concerns not merely *whether* these things are important but also *how* important they are and *why* so. Utilitarianism regards them as worthless in themselves and valuable only

---

[7] This applies to both 'classical' and 'average' utilitarianism. The latter divides the total utility by the number of people, but that obviously does not restore the lost information.
[8] On this issue see Williams 1976a.
[9] See Williams 1973 and 1976b.

to the extent of their effects on utility. They are not any more important than what happens to be caught in the impersonal metric of utility.

Two types of objections may be raised about measuring importance through utility. First, even if it is accepted that for something to be important it must be desired by someone (or must give pleasure or reduce pain, i.e. in some sense yield utility), it may be questioned whether the *metric* of utility provides the appropriate measure. There is a substantial difference between its being a necessary condition for something to be valuable that it be desired by someone (i.e. utility being an 'admission condition' of moral importance), and equating the importance of a thing with the *extent* of the desire for it or with the pleasure generated by it (i.e. utility being the measure of importance). If the first idea is accepted but not the second, it is possible to attach greater importance to the utility generated in, say, 'self-regarding' activities than in 'other-regarding' activities, or to value more highly 'personal preference' than 'external preference'.[10] This involves a rejection of welfarism, and thus *a fortiori* of utilitarianism, even though some very special role is still given to utility in moral judgement.

One difficulty with the view which accepts merely the admission condition is the 'discontinuity' it generates. Something may remain highly valuable independently of the size of the utility associated with it as long as the utility value is positive – however tiny – but if the utility value falls from the infinitesimal to zero, then that thing suddenly drops from being highly valuable to being totally valueless.[11]

A second type of objection goes deeper, claiming that something can be valuable even if it is not desired by anyone. A person may not have the courage to desire freedom under a severely oppressive régime,[12] or may not have the wits to do so because of lack of experience, or social conditioning. Further, a person's experience may affect what he actually desires – Elster's paper takes up this issue. Also, a 'fair deal' being given to a person may be important even if he does not, specifically, desire it.

Rights

One particular area in which the measurement of moral importance through utility is especially questionable is that of rights. Mr *A* may not wish to read a book but desire even more strongly that Ms *B* should not read it. But this need not by itself make the latter desire morally more

---

[10] Cf. Dworkin 1977.

[11] It is possible to give utility a role that is stronger than an admission condition but weaker than what welfarism gives: e.g. the class of 'utility-supported moralities' (see Sen 1981).

[12] This question has been discussed by Isaiah Berlin: see Berlin 1969, pp. 139–40.

important than the former. The former desire relates to A's own reading activity on which he may be taken to have a right, while the latter desire deals with a field outside it, viz., B's reading activity, and furthermore it may go counter to B's exercising *her* rights. This type of right-based consideration not merely goes against utilitarianism and welfarism, but can be inconsistent even with Pareto optimality – perhaps the mildest utility-based condition and the most widely used welfare criterion in economics.[13]

There are two distinct issues related to this 'impossibility of the Paretian liberal' that figure in the contributions to this volume. There is, first, the problem that, if people are given the right to decide certain things about their own life, then the outcome need not be Pareto optimal in cases of this kind. Levi's paper analyses how Pareto optimality might nevertheless come about under certain types of belief-based behaviour.

The second issue concerns the moral importance of Pareto optimality. If utility is the only thing of value and the only scale of value, then clearly Pareto optimality must be important. If, however, rights are valuable in themselves, or – alternatively – influence the moral value of utility (e.g. increasing the importance of Mr A's desire for what he should read and reducing the importance of his desire for what Ms B should read), then Pareto optimality, which deals only with the crude calculus of utility, may well need rejection. Mirrlees accepts part of the point and proposes 'ignoring some external effects' when, say, A 'could just decide not to be unhappy' about B's reading, and endorses a 'rather elastic sense of utility that makes utilitarianism an acceptable doctrine' p. 83. Hammond goes further, and shows how preference-based valuation may have to be revised to take account of issues of rights, among other considerations. While he chooses to call the redefined value also 'utility', he explains that it 'may bear little relation to individual preferences'.

The materials of utilitarianism

Hammond's procedure obviously raises the question of how far it is reasonable to revise the definition of utilitarianism, for instance by re-defining 'utility', and so to keep the old name for a theory which is now substantially different, in particular by having a richer informational input. How far does one have to go, and in what directions, to get 'beyond' utilitarianism? In the end, this must be a question of the basic point and motivation of the utilitarian outlook.

In this connexion, it is important to consider some ways in which

[13] For a formal analysis and informal discussion of this conflict, see Sen 1970b, 1976, and 1979a.

utilities are treated by theories which on any current understanding of the term are utilitarian. The most elementary, intuitive, recommendation for the utilitarian approach presumably lies in the thought that it must be sensible to bring about what people want. As Scanlon argues in his paper, this thought seems to offer an account both of the subject matter of morality and of its motivations.

The utilitarian handling of 'what people want', however, is not as simple, nor yet as intuitively obvious, as that elementary thought implies. We shall consider three devices which, in various degrees, are character-istic of the treatment, in utilitarian theories, of desires or preferences. The first, which we shall call *reduction*, is essential to all utilitarian theories; the second, which we label *idealisation*, is used in varying degrees by different utilitarian theorists; the third, *abstraction*, raises problems par-ticularly for indirect utilitarianism.

Reduction

Reduction is the device of regarding all interests, ideals, aspirations, and desires as on the same level, and all representable as preferences, of different degrees of intensity, perhaps, but otherwise to be treated alike. This is brought out in a marked way in Hare's article, which starts from the equality of consideration for *interests* and then extends this to preferences in general, including ideals among such preferences. There may be some purposes of psychological explanation or interpretation to which this degree of assimilation is appropriate, but it is a matter of profound disagreement between utilitarians and their critics whether it is appropriate to the context of justification, criticism and practical deliber-ation. This is for at least two reasons. One is to be found in the moral and other concepts to which interests, desires, etc., are variously linked. A moral outlook which uses the notion of *rights*, for instance, will relate these differently to some at least of the person's interests than it will to what are merely his or her desires. We have already touched on this point in considering the paradox of the Paretian Liberal, and the loss of informa-tion about persons' situations that is entailed by utilitarianism and other utility-based approaches.

Second, the agent's own critical and practical relation to motivations of different kinds or types is itself different. In a terminology which some have found useful,[14] the agent's application of second-order preferences to these various kinds of motivation will be different. Anyone who is sane can criticise, reject, or forgo some of his preferences when they are merely

[14] See Frankfurt 1971; Sen 1974; Jeffery 1974; Körner 1976; Hirschman 1982.

what everyone calls 'preferences', but a critique of one's own ideals (which are themselves, in one aspect, second-order preferences) raises much wider questions, some of them very puzzling. Here a substantial theory is needed about the psychological reality of utilitarianism, and a substantial question is raised about the concept of rationality that it presupposes.

Idealisation

While utilitarianism is exceptionally generous about what it is prepared to count as a preference, at the same time it can be rather demanding about the preferences that it allows to count. Thus, on Hare's view, the correct principle should be based not on actual preferences of agents, but on their 'perfectly prudent preferences' – what someone would desire if fully informed and unconfused. Harsanyi and Mirrlees take a similar position. Harsanyi accepts 'the important philosophical principle' of *preference autonomy* to the effect that 'in deciding what is good and what is bad for an individual, the ultimate criterion can only be his wants and his own preferences', but this has to allow for the possibility that 'his own preferences at some deeper level are inconsistent with what he is now trying to achieve'. 'All we have to do,' Harsanyi says, 'is to distinguish between a person's manifest preferences and his true preferences', where his 'true' preferences are those that 'he *would* [Harsanyi's emphasis] have if he had all the relevant information, always reasoned with the greatest possible care, and were in a state of mind most conducive to rational choice' (p. 55).

Harsanyi indeed goes further than this in the 'correction' of preferences. From the choice-based utilities which have been already purged of 'irrational preferences', he proceeds to 'exclude all antisocial preferences, such as sadism, envy, resentment, and malice' (p. 56). There is quite a substantial mathematical problem in retaining the scaling of utility after all these 'antisocial preferences' have been taken out, since the scaling proceeds on consistency, which is not easy to retain when one integrated set of preferences is purged of elements of malice, resentment, etc. But be that as it may, there are important questions both about the motivation of such steps, and, relatedly, about what is to count as an 'antisocial' preference. Presumably they do not include, for instance, all preferences the satisfaction of which will as a matter of fact exclude the satisfaction of others, as in competition. Do they include only those preferences which refer, negatively, to other preferences? That condition would certainly need some further refinement, since it would apply to a wide range of moral attitudes, including, incidentally, Harsanyi's own objection to envy, etc. In fact, however, the motivation for these exclusions seems to be a simple moral one, not to be captured by any purely formal constraint on the preferences in question, and rests on the consideration that 'the fundamental basis of all our moral commitments to other people is a general goodwill and human sympathy' (p. 56).

In this version, then, idealisation extends very far, and the conception that all that matters to morality is impartial benevolence determines not only the form of the moral theory, but also, to some extent, the preferences that it is prepared even to count.

Any degree of idealisation, even those less radical than this, such as those suggested by Hare and by Mirrlees, which require only the correction of preferences to what would be preferred under conditions of reflection and improved information, still of course leave one with the fact that a 'true' preference is not necessarily an actual preference at all. This in itself raises a problem in utilitarian terms. How should allowance be made for the fact that actual preferences will not be 'true' preferences? (This is one of the questions discussed in Schick's paper.) If people do not, in fact, get round to actually wanting what, in this sense, it would be rational for them to want, people may always be actually unsatisfied by the results of the correct policy, and this is a large step from what was promised in the intuitive justification of utilitarianism. There is, in fact, as this point illustrates, a conflict in spirit between reduction and idealisation: the simplifications of reduction are the product of the hard-headed desire to take as they come the world and the wants that it contains, while idealisation starts already to adjust them towards what they might better be.

These exclusions from the input, moreover, may go beyond preferences which are 'irrational' for the individual agent, as in the minimal degree of idealisation, and even beyond the anti-social desires such as malice and envy, excluded on the more ambitious versions. It can be argued that they should extend to all preferences which are not consistent with utilitarianism itself, or even to all preferences which, as a matter of fact, are the product of outlooks other than utilitarianism.[15] Most utilitarians regard non-utilitarian outlooks as confused. Some writers indeed associate utilitarianism intimately with the very definition of morality. Thus Harsanyi, who writes '[an agent's] moral preferences . . . will by definition always assign the same weight to all individuals' interests, including his own' (p. 47), where 'interests', it seems clear, stands generally for preferences. If anti-utilitarian theories or moralities are the product of not thinking clearly enough (about the nature of morality), and if those preferences are to be discounted which are based on confused thinking, no preference

[15] This is a traditional issue in utilitarianism. For discussion in relation to John Stuart Mill, see Wollheim 1973.

which flows from non-utilitarian thoughts will, on this showing, be allowed to count.

Preferences

The techniques of reduction and idealisation also give rise to a deep question about the whole basis of modern utilitarian theory as lying in *preferences*. This question concerns not only the correct formulation of utilitarianism, but its moral plausibility.

It is useful to contrast the different views of utility adopted in the alternative defences of utilitarianism provided by Hare, Harsanyi and Mirrlees. The contrasts involve both the definitions of utility as well as what gives utility its alleged moral force. Hare's view of utility is entirely in line with the utilitarian tradition of viewing utility in terms of desires and their fulfilment. While this differs from the Benthamite description of utility in terms of pleasure and pain, the desire-based approach represents a long-standing tradition. It is such a reference to desires which – particularly when they are assimilated to interests – underlies the intuitive justification of utilitarianism referred to earlier. There is nothing peculiar about Hare's characterisation of utility as such, and in this respect he has provided new arguments for defending an old tradition rather than reformulating the content of utilitarianism.

Choice and valuation

Harsanyi and Mirrlees, however, like many other contemporary writers, depart from the older utilitarian traditions and define utility in terms of *choice*. The force of these departures is somewhat tempered by certain *empirical* assumptions made about how people do, in fact, choose. It is fair to say that despite defining utility entirely through choice, Harsanyi and Mirrlees both adopt a *dual* characterisation of utility, reflecting choice characteristics, on the one hand, and what we may call content characteristics, on the other. Their respective views of both choice characteristics and content characteristics differ, but both use a *dual* characterisation of utility, which is important for their respective analyses of the moral force of utilitarianism. The moral force rests partly on the respective empirical readings of the world.

For Harsanyi, utility reflects choice, with the cardinalisation derived from choosing in situations of uncertainty, and at the same time the utility indicators provide 'measures for the relative personal importance [the agent] assigns to various economic (and non-economic) alternatives' (p. 53). For Mirrlees utility reflects choice, with the cardinalisation obtained from 'separability' of choice, and at the same time utility also reflects each person's well-being. Since Mirrlees also insists that it is 'convenient to let the term "utility" describe the well-being rather than the conception of it' (p. 64), he is led to the position that 'it is not right to let utility rest entirely on individual tastes' (p. 69).

What emerges is, once more, some doctoring or idealisation of choice-based utility – on the ground that 'it cannot be wrong in principle to try to get someone to do what would be better for him even though he does not recognise it' – with the hope that 'with full understanding, he would come to accept the rightness of the altered utility function, or, rather, of the underlying preferences' (p. 69).[16] So Mirrlees' notion of utility both reflects choice 'with full understanding' and the 'well-being' of the person concerned.

There is by now a well-established tradition in modern economics of defining utility entirely in terms of choice, and at the same time insisting that it must also have a particular content in terms of what is maximised. The choice-based characterisation comes from explicit definition (e.g. of 'revealed preferences'),[17] while the content characterisation, usually in the form of maximising the person's 'self-interest', or 'well-being', is either introduced through *defining* self-interest or well-being that way (and is thus used in a tautologous form), or through an explicit or implicit empirical assumption about how people do choose (or would choose under some 'ideal' circumstances).[18] The ambiguity of the term 'preference' facilitates this dual picture of utility, since linguistic convention seems to permit the treatment of 'preferring' as choosing as well as taking what a person (really) 'prefers' as what would make him better off. In welfare-economic arguments it is not unconventional to appeal to both characteristics, even though this involves a strong empirical assumption about how people do choose (or would choose under some 'ideal' conditions) – an assumption for which the empirical evidence is, to say the least, inconclusive.

When one has separated out these two types of characteristics, one must ask what kind of moral force the choice characteristics, in themselves, provide to utility (assuming that utility is defined entirely in terms of choice). Is the mere fact that someone chooses something a source of value for the thing chosen? It is natural to think of choosing and valuing as related, but it is hard to avoid the suspicion that, in this representation, the direction of the linkage has been inverted. It is not by any means unreasonable to respond to the question: 'What should I choose?', by answering,

[16] Harsanyi discusses similar corrections, pp. 55–6.
[17] Discussed originally by Paul Samuelson: see Samuelson 1938.
[18] On this see Sen 1977b; Broome 1978a; Hahn and Hollis 1979.

'Whatever is most valuable'. But to respond to the question, 'What is most valuable?', or even 'What is most valuable to me?', by answering, 'Whatever I would choose', would seem to remove the content from the notion of valuing, even when qualifications are added to the supposed choice in the form of 'under ideal conditions' or 'with full understanding'. Basing choice on valuation is cogent in a way that basing valuation on choice is not.

The derivation of importance of the thing chosen from the fact of choice must not be confused with regarding the ability of people to choose as important in itself. 'Autonomy' as a value is concerned with the latter, but it belongs to an approach altogether different from utilitarianism, and is concerned with valuing the *capability to choose* rather than valuing *the thing chosen*. Valuing autonomy works directly in favour of supporting choice, and not via enhancing the value of the *object* of choice through the increase in a utility-giving property which is defined in terms of choice.

In Harsanyi's case, the subtraction of 'anti-social' preferences, which has already been discussed, seems to reveal a considerable scepticism about the force of simply choice-based utility, as opposed to the desirable content of choices, even though the framework he offers is based on choice, in the form of 'as if' uncertainty about who is going to be whom. The force of choice seems somewhat stronger in Mirrlees's framework and even the permitted idealisations are justified through the hypothesis of what would be chosen 'with full understanding'. However, it is difficult to determine whether choice is acting as the basis of valuation, or whether one is being advised to choose what is valued. At an early stage of the argument it is explained that 'one can imagine inviting the person to consider what he would choose' under certain conditions, and 'in this way one can hope to assign utility to the consumption of alternative selves in different states' (p. 66). But later the relation is turned around, after noting that 'for any one of the individuals the sum of his utilities describes his considered preferences regarding the lives of his alternative selves', and 'therefore in choosing among outcomes for himself alone, i.e. with outcomes the same for everyone else, he ought to choose the pattern of outcomes with greatest total utility' (p. 70).[19] It could certainly be the

---

[19] Giving total utility the role of *describing* choice as well as *justifying* it leads to some ambiguity in the assessment of arguments based on other definitions of utility. This can be seen in Mirrlees' comments on the argument that a person may be right in not maximising the sum-total of his utility over his life time irrespective of the distribution of utility over time. The definition of utility used in that argument was in terms of pleasure and pain, or desire-fulfilment at each period. Mirrlees remarks that if this 'form of argument were applied' to the framework used by Mirrlees, then that moral intuition would present 'itself as a hair-shirt morality in conflict with the individual's preferences' (p. 71). But in fact if the person was inclined not to maximise the pleasure-sum over his life time but some other magnitude, then the new choice will also reflect maximisation of 'total utility' under the choice-based definition of utility.

case that one ought to choose what one does choose, but such a claim will, of course, need justification.

In fact, it is quite clear that Mirrlees does rely quite substantially on the content of choice, and the moral appeal of promoting well-being. So the empirical assumptions on which the identification works are important for his moral system, as indeed are other empirical assumptions invoked in the process of establishing his claims, to wit, a strong version of 'separability' holding in one's 'preference' (i.e. in one's choices *as well as* in characterisations of well-being), and what Mirrlees calls 'isomorphy' of preferences. Thus the conflict between different notions of well-being, different views of interests of persons, etc., are not resolved by the adoption of the choice perspective on utility.[20]

Abstraction

The techniques of reduction and idealisation which we have discussed concern the content of the information which supposedly forms the input to the welfarist assessment. The third device, *abstraction*, concerns the *location* of that information. There is a strong tendency in the utilitarian tradition (one very clearly expressed in the early and continuing fiction of the ideal observer, to which Harsanyi refers) that this information is transcendental to the social world to which it refers, and is not actually present in that world at all. But this is a fiction. If this information is to exist it must exist somewhere, and, if it is to contain both the degree of detail and the social-scientific robustness that utilitarian pretensions require of it, it must be sustained by a substantial and strategically placed research effort. The mere existence of such information and hence of such an effort in any concrete social sense requires some institutions rather than others, and is not compatible with any arbitrary form either of social organisation or of public consciousness. In particular, there is no reason at all to suppose that it is compatible with traditionalist arrangements.

The requirements of the process of idealisation, just discussed, lend further weight to the same point. If the assumptions about the 'true' preferences of citizens are not simply dogmatic, something will have to be known – and that implies, presumably, found out – about true preferences, and that will in turn require institutions which will themselves form and alter preferences. Any institutionalised or concretely realised

---

[20] It will not help with the further deep problems that arise when one considers what kinds of preference should be allowed to count in comparing people's 'all-in welfare' or 'overall success', with regard, for instance, to the problem of expensive tastes. Dworkin has powerfully argued that a notion such as 'reasonable regret' is required here – a notion which, he claims, must *already* involve ideas of fairness. See Dworkin 1981.

processes of social distribution and policy will modify preferences, as Elster emphasises in his paper. *Abstraction* is the use of the assumption that the preferences on which utilitarianism operates are given – at least for all important purposes – independently of the processes of the utilitarian running of society itself. This assumption seems less plausible as soon as one is prepared to be reminded that utilitarianism needs *some* embodiment, and that a utilitarian society is not simply a society which happens to satisfy utilitarian requirements, but a society which is run in accordance with these requirements.

Two-level theories

This very basic consideration casts grave doubts on the efficacy of indirect versions of utilitarianism, and this point naturally[21] applies as much to utilitarianism as a personal morality as it does to public policy applications of such theories. Hare's article, which presents an authoritative version of indirect utilitarianism, explores two levels of moral thought, at one of which the agent deploys very simple principles which are instilled in childhood, but which are themselves selected, criticised, etc., by reflection at a second level of (effectively) utilitarian thought. These first principles are not merely rules of thumb: they are internalised as dispositions to action, and are departed from only with the 'greatest repugnance', while their violation by others elicits 'the highest indignation'. So far the requirement would seem to be for principles which have some meaning for the agent, which structure his or her view of the world and are something in which he or she believes. They would naturally be expected to express or be associated with those 'ideals' for human life and society to which Hare also refers. Yet they have to coexist with utilitarian reflections which justify those principles as devices, to deal with problems of 'practical moral thinking especially under conditions of stress', and which also (under what we have called 'reduction') regard those ideals as just one set of 'desires' or 'likings' among others. How and where do these two bodies of thought coexist?

In Hare's article, as more generally in the utilitarian tradition, there are suggestions of two different (though certainly compatible) answers to this question. One separates the two sorts of thoughts by time and circumstances: on this showing, second level utilitarian thought is appropriate to 'a cool hour' when there is 'time for unlimited investigation of the facts' and 'no special pleading'. On the other model, the distinction is rather between persons: on the one side, 'the ordinary man, whose principles are

---

[21] See above, p. 3.

not designed to cope with such cases', and, on the other, people of a more philosophical or enquiring bent who may be expected to reflect on the utilitarian justification of their own and others' dispositions. Once these models are taken seriously as a specification of a possible psychological or social reality, these are pressing questions of how realisable and how stable these kinds of dissociation might prove to be. To take the psychological model, it must be an empirical question, as well as one inviting philosophical reflection, how far considerations of the cool hour could remain impartial towards the agent's own moral dispositions and ideals, or, in the other direction, how undisturbed those dispositions and ideals will remain by the consciousness that they are basically an instrumental device.

Regarded from a social point of view, the required dissociation is naturally expressed in what might be called 'Government House utilitarianism', an outlook favouring social arrangements under which a utilitarian élite controls a society in which the majority may not itself share those beliefs. In the past, some utilitarians have recommended such arrangements and, indeed, some have participated in them; others, and more recently, have at any rate left little alternative to them. We take it that few utilitarians would welcome these institutions, and that no-one else has good reason to welcome them; but it is a pressing question, what alternatives there are, once 'abstraction' is rejected and indirect utilitarianism is required to take some concrete social form.[22]

Pluralism and rationality

We remarked earlier that not all critics of utilitarianism would like to go 'beyond' utilitarianism, in the sense of constructing some general theory, with comparably wide scope, which would be superior to utilitarianism. Indeed, they would be critical of any theory which displayed that degree of ambition. It is true, however, that the ambitiousness of utilitarianism has itself served as a source of its appeal. In promising to resolve all moral issues by relying on one uniform ultimate criterion, utilitarianism has appeared to be the 'rational' moral theory *par excellence*. We have already commented on some devices that utilitarianism employs in order to apply that criterion, devices which distance it from its primitive intuitive appeal. From a formal point of view, however, the neat model of maximising one homogeneous magnitude offers a standard of consistency and completeness that might seem unachievable by a pluralist moral theory of any kind. While moral theories which are rivals to utilitarianism need not necessarily

[22] For some further remarks on the social embodiment of indirect utilitarianism, and, in particular, the notion of a utilitarian élite, see Williams 1973, pp. 138–40.

be pluralist, they very often are indeed so, and the issue of the consistency of pluralism with rational choice requires a closer examination.

The characteristics of rationality are not easy to identify even for prudential theories, and the problem is certainly no easier for evaluating moral theories. There is, however, a well-established tradition according to which *inconsistency* of judgement or choice is regarded as displaying irrationality.[23] That criterion itself is not fully compelling. It makes a difference how inconsistency is generated. Nevertheless, it is useful to begin with the question of consistency. Plural theories which require the maximisation of several distinct magnitudes *simultaneously* can, of course, lead to inconsistency. But the culprit there is not pluralism itself, but the incoherent form of maximisation that is adopted. Indeed, underlying any multi-magnitude maximisation question is the well-defined problem of finding the consistent partial ordering of 'dominance': x weakly dominates y if and only if x is no lower than y in terms of each of the respective dimensions. If, furthermore, x is *higher* than y in some dimension, then it strictly dominates y. Non-hierarchical pluralism thus leads naturally to a possibly incomplete, but certainly consistent, ordering.

Does rationality require *completeness*? It is difficult to see why it should. To be unable to rank may be frustrating, but by itself it could scarcely be a failure of rationality. To insist, following the lead of 'revealed preference' theory, that rational choice requires that x can be chosen when y is available *only if* – everything considered – x is regarded as at least as good as y, imposes a peculiar limitation on choice. The real 'irrationality' of Buridan's ass rested not in its inability to rank the two haystacks, but in its refusal to choose either haystack without being perfectly sure that that haystack was better than, or at least as good as, the other (surely an asinine attempt to be faithful to an odd theory of 'rational choice'). It can be argued that rational choice based on an incomplete ordering requires only that a not inferior alternative be picked. This would have required Buridan's ass to pick either haystack, but not *neither*, which was clearly an inferior alternative.

It is, of course, true that completeness is often seen as a merit, and it is a characteristic that utilitarianism pretends to enjoy. That pretension is not altogether well grounded, since depending on the nature of interpersonal comparison of utility, the utilitarian ranking may or may not be complete. It is only in the special case of full cardinal comparability (more technically, with 'unit comparability' or more) that utilitarianism yields a complete ordering, and for less exacting frameworks of inter-personal

[23] See Arrow 1951, chapters 1 and 2; Hahn and Hollis 1979.

comparison utilitarianism yields partial orderings of states of affairs (and thus of actions, rules, etc.).[24]

It is also far from clear that completeness should really be seen as a virtue. In many-dimensional moral conflicts the presumption of completeness of ranking may well be quite artificial. Indeed, the insistence on completeness in cost–benefit analysis applied to such subjects as the 'valuation of life' has, quite apart from its vulgarity, been shown to be theoretically problematic.[25]

It seems reasonable to argue that completeness is in itself neither a merit nor a demerit. If a pluralist moral theory is accepted on other grounds, there is no particular reason either to reject that acceptance, or to affirm it more strongly, on the ground of the incompleteness of orderings that it might yield. The issue of rational *choice* consistent with *incomplete orderings* does, of course, remain, but that – as was noted earlier – poses no remarkable challenge.

Finally, pluralist moralities need not necessarily admit incompleteness, even though many of them in fact do that. There could be a hierarchy of criteria (as in, say, Rawls's two principles of justice), or a resolving rule if there is a conflict between the different criteria. In these cases, the contrast with 'monist' moralities like utilitarianism does not rest on the issue of completeness as such, but on *the way* completeness is achieved when it is achieved. In the case of utilitarianism the complete ordering takes the form of simply recording the numerical ordering of some allegedly homogeneous magnitude – total utility, to be exact – whereas for complete plural moralities there is no such homogeneous magnitude with independent descriptive content. ('Moral goodness' does not, of course, have that descriptive content.)

This may well be an interesting distinction, but there is no obvious reason why congruence with the numerical order of some homogeneous descriptive magnitude should be seen to be more sensible or rational. It is surely an issue of the substantive content of moral theory whether moral goodness or rightness should correspond in this way to some homogeneous descriptive magnitude. To require it *a priori* is surely to beg an important question. A sensible judge and rational chooser may indeed be more than a teller.

Utilitarianism's claim to be peculiarly in conformity with the requirements of rational judgement and choice is, thus, difficult to sustain. And this is so, no matter whether we try to see the contrast with pluralism in terms of (i) consistency, (ii) completeness, or (iii) congruence with some homogeneous descriptive magnitude.

[24] See Sen 1970a, chapters 7 and 7*. See also Basu 1979 and Levi 1980.
[25] See Broome 1978b.

Primary goods and rights

One field in which the pluralist form is quite crucial is that of rights. In contrast to the utilitarian conception of aggregate utility, rights of different people cannot be merged into some allegedly homogeneous total magnitude. In the formulation of rights in the shape of deontological constraints (as in, say, Robert Nozick's system[26]), different people's rights stand incommensurable with each other – each imposing its own constraints on the actions of all. The absence of 'trade-offs' between different types of rights in such a formulation has been criticised by Herbert Hart[27] and others. But even when trade-offs are permitted,[28] rights of different people and of different types do not get merged into one homogeneous total, yielding a 'monist' morality based on the maximisation of such a magnitude. Rather, each of the different rights is seen as having moral value, and if they are combined – and even scaled against each other in terms of moral importance – this aggregation is *within* an essentially pluralist approach.

Even if rights are made a part of *consequential* evaluation,[29] this pluralist character remains. The metric of goodness of states of affairs, in such a formulation, will take systematic account of rights, and their fulfilments and violations, but the moral goodness of states will not correspond to some descriptive magnitude of the same type as 'total utility'. Indeed, consequential evaluation including goals of rights-fulfilment among other goals could even admit a great deal of incompleteness and restricted comparability, leading to no more than partial orderings of states of affairs.

Aside from the feature of pluralism, rights-based moral theories differ from utilitarianism also in their concentration on *opportunities* rather than on the value of the exact *use* made of these opportunities. In his paper in this volume, John Rawls has supported his focus on 'primary goods' by linking such goods with the opportunities offered, taking the use citizens make of their rights and opportunities as their own responsibility, since they are 'responsible for their ends' (p. 169).[30]

While Rawls himself has postponed the problem of how to make explicit provision for handicaps and other differences in people's ability to make use of primary goods, the ultimate concern with opportunities can perhaps be made more direct in an extension of the Rawlsian system,

[26] Nozick 1974.
[27] Hart 1979.
[28] See Thomson 1976 and Mackie 1978.
[29] Sen 1982.
[30] While Rawls did present this argument in his earlier writings (e.g. in Rawls 1971), the emphasis on this point emerges more clearly in this paper.

focussing not on primary goods as such but on primary 'capabilities' of people, e.g. the capability to meet nutritional requirements, or the capability to move freely. Such a formulation will be sensitive to differences in people's 'needs', reflected in differences in the conversion of goods into capabilities (e.g. being sensitive to the greater nutritional needs of larger persons, or greater transport needs of disabled people, etc.).[31]

This is really one method of dealing with the so-called 'positive' freedoms, and primary goods are treated just as the *means* of achieving such freedoms. The focus is not on primary goods as such, but on the actual capabilities that the primary goods provide. The question then arises of interpersonal variation in the transformation of primary goods into actual freedoms: e.g. of income into freedom from nutritional deficiency (taking note of variation of nutritional needs), or of the 'social basis of self-respect' into the actual capability to have self-respect (taking note of variation of personal characteristics). While this goes beyond Rawls' concern with the index of primary goods as such, it follows his lead in rejecting the utilitarian tradition of judging freedoms by the collateral utilities that are associated with using those freedoms.

Beyond utilitarianism

By the criteria of rationality familiar from general choice theory, a pluralist theory can be as 'rational' as utilitarianism or any other monistic theory, and has a chance of being a good deal more realistic. The question still remains, of course, not only whether a 'theory' is what is required, but how much a theory can be expected to determine – how far it extends, both within a given culture, and also over various cultures. Hampshire's paper suggests that we should distinguish between two different dimensions of moral thought. One set of considerations (roughly, the theory of justice) is conceived as applying universally, but within those considerations there are other and more local constitutions of the moral life, to which it is essential that they have a particular historical existence, through which alone, and by the use of the imagination, they are to be understood.

Scanlon's paper argues for a general theoretical basis alternative to that of utilitarianism, embodying the contractual thought that institutions, rules or actions should be tested by the question whether they could be justified to other people on grounds which those other people could not reasonably reject. That theoretical basis would offer, as Scanlon puts it, an alternative view to that of utilitarianism about the subject matter of morality, and would also speak to a different moral motivation, one which

---

[31] Such a formulation is presented and defended in Sen 1980.

is nevertheless psychologically recognisable; it would at the same time no doubt admit a fair measure of pluralism within the moral thought of the culture, as well as, once again, legitimate and comprehensible variation between cultures.

However theoretically ambitious or modest an alternative to utilitarianism may be, to whatever degree it may be pluralist, and whatever room it may leave for morally tolerable variation between cultures, it must at least be compatible with, and preferably suggest, a credible psychology and a credible conception of politics and of the relation of politics to moral reflection.

Some of the criticisms of utilitarianism that have been made in this Introduction (those concerning 'abstraction', to take one area) can be summed up in the consideration that utilitarianism, whether as a moral or as a social doctrine, lacks a psychology and a politics. The questions that need to be pressed are 'How could it be lived by anyone?', 'How could it be lived here and now and in the foreseeable future?', 'What institutions would it need? – in particular, institutions that could be formed, adapted or introduced by us?' One such question, a central one, is presented in Gutman's paper on education: 'How could a utilitarian society replicate itself through learning?'

Utilitarianism was born of a distinctive psychological theory and, to some extent, a distinctive attitude to politics, though even in its earlier developments there were divergent conservative and radical applications of it. It is a strange but very striking fact that in its more recent existence as contributing to moral and economic theory it has lost those connections with psychological and political reality.

This fact has implications not only for the credibility of utilitarianism but for the style of the debate about what, if anything, should replace it. Many utilitarians accuse other theories of 'prejudice', 'dogma', 'irrational tradition', and so forth, and similar charges are directed at some people who claim no theory, but only moral convictions or sentiments. In the absence of some concrete account of the psychology and politics of the utilitarian life, that rhetoric is totally empty and lacks the mass to dent anything.

Its materials obviously have, in their own right, some weight. One hardly needs reminding that there is such a thing as irrational prejudice, or a selfish and complacent refusal to face newer and wider demands. The important questions come after the recognition of that. One question is whether utilitarianism is particularly fitted either to express that recognition or to equip one to respond to it, and it is our belief, as of many of our contributors, that the answer to that is negative. Most human beings have needed, and assuredly will need, to use notions which utilitarianism can neither accommodate nor explain.

1 Ethical theory and utilitarianism

R. M. HARE

Contemporary moral philosophy (and the British is no exception) is in a phase which must seem curious to anybody who has observed its course since, say, the 1940s. During all that time moral philosophers of the analytic tradition have devoted most of their work to fundamental questions about the analysis of the meaning of the moral words and the types of reasoning that are valid on moral questions. It may be that some of them were attracted by the intrinsic theoretical interest of this branch of philosophical logic; and indeed it is interesting. But it may surely be said that the greater part, like myself, studied these questions with an ulterior motive: they saw this study as the philosopher's main contribution to the solution of practical moral problems such as trouble most of us. For if we do not understand the very terms in which the problems are posed, how shall we ever get to the root of them? I, at least, gave evidence of this motive in my writings and am publishing many papers on practical questions.[1] But, now that philosophers in greater numbers have woken up to the need for such a contribution, and whole new journals are devoted to the practical applications of philosophy, what do we find the philosophers doing? In the main they proceed as if nothing had been learnt in the course of all that analytical enquiry – as if we had become no clearer now than in, say, 1936, or even 1903, how good moral arguments are to be distinguished from bad.

I cannot believe that we need be so pessimistic; nor that I am alone in thinking that logic can help with moral argument. But surprisingly many philosophers, as soon as they turn their hands to a practical question, forget all about their peculiar art, and think that the questions of the market place can be solved only by the methods of the market place – i.e. by a combination of prejudice (called intuition) and rhetoric. The

Reprinted from *Contemporary British Philosophy*, edited by H. D. Lewis, London: Allen and Unwin, 1976. For a fuller and more recent exposition of the views expressed here, see R. M. Hare, *Moral Thinking: its Levels, Method and Point*, Oxford: Oxford University Press, 1982.
[1] See, for example, Hare 1963, ch. 11; 1972a; 1972b; 1973a; 1975a; 1975b.

philosopher's special contribution to such discussions lies in the ability that he ought to possess to clarify the concepts that are being employed (above all the moral concepts themselves) and thus, by revealing their logical properties, to expose fallacies and put valid arguments in their stead. This he cannot do unless he has an understanding (dare I say a theory?) of the moral concepts; and that is what we have been looking for all these years. And yet we find philosophers writing in such a way that it is entirely unclear what understanding they have of the moral concepts or of the rules of moral reasoning.[2] It is often hard to tell whether they are naturalists, relying on supposed equivalences between moral and non-moral concepts, or intuitionists, whose only appeal is to whatever moral sentiments they can get their readers to share with them. Most of them seem to be some sort of descriptivists; but as they retreat through an ever vaguer naturalism into a hardly avowed intuitionism, it becomes more and more obscure what, in their view, moral statements say, and therefore how we could decide whether to accept them or not. Philosophy, as a rational discipline, has been left behind.

It is the object of this paper to show how a theory about the meanings of the moral words can be the foundation for a theory of normative moral reasoning. The conceptual theory is of a non-descriptivist but nevertheless rationalist sort.[3] That this sort of theory could claim to provide the basis of an account of moral reasoning will seem paradoxical only to the prejudiced and to those who have not read Kant. It is precisely that sort of prejudice which has led to the troubles I have been complaining of: the belief that only a descriptivist theory can provide a rational basis for morality, and that therefore it is better to explore any blind alley than expose oneself to the imputation of irrationalism and subjectivism by becoming a non-descriptivist.

The normative theory that I shall advocate has close analogies with utilitarianism, and I should not hesitate to call it utilitarian, were it not that this name covers a wide variety of views, all of which have been the victims of prejudices rightly excited by the cruder among them. In calling my own normative theory utilitarian, I beg the reader to look at the theory itself, and ask whether it cannot avoid the objections that have been made against other kinds of utilitarianism. I hope to show in this paper that it can avoid at least some of them. But if I escape calumny while remaining both a non-descriptivist and a utilitarian, it will be a marvel.

In my review of Professor Rawls's book[4] I said that there were close

---

[2] See the beginning of Hare 1975a.

[3] It is substantially that set out in Hare 1963. For the distinction between non-descriptivism and subjectivism, see Hare 1974.

[4] Hare 1973b; cf. Hare 1972b, and B. Barry 1973, pp. 12–13.

formal similarities between rational contractor theories such as Rawls's, ideal observer theories such as have been advocated by many writers[5] and my own universal prescriptivist theory. I also said that theories of this form can be made to lead very naturally to a kind of utilitarianism, and that Rawls avoided this outcome only by a very liberal use of intuitions to make his rational contractors come to a non-utilitarian contract. Rawls advocates his theory as an alternative to utilitarianism. Whether the system which I shall sketch is to be regarded as utilitarian or not is largely a matter of terminology. The form of argument which it employs is, as I have already said, formally extremely similar to Rawls's; the substantive conclusions are, however, markedly different. I should like to think of my view as, in Professor Brandt's expression, 'a credible form of utilitarianism';[6] no doubt Rawls would classify it as an incredible form of utilitarianism; others might say that it is a compromise between his views and more ordinary kinds of utilitarianism. This does not much matter.

I try to base myself, unlike Rawls, entirely on the formal properties of the moral concepts as revealed by the logical study of moral language; and in particular on the features of prescriptivity and universalisability which I think moral judgements, in the central uses which we shall be considering, all have. These two features provide a framework for moral reasoning which is formally similar to Rawls's own more dramatic machinery. But, rather than put the argument in his way, I will do overtly what he does covertly – that is to say, I do not speculate about what some fictitious rational contractors *would* judge if they were put in a certain position subject to certain restrictions; rather, I subject myself to certain (formally analogous) restrictions and put myself (imaginatively) in this position, as Rawls in effect does,[7] and *do* some judging. Since the position and the restrictions are formally analogous, this ought to make no difference.

In this position, I am prescribing universally for all situations just like the one I am considering; and thus for all such situations, *whatever* role, among those in the situations, I might myself occupy. I shall therefore give equal weight to the equal interests of the occupants of all the roles in the situation; and, since any of these occupants might be myself, this weight will be positive. Thus the impartiality which is the purpose of Rawls's 'veil of ignorance' is achieved by purely formal means; and so is the purpose of his insistence that his contractors be rational, i.e. prudent. We have therefore, by consideration of the logic of the moral concepts alone, put ourselves in as strong a position as Rawls hopes to put himself by his more

[5] See, for example, the discussion between R. Firth and R. B. Brandt, Firth 1952 and Brandt 1955; also Haslett 1974.
[6] Brandt 1963.
[7] See my review of Rawls (Hare 1973b), p. 249.

elaborate, but at the same time, as I have claimed, less firmly based apparatus.

Let us now use these tools. Rawls himself says that an ideal observer theory leads to utilitarianism; and the same ought to be true of the formal apparatus which I have just sketched. How does giving equal weight to the equal interests of all the parties lead to utilitarianism? And to what kind of utilitarianism does it lead? If I am trying to give equal weight to the equal interests of all the parties in a situation, I must, it seems, regard a benefit or harm done to one party as of equal value or disvalue to an equal benefit or harm done to any other party. This seems to mean that I shall promote the interests of the parties most, while giving equal weight to them all, if I maximise the total benefits over the entire population; and this is the classical principle of utility. For fixed populations it is practically equivalent to the average utility principle which bids us maximise not total but average utility; when the size of the population is itself affected by a decision, the two principles diverge, and I have given reasons in my review of Rawls's book for preferring the classical or total utility principle. In these calculations, benefits are to be taken to include the reduction of harms.

I am not, however, going to put my theory in terms of benefits and the reduction of harms, because this leads to difficulties that I wish to avoid. Let us say, rather, that what the principle of utility requires of me is to do for each man affected by my actions what I wish were done for me in the hypothetical circumstances that I were in precisely his situation; and, if my actions affect more than one man (as they nearly always will) to do what I wish, all in all, to be done for me in the hypothetical circumstances that I occupied all their situations (not of course at the same time but, shall we say?, in random order). This way of putting the matter, which is due to C. I. Lewis,[8] emphasises that I have to give the same weight to everybody's equal interests; and we must remember that, in so far I am one of the people affected (as in nearly all cases I am) my own interests have to be given the same, and no more, weight – that is to say, my own actual situation is one of those that I have to suppose myself occupying in this random order.

Some further notes on this suggestion will be in place here. First, it is sometimes alleged that justice has to be at odds with utility. But if we ask how we are to be just between the competing interests of different people, it seems hard to give any other answer than that it is by giving equal weight, impartially, to the equal interests of everybody. And this is precisely what yields the utility principle. It does not necessarily yield equality in the resulting distribution. There are, certainly, very good utilitarian

---

[8] Lewis 1946, p. 547; see also Haslett 1974, ch. 3.

reasons for seeking equality in distribution too; but justice is something distinct. The utilitarian is sometimes said to be indifferent between equal and unequal distributions, provided that total utility is equal. This is so; but it conceals two important utilitarian grounds for a fairly high degree of equality of actual goods (tempered, of course, as in most systems including Rawls's, by various advantages that are secured by moderate inequalities). The first is the diminishing marginal utility of all commodities and of money, which means that approaches towards equality will tend to increase total utility. The second is that inequalities tend to produce, at any rate in educated societies, envy, hatred and malice, whose disutility needs no emphasising. I am convinced that when these two factors are taken into account, utilitarians have no need to fear the accusation that they could favour extreme inequalities of distribution in actual modern societies. Fantastic hypothetical cases can no doubt be invented in which they would have to favour them; but, as we shall see, this is an illegitimate form of argument.

Secondly, the transition from a formulation in terms of interests to one in terms of desires or prescriptions, or vice versa, is far from plain sailing. Both formulations raise problems which are beyond the scope of this paper. If we formulate utilitarianism in terms of interests, we have the problem of determining what are someone's true interests. Even if we do not confuse the issue, as some do, by introducing moral considerations into this prudential question (i.e. by alleging that becoming morally better, or worse, in itself affects a man's interests),[9] we still have to find a way of cashing statements about interests in terms of such states of mind as likings, desires, etc., both actual and hypothetical. For this reason a formulation directly in terms of these states of mind ought to be more perspicuous. But two difficult problems remain: the first is that of how present desires and likings are to be balanced against future, and actual desires and likings against those which would be experienced if certain alternative actions were taken; the second is whether desires need to be mentioned at all in a formulation of utilitarianism, or whether likings by themselves will do. It would seem that if we arrive at utilitarianism via universal prescriptivism, as I am trying to do, we shall favour the former of the last pair of alternatives; for desires, in the required sense, are assents to prescriptions. All these are questions within the theory of prudence, with which, although it is an essential adjunct to normative moral theory, I do not hope to deal in this paper.[10]

I must mention, however, that when I said above that I have to do for each man affected by my actions what I wish were done for me, etc., I was

[9] Cf. Plato, *Republic*, 335.
[10] The theory of prudence is ably handled in Richards 1971; Haslett 1974; and Brandt 1979.

speaking inaccurately. When I do the judging referred to on page 25, I have to do it as rationally as possible. This, if I am making a moral judgement, involves prescribing universally; but in prescribing (albeit universally) I cannot, if rational, ignore prudence altogether, but have to universalise this prudence. Put more clearly, this means that, whether I am prescribing in my own interest or in someone's else's (see the next paragraph), I must ask, not what I or he does actually at present wish, but what, prudentially speaking, we should wish. It is from this rational point of view (in the prudential sense of 'rational') that I have to give my universal prescriptions. In other words, it is *qua* rational that I have to judge; and this involves at least judging with a clear and unconfused idea of what I am saying and what the actual consequences of the prescription that I am issuing would be, for myself and others. It also involves, when I am considering the desires of others, considering what they would be if those others were perfectly prudent – i.e. desired what they would desire if they were fully informed and unconfused. Thus morality, at least for the utilitarian, can only be founded on prudence, which has then to be universalised. All this we shall have to leave undiscussed, remembering, however, that when, in what follows, I say 'desire', 'prescribe', etc., I mean 'desire, prescribe, etc., from the point of view of one who is prudent so far as his own interest goes'. It is important always to supply this qualification whether I am speaking of our own desires or those of others; but I shall omit it from now on because it would make my sentences intolerably cumbrous, and signalise the omission, in the next paragraph only, by adding the subscript '$_p$' to the words 'desire', etc., as required, omitting even this subscript thereafter. I hope that one paragraph will suffice to familiarise the reader with this point.

Thirdly, when we speak of the 'situations' of the various parties, we have to include in the situations all the desires$_p$, likings$_p$, etc., that the people have in them – that is to say, I am to do for the others what I wish$_p$ to be done for me were I to have their likings$_p$, etc., and not those which I now have. And, similarly, I am not to take into account (when I ask what I wish$_p$ should be done to me in a certain situation) my own present desires$_p$, likings$_p$, etc. There is one exception to this: I have said that one of the situations that I have to consider is my own present situation; I have to love$_p$ my neighbour *as*, but *no more than* and *no less than*, myself, and likewise to do to others *as* I wish$_p$ them to do to me. Therefore just as, when I am considering what I wish$_p$ to be done to me were I in X's situation, where X is somebody else, I have to think of the situation as including *his* desires$_p$, likings$_p$, etc., and discount my own, so, in the single case where X is myself, I have to take into account *my* desires$_p$, likings$_p$, etc. In other words, *qua* author of the moral decision I have to discount my own desires$_p$, etc., and consider only the desires$_p$, etc., of the affected party; but where (as normally) I am one of the affected parties, I have to consider my own desires$_p$, etc., *qua* affected party, on equal terms with those of all the other affected parties.[11]

It will be asked: if we strip me, *qua* author of the moral decision, of all desires and likings, how is it determined what decision I shall come to? The answer is that it is determined by the desires and likings of those whom I take into account as affected parties (including, as I said, myself, but only *qua* affected party and not *qua* author). I am to ask, indeed, what I do wish should be done for me, were I in their situations; but were I in their situations, I should have their desires, etc., so I must forget about my own present desires (with the exception just made) and consider only the desires which *they* have; and if I do this, what I *do* wish for will be the satisfaction of *those* desires; that, therefore, is what I shall prescribe, so far as is possible.

I wish to point out that my present formulation enables me to deal in an agreeably clear way with the problem of the fanatic, who has given me so much trouble in the past.[12] In so far as, in order to prescribe universally, I have to strip away (*qua* author of the moral decision) all my present desires, etc., I shall have to strip away, among them, all the ideals that I have; for an ideal is a kind of desire or liking (in the generic sense in which I am using those terms); it is, to use Aristotle's word, an *orexis*.[13] This does not mean that I have to give up having ideals, nor even that I must stop giving any consideration to my ideals when I make my moral decisions; it means only that I am not allowed to take them into account *qua* author of the moral decision. I am, however, allowed to take them into account, along with the ideals of all the other parties affected, when I consider my own position, among others, as an affected party. This means that for the purposes of the moral decision it makes no difference *who has* the ideal. It means that we have to give impartial consideration to the ideals of ourselves and others. In cases, however, where the pursuit of our own ideals does not affect the ideals of the interests of others, we are allowed and indeed encouraged to pursue them.

[11] Professor Bernard Williams says, 'It is absurd to demand of such a man, when the sums come in from the utility network which the projects of others have in part determined, that he should just step aside from his own project and decision and acknowledge the decision which utilitarian calculation requires' (Williams 1973, p. 116, and cf. p. 117n). Christian humility and *agape* and their humanist counterparts are, then, according to Williams's standards, an absurd demand (which is hardly remarkable). What is more remarkable is the boldness of the persuasive definition by which he labels the self-centred pursuit of one's own projects 'integrity' and accounts it a fault in utilitarianism that it could conflict with this.

[12] Hare 1963, ch. 9; 'Wrongness and Harm', in Hare 1972c.

[13] *De Anima*, 433a 9ff.

All this being so, the only sort of fanatic that is going to bother us is the person whose ideals are so intensely pursued that the weight that has to be given to them, considered impartially, outbalances the combined weights of all the ideals, desires, likings, etc., that have to be frustrated in order to achieve them. For example, if the Nazi's desire not to have Jews around is intense enough to outweigh all the sufferings caused to Jews by arranging not to have them around, then, on this version of utilitarianism, as on any theory with the same formal structure, it ought to be satisfied. The problem is to be overcome by, first, pointing out that fanatics of this heroic stature are never likely to be encountered (that no *actual* Nazis had such intense desires is, I think, obvious); secondly, by remembering that, as I shall be showing in a moment, cases that are never likely to be actually encountered do not have to be squared with the thinking of the ordinary man, whose principles are not designed to cope with such cases. It is therefore illegitimate to attack such a theory as I have sketched by saying 'You can't ask us to believe that it would be right to give this fantastic fanatical Nazi what he wanted'; this argument depends on appealing to the ordinary man's judgement about a case with which, as we shall see, his intuitions were not designed to deal.

A similar move enables us to deal with another alleged difficulty (even if we do not, as we legitimately might, make use of the fact that all desires that come into our reasoning are desires$_p$, i.e. desires that a man will have after he has become perfectly prudent). It is sometimes said to be a fault in utilitarianism that it makes us give weight to bad desires (such as the desire of a sadist to torture his victim) solely in proportion to their intensity; received opinion, it is claimed, gives no weight at all, or even a negative weight, to such desires. But received opinion has grown up to deal with cases likely to be encountered; and we are most *un*likely, even if we give sadistic desires weight in accordance with their intensity, to encounter a case in which utility will be maximised by letting the sadist have his way. For first, the suffering of the victim will normally be more intense than the pleasure of the sadist. And, secondly, sadists can often be given substitute pleasures or even actually cured. And, thirdly, the side-effects of allowing the sadist to have what he wants are enormous. So it will be clear, when I have explained in more detail why fantastic cases in which these disutilities do not occur cannot legitimately be used in this kind of argument, why it is perfectly all right to allow weight to bad desires.

We have now, therefore, to make an important distinction between two kinds or 'levels' of moral thinking. It has some affinities with a distinction made by Rawls in his article 'Two Concepts of Rules'[14] (in which he was by

[14] Rawls 1955.

way of defending utilitarianism), though it is not the same; it also owes
something to Sir David Ross,[15] and indeed to others. I call it the difference
between level-1 and level-2 thinking, or between the principles employed
at these two levels.[16] Level-1 principles are for use in practical moral
thinking, especially under conditions of stress. They have to be general
enough to be impartable by education (including self-education), and to be
'of ready application in the emergency',[17] but are not to be confused with
rules of thumb (whose breach excites no compunction). Level-2 principles
are what would be arrived at by leisured moral thought in completely
adequate knowledge of the facts, as the right answer in a specific case.
They are universal but can be as specific (the opposite of 'general', not of
'universal'[18]) as needs be. Level-1 principles are inculcated in moral education; but the selection of the level-1 principles for this purpose should be
guided by leisured thought, resulting in level-2 principles for specific
considered situations, the object being to have those level-1 principles
whose general acceptance will lead to actions in accord with the best
level-2 principles in most situations that are actually encountered. Fantastic and highly unusual situations, therefore, need not be considered for
this purpose.

I have set out this distinction in detail elsewhere;[19] here we only need to
go into some particular points which are relevant. The thinking that I have
been talking about so far in this paper, until the preceding paragraph, and
indeed in most of my philosophical writings until recently, is level-2. It
results in a kind of act-utilitarianism which, because of the universalisability of moral judgements, is practically equivalent to a rule-utilitarianism
whose rules are allowed to be of any required degree of specificity. Such
thinking is appropriate only to 'a cool hour', in which there is time for
unlimited investigation of the facts, and there is no temptation to special
pleading. It can use hypothetical cases, even fantastic ones. In principle it
can, given superhuman knowledge of the facts, yield answers as to what
should be done in any cases one cares to describe.

The commonest trick of the opponents of utilitarianism is to take
examples of such thinking, usually addressed to fantastic cases, and confront them with what the ordinary man would think. It makes the utilitarian look like a moral monster. The anti-utilitarians have usually confined their own thought about moral reasoning (with fairly infrequent
laspses which often go unnoticed) to what I am calling level 1, the level of

---

[15] Ross 1930, pp. 19ff.
[16] See my review of Rawls (Hare 1973b), p. 153; Hare 1972/3; 1972b; 1963, pp. 43–5.
[17] Burke; see Hare 1963, p. 45.
[18] See Hare 1972/3.
[19] See note 16.

everyday moral thinking on ordinary, often stressful, occasions in which information is sparse. So they find it natural to take the side of the ordinary man in a supposed fight with the utilitarian whose views lead him to say, if put at the disconcertingly unfamiliar standpoint of the archangel Gabriel, such extraordinary things about these carefully contrived examples.

To argue in this way is entirely to neglect the importance for moral philosophy of a study of moral education. Let us suppose that a fully-informed archangelic act-utilitarian is thinking about how to bring up his children. He will obviously not bring them up to practise on every occasion on which they are confronted with a moral question the kind of archangelic thinking that he himself is capable of; if they are ordinary children, he knows that they will get it wrong. They will not have the time, or the information, or the self-mastery to avoid self-deception prompted by self-interest; this is the real, as opposed to the imagined, veil of ignorance which determines our moral principles.

So he will do two things. First, he will try to implant in them a set of good general principles. I advisedly use the word 'implant'; these are not rules of thumb, but principles which they will not be able to break without the greatest repugnance, and whose breach by others will arouse in them the highest indignation. These will be the principles they will use in their ordinary level-1 moral thinking, especially in situations of stress. Secondly, since he is not always going to be with them, and since they will have to educate *their* children, and indeed continue to educate themselves, he will teach them, as far as they are able, to do the kind of thinking that he has been doing himself. This thinking will have three functions. First of all, it will be used when the good general principles conflict in particular cases. If the principles have been well chosen, this will happen rarely; but it will happen. Secondly, there will be cases (even rarer) in which, though there is no conflict between general principles, there is something highly unusual about the case which prompts the question whether the general principles are really fitted to deal with it. But thirdly, and much the most important, this level-2 thinking will be used to *select* the general principles to be taught both to this and to succeeding generations. The general principles may change, and should change (because the environment changes). And note that, if the educator were not (as we have supposed him to be) archangelic, we could not even assume that the best level-1 principles were imparted in the first place; perhaps they might be improved.

How will the selection be done? By using level-2 thinking to consider cases, both actual and hypothetical, which crucially illustrate, and help to adjudicate, disputes between rival general principles. But, because the general principles are being selected for use in actual situations, there will have to be a careful proportioning of the weight to be put upon a particular case to the probability of its actually occurring in the lives of the people who are to use the principles. So the fantastic cases that are so beloved of anti-utilitarians will have very little employment in this kind of thinking (except as a diversion for philosophers or to illustrate purely logical points, which is sometimes necessary). Fantastic unlikely cases will never be used to turn the scales as between rival general principles for practical use. The result will be a set of general principles, constantly evolving, but on the whole stable, such that their use in moral education, including self-education, and their consequent acceptance by the society at large, will lead to the nearest possible approximation to the prescriptions of archangelic thinking. They will be the set of principles with the highest acceptance-utility. They are likely to include principles of justice.

It is now necessary to introduce some further distinctions, all of which, fortunately, have already been made elsewhere, and can therefore be merely summarised. The first, alluded to already, is that between specific rule-utilitarianism (which is practically equivalent to universalistic act-utilitarianism) and general rule-utilitarianism.[20] Both are compatible with act-utilitarianism if their roles are carefully distinguished. Specific rule-utilitarianism is appropriate to level-2 thinking, general rule-utilitarianism to level-1 thinking; and therefore the rules of specific rule-utilitarianism can be of unlimited specificity, but those of general rule-utilitarianism have to be general enough for their role. The thinking of our archangel will thus be of a specific rule-utilitarian sort; and the thinking of the ordinary people whom he has educated will be for the most part of a general rule-utilitarian sort, though they will supplement this, when they have to and when they dare, with such archangelic thinking as they are capable of.

The second distinction is that between what Professor Smart[21] calls (morally) 'right' actions and (morally) 'rational' actions. Although Smart's way of putting the distinction is not quite adequate, as he himself recognises, I shall, as he does, adopt it for the sake of brevity. Both here, and in connexion with the 'acceptance-utility' mentioned above, somewhat more sophisticated calculations of probability are required than might at first be thought. But for simplicity let us say that an action is rational if it is the action most likely to be right, even if, when all the facts are known, as they were not when it was done, it turns out not to have been right. In such a society as we have described, the (morally) rational action will nearly always be that in accordance with the good general principles of level 1, because they have been selected precisely in order to make this the case. Such actions may not always turn out to have been (morally) right in Smart's sense when the cards are turned face upwards; but the agent is not to be blamed for this.

[20] See Hare 1972/3.   [21] Smart and Williams 1973, pp. 46f.

It is a difficult question, just how simple and general these level-1 principles ought to be. If we are speaking of the principles to be inculcated throughout the society, the answer will obviously vary with the extent to which the members of it are sophisticated and morally self-disciplined enough to grasp and apply relatively complex principles without running into the dangers we have mentioned. We might distinguish sub-groups within the society, and individuals within these sub-groups, and even the same individual at different stages, according to their ability to handle complex principles. Most people's level-1 principles become somewhat more complex as they gain experience of handling different situations, and they may well become so complex as to defy verbal formulation; but the value of the old simple maxims may also come to be appreciated. In any case, level-1 principles can never, because of the exigencies of their role, become as complex as level-2 principles are allowed to be.

A third distinction is that between good actions and the right action.[22] The latter is the action in accordance with level-2 principles arrived at by exhaustive, fully-informed and clear thinking about specific cases. A good action is what a good man would do, even if not right. In general this is the same as the morally rational action, but there may be complications, in that the motivation of the man has to be taken into account. The good (i.e. the morally well-educated) man, while he is sometimes able and willing to question and even to amend the principles he has been taught, will have acquired in his upbringing a set of motives and dispositions such that breaking these principles goes very much against the grain for him. The very goodness of his character will make him sometimes do actions which do not conform to archangelic prescriptions. This may be for one of at least two reasons. The first is that when he did them he was not fully informed and perhaps knew it, and knew also his own moral and intellectual weaknesses, and therefore (humbly and correctly) thought it morally rational to abide by his level-1 principles, and thus did something which turned out in the event not to be morally right. The second is that, although he could have known that the morally rational action was on this unusual occasion one in breach of his ingrained principles (it required him, say, to let down his closest friend), he found it so much against the grain that he just could not bring himself to do it. In the first case what he did was both rational and a morally good action. In the second case it was morally good but misguided – a wrong and indeed irrational act done from the best of motives. And no doubt there are other possibilities.

The situation I have been describing is a somewhat stylised model of our own except that we had no archangel to educate us, but rely on the

[22] See Hare 1952, p. 186.

deliverances, not even of philosopher kings, but of Aristotelian *phronimoi* of very varying degrees of excellence. What will happen if a lot of moral philosophers are let loose on this situation? Level-1 thinking forms the greater part of the moral thinking of good men, and perhaps the whole of the moral thinking of good men who have nothing of the philosopher in them, including some of our philosophical colleagues. Such are the intuitionists, to whom their good ingrained principles seem to be sources of unquestionable knowledge. Others of a more enquiring bent will ask why they should accept these intuitions, and, getting no satisfactory answer, will come to the conclusion that the received principles have no ground at all and that the only way to decide what you ought to do is to reason it out on each occasion. Such people will at best become a crude kind of act-utilitarians. Between these two sets of philosophers there will be the sort of ludicrous battles that we have been witnessing so much of. The philosopher who understands the situation better will see that both are right about a great deal and that they really ought to make up their quarrel. They are talking about different levels of thought, both of which are necessary on appropriate occasions.

What kind of philosopher will this understanding person be? Will he be any kind of utilitarian? I see no reason why he should not be. For, first of all, level-2 thinking, which is necessary, is not only utilitarian but act-utilitarian (for, as we have seen, the specific rule-utilitarian thinking of this level and universalistic act-utilitarianism are practically equivalent). And there are excellent act-utilitarian reasons for an educator to bring up his charges to follow, on most occasions, level-1 thinking on the basis of a set of principles selected by high-quality level-2 thinking. This applies equally to self-education. So at any rate all acts that could be called educative or self-educative can have a solid act-utilitarian foundation. To educate oneself and other men in level-1 principles *is* for the best, and only the crudest of act-utilitarians fails to see this. There will also be good act-utilitarian reasons for *following* the good general principles in nearly all cases; for to do so will be rational, or most likely to be right; and even an act-utilitarian, when he comes to tell us how we should proceed when choosing what to do, can only tell us to do what is *most probably* right, because we do not know, when choosing, what *is* right.

There will be occasions, as I have said, when a man brought up (on good general principles) by a consistent act-utilitarian will do a rational act which turns out not to be right; and there will even be occasions on which he will do a good action which is neither rational nor right, because, although he could have known that it would be right on this unusual occasion to do an act contrary to the good general principles, he could not bring himself to contemplate it, because it went so much against the grain.

And since one cannot pre-tune human nature all that finely, it may well be that the act-utilitarian educator will have to put up with the possibility of such cases, in the assurance that, if his principles are well chosen, they will be rare. For if he attempted to educate people so that they would do the rational thing in these cases, it could only be by incorporating into their principles clauses which might lead them, in other more numerous cases, to do acts most likely to be wrong. Moral upbringing is a compromise imposed by the coarseness of the pupil's discrimination and the inability of his human educators to predict with any accuracy the scrapes he will get into.

The exclusion from the argument of highly unusual cases, which I hope I have now achieved, is the main move in my defence of this sort of utilitarianism. There are also some subsidiary moves, some of which I have already mentioned, and all of which will be familiar. It is no argument against act-utilitarianism that in some unusual cases it would take a bad man to do what according to the utilitarian is the morally right or even the morally rational thing; good men are those who are firmly wedded to the principles which *on nearly all actual occasions* will lead them to do the right thing, and it is inescapable that on unusual occasions moderately good men will do the wrong thing. The nearer they approach archangelic status, the more, on unusual occasions, they will be able to chance their arm and do what they think will be the right act in defiance of their principles; but most of us ordinary mortals will be wise to be fairly cautious. As Aristotle said, we have to incline towards the vice which is the lesser danger for *us*, and away from that extreme which is to *us* the greater temptation.[23] For some, in the present context, the greater danger may be too much rigidity in the application of level-1 principles; but perhaps for more (and I think that I am one of them) it is a too great readiness to let them slip. It is a matter of temperament; we have to know ourselves (empirically); the philosopher cannot tell each of us which is the greater danger for him.

The moves that I have already made will, I think, deal with some other cases which are well known from the literature. Such are the case of the man who is tempted, on utilitarian grounds, to use electricity during a power crisis, contrary to the government's instructions; and the case of the voter who abstains in the belief that enough others will vote. In both these cases it is alleged that some utility would be gained, and none lost, by these dastardly actions. These are not, on the face of it, fantastic or unusual cases, although the degree of knowledge stipulated as to what others will do is perhaps unusual. Yet it would be impolitic, in moral education, to

---

[23] *Nicomachean Ethics*, 1109 b 1.

bring up people to behave like this, if we were seeking level-1 principles with the highest acceptance-utility; if we tried, the result would be that nearly everyone would consume electricity under those conditions, and hardly anybody would vote. However, the chief answer to these cases is that which I have used elsewhere[24] to deal with the car-pushing and death-bed promise cases which are also well canvassed. It is best approached by going back to the logical beginning and asking whether I am prepared to prescribe, or even permit, that others should (*a*) use electricity, thus taking advantage of my law-abidingness, when I am going without it; (*b*) abstain from voting when I do so at inconvenience to myself, thereby taking advantage of my public spirit; (*c*) only pretend to push the car when I am rupturing myself in the effort to get it started; (*d*) make death-bed promises to me (for example to look after my children) and then treat them as of no weight. I unhesitatingly answer 'No' to all these questions; and I think that I should give the same answer even if I were perfectly prudent and were universalising my prescriptions to cover other perfectly prudent affected parties (see above, page 28). For it is not imprudent, but prudent rather, to seek the satisfaction of desires which are important to me, even if I am not going to know whether they have been satisfied or not. There is nothing in principle to prevent a fully informed and clear-headed person wanting above all that his children should not starve after his death; and if that is what he wants above all, it is prudent for him to seek what will achieve it, and therefore prescribe this.

Since the logical machinery on which my brand of utilitarianism is based yields these answers, so should the utilitarianism that is based on it; and it is worth while to ask, How? The clue lies in the observation that to frustrate a desire of mine is against my interest even if I do not know that it is being frustrated, or if I am dead. If anybody does not agree, I ask him to apply the logical apparatus direct and forget about interests. Here is a point at which, perhaps, some people will want to say that my Kantian or Christian variety of utilitarianism, based on giving equal weight to the prudent prescriptions or desires of all, diverges from the usual varieties so much that it does not deserve to be called a kind of utilitarianism at all. I am not much interested in that terminological question; but for what it is worth I will record my opinion that the dying man's interests *are* harmed if promises are made to him and then broken, and even more that mine are harmed if people are cheating me without my knowing it. In the latter case, they are harmed because I very much want this not to happen; and my desire that it should not happen is boosted by my level-1 sense of justice, which the utilitarian educators who brought me up wisely inculcated in me.

[24] See my paper 'The Argument from Received Opinion' in Hare 1972d, pp. 128ff.; Hare 1963, pp. 132ff.

Whichever way we put it, whether in terms of what I am prepared to prescribe or permit universally (and therefore also for when I am the victim) or in terms of how to be fair as between the interests of all the affected parties, I conclude that the acts I have listed will come out wrong on the act-utilitarian calculation, because of the harms done to the interests of those who are cheated, or the non-fulfilment of prescriptions to which, we may assume, they attach high importance. If we add to this move the preceding one which rules out fantastic cases, and are clear about the distinction between judgements about the character of the agent, judgements about the moral rationality of the action, and judgements about its moral rightness as shown by the outcome, I think that this form of utilitarianism can answer the objections I have mentioned. Much more needs to be said; the present paper is only a beginning, and is not very original.[25] I publish it only to give some indication of the way in which ethical theory can help with normative moral questions, and to try to get the discussion of utilitarianism centred round credible forms of it, rather than forms which we all know will not do.

[25] Among many others from whose ideas I have learnt, I should like in particular to mention Dr Lynda Sharp (Mrs Lynda Paine), in whose thesis 'Forms and Criticisms of Utilitarianism' (deposited in the Bodleian Library at Oxford) some of the above topics are discussed in greater detail.

2 Morality and the theory of rational behaviour

1 Historical background

The ethical theory I am going to describe in this paper is based on three different time-honoured intellectual traditions in moral philosophy. It also makes essential use of a great intellectual accomplishment of much more recent origin, namely, the modern Bayesian theory of rational behaviour under risk and uncertainty.

One of the three moral traditions I am indebted to goes back to Adam Smith, who equated the moral point of view with that of an impartial but sympathetic spectator (or observer).[1] In any social situation, each participant will tend to look at the various issues from his own self-centred, often emotionally biassed, and possibly quite one-sided, partisan point of view. In contrast, if anybody wants to assess the situation from a *moral* point of view in terms of some standard of justice and equity, this will essentially amount to looking at it from the standpoint of an impartial but humane and sympathetic observer. It may be interesting to note that modern psychological studies on the development of moral ideas in children have come up with a very similar model of moral value judgements.[2]

Another intellectual tradition I have benefited from is Kant's. Kant claimed that moral rules can be distinguished from other behavioural rules by certain formal criteria and, in particular, by the criterion of universality (which may also be described as a criterion of reciprocity).[3] For example, if I really believe that other people should repay me any money they have borrowed from me, then I must admit that *I* am under a similar moral obligation to repay any money I have borrowed from other persons under comparable circumstances. Thus, in ethical content, Kant's principle of universality says much the same thing as the golden rule of the Bible: 'Treat other people in the same way as you want to be treated by them.' Among contemporary authors, the Oxford moral philosopher Hare has

Reprinted from *Social Research*, Winter 1977, vol. 44, no. 4.
[1] Adam Smith 1976.
[2] See, for example Piaget 1962.
[3] Immanuel Kant 1785.

advocated a moral theory based specifically on the Kantian universality requirement (which he calls the 'universalisation' requirement).[4]

My greatest intellectual debt, however, goes to the utilitarian tradition of Bentham, John Stuart Mill, Sidgwick, and Edgeworth, which made maximisation of social utility the basic criterion of morality – social utility being defined either as the sum, or the arithmetic mean, of the utility levels of all individuals in the society.[5] (What these classical utilitarians called 'social utility' is often called the 'social welfare function' in modern welfare economics. But in many cases the term 'social welfare function' is now used in a less specific sense, without any utilitarian connotations.)

Though many details of the classical utilitarian position may be unacceptable to us today, we must not forget what basic political and moral principles they were fighting for. Basically, both in politics and in ethics, they fought for reason against mere tradition, dogmatism, and vested interests. In politics, they conceived the revolutionary idea of judging existing social institutions by an impartial rational test, that of social utility, and did not hesitate to announce it in clear and unmistakable terms if they felt that many of these institutions had definitely failed to pass this test. Likewise, in ethics, they proposed to subject all accepted moral rules to tests of rationality and social utility.

Their main opponents in moral philosophy were the intuitionists, who claimed that we can discover the basic moral rules by direct intuition, which, of course, made any rational evaluation of such moral rules both impossible and unnecessary. Apparently, these intuitionist philosophers were not particularly troubled by the well-known empirical fact that people's 'moral intuitions' seem to be highly dependent on accidents of their own upbringing and, more fundamentally, on the accident of being raised in one particular society rather than another. Though there were many notable exceptions, most people raised in a warlike society or a slave-holding society or a caste society always claimed to have the clear 'moral intuition' that the social practices of their society had full moral justification. It was this uncritical acceptance of existing social practices that the utilitarians fought against by their insistence on subjecting all moral beliefs to a rational test.

In our own time, these crude forms of obscurantism in ethics have largely disappeared. But it is still true, it seems to me, that the updated version of classical utilitarianism is the only ethical theory which consistently abides by the principle that moral issues must be decided by rational tests and that moral behaviour itself is a special form of rational behaviour. I think it can be easily shown that all nonutilitarian theories of

[4] Hare 1952.
[5] Bentham 1948; John Stuart Mill 1962; Sidgwick 1962; Edgeworth 1881.

morality, including John Rawls's very influential theory[6] and several others, at one point or another involve some highly irrational moral choices, representing major departures from a rational pursuit of common human and humane interests, which, in my view, is the very essence of morality.

Yet, notwithstanding its very considerable intellectual accomplishments, classical utilitarianism was open to some major objections. The most important step toward resolving most of these objections was taken by Keynes's friend, the Oxford economist Harrod, who was the first to point out the advantages of *rule* utilitarianism over *act* utilitarianism.[7] (But he did not actually use this terminology. The terms 'act utilitarianism' and 'rule utilitarianism' were introduced only by Brandt.[8]) Act utilitarianism is the view that each individual act must be judged directly in terms of the utilitarian criterion. Thus a morally right act is one that, in the situation the actor is actually in, will maximise social utility. In contrast, rule utilitarianism is the view that the utilitarian criterion must be applied, in the first instance, not to individual acts but rather to the basic general rules governing these acts. Thus a morally right act is one that conforms to the correct moral rule applicable to this sort of situation, whereas a correct moral rule is that particular behavioural rule that would maximise social utility if it were followed by everybody in all social situations of this particular type.

I will discuss the moral implications of these two versions of utilitarian theory in section 9. As I will argue, only rule utilitarianism can explain why a society will be better off if people's behaviour is constrained by a network of moral rights and moral obligations which, barring extreme emergencies, must not be violated on grounds of mere social-expediency considerations. Prior to the emergence of rule-utilitarian theory, utilitarians could not convincingly defend themselves against the accusation that they were advocating a super-Machiavellistic morality, which permitted infringement of all individual rights and all institutional obligations in the name of some narrowly defined social utility.

Virtually all the moral content of the ethical theory I am going to propose will come from these three intellectual traditions: Adam Smith's, Kant's, and that of the utilitarian school. Yet it would not have been possible to put all these pieces together into an intellectually satisfactory theory of morality before the emergence, and without an extensive use, of the modern theory of rational behaviour and, in particular, the modern

---

[6] Rawls 1971. For a detailed critique of Rawls' theory, see Harsanyi 1975a. For a discussion of some other nonutilitarian theories, see Harsanyi 1975c.
[7] Harrod 1936.
[8] Brandt 1959, pp. 369, 380.

theory of rational behaviour under risk and uncertainty, usually described as Bayesian decision theory. The Bayesian concept of rationality is a very crucial ingredient of my theory.

2 Ethics as a branch of the general theory of rational behaviour

I propose to argue that the emergence of modern decision theory has made ethics into an organic part of the general theory of rational behaviour. The concept of rational behaviour (practical rationality) is important in philosophy both in its own right and because of its close connection with theoretical rationality. It plays a very important role also in the empirical social sciences, mainly in economics but also in political science and in sociology (at least in the more analytically oriented versions of these two disciplines). What is more important for our present purposes, the concept of rational behaviour is the very foundation of the normative disciplines of decision theory, of game theory, and (as I will argue) of ethics.

The concept of rational behaviour arises from the empirical fact that human behaviour is to a large extent goal-directed behaviour. Basically, rational behaviour is simply behaviour consistently pursuing some well defined goals, and pursuing them according to some well defined set of preferences or priorities.

We all know that, as a matter of empirical fact, even if human behaviour is usually goal-directed, it is seldom sufficiently consistent in its goals, and in the priorities it assigns to its various goals, to approach the ideal of full rationality. Nevertheless, in many fields of human endeavour – for example, in most areas of economic life, in many areas of politics (including international politics), and in some other areas of social interaction – human behaviour does show sufficiently high degrees of rationality as to give a surprising amount of explanatory and predictive power to some analytical models postulating full rationality. (Of course, it is very possible that we could further increase the explanatory and predictive power of our theories if we paid closer attention to the actual limits of human rationality and information-processing ability, in accordance with Simon's theory of limited rationality.[9])

Moreover, whether people actually do act rationally or not, they are often interested in increasing the rationality of their behaviour; and they are also interested in the conceptual problem of what it would actually mean to act fully rationally in various situations. It is the task of the normative disciplines of decision theory, game theory, and ethics to help

[9] See, for example, Simon 1960.

people to act more rationally and to give them a better understanding of what rationality really is.

For reasons I will describe presently, I propose to consider these three disciplines as parts of the same general theory of rational behaviour. Thus one part of this general theory[10] will be:

(1) The theory of *individual* rational behaviour, which itself comprises the theories of rational behaviour

(1A) Under certainty,

(1B) Under risk (where all probabilities are known objective probabilities), and

(1C) Under uncertainty (where some or all probabilities are unknown, and may be even undefined as objective probabilities).

(1A), (1B), and (1C) together are often called utility theory while (1B) and (1C) together are called decision theory.

The two other branches of the general theory of rational behaviour both deal with rational behaviour in a *social* setting. They are:

(2) Game theory, which is a theory of rational interaction between two or more individuals, each of them rationally pursuing his own objectives against the other individual(s) who rationally pursue(s) his (or their) own objectives. Any individual's objectives may be selfish or unselfish, as determined by his own utility function. (A nontrivial game situation can arise just as easily among altruists as it can among egoists – as long as these altruists are pursuing partly or wholly divergent altruistic goals.)

(3) Ethics, which is a theory of rational behaviour in the service of the common interests of society as a whole.

I think it is useful to regard (1), (2), and (3) as branches of the same basic discipline, for the following reasons:

(i) All three normative disciplines use essentially the same method. Each starts out by defining rational behaviour in its own field either by some set of axioms or by a constructive decision model. In either case, this initial definition may be called the primary definition of rationality in this particular field. Then, from this primary definition, each derives a secondary definition of rationality, which is usually much more convenient than the primary definition in itself would be in its axiomatic or constructive form, both for practical applications and for further philosophical analysis. For example, in case (1A) the secondary definition of rationality is *utility maximisation* – which is for many purposes a much more convenient characterisation of rational behaviour under certainty than is its primary definition in terms of the usual axioms (the complete preordering requirement and the continuity axiom).

---

[10] The remaining part of this section will be somewhat technical, but it can be omitted without loss of continuity.

In cases (1B) and (1C), the secondary definition of rationality is *expected-utility maximisation* (with objective probability weights in case (1B) and with subjective probability weights in case (1C)).

In the game-theoretical case (2), the secondary definition is provided by various game-theoretical solution concepts.

Finally, in the case of ethics (case (3)), as we will see, the secondary definition of rationality (or of morality) is in terms of *maximising the average utility level* of all individuals in the society.

This common method that these normative disciplines use represents a unique combination of philosophical analysis and of mathematical reasoning. In each case, a movement from the primary definition of rationality to its secondary definition is a straightforward mathematical problem. But discovery of an appropriate primary definition is always essentially a philosophical – that is, a conceptual – problem (with the possible exception of case (1A), where the philosophical dimension of the problem seems to be less important). People familiar with research work in these areas know the special difficulties that arise from this unusual interdependence of philosophical and mathematical problems. These are definitely not areas for people who prefer their mathematics without any admixture of philosophy, or who prefer their philosophy without any admixture of mathematics.

(ii) The axioms used by decision theory, game theory, and ethics are mathematically very closely related. In all three disciplines they are based on such mathematical properties as efficiency, symmetry, avoidance of dominated strategies, continuity, utility maximisation, invariance with respect to order-preserving linear utility transformations, etc.

(iii) Yet the most important link among the three disciplines lies in the fact that recent work has made it increasingly practicable to reduce some basic problems of game theory and of ethics partly or wholly to decision-theoretical problems.[11]

3 The equiprobability model for moral value judgements

After the two introductory sections, I now propose to describe my theory of morality. The basis of this theory is a model for moral value judgements.

Any moral value judgement is a judgement of preference, but it is a judgement of preference of a very special kind. Suppose somebody tells us: 'I much prefer our capitalist system over any socialist system because

---

[11] In game theory, one step in this direction has been a use of probability models for analysing games with incomplete information (Harsanyi 1967–8). More recently, a decision-theoretical approach to defining a solution for noncooperative games has been proposed (Harsanyi 1975b). On uses of decision theory in ethics, see Harsanyi 1977.

under our capitalist system I happen to be a millionaire and have a very satisfying life, whereas under a socialist system I would be in all probability at best a badly paid minor government official.' This may be a very reasonable judgement of personal preference from his own individual point of view. But nobody would call it a *moral* value judgement because it would be obviously a judgement based primarily on self-interest.

Compare this with a situation where somebody would express a preference for the capitalist system as against the socialist system without knowing in advance what particular social position he would occupy under either system. To make it more precise, let us assume that he would choose between the two systems under the assumption that, in either system, he would have the same probability of occupying any one of the available social positions. In this case, we could be sure that his choice would be independent of morally irrelevant selfish considerations. Therefore his choice (or his judgement of preference) between the two systems would now become a genuine moral value judgement.

Of course, it is not really necessary that a person who wants to make a moral assessment of the relative merits of capitalism and of socialism should be literally ignorant of the actual social position that he does occupy or would occupy under each system. But it *is* necessary that he should at least try his best to disregard this morally irrelevant piece of information when he is making his moral assessment. Otherwise his assessment will not be a genuine moral value judgement but rather will be merely a judgement of personal preference.

For short reference, the fictitious assumption of having the same probability of occupying any possible social position will be called the *equiprobability postulate*, whereas the entire preceding decision model based on this assumption will be called the *equiprobability model of moral value judgements*.

We can better understand the implications of this model if we subject it to decision-theoretical analysis. Suppose the society we are considering consists of n individuals, numbered as individual $1, 2, \ldots, n$, according to whether they would occupy the 1st (highest), 2nd (second highest), $\ldots$, nth (lowest) social position under a given social system. Let $U_1, U_2, \ldots, U_n$, denote the utility levels that individuals $1, 2, \ldots, n$ would enjoy under this system. The individual who wants to make a moral value judgement about the relative merits of capitalism and of socialism will be called individual i. By the equiprobability postulate, individual i will act in such a way as if he assigned the *same* probability $1/n$ to his occupying *any* particular social position and, therefore, to his utility reaching any one of the utility levels $U_1, U_2, \ldots, U_n$.

Now, under the assumed conditions, according to Bayesian decision theory, a rational individual will always choose that particular social system that would maximise his expected utility, that is, the quantity

$$(1) \quad W_i = \frac{1}{n} \sum_{j=1}^{n} U_j,$$

representing the arithmetic mean of all individual utility levels in society. We can express this conclusion also by saying that a rational individual will always use this mean utility as his social welfare function; or that he will be a utilitarian, who defines social utility as the mean of individual utilities (rather than as their sum, as many utilitarians have done).[12]

Of course, this conclusion makes sense only if we assume that it is mathematically admissible to *add* the utilities of different individuals, that is, if we assume that interpersonal comparisons of utility represent a meaningful intellectual operation. I will try to show that this is in fact the case.

In describing this equiprobability model, I have assumed that individual *i*, who is making a moral value judgement on the merits of the two alternative social systems, is one of the *n* members of the society in question. But exactly the same reasoning would apply if he were an interested outsider rather than a member. Indeed, for some purposes it is often heuristically preferable to restate the model under this alternative assumption. Yet, once we do this, our model becomes a modern restatement of Adam Smith's theory of an impartially sympathetic observer. His impartiality requirement corresponds to my equiprobability postulate, whereas his sympathy requirement corresponds to my assumption that individual *i* will make his choice in terms of interpersonal utility comparisons based on empathy with various individual members of society (see section 5).

This equiprobability model of moral value judgements gives us both a powerful analytical criterion and a very convenient heuristic criterion for deciding practical moral problems. If we want to decide between two alternative moral standards A and B, all we have to do is ask ourselves the question, 'Would I prefer to live in a society conforming to standard A or in a society conforming to standard B? – assuming I would not know in advance what my actual social position would be in either society but rather would have to assume to have an equal chance of ending up in any one of the possible positions.'

[12] For most purposes the two definitions of social utility are mathematically equivalent. This is always true when *n*, the number of people in society, can be regarded as a constant. The two definitions, however, yield different decision criteria in judging alternative population policies. In this latter case, in my view, the mean-utility criterion gives incomparably superior results.

Admittedly, this criterion – or any conceivable moral criterion – will still leave each of us with the great moral responsibility, and the often very difficult intellectual task, of actually choosing between these two alternative moral standards in terms of this criterion. But by using this criterion we will know at least *what* the actual intellectual problem is that we are trying to solve in choosing between them.

My equiprobability model was first published in 1953, and was extended in 1955.[13] Vickrey had suggested a similar idea,[14] but my work was independent of his. Later John Rawls again independently proposed a very similar model, which he called the 'original position', based on the 'veil of ignorance'.[15] But while my own model served as a basis for a utilitarian theory, Rawls derived very nonutilitarian conclusions from his own. Yet the difference does not lie in the nature of the two models, which are based on almost identical qualitative assumptions. Rather, the difference lies in the decision-theoretical analysis applied to the two models. One difference is that Rawls avoids any use of numerical probabilities. But the main difference is that Rawls makes the technical mistake of basing his analysis on a highly irrational decision rule, the maximin principle, which was fairly fashionable thirty years ago but which lost its attraction a few years later when its absurd practical implications were realised.[16]

Our model of moral value judgements can also be described as follows. Each individual has two very different sets of preferences. On the one hand, he has his *personal preferences*, which guide his everyday behaviour and which are expressed in his utility function U_i. Most people's personal preferences will not be completely selfish. But they will assign higher weights to their own interests and to the interests of their family, their friends, and other personal associates than they will assign to the interests of complete strangers. On the other hand, each individual will also have *moral preferences* which may or may not have much influence on his everyday behaviour but which will guide his thinking in those – possibly very rare – moments when he forces a special impersonal and impartial attitude, that is, a moral attitude, upon himself. His moral preferences, unlike his personal preferences, will by definition always assign the same weight to all individuals' interests, including his own. These moral preferences will be expressed by his social-welfare function W_i. Typically, different individuals will have very different utility functions U_i but, as can be seen from Equation (1) above, in theory they will tend to have identical social-welfare functions – but only if they agree in their factual assump-

[13] Harsanyi 1953 and 1955.
[14] Vickrey 1945.
[15] Rawls 1957; 1958; and 1971.
[16] First by Radner and Marschak 1954, pp. 61–8. See also Harsanyi 1975a.

tions on the nature of the individual utility functions U_i and on the conversion ratios between different individuals' utilities (as decided by interpersonal utility comparisons) – which, of course, may not be the case.

By definition, a moral value judgement is always an expression of one's moral preferences. Any evaluative statement one may make will automatically lose its status of a moral value judgement if it is unduly influenced by one's personal interests and personal preferences.

4   An axiomatic justification for utilitarian theory

I now propose to present an alternative, this time *axiomatic*, justification for utilitarian theory. This axiomatic approach yields a lesser amount of philosophically interesting information about the nature of morality than the equiprobability model does, but it has the advantage of being based on much weaker – almost trivial – philosophical assumptions. Instead of using very specific philosophical assumptions about the nature of morality, it relies merely on Pareto optimality and on the Bayesian rationality postulates.

We need three axioms:

Axiom 1: Individual rationality. The personal preferences of all n individuals in society satisfy the Bayesian rationality postulates.[17]

Axiom 2: Rationality of moral preferences. The moral preferences of at least one individual, namely, individual i, satisfy the Bayesian rationality postulates.

Axiom 3: Pareto optimality. Suppose that at least one individual j ($j = 1$, ..., n) personally prefers alternative A to alternative B, and that no individual has an opposite personal preference. Then individual i will morally prefer alternative A over alternative B.

Axiom 3 is a very weak and hardly objectionable moral postulate. Axiom 1 is a rather natural rationality requirement. Axiom 2 is an equally natural rationality requirement: in trying to decide what the common interests of society are, we should surely follow at least as high standards of rationality as we follow (by Axiom 1) in looking after our own personal interests.

[17] Most philosophers and social scientists do not realise how weak the rationality postulates are that Bayesian decision theory needs for establishing the expected-utility maximisation theorem. As Anscombe and Aumann have shown (Anscombe and Aumann 1963), all we need is the requirement of consistent preferences (complete preordering), a continuity axiom, the sure-thing principle (avoidance of dominated strategies), and the requirement that our preferences for lotteries should depend only on the possible prizes and on the specific random events deciding the actual prize. (The last requirement can be replaced by appropriate axioms specifying the behaviour of numerical probabilities within lotteries. In the literature, these axioms are usually called 'notational conventions'.)

Axiom 1 implies that the personal preferences of each individual j ($j = 1,$ $\ldots, n$) can be represented by a von Neumann–Morgenstern ($=$vNM) utility function U_j. Axiom 2 implies that the moral preferences of individual i can be represented by a social welfare function W_i, which mathematically also has the nature of a vNM utility function. Finally, the three axioms together imply the following theorem:

Theorem T. The social welfare function W_i of individual i must be of the mathematical form:

(2) $$W_i = \sum_{j=1}^{n} a_j U_j \text{ with } a_j > 0 \text{ for } j = 1, \ldots, n.$$

This result[18] can be strengthened by adding a fourth axiom:

Axiom 4: Symmetry. The social-welfare function W_i is a symmetric function of all individual utilities. (That is, different individuals should be treated equally.)

Using this axiom, we can conclude that

(3) $$a_1 = \ldots = a_n > 0.$$

Equations (2) and (3) together are essentially equivalent to Equation (1).[19]

I realise that some people may feel uncomfortable with the rather abstract philosophical arguments I used to justify my equiprobability model. In contrast, the four axioms of the present section make only very weak philosophical assumptions. They should appeal to everbody who believes in Bayesian rationality, in Pareto optimality, and in equal treatment of all individuals. Yet these very weak axioms turn out to be sufficient to entail a utilitarian theory of morality.

5 Interpersonal utility comparisons

In everyday life we make, or at least attempt to make, interpersonal utility comparisons all the time. When we have only one nut left at the end of a trip, we may have to decide which particular member of our family is in greatest need of a little extra food. Again, we may give a book or a concert ticket or a free invitation to a wine-tasting fair to one friend rather than to another in the belief that the former would enjoy it more than the latter would. I do not think it is the task of a philosopher or a social scientist to

---

[18] For proof, see Harsanyi 1955.

[19] There is, however, the following difference. Equation (1) implies that social utility must be defined as the mean of individual utilities rather than as their sum. In contrast, Equations (2) and (3) do not favour either definition of social utility over its alternative.

deny the obvious fact that people often feel quite capable of making such comparisons. Rather, his task is to explain how we ever managed to make such comparisons – as well or as badly as we do make them.

Simple reflection will show that the basic intellectual operation in such interpersonal comparisons is imaginative empathy. We imagine ourselves to be in the shoes of another person, and ask ourselves the question, 'If I were now really in *his* position, and had *his* taste, *his* education, *his* social background, *his* cultural values, and *his* psychological make-up, then what would now be *my* preferences between various alternatives, and how much satisfaction or dissatisfaction would *I* derive from any given alternative?' (An 'alternative' here stands for a given bundle of economic commodities plus a given position with respect to various noneconomic variables, such as health, social status, job situation, family situation, etc.)

In other words, any interpersonal utility comparison is based on what I will call the *similarity postulate*, to be defined as the assumption that, once proper allowances have been made for the empirically given differences in taste, education, etc., between me and another person, then it is reasonable for me to assume that our basic psychological reactions to any given alternative will be otherwise much the same. Of course, it is only too easy to misapply this similarity postulate. For instance, I may fail to make proper allowances for differences in our tastes, and may try to judge the satisfaction that a devoted fish eater derives from eating fish in terms of my own intense dislike for any kind of sea food. Of course, sensible people will seldom make such an obvious mistake. But they may sometimes make much subtler mistakes of the same fundamental type.

In general, if we have enough information about a given person, and make a real effort to attain an imaginative empathy with him, we can probably make reasonably good estimates of the utilities and disutilities he would obtain from various alternatives. But if we have little information about him, our estimates may be quite wrong.

In any case, utilitarian theory does not involve the assumption that people are very good at making interpersonal utility comparisons. It involves only the assumption that, in many cases, people simply *have* to make such comparisons in order to make certain moral decisions – however badly they may make them. If I am trying to decide which member of my family is in greatest need of food, I may sometimes badly misjudge the situation. But I simply *have* to make *some* decision. I cannot let *all* members of my family go hungry because I have philosophical scruples about interpersonal comparisons and cannot make up my mind.

Nevertheless, interpersonal utility comparisons do pose important philosophical problems. In particular, they pose the problem that they require us to use what I have called the similarity postulate. Yet this postulate, by its very nature, is not open to any direct empirical test. I may very well assume that different people will have similar psychological feelings about any given situation, once differences in their tastes, educations, etc. have been allowed for. But I can never verify this assumption by direct observation since I have no direct access to their inner feelings.

Therefore, the similarity postulate must be classified as a nonempirical a priori postulate. But, of course, interpersonal utility comparisons are by no means unique among empirical hypotheses in their dependence on such nonempirical postulates. In actual fact, whenever we choose among alternative empirical hypotheses, we are always dependent on some nonempirical choice criteria. This is so because the empirical facts are always consistent with infinitely many alternative hypotheses, and the only way we can choose among them is by using a priori nonempirical choice criteria, such as simplicity, parsimony, preference for the 'least arbitrary' hypothesis, etc.

Our similarity postulate is a nonempirical postulate of the same general type. Its intuitive justification is that, if two individuals show exactly identical behaviour — or, if they show different behaviour but these differences in their observable behaviour have been properly allowed for — then it will be a completely arbitrary and unwarranted assumption to postulate some further hidden and unobservable differences in their psychological feelings.

We use this similarity postulate not only in making interpersonal utility comparisons but also in assigning other people human feelings and conscious experiences at all. From a purely empirical point of view, a world in which I would be the only person with real conscious experiences while all other people were mindless robots would be completely indistinguishable from our actual world where all individuals with human bodies are conscious human beings. (Indeed, even a world in which I alone would exist, and all other people as well as the whole physical universe would be merely my own dream — solipsism — would be empirically indistinguishable from the world we actually live in.) When we choose the assumption that we actually live in a world populated by millions of other human beings, just as real and just as conscious as we are ourselves, then we are relying on the same similarity postulate. We are essentially saying that, given the great basic similarity among different human beings, it would be absurd to postulate fundamental hidden differences between them by making one person a conscious human being while making the others mere robots, or by making one person real while making the others mere dream figures. (Strictly speaking, we cannot exclude the possibility that somebody who looks human will turn out to be an unfeeling robot; but we have no scientific or moral justification to treat him like a robot before the evidence for his being a robot becomes overwhelming.)

There is no logical justification for using the similarity postulate to reject the hypothesis that other people are mere robots (or mere dream figures) yet to resist interpersonal utility comparisons based on the very same similarity postulate. It is simply illogical to admit that other people do have feelings and, therefore, do derive *some* satisfaction from a good meal in the same way we do; yet to resist the quantitative hypothesis that the *amount* of satisfaction they actually obtain from a good dinner – that is, the personal importance they attach to a good dinner – must be much the same as it is in our own case, after proper allowances have been made for differences in our tastes, in the food requirements of our bodies, in our state of health, etc. A willingness to make interpersonal comparisons is no more than an admission that other people are just as real as we are, that they share a common humanity with us, and that they have the same basic capacity for satisfaction and for dissatisfaction, in spite of the undeniable individual differences that exist between us in specific detail.

The long-standing opposition by many philosophers and social scientists to interpersonal utility comparisons goes back to the early days of logical positivism, when the role of nonempirical a priori principles, like the similarity postulate, in a choice among alternative empirical hypotheses was very poorly understood. We owe an immense intellectual debt to the logical positivists for their persistent efforts to put philosophy on truly scientific foundations by combining strict empiricism with the strict mathematical rigour of modern logic. But there is no denying that many of their specific philosophical views were badly mistaken, and that they had little appreciation in their early period for the importance of a priori principles and, more generally, for the importance of theoretical ideas in empirical science.

One would think that after so many years the time had come to escape the narrow confines of a long-obsolete logical-positivist orthodoxy and to have a fresh look at the problem of interpersonal utility comparisons.

6 The use of von Neumann–Morgenstern utility functions

The utilitarian theory I have proposed makes an essential use of von Neumann–Morgenstern (= vNM) utility functions. Many critics have argued that any use of vNM utility functions is inappropriate, because they merely express people's attitudes toward gambling, and these attitudes have no moral significance.[20] This objection is based on a rather common misinterpretation of vNM utility functions. These utility func-

[20] See, for example, Rawls 1971, pp. 172, 323.

tions do express people's attitudes to risk taking (in gambling, buying insurance, investing and other similar activities). But they do not merely register these attitudes; rather, they try to explain them in terms of the relative importance (relative utility) people attach to possible gains and to possible losses of money or of other economic or noneconomic assets.

For example, suppose that Mr X is willing to pay \$5 for a lottery ticket that gives him a $1/1,000$ chance of winning \$1,000. Then we can explain his willingness to gamble at such very unfavourable odds as follows. He must have an unusually high utility for winning \$1,000, as compared with his disutility for losing \$5. In fact, even though the ratio of these two money amounts is only $1,000 : 5 = 200 : 1$, the ratio of the corresponding utility and disutility must be at least $1,000 : 1$. (If we know Mr X's personal circumstances, then we will often be able to carry this explanation one step – or several steps – further. For instance, we may know that his strong desire for winning \$1,000 arises from the fact that he needs the money for a deposit on a badly needed car, or for some other very important large and indivisible expenditure; while his relative unconcern about losing \$5 is due to the fact that such a loss would not seriously endanger his ability to pay for his basic necessities – food, lodging, etc.[21])

In other words, even though a person's vNM utility function is always estimated in terms of his behaviour under risk and uncertainty, the real purpose of this estimation procedure is to obtain cardinal-utility measures for the relative personal importance he assigns to various economic (and noneconomic) alternatives.

No doubt, since social utility is defined in terms of people's vNM utility functions, our utilitarian theory will tend to assign higher social priorities to those individual desires for which people are willing to take considerable risks in order to satisfy them. But this is surely as it should be. Other things being equal, we *should* give higher social priorities to intensely felt human desires; and one indication that somebody feels strongly about a particular desired objective is his willingness to take sizable risks to attain it. For example, if a person is known to have risked his life in order to obtain a university education (e.g., by escaping from a despotic government which had tried to exclude him from all higher education), then we can take this as a reasonably sure sign of his attaching very high personal importance (very high utility) to such an education; and I cannot see anything wrong with our assigning high social priority to helping him to such an education on the basis of this kind of evidence.

[21] Fundamentally, any explanation of why a given person's vNM utility function has any specific shape and, in particular, why its convex and concave segments are distributed in the way they are, will be typically in terms of substitution and complementarity relations among the commodities consumed by him. Mathematically, indivisible commodities are a special case of complementarity.

7 Preference utilitarianism, hedonism, ideal utilitarianism, and the question of irrational preferences

The utilitarian theory I have proposed defines social utility in terms of individual utilities, and defines each person's utility function in terms of his personal preferences. Thus, in the end, social utility is defined in terms of people's personal preferences. This approach may be called *preference utilitarianism*. It is not the same approach that was used by the nineteenth-century utilitarians. They were *hedonists* (hedonistic utilitarians), and defined both social utility and individual utility functions in terms of feelings of pleasure and pain. A third approach, called *ideal utilitarianism*, was proposed by the Cambridge philosopher Moore, who defined both social utility and individual utilities in terms of amounts of 'mental states of intrinsic worth', such as the mental states involved in philosophy, science, aesthetic appreciation of works of art, experiences of personal friendship, etc.[22]

Both hedonistic and ideal utilitarianism are open to serious objections. The former presupposes a now completely outdated hedonistic psychology. It is by no means obvious that all we do we do only in order to attain pleasure and to avoid pain. It is at least arguable that in many cases we are more interested in achieving some objective state of affairs than we are interested in our own subjective feelings of pleasure and pain that may result from achieving it. It seems that when I give a friend a present my main purpose is to give *him* pleasure rather than to give pleasure to myself (though this may very well be a secondary objective). Even if I want to accomplish something for myself, it is by no means self-evident that my main purpose is to produce some feelings of pleasure in myself, and it is not the actual accomplishment of some objective condition, such as having a good job, solving a problem, or winning a game, etc. In any case, there is no reason whatever why any theory of morality should try to prejudge the issue whether people are always after pleasure or whether they also have other objectives.

As to ideal utilitarianism, it is certainly not true as an empirical observation that people's only purpose in life is to have 'mental states of intrinsic worth'. But if this is not in fact the case, then it is hard to see how we could prove that, even though they may not in fact act in this way, this is how they *should* act. Moreover, the criteria by which 'mental states of intrinsic worth' can be distinguished from other kinds of mental states are extremely unclear. (Moore's own theory that they differ from other mental states in having some special 'nonnatural qualities' is a very unconvincing

[22] Moore 1903.

old-fashioned metaphysical assumption lacking any kind of supporting evidence.)

More fundamentally, preference utilitarianism is the only form of utilitarianism consistent with the important philosophical principle of *preference autonomy*. By this I mean the principle that, in deciding what is good and what is bad for a given individual, the ultimate criterion can only be his own wants and his own preferences. To be sure, as I will myself argue below, a person may irrationally want something which is very 'bad for him'. But, it seems to me, the only way we can make sense of such a statement is to interpret it as a claim to the effect that, in some appropriate sense, his own preferences at some deeper level are inconsistent with what he is now trying to achieve.

Any sensible ethical theory must make a distinction between rational wants and irrational wants, or between rational preferences and irrational preferences. It would be absurd to assert that we have the same moral obligation to help other people in satisfying their utterly unreasonable wants as we have to help them in satisfying their very reasonable desires. Hedonistic utilitarianism and ideal utilitarianism have no difficulty in maintaining this distinction. They can define rational wants simply as ones directed toward objects having a real ability to produce pleasure, or a real ability to produce 'mental states of intrinsic worth'; and they can define irrational wants as ones directed toward objects lacking this ability. But it may appear that this distinction is lost as soon as hedonistic and ideal utilitarianism are replaced by preference utilitarianism.

In actual fact, there is no difficulty in maintaining this distinction even without an appeal to any other standard than an individual's own personal preferences. All we have to do is to distinguish between a person's manifest preferences and his true preferences. His manifest preferences are his actual preferences as manifested by his observed behaviour, including preferences possibly based on erroneous factual beliefs, or on careless logical analysis, or on strong emotions that at the moment greatly hinder rational choice. In contrast, a person's true preferences are the preferences he *would* have if he had all the relevant factual information, always reasoned with the greatest possible care, and were in a state of mind most conducive to rational choice. Given this distinction, a person's rational wants are those consistent with his true preferences and, therefore, consistent with all the relevant factual information and with the best possible logical analysis of this information, whereas irrational wants are those that fail this test.

In my opinion, social utility must be defined in terms of people's true preferences rather than in terms of their manifest preferences. But, while it is only natural to appeal from a person's irrational preferences to his underlying 'true' preferences, we must always use his own preferences in some suitable way as our final criterion in judging what his real interests are and what is really good for him.

8 Exclusion of antisocial preferences

I have argued that, in defining the concept of social utility, people's irrational preferences must be replaced by what I have called their true preferences. But I think we have to go even further than this: some preferences, which may very well be their 'true' preferences under my definition, must be altogether excluded from our social-utility function. In particular, we must exclude all clearly antisocial preferences, such as sadism, envy, resentment, and malice.[23]

According to utilitarian theory, the fundamental basis of all our moral commitments to other people is a general goodwill and human sympathy. But no amount of goodwill to individual X can impose the moral obligation on me to help him in hurting a third person, individual Y, out of sheer sadism, ill will, or malice. Utilitarian ethics makes all of us members of the same moral community. A person displaying ill will toward others does remain a remember of this community, but not with his whole personality. That part of his personality that harbours these hostile antisocial feelings must be excluded from membership, and has no claim for a hearing when it comes to defining our concept of social utility.[24]

9 Rule utilitarianism vs. act utilitarianism

Just as in making other moral decisions, in choosing between rule utilitarianism and act utilitarianism the basic question we have to ask is this: Which version of utilitarianism will maximise social utility? Will society be better off under one or the other? This test very clearly gives the advantage to rule utilitarianism.

In an earlier paper[25] I proposed the following decision-theoretical model for studying the moral implications of the two utilitarian theories. The

[23] For a contrary view, see Smart 1961, pp. 16–17.
[24] The German neo-Kantian utilitarian philosopher Leonard Nelson proposed a distinction between legitimate and illegitimate personal interests (Nelson 1917–32). He argued that the only interests we are morally obliged to respect are legitimate interests. Thus, under his theory, exclusion of antisocial preferences from our concept of social utility is merely a special case of the general principle of disregarding all illegitimate interests. Unfortunately, Nelson did not offer any clear formal criterion for defining legitimate and illegitimate interests. But it seems to me that a really satisfactory theory of legitimate and illegitimate interests would be a major step forward in utilitarian moral philosophy. Yet discussion of this problem must be left for another occasion. (The reference to Nelson's work I owe to Reinhard Selten.)
[25] Harsanyi 1977.

problem we want to consider is that of making moral decisions, that is, the problem of deciding what the morally right action is in a given situation or in a given class of situations. In actual fact, analytically it is preferable to redefine this problem as one of choosing a morally right strategy. Here the term 'strategy' has its usual decision-theoretical and game-theoretical meaning. Thus a strategy is a mathematical function assigning a specific action to any possible situation, subject to the requirement that, if the agent has insufficient information to distinguish one situation from another, then any strategy of his must assign the same specific action to both situations. (In technical language, all choice points belonging to the same information set must have the same specific action assigned to them.)

The two utilitarian theories use different decision rules in solving this moral decision problem. For both theories, a moral decision problem is a maximisation problem involving maximisation of the same quantity, namely, social utility. But the two theories impose very different mathematical constraints on this maximisation problem. An act-utilitarian moral agent assumes that the strategies of all other moral agents (including those of all other utilitarian agents) are given and that his task is merely to choose his own strategy so as to maximise social utility when all other strategies are kept constant. In contrast, a rule-utilitarian moral agent will regard not only his own strategy but also the strategies of all other rule-utilitarian agents as variables to be determined during the maximisation process so as to maximise social utility. For him this maximisation process is subject to two mathematical constraints: one is that the strategies to be chosen for all rule-utilitarian agents must be identical (since, by the definition of rule utilitarianism, all rule-utilitarian agents are always required to follow the same general moral rules); the other is that the strategies of all nonutilitarian agents must be regarded as given. (On this last point both utilitarian theories agree: people known not to believe in a utilitarian philosophy cannot be expected to choose their strategies by trying to maximise social utility. They may follow traditional morality, or some other nonutilitarian morality, or may simply follow self-interest, etc. But, in any case, for the purposes of a utilitarian decision problem, their strategies must be regarded as being given from outside of the system.)

These differences in the decision rules used by the two utilitarian theories, and in particular the different ways they define the constraints for the utilitarian maximisation problem, have important practical implications. One implication is that rule utilitarianism is in a much better position to organise cooperation and strategy coordination among different people (coordination effect).

For example, consider the problem of voting when there is an important measure on the ballot but when voting involves some minor inconvenience. Suppose there are 1,000 voters strongly favouring the measure, but it can be predicted with reasonable certainty that there will also be 800 negative votes. The measure will pass if it obtains a simple majority of all votes cast. How will the two utilitarian theories handle this problem?

First suppose that all 1,000 voters favouring the measure are act utilitarians. Then each of them will take the trouble to vote only if he thinks that his own vote will be decisive in securing passage of the measure, that is, if he expects *exactly* 800 other people favouring the measure to vote (since in this case his own vote will be needed to provide the 801 votes required for majority). But of course each voter will know that it is extremely unlikely that his own vote will be decisive in this sense. Therefore, most act-utilitarian voters will not bother to vote, and the measure will fail, possibly with disastrous consequences for their society.

In contrast, if the 1,000 voters favouring the measure are rule utilitarians, then all of them will vote (if mixed strategies are not permitted). This is so because the rule-utilitarian decision rule will allow them a choice only between two admissible strategies: one requiring everybody to vote and the other requiring nobody to vote. Since the former will yield a higher social utility, the strategy chosen by the rule-utilitarian criterion will be for everybody to vote. As this example shows, by following the rule-utilitarian decision rule people can achieve successful spontaneous cooperation in situations where this could not be done by adherence to the act-utilitarian decision rule (or at least where this could not be done without explicit agreement on coordinated action, and perhaps without an expensive organisation effort).

Though in some situations this coordination effect may be quite important, it seems to me that the main advantage of rule utilitarianism over act utilitarianism really lies in a different direction, namely, in its ability to take proper account of the implications that alternative systems of possible moral rules would have for people's expectations and incentives (expectation and incentive effects).

For example, consider the problem of keeping promises. Traditional morality says that promises should be kept, with a possible exception of cases where keeping a promise would impose excessive hardship on the promise maker (or perhaps on third persons). In contrast, act utilitarianism would make the breaking of a promise morally permissible whenever this would yield a slightly higher social utility — perhaps because of unexpected changes in the circumstances — than keeping of the promise would yield. But this would greatly reduce the social benefits associated with the making of promises as an institution. It would make it rather uncertain in most cases whether any given promise would be kept. People would be less able to form definite expectations about each other's future behaviour and would have a general feeling of insecurity about the future. Moreover, this uncertainty would greatly reduce their incentives to engage in various socially very useful activities on the expectation that promises given to them would be kept. (For instance, they would become much less willing to perform useful services for other people for promised future rewards.)

As compared with act utilitarianism, rule utilitarianism will be much closer to traditional morality in maintaining that promises should be kept, subject only to rather rare exceptions. An act utilitarian always asks the question, 'Would this one act of possible promise breaking increase or decrease social utility?' In contrast, a rule utilitarian has to ask, 'What particular moral rule for promise keeping would maximise social utility?'

As a result, an act utilitarian can consider the socially unfavourable effects of promise breaking only to the extent that these have the nature of causal consequences of individual acts of promise breaking. No doubt, one act of promise breaking already will somewhat reduce people's trust in promises, but normally this effect will be quite small. In contrast, a rule utilitarian can also consider the causal consequences of a general practice of repeated promise breaking. But, more importantly, he can also consider the noncausal logical implications of adopting a moral rule permitting many easy exceptions to promise keeping.

More particularly, he will always have to ask the question, 'What would be the social implications of adopting a moral rule permitting that promises should be broken under conditions *A, B, C,* etc. – assuming that all members of the society would know[26] that promise breaking would be permitted under these conditions?' Thus he will always have to balance the possible direct benefits of promise breaking in some specific situations against the unfavourable expectation and incentive effects that would arise if people knew in advance that in these situations promises would not be kept. In other words, rule utilitarianism not only enables us to make a rational choice among alternative possible general rules for defining morally desirable behaviour. Rather, it also provides a rational test for determining the exceptions to be permitted from these rules.

Limitations of space do not allow me to discuss the moral implications of rule utilitarianism here in any greater detail.[27] It can be shown, however, that rule utilitarianism comes fairly close to traditional morality in recognising the importance of social institutions which establish a network of

---

[26] In trying to evaluate a possible moral rule from a rule-utilitarian point of view, we must always assume that everybody would know the content of this moral rule. This is so because in principle everybody can always find out by direct computation what particular set of moral rules (i.e., what particular moral strategy) is optimal in terms of the rule-utilitarian criterion.

[27] But see Harsanyi 1977.

moral rights and of moral obligations among different people in society; and in maintaining that these rights and obligations must not be infringed upon on grounds of immediate social utility, with the possible exception of some very rare and very special cases. (The main social advantages of such stable rights and stable obligations, once more, lie in their beneficial expectation and incentive effects.) But of course we cannot expect that the rule-utilitarian criterion would confirm traditional views on these matters in all particulars.

10 The utility of free personal choice

As Rawls has rightly pointed out,[28] traditional utilitarianism tries to impose unreasonably strict moral standards on us, because it requires us to choose every individual action of ours so as to maximise social utility. Thus, if I feel like reading a book for entertainment, I must always ask myself whether my time could not be more usefully devoted to looking after the poor, or to converting some as yet unconverted colleagues to utilitarianism, or to taking part in some other socially beneficial project, etc. The only ways I could possibly justify my taking out time for reading this book would be to argue that reading it would give me exceptionally high direct utility (so as to exceed any social utility I could possibly produce by alternative activities), or that my reading the book would have great instrumental utility – for example, by restoring my temporarily depleted mental and physical energy for future socially very beneficial activities.

There is obviously something wrong with this moral choice criterion. It is not hard to see where the problem lies. Any reasonable utilitarian theory must recognise that people assign a nonnegligible positive utility to free personal choice, to freedom from unduly burdensome moral standards trying to regulate even the smallest details of their behaviour. Suppose we could choose between a society with the highest possible moral standards, regulating every minute of our waking lives in full detail, and a society with somewhat more relaxed moral standards, leaving us a reasonable amount of free choice in planning our everyday activities. It is very possible (though it is by no means certain) that, by imposing much stricter standards, the former society would attain higher levels of economic and cultural achievement than the latter would. Nevertheless, many of us might very well prefer to live in the latter society – at least if the differences in the economic and cultural standards between the two societies were not unduly large.

[28] Rawls 1971, p. 117.

What this means analytically is that, apart from the social utility W we assign to the outcome of any given activity, we must also assign some procedural utility $V > 0$ to our having a free personal choice among alternative activities. Suppose we have to choose between two alternative strategies S^* and S^{**} likely to yield the outcome utilities W^* and W^{**}, with $W^* > W^{**}$. Then classical utilitarianism would select strategy S^* as the *only* morally permissible strategy. But, it seems to me, we must recognise S^{**} as being an equally permissible strategy, provided that $W^{**} + V \geqq W^*$.

11 Conclusion

I have tried to show that there is a unique rational answer to the philosophical question, 'What is morality?' I have argued that, by answering this question, we obtain a very specific decision rule for choosing between alternative possible moral codes.

Even if this conclusion is accepted, this will not mean that practical moral problems from now on will become simply matters of solving some well-defined mathematical maximisation problems. Solving such problems will always involve extremely important questions of personal judgement because we have to use our own best judgement whenever we lack completely reliable factual information about some of the relevant variables. We will often lack reliable information about other people's manifest preferences and, even more so, about their true preferences. Our interpersonal utility comparisons may also be based on insufficient information, etc.

But the most fundamental source of uncertainty in our moral decisions will always lie in our uncertainty about the future, including our uncertainty about the future effects of our present policies, both in the short run and in the long run. It seems to me that careful analysis will almost invariably show that the most important source of moral and political disagreements among people of goodwill lies in divergent judgements about future developments and about the future consequences of alternative policies.

I have tried to show that an updated version of classical utilitarianism is the only ethical theory consistent with both the modern theory of rational behaviour and a full commitment to an impartially sympathetic humanitarian morality.

On the other hand, neither the concept of rationality alone, nor a commitment to a humanitarian morality alone, could yield a useful ethical theory. Rather, we need a combination of both. As I have argued in discussing Rawls's theory, even the best intuitive insight into the nature of morality will yield a highly unsatisfactory ethical theory if these insights are conjoined with a highly irrational decision rule like the maximin principle. Conversely, even the most careful analysis of the concept of rationality cannot show that rationality entails a commitment to a humanitarian morality.

Kant believed that morality is based on a categorical imperative so that anybody who is willing to listen to the voice of reason must obey the commands of morality. But I do not think he was right. All we can prove by rational arguments is that anybody who wants to serve our common human interests in a rational manner must obey these commands. In other words, all we can prove are hypothetical imperatives of the form: 'If you want to act in a way that an impartially sympathetic observer would approve of, then do such and such', or: 'If you want your behaviour to satisfy the axioms . . . then do such and such.'[29] But I do not think that this negative conclusion is a real setback for moral philosophy, or has any important practical implications at all. As a practical matter, all of us have always known that rational discussion about moral issues is possible only between people who share some basic moral commitments, such as a common interest in a truly humanitarian morality.

Let me end with a disclaimer. I think the utilitarian theory I have described in principle covers all interpersonal aspects of morality. But I do not think it covers *all* morality. There are some very important moral obligations it fails to cover because they are matters of individual morality and of individual rationality. Perhaps the most important such obligation is that of intellectual honesty, that is, the duty to seek the truth and to accept the truth as far as it can be established – regardless of any possible positive or negative social utility this truth may have. (Telling the truth to others may be constrained by tact, respect for other people's feelings, or commitments to secrecy, etc. But admitting the truth to ourselves is not.)

Intellectual honesty requires us to accept even very unpleasant truths rather than withdraw into a dream world or a fool's paradise based on self-deception. It also requires us to accept wholeheartedly the truth that we are not alone in this world but rather share a common human nature with many millions of others. Acceptance of this particular truth is, of course, not merely a matter of theoretical rationality; rather, it is also the intellectual basis of all social morality.

[29] Harsanyi 1958.

* The author wants to thank the National Science Foundation for supporting this research through Grant Soc 77–06394 to the Center for Research in Management Science, University of California, Berkeley.

3 The economic uses of utilitarianism[1]

J. A. MIRRLEES

Some economists, when evaluating alternative economic policies, are utilitarians. At any rate they look at something they call the total utility of the outcome. This paper is intended to argue in favour of this procedure.[2] It may be as well first to exemplify it.

An interesting question is how much income ought to be redistributed from those with high wages and salaries to those with low wages. To answer it, one can set up a model in which each individual's utility is a numerical function of his net income, after taxes and subsidies, and of the quantity of labour he supplies. Each individual, supposedly knowing how his income depends on the labour he supplies, decides how much to supply by computing what will maximise his utility. All these labour supply decisions taken together determine the output of the economy. A redistributive system, consisting of taxes and subsidies, is feasible provided that the output of the economy is sufficient to provide for public and private expenditures, private expenditures being determined by private net incomes. The object of the exercise is to find which feasible redistributive system yields the greatest total utility.

This is not the place to defend the simplifications of such an economic analysis, far less to discuss how it might be improved. Even within the model outlined, assumptions as to the kinds of taxes and subsidies that are possible have a substantial effect on the results. I shall want to return to

[1] A public lecture with the same title was given at University College, London, in February 1977. The main arguments were the same, but it is doubtful whether there are any common sentences. Nevertheless I am grateful for that invitation and the opportunity it provided to attempt to articulate an economist's defence of utilitarian methods, as used in much contemporary welfare economics. I should like to acknowledge valuable discussions on these questions with J. R. Broome, P. A. Diamond, and A. K. Sen, and their comments on the first draft of this paper. Comments by P. S. Dasgupta and Q. R. D. Skinner were also useful.
[2] There have been so many papers presenting versions of utilitarianism, or defending it against criticism (many of which I have read only cursorily or not at all), that it is hard to defend writing another. But there are differences of emphasis from the major statement by Vickrey (1960), and more substantial differences from Harsanyi (1953, 1955, and later books), both of whom discuss these matters from the point of view of economic problems. Taking that point of view, I found that I wanted to deal with a number of matters not discussed by Hare (1976) and Smart (1973) in their statements.

this aspect later, by way of illustration. The first issue is whether it is possible to specify numerical utility functions, in order to carry out such an analysis of redistributive policies.

The utility functions are partly tied down by the assumption that individuals' labour supplies are determined by utility maximisation. Observations on labour supply behaviour can therefore provide some check on the correctness of the utility functions; but only to a limited extent. Many distinct utility functions predict the same behaviour. When choosing a particular specification, do economists believe they are talking about quantities of pleasure less pain? If so, they show remarkably little interest in devising methods of actually measuring pleasure and pain. Edgeworth's ingenious suggestion that an absolute unit of utility is provided by the smallest perceptible change for the better has not found much favour.[3] I shall want to return to the question why this is not an acceptable measure of utility – as I think it is not – despite being the only one that seems to provide an objective basis for interpersonally comparable measurement.

Sen, in a recent discussion of utilitarianism (1979b), says, that he will take 'utility . . . to stand for a person's conception of his own well-being', a formulation which, though adopted specifically to emphasise its factual character, might be accepted by many economists as an adequate definition. But on one count it is not acceptable; and on another it may not be, if its meaning is made more precise. In the first place a person's *own* conception of his well-being should not always determine, other things being equal, the outcome for him. In the economic analysis sketched above, it was assumed that it should: that assumption might be wrong. People sometimes have mistaken conceptions of their well-being. At least the conception must somehow be purified of obvious errors of foresight or memory. More, one ought to be willing to entertain the possibility that some experiences are not usually correctly valued by the individual: that, in certain respects, people do not know what is good for them. For example, it has been claimed that many give too little weight to future experiences. Provided that the modification of measured well-being thus contemplated is empirically based, it is surely convenient to let the term 'utility' describe the well-being rather than the conception of it. Sen would, I think, regard this as too elastic a definition of 'utility', and prefers to make the same kind of point by saying that non-utility information about outcomes is sometimes relevant; though he would go further and allow 'non-utility information' that is not simply empirical evidence as to what is in fact a person's

---

[3] Edgeworth (1881) was very clear that one must provide an operational definition of utility. Sen (1970a, Chapter 7) gives references, and adds to the stock of negative opinions. Ng (1975) has analysed the possibilities further in an interesting way.

well-being. At any rate, I would use 'utility' in a wider sense, and think that other economists sometimes do too.[4]

Sen is right to emphasise the factual nature of utility. Yet his definition does not help one understand how it might be numerically measured. This is the second count on which the definition may not be acceptable. It is precisely the difficulty Utilitarians have in explaining how their method for evaluating outcomes could be effected in specific instances, so as to yield definite conclusions, that makes many people sceptical of the method. As far as I can see, there is one and only one way in which measurability of utility can be achieved. A person who conceives of himself in two alternative states can have preferences regarding different combinations of outcomes for himself in these states. He can arbitrarily fix two very similar outcomes A and B in state 1 as the standards of comparison, A being assigned zero utility and B unit utility. The utility difference between outcomes P and Q in state 2 is taken to be unity if he is indifferent between the combinations (A,Q) and (B,P). In this way the relative utility of all outcomes in state 2 can be calibrated, to within the standard of accuracy given by the degree of similarity of A and B. To calibrate utility in state 1, the same procedure is used, with particular P and Q in state 2 as the standard outcomes.

This must be what economic Utilitarians have usually had in mind. Ways of calibrating utility that are equivalent to it are to be found in the writings of Irving Fisher, Paul Samuelson, William Vickrey, and John Harsanyi, among many others.[5] For the method to be satisfactory, it is necessary:

(1) to identify situations in which individuals express preferences among outcomes for alternative selves; and to show that the observer should always deduce essentially[6] the same utility function if he applies the method with different standard outcomes, or to different situations in which there is choice on behalf of alternative selves;

(2) to show how the utility function obtained allows inter-personal comparability; and

(3) to explain why this way of measuring utility leads to a way of evaluating alternative economic outcomes that has moral force.

In what follows, I endeavour to deal with these issues. Then I discuss

---

[4] Sen (1970a p.98, 16) has remarked on the way that economists customarily extend the meaning of 'utility', as compared to the classical Utilitarians. Indeed, most economists recognise that the psychological theory on which Utilitarianism was first based is incorrect. The term 'utility' is still used to suggest that, in many ways, it can be used as Bentham used it.

[5] Fisher 1927, Samuelson 1937, Vickrey 1945, Harsanyi 1953.

[6] I.e. apart from addition of a constant of multiplication by a positive constant, transformations that evidently do not matter.

some implications, and deal sketchily with some possible objections. The paper concludes with a summary.

Alternative selves

What a person plans to do can be described as the totality of what he plans to do at particular times, and under particular circumstances. He could be a rational economic man, whose choices always conform to an underlying preference ordering, without it being logically possible to assign numerical utilities to his actions and experiences in particular time-periods and circumstances. For it to be possible to introduce numerical measurement of utility in the way just mentioned, it is necessary that his preferences regarding what he will be doing at one particular time in one particular set of circumstances be independent of what he may be planning for all other times and circumstances. For someone whose preferences display this degree of what economists have come to call separability, his choices can be represented as maximising some function of the utilities generated in the various periods and eventualities of his life. Symbolically, he can be said to maximise $W(\ldots, u(c_s,s), \ldots)$, where c_s represents his 'consumption' – i.e. all he does – in state s, and s is a short period of time in one particular possible development of his life.

It is unlikely that many people have preferences conforming to this model. Everything that has to do with life as a connected whole – such as habit, memory, preparation for future action, anticipation, achievement and failure – seems to have been ignored. But one can imagine inviting the person to consider what he would choose for one state if there were to be no consequential effects of outcomes in other states, e.g. if consumption in that state would be neither foreseen nor remembered. He could even be invited to consider choices among alternative memories, backgrounds, and prospects, as well as the more obvious choices among consumer goods and work activities. In this way one can hope to assign utility to the consumption of alternative selves in different states. It remains an empirical issue whether persons performing these thought-experiments have separable preferences. It appears plausible that they should, for what is happening in one state is, by the terms of the experiment, irrelevant to experience in other states. The possibility of doing the thought experiment shows what utility is. It involves insisting that what is good for me can be analysed into experiences in different states, experiences in a larger context certainly, but experiences that are tied to time and circumstance.

Standard Utilitarianism requires something more, for in that method it is required that individual preferences can be represented as a sum of utilities, not just as a function of utilities. This is the case if the individual's preferences about consumption in any two states, taken together, are independent of what he may be planning for other states. Thus one requires a stronger formulation of the principle that what is going to happen at another time, or under different circumstances, should be ignored, except insofar as memory, anticipation, and so on, are affected. This is an empirical claim, but one that is not, or, at any rate, not entirely, a claim about the behaviour of people in the ordinary business of life. It is a claim about the preferences that they would have if they had clearly understood the artificial choices that would have to be put to them, and had honestly observed and appreciated the consequences of these choices for themselves. We might insist that, for example, experiences that will have been forgotten ought to have no influence on preferences for activities at yet later times, even when early plans are being made. Better for Utilitarianism if we can claim that in fact they would have no influence. The evidence in favour of that view is primarily that it seems so unreasonable that such forgettable experiences should have relevance to choices about later times.

The argument I have put is that utility must be given meaning, if at all, in terms of individuals' preferences. It is often said that the Utilitarian view sees people as though they conformed to the model of rational economic man. Certainly people often do not conform to that model. They do many things that they would not if they had carefully, coolly, and in full knowledge of the facts, considered what to do, and been able to do what they had decided to do. Experiences determine behaviour, as well as considered choices. But we can ask what people would do if they could succeed in conforming to the simple rational-choice model and use that as a standard for judging what is best for them, individually.

Many of the difficulties about memory, anticipation, and so on, which can make the model of rational man seeking to maximise the sum of his utilities over time seem implausible, are avoided if instead one considers choice under uncertainty, where the individual is asked to choose the lives he would follow under different circumstances. This way of deducing utility has been the subject of many contributions.[7] It is, after all, natural to assign probabilities to possible worlds, and consumers do sometimes enter into well-considered insurance contracts. In many situations, actual decisions under uncertainty appear not to conform well to the utility model, even when there is no obvious doubt about the relevant probabilities.[8] This is hardly surprising, for skill at taking decisions under uncertainty is rare and requires training. The merit of considering choices among

---

[7] Vickrey 1945, Harsanyi 1953 and 1955. The method has been criticised by Pattanaik (1968) and Sen (1970a, Chapter 9).
[8] Kahneman and Tversky 1979.

probabilistic lotteries for alternative selves, only one of whom will actually occur, is that what is planned for some alternatives would plausibly have no effect on considered preferences regarding what happens to the other alternative selves. Such emotions as regret have to be discounted. Nevertheless, it should be possible to perform the thought-experiments required to calculate utility.

While choices among alternative uncertain outcomes can define and measure utility for alternative lives taken as wholes, it would be more useful for many purposes if one could assign utility to subperiods of lives, as my earlier discussion suggested one could. If one can deduce utility from consideration of alternatives for one set of circumstances only, it would be a pity if choices among lotteries did not maximise the mathematical expectation of the lifetime sum of utilities. Again there is no logical necessity that they should. An independence property analogous to that mentioned above is required.[9] Specifically, preferences with respect to outcomes in two possible states of nature at one time should be independent of what is planned for all other states of nature, and all other times in these states of nature; and, similarly, preferences with respect to outcomes at two times in one state of nature should be independent of all other plans. As far as I can judge, it does not seriously violate observation of carefully considered consumer decisions in real-life situations to assume this independence property. As in the previous case, it seems reasonable, and therefore probably true, that what is irrelevant would not be allowed to influence rational choice. It surely might become difficult to maintain the assumptions in the face of an accumulation of certain kinds of evidence. If so, we should bear in mind the possibility that a weaker kind of independence might hold for rational preferences. In that case, it would still be possible to define utility, and show how it could be measured; but it would be best for individuals to maximise, not the sum of utilities, but some other function of utility levels. A reconstruction of utilitarianism would then be required and possible.

The deduction of utility from individual behaviour presupposes that, at some level, man has immutable preferences. It is sometimes said that this assumption is contrary to fact. Many of the tastes expressed by consumers are, it seems, easily influenced: does advertisement change tastes, or change the consumer's knowlege of his own tastes, one way or the other, and how in any case can we hope to decide that? Do we not often find, when important issues are at stake, that it is very hard to be sure what our preferences are? If all taste is whim, these are not the data on which to base large moral judgements. These issues deserve extended treatment, but one

9 Gorman 1968

can surely hope to conclude that most people do have firm preferences for many possible choices, and also that they do not have firm or certain preferences for many choices that a utilitarian would like them to be able to make. Utilitarianism will sometimes be usable, but not always: I shall develop this claim in a later section. It should be emphasised that uncertainty about one's tastes, and consequent openness to suggestion, whether from advertisers or music critics, is not evidence that firm preferences are absent. One does not know what visiting the Taj Mahal is going to be like: but, when one is there, uncertainty about tastes is much diminished.

Yet it is not right to let utility rest entirely on individual tastes. Though the meaning of utility, and the calibration of the utility function, is, in principle, derived from individual preferences, it must be possible to allow for convictions about what is good for one that, though unshakable, are nevertheless mistaken. In formulating my preferences, I may be unable to free myself from the conventional view that more money would always make me better off; yet there may be good evidence that, beyond a point, more money leads similar individuals into alcoholism, excessive self-concern, and other phenomena that I would, if I understood them, dislike. Such facts should influence the utility function. It must be legitimate, in principle, to advance arguments in favour of modifying the utility function that exactly represents my existing tastes. It cannot be wrong in principle to try to get someone to do what would be better for him even though he does not recognise it: but there must be some basis for saying that, with full understanding, he would come to accept the rightness of the altered utility function, or, rather, of the underlying preferences. Those who jump to the defence of consumer sovereignty at any mention of attempts to supplant individual tastes must be asked to wait for a later section in which policy procedures will be discussed. At the present stage of the argument, only the evaluation of outcomes is under consideration. There may well be arguments in favour of *procedures* that respect individual preferences even if there are none in favour of moral evaluations that completely respect them.

Having seen how utility can be defined, we can see why the proposal to measure utility in units of minimum perceptible improvement is not acceptable. On many occasions, a just perceptible improvement in musical performance means much more to me than a just perceptible quantity of drink; there is no reason to regard this as an ill-informed or unconsidered preference. There is no plausible connection between intensity of preference and the number of perceptible steps, even for one individual considered in isolation.

Interpersonal comparisons

Having constructed utility for an individual, we can proceed to apply it to evaluating outcomes in a society of identical individuals.[10] Such a society exists only as a theoretical model. It is often said to be of little importance: 'Any genuine attempt at evaluating social welfare must take into account the differences in preference patterns of individuals' (Pattanaik 1968). I believe that this view is seriously misleading if it is thought to imply that the model society of identical individuals is irrelevant to our moral judgements on social policy. In this section, I shall argue that there are at least three reasons why the simplest case of social choice is important.

In the first place, we can make the model correspond to the real world much more closely than is initially apparent. This can be done by extending the concept of identity, which is I suppose fairly straightforward in the present context, to that of isomorphy. It will be shown that it is possible to regard individuals who are, by reason of age, skills, sex, strength, or culture, apparently very different, as nevertheless identical for the purposes of social judgement. This effective identity is achieved by setting up an isomorphism between the different individuals, relating like experience to like experience. In this way, it is possible to apply the utilitarian methodology in a disciplined way to such issues as that of income distribution alluded to at the beginning of the paper.

The second, and somewhat less important, use of the simple model is as an approximation to more complex worlds, in which individuals, though not identical, or even isomorphic, are rather similar. What judgements one would make for the more complex world should be similar to the judgements that are correct for the simpler world.

The third reason why the simple model is useful is that it provides a test for other moral theories. If it were agreed that Utilitarianism tells us which outcomes to prefer in the simple world of identical individuals, then any acceptable moral theory must come to the same conclusions in this special case. I claim that this use of the model leads to the rejection of the standard alternatives to utilitarianism.

The argument of utilitarianism in a society of identical individuals runs as follows.[11] For any one of the individuals, the sum of his utilities describes his considered preferences regarding the lives of his alternative selves. Therefore in choosing among outcomes for himself alone, i.e. with outcomes the same for everyone else, he ought to choose the pattern of outcomes with greatest total utility. With individuals identical, there is no

[10] Vickrey highlighted this case (1960), but even he moves on quickly to worry about non-identical (and non-isomorphic) individuals.

[11] A related approach is taken by Parfit (1973).

reason for treating a fully-described outcome for one of his own selves any differently from that outcome for the self of another individual in corresponding circumstances. Roughly speaking, the totality of all individuals can be regarded as a single individual. Therefore total social utility, the sum of the total utilities of the separate individuals, is the right way to evaluate alternative patterns of outcomes for the whole society. That should be the view of any individual in the society, and therefore also of any outside observer.

None of the three steps of this argument is a logically necessary implication. The first step, from preferences to individual values, has been challenged by Sen,[12] who suggests one might, for example, decide it is right to have greater equality of utilities in one's own life than maximising the sum of utilities implies. I understand that, for Sen, utility is defined in a different way from the one I have used, though I remain unconvinced that there is a different way of doing it. If Sen's form of argument were applied to the first step in the social argument as I have presented it, I should want to object when 'moral intuition' presents itself as a hair-shirt morality in conflict with the individual's preferences: that intuition is not moral, and should be resisted. There is more to be said about equality, and I return to it below.

The second step in the argument is an expression of impartiality and universalizability, which I take to have enormous weight in matters of morality. Certainly there are circumstances in which loyalty to one's own self, or to one's family, should be given special weight, even in the absence of explicit or implicit contracts and promises (which anyone would agree sometimes have utility). But that seems to me to have to do with the right way for an individual to behave, taking account of the influence of behaviour on future experience, understanding, and behaviour. Thus we are in the realm of procedures rather than the evaluation of outcomes. In the evaluation of the outcomes of public policy, loyalty and other kinds of partiality should be excluded.[13]

12 Sen 1979b, pp. 470–1, commenting on Parfit's argument.
13 Hare (Chapter 1, above) argues against Williams (1973) that pursuing one's own projects (almost) regardless can hardly count as moral behaviour. The same must be true of any restriction on the group whose ends are to count. Where the Williams case has force is in the suggestion that acting as a utilitarian is inconsistent with what is best for one as an individual, not just because effects on others must be counted, but because this kind of selflessness is inconsistent with the pursuit or achievement of certain high ends. A possible example is artistic creation. More generally, it is unlikely that having everyone constantly attempt to add to social utility is an arrangement calculated to maximise social utility. But I want government ministers to try to maximise utility, even if their personal sense of achievement is gravely compromised, their crazy industrial dreams unfulfilled: the ministers' utility deserves no significant weight in our assessments of utility in comparison to the millions who may suffer. To this extent, the morality of economic policy is simpler than that of personal life or culture.

The final step in the argument treats moral principles as though they were proposals put forward for assent or rejection, and appears to suggest that rejection would nullify them, perhaps even rejection by one person. We are accustomed to think that when Tom says A is right and Dick says B is wrong, then they are disagreeing. One reason why that is a valuable way to think is that it encourages Tom and Dick to explore their evidence and arguments and the sources of their 'disagreement'. But if these values were otherwise recognised, it is hard to see why it should be advantageous to insist that the logic of values follow the same rules as the logic of fact or deduction. Some degree of acceptance of the usage 'good in Tom's opinion' rather than 'good' understood absolutely seems reasonable, even desirable. In this spirit, when moral judgements are agreed (after 'serious consideration') matters should be concluded in that sense. That is why I find the final step persuasive.

We must now extend the argument to cover models of societies consisting of isomorphic individuals. Two individuals are isomorphic if they are described in formally identical terms by means of changes in the variables that describe their situations. The simplest example of isomorphy, which is indisputably acceptable, is that of individuals who are identical except for being born at different times or (perhaps) in different places. More disputable examples are:

(i) A strong man might be regarded as identical to a weak man, except that the same subjective effort by the former exerts twice the force.

(ii) A child may be regarded as an adult for whom a unit consumption of ice-cream means twice as much and a unit consumption of quiet conversation half as much as for a 'normal' adult; and so on for all aspects of consumption. This isomorphy is commonly used in econometric analysis of consumer behaviour, and is important for the construction and interpretation of 'family equivalence scales'.[14]

(iii) A person receiving a high annual labour income may be related isomorphically to another person receiving half of his earned income by supposing that they are identical except that the first takes half as much time to earn a pound sterling as does the second. In the models of redistribution, briefly described at the outset, a plausible, though still very approximate, correspondence between the model and reality is obtained in this way.

The idea of picturing a complex reality, where individuals are, by common agreement, not at all similar to one another in many important respects, by mapping it to a formal model in which individuals are, by suitable change of variables, isomorphic to one another, has proved to be

---

[14] Deaton and Muellbauer 1980, Chapter 8.

rather powerful in recent economics. The technique has limitations. One cannot claim that every important question of economic policy can be handled by such a model – only that many can. When they can, Utilitarianism provides a method for evaluating policies.

The possibility of setting up an isomorphism between individuals does not automatically make their utility functions comparable. The very fact that there is some identifiable way in which they differ, so that one is seen to be rich, another poor, allows us the mathematical possibility of relating the utility functions in all kinds of ways. Some simple formalism is needed to bring this out. Suppose that, for everyone, utility is a function of disposable income, labour earnings, and labour efficiency; and that we want to use the isomorphism that treats labour earnings divided by labour efficiency as meaning the same thing for different people. Then we write the utility function as[15]

$$u(x, \tfrac{z}{n}), \quad x = \text{disposable income}$$
$$z = \text{labour earnings}$$
$$n = \text{labour efficiency.}$$

But why should one not write

$$nu(x, \tfrac{z}{n})$$

instead? The two individuals still have the same preferences in regard to x and z/n, so there is no economic–empirical way in which we can distinguish the two procedures. I have no doubt that the first is much the more plausible procedure. This means that I think there is some warrant for the belief that the isomorphism relates similar experiences: that when two persons, rich and poor, have the same z/n, the same x means the same to both, in terms of subjective feelings. The particular example may suggest that this is an easier matter to settle than it usually is. Some economists seem to have made a particular choice of utility correspondence by inadvertence rather than after due consideration of the possible alternatives. That does not mean that there is no evidence to allow intelligent choice: it is an empirical matter, to which the kinds of evidence economists usually use is not relevant.

The conception of an economic model as an imperfect picture of the real society suggests also how utilitarianism could say something about societies of non-isomorphic individuals. In two economies that are fairly similar (say, one a simplified version of the other), the way we evaluate outcomes should be fairly similar too. More precisely, the method of

[15] For the sake of the illustration, let us take u to be always positive.

evaluation should be a continuous function of the collection of individuals that constitute the society.[16] Therefore one should not strongly disapprove of a method of evaluation applied to a simplified but apparently rather similar society in which individuals are isomorphic.

There are ways in which utilitarianism can be extended to societies of non-isomorphic individuals. So long as individuals can accurately imagine themselves being other individuals, each individual has a basis for his values in preferences by the method already described. A normal white adult may not be very good at imagining himself a child, a genius, or a black, if he is not one already. That does not affect the principle. The difficulty is to decide what should be done about the different utility functions that different, though careful and prudent, individuals would presumably discover in their preferences. This will be discussed further below. The point I want to make here is that, whatever general method of evaluation is proposed to deal with societies of non-isomorphic individuals, it must be consistent with utilitarianism when society consists of isomorphic individuals. Plainly this is not true of a maximin criterion, or of the more sophisticated, less precise version of this criterion advanced by Rawls.

It is interesting to note that a theory of the maximin type runs into difficulties that appear to be more severe than those of utilitarianism. The trouble is that it is sometimes not possible to use preferences about outcomes for alternative selves who are different, such as man and child, clever and stupid, or whole and handicapped, to determine whether, with specific outcomes, one or other of the two selves has greater utility. Relative marginal utilities can be deduced from preferences, but not relative absolute utilities. I can reveal how much I think money would help me if I had no arms, but not how much I would pay to avoid losing them – unless I can affect the probability. Claims about which self is better off cannot therefore be checked, however imperfectly, by market behaviour revealing preference; and indeed the meaning of such claims must be in doubt. I think such a claim involves an implicit belief that there is an isomorphism of some kind between the individuals.

Equality

As is quite well known, utilitarianism implies that, in general, a society of isomorphic, though not completely identical, individuals should *not* have

---

[16] At this level, continuity is an ambiguous notion, and anyway one has something much more demanding, but less precise, in mind: that one can roughly tell whether the likeness of two economies is great enough for the utility costs of following the optimal policies for one in the other to be small enough to justify terminating the analysis.

equal utility. Thus the equal treatment implicit in the utilitarian procedure does not guarantee equal outcomes, or even equally valued outcomes. An example will show what is involved. Consider a society of two individuals, Tom and Dick, who have the same utility as a function of income, and of hours worked. Incomes are spent on output, which comes from the labour of these two. One hour of Tom's labour produces twice as much as an hour of Dick's. Utility obeys the law of diminishing marginal utility – more income makes extra income less valuable, and less work makes extra leisure less valuable. It is also reasonable – because apparently realistic – to assume that more income would make them more eager to substitute leisure for income.[17] Utilitarianism says that in the ideal state of this society, Tom and Dick are called upon to work such amounts, and given such income, that producing an extra unit of output would reduce either one's utility by the same amount.

A fairly easy piece of economic theory shows that (i) Tom, the more productive, should work more than Dick; but that (ii) Tom's income should be less than Dick's; and indeed that (iii) Tom's utility should be less than Dick's.[18] The principle is, of course, 'From each according to his ability, to each according to his need'; and it turns out that Utilitarianism can recommend that this redistribution should be extremely radical. The wrong reaction is to reject utilitarianism as failing to conform with our moral intuitions. I, for one, had no prior intuitions about this simple economic problem, moral or otherwise. Anyway, appeal to prior moral opinions or beliefs is inappropriate. If utilitarianism is to be a valuable moral theory, one had better be surprised sometimes by its conclusions. Instinctive rejection of the conclusions of a utilitarian argument can be a good reason to check the argument, particularly for omitted considerations; not a reason for rejection.

A more interesting response to the example, which is intended, after all, to represent an important feature of human society, is to point out that, under a utilitarian government, Tom, if he acts selfishly – as well he might, however he votes – will pretend to be no more productive than Dick. That should not be hard for him. Therefore the proposed allocation, subject to the constraint that Tom should not be worse off than Dick – so as to ensure that he has no incentive to dissemble his productivity – is one that provides each with the same utility (though Tom still works more than Dick). This is the way in which utilitarianism is most likely to recommend equality: as the weakest way of not destroying incentives. Where incentives must be positively preserved – as when the government can identify Tom and Dick

[17] The technical, and precise, statement of these assumptions is that utility is a concave function of income and leisure, and that leisure is not an inferior good.
[18] This is proved in Mirrlees 1974, p. 258.

only by the amounts they choose to produce, so that the one who works more (Tom) must not want to work less and be content with Dick's income – then inequality can go the other way, with the more productive having more utility.

The example emphasises that utilitarianism can lead to all kinds of inequality. It can even recommend inequality between individuals who are similar in all respects – truly identical, not just isomorphic. It is theoretically possible that randomising the income tax would increase total utility.[19] This is a sophisticated version of the simple idea that two castaways in a rowing boat with one oar may be wise to allocate most food to the oarsman, even if they both like rowing.

It is the case that many people are affected by inequality, and have tastes about it. Therefore inequality in the society affects their utility, in some ways increasing it, but mostly, I suppose, decreasing it. We have, to my knowledge, no estimates of the magnitude of these effects. Indeed hardly any economist has addressed the question of formulating the kind or kinds of inequality people care about. The indexes of inequality developed by statisticians and economists have been carefully and thoughtfully examined by statisticians and economists, but not checked for relevance. None of them corresponds well to the fairly well substantiated, though not formally precise, notion of relative deprivation.[20] One reason for not finding out how much people care about which kinds of inequality is the conceptual difficulty of determining the influence of external facts on utility. Probably one can do little better than ask oneself and others how much they would pay for changes in inequality. Another reason for not attempting an empirical analysis of the influence of inequality on utility is the difficulty of distinguishing values from preferences. Inequality can affect the morally insensitive, by inducing envy, pride, or discomfort at adjusting to the behaviour of the rich or the poor. But these are feelings that have some tendency to melt away under the close self-scrutiny required. On the other hand, many have an aversion to inequality which is the outcome of moral considerations, and this aversion might be increased by self-scrutiny. Is this an aspect of preferences, or a matter of values not relevant to the estimation of utility? All of this emphasises the practical difficulty of estimating the effect of inequality on utility: it does not imply that inequality should be allowed for separately and additionally.

Inequality, like torture and slavery, attracts strong moral and political feelings. Expressed values about it form a test of moral soundness within systems of intellectual, social and political commitment. So someone might be apprehensive about committing himself to a moral calculus

[19] Weiss 1976.
[20] Runciman 1966.

that cannot be guaranteed to come up with conclusions that fit. Commitments to concrete policies may be necessary for influence and action. But in considering methods of policy evaluation, nothing should be taken for granted, everything subjected to critical analysis. Inequality would in any case have to be analysed, because it is quite unclear, in advance, what it is, i.e. how it is supposed to be measured. This makes clear, what I suppose is in any case an evident requirement, the need to derive badness of inequality from something else – if not its unpleasantness, or the utility-increasing effects of redistribution, or its bad incentive effects, then what?

Lest it be suspected that these considerations do not fully deal with inequalities, I readily agree that there are other ways, besides the direct effect on individual utilities, in which inequality comes into a satisfactory analysis of economic policies. The processes of public and private decision-taking are affected by the inequalities in society. Thus the connections between the levers of economic policy and the outcomes whose utility is to be measured vary with the degrees and kinds of inequalities. The kind of thing I have in mind is that special tax allowances designed to encourage the movement of resources to where they are needed in the medium term may provide interested parties with resources to resist desirable later removal of these tax allowances. As everyone knows, inequality can be associated with concentration of power to pursue narrow interests.

One would surely not capture considerations of this kind by combining utilities in a social maximand that tries to make them equal, as with the maximin welfare function. There are many less extreme ways of giving weight to the equality of utilities.[21] They have no rationale, because they are not directed at any of the identifiable flaws in simple utilitarianism: that it neglects the unpleasantness of inequality, and its effects on the distribution of power. In any case, these external effects of inequality may be quite small. Most of us, most of the time, are totally forgetful of inequality and our places in it. It will, and should, require some empirical arguments and evidence to change the models that economists are inclined to treat currently as standard.

None of this discussion is intended to argue that people's utility is likely to display a low degree of aversion to inequality in the distribution of goods. Despite what was said at the outset, about utilitarianism implying the desirability of inequality, the optimal degree of inequality in utilities

---

[21] Sen 1979b describes one class of such methods, namely replacing the sum of utilities by the sum of a concave function of utilities, as 'Mirrleesian'. I wish he had not. At the time I used it, I had no intention of avoiding the addition of utilities, but rather of looking at the effect on optimal policies of having a more inequality-averse utility function.

may be rather small. That depends on the form of utility functions that describe preferences among alternative selves. If people would be very reluctant to plan different levels of well-being for themselves in different states of nature, e.g. depending on the wage or family-responsibilities they would then have, it follows that the sum of utilities will, as a criterion, display considerable aversion to inequalities of incomes, or indeed of utilities. I think that people behave in ways that make them seem not very averse to large variations in their fates, e.g. by gambling, for excitement or not having enough of the right kinds of insurance, because they are in these areas ill-informed, not very rational, and anyway rightly sceptical about the terms insurance companies offer. Their coolly considered preferences would be much more inequality-averse, and not only for the reason – irrelevant to social utility – that adjustment to new standards of living is costly.

Unlike individuals

It would be good if utilitarianism (or anything else) could provide us with a compelling method of evaluating outcomes for a society in which people have (substantially) different utility functions. But it is hard to conceive how individuals, who have after careful, critical, well-informed study discovered in themselves essentially different assessments of utility, could have their moral opinions aggregated by a morally compelling social decision function. There is no way of deducing what is absolutely good from what Tom thinks good and Dick thinks good. A social decision function could be a device for cutting the argument short, because it is agreed to be too costly to go on postponing decision in the hope of reaching agreement by further consideration of arguments and facts. The criteria for an aggregation device to be good for that purpose are quite different from the criteria for a good method of combining individual tastes into evaluations of social welfare.

It seems likely that discussion and further consideration among people who have abandoned entrenched positions, or at least among open-minded utilitarians, will tend to reduce divergence among their evaluations of social outcomes. I do not rely on the well-known socio-biological methods of achieving agreement through Johnson's principle that 'No two men can be half an hour together, but one shall acquire an evident superiority over the other.' We might rather imagine discussion about utilities taking the following form:

Tom: I have been thinking very seriously about my pension and savings, and about my car insurance and investments, and I find that the square root of consumption[22] accurately represents my utility now and in the future, so long as I am healthy. Of course, you, Dick, are a rather different kind of person from me, not sleeping so long and enjoying giving parties and all that. I've thought about what I would feel being you, and I must say, I think you get more out of the things money can buy than I do, even if you don't get much pleasure from long walks in the country. Allowing for that, I can see your utility is the square root of consumption multiplied by 1.2.

Dick: It's nice of you to allow me that extra twenty per cent, but I don't think you realise how boring I often find these bigger parties are. If I could agree with the square root of consumption, I would say that ten per cent was ample allowance for my monetary needs. But I find my utility is proportional to the cube root of consumption, and it does not seem to me that being you would make any difference to that. It would just mean that I spent a bit less time on enjoying the things money can buy. My enjoyment of extra consumption in the week really does fall off faster than your square-root function suggests, and I must say I would not coolly take quite as many risks with my investments as that utility function implies.

Tom: Well, it seems people aren't as like one another as I thought, and I do see, now you draw my attention to it, that a big dip in your consumption affects you relatively more than it would me. You've persuaded me that the cube root is right for your utility function. And now I realise why we were disagreeing about ten or twenty per cent. It wasn't conventional politeness: after all, we *are* Utilitarians. It was just that I had last year's consumption in mind, before we got our rises. Now that we both get £10,000 a year, I suggest that we measure our consumption in pennies, thus making us both millionaires, and allow us to take the square root of consumption for my utility, and eleven times the cube root of consumption for yours.[23]

Dick: Fine, but now what about Harry? He claims his utility function reaches its maximum at £5,000 a year, and that he can see we aren't any better off for being richer than that either. I know he means it, and behaves accordingly, but it's absurd . . .

Thus reasonable men may tend towards agreement; but they need not – Harry will be a problem. Apparently disagreement can be about facts, or about the way the facts are experienced. When there is disagreement,

[22] On almost any reasonable view, the utility functions discussed by Tom and Dick are far from sufficiently inequality-averse. The square root and cube root were chosen for their relative euphony – compared to 'minus the reciprocal of the square of consumption', say.

[23] Martin Gardner addicts will want to work out what rise they got.

quick compromise seems to be the right answer, because there is no right answer.

Open judgements

The utilitarian method does not answer all questions. Is there any reason to think we are in a better position to decide how much to spend on kidney machines, than we are to decide how long this universe will last? That one does not know the answer to many moral questions is a reason for developing systematic procedures. But even after attempted analysis, not knowing may be the correct answer. Two examples of this are the treatment of handicapped people, and the question of optimum population.

In his lectures on inequality (1973), Sen has directed particular attention to the allocation of resources between whole and handicapped individuals. If nothing will improve the well-being of the handicapped individual, e.g. because he is permanently in coma, the utilitarian finds it easy to say that no further resources should be transferred to that person. By continuity, he must be prepared to contemplate providing the handicapped individual with rather few resources if his capability of enjoyment is very low – say because he is conscious for only a minute a day. That is how I would allocate resources to myself in such a state, if I could control the allocation, and consequently I take the same view about others. Most cases of handicap are, however, unclear. It is difficult to get inside the other person's skin when the other person's situation is very different from one's own. There are no good tests of whether one's beliefs, as to what it is like, are correct. It would not be unreasonable to refuse to make a judgement. Then one should not mind what is done about the handicapped person. Maybe others know what is right, and even if one thinks they do not, having no basis for an opinion, one cannot object to whatever they decide to do. The best hope for comparison is partial isomorphism: in some situations people are alike, but some people have good information for appreciating modulations into states of handicap.

Consideration of extreme proposals – half the national product to the blind, nothing for the deaf – strongly suggests that total ignorance is not a sustainable position about handicap. Rather, uncertainty about the nature of the experiences should be expressed by means of probabilities, and the mathematical expectation of utilities used as the measure of utility. But the example helps to show what moral ignorance implies.

In the case of variations in population size,[24] moral ignorance may

---

[24] I am referring to variations in the population of a closed society, e.g. the whole world. Migration from one country to another poses no special problems for evaluating outcomes, just for getting people to accept right policies.

appear to be almost irresistibly the correct position. To get preference information relevant to comparing states of the society with different numbers, the individual has to perform a thought experiment in which the number of alternative selves varies, and to decide which of the two positions he prefers. I suppose this is the purified question of choice about length of life. Can one consider this question without the corruption of thinking about it as one's own life, rather than variation in the number of experiences? The value of a year of human life has been discussed,[25] and estimated, and used in cost–benefit analysis by the Road Research Laboratory. If one can decide about that without – as in practice one does – getting it confused with the impact on family, etc., then one has a utilitarian basis for evaluating alternative population sizes.

It seems to me a reasonable position that one cannot decide whether one would like another year of life, nor therefore whether more or fewer people in the world is desirable. It is not reasonable to take this position totally. Another year of bliss is good: a year during which one is torturing others is certainly bad. Correspondingly, more people at a high standard of living is good, and more people at very low standards of living is bad. Specifically, one might argue that the population of the world is now too large, without claiming that no-one should have a child until it has come right and without wishing to claim that one knew what the optimum size of the world population is. But even in so difficult a case as this, extensive research on the value of human life might make so open an opinion on the question difficult to sustain.

Procedures and outcomes

There are many reasons why a utilitarian should not, in practice, insist that the utility functions he has come to believe in must govern economic policy, even if he has the power to do so. I (like others) may have made random errors in estimating utility functions, neglecting evidence or even simply calculating wrongly. I may have a tendency to be biassed in favour of, or even against, people like myself. It might be costly, in my view, to have my evaluation prevail. In order to gain influence for my evaluations (which, allowing for the first two points, are nevertheless my view of what is right), it may be necessary to agree to some degree of influence for the considered valuations, or even the tastes, passions and whims of others. All of these are reasons for taking account of the views of others; and they are reasons why the external observer should adopt evaluations influenced

[25] See Jones-Lee 1976. This approach, which assumes expected utility maximisation, has been criticised by Broome (1978b) on the ground, unacceptable to a utilitarian, that it is in principle impossible to compare the value of a life with the value of (mere) commodities.

by the evaluations of all individuals. The first two reasons, at least, are also, be it noted, reasons why evaluations of outcomes for a particular society should be influenced, perhaps rather strongly, by the assessments of those who do not belong to it, e.g. those who lived a long time ago. On the basis of all these considerations, I conclude that a utilitarian should not be much in favour of dictatorship, even benign dictatorship; but that he should favour methods of compromise among alternative evaluations, in which the weight accorded to particular evaluations is related to the quality of the arguments on which they are based. Intuitions, beliefs in rights, and responses to polls and questionnaires should count only to the extent that political necessity warrants – which may be considerable.

This line of argument goes some way to meet the claim that, to paraphrase Diamond (1967a), 'Utilitarianism is concerned only to evaluate outcomes, whereas in considering, e.g., the determination of economic policies, we should also be concerned about the process of choice.' This claim has often been advanced, but the example Diamond provides is a particularly cogent one. It compares a policy which always leaves Tom with a low utility and Dick with a high to one in which Tom and Dick experience an equivalent lottery. It must be agreed that a utility-maximising government may not be the best kind to try to have, because it would not in fact be a utility-maximising government, but would respond to pressures, have quirks, thoughtless tastes, loyalties to particular interests, etc., just as governments always have had. It may be better to have a constitution-constrained government, in part controlled also by conventions that it should consult all concerned groups on issues, and not discriminate against particular groups, or between people who are in certain superficial respects alike. One way of making it hard for officials to be corrupt, or partial, is to insist that large classes of people be treated the same. This conflicts with crude utilitarianism. In Diamond's example, the government might or might not plan to give different people different positions in the income distribution in different states of nature. If I happen never to get a good job from the government, I shall probably suspect it of bias. If I *knew* it was utilitarian, I would not, and would have no grounds for objection to always being the less fortunate one.

A rather different claim, that utilitarianism (or indeed a larger class of doctrines) is inconsistent with the proper respect of individual liberty is Sen's liberalism argument[26] that utilitarianism conflicts with rights to free choice by the individual over matters that are his own prerogative. Sen's argument rests on a moral intuition that in some kinds of situation Tom's pleasure from Tom's consumption should count for more than Dick's

---

[26] This is expounded in detail in Sen 1970a, Chapter 6*, and the discussion in Sen 1979b is particularly illuminating.

pleasure from Tom's consumption. I try not to suffer from moral intuitions, but I can think of reasons why we should give less weight to evidence that Dick's utility is affected by Tom's consumption than to evidence that Tom's utility is so affected, e.g. that it is cheap for Dick to pretend; and of reasons why publicly known decision procedures should give less weight to Dick's negative feelings about Tom's consumption, e.g. that these are feelings it is possible, and desirable, to discourage. Note that it is possible for some, perhaps any, of us to stop being upset by someone doing something we believe to be wrong. This in no way weakens the force of our disapproval. There is no virtue, very much the contrary, in being miserable about wrong things happening; unless we need that as motivation to act to diminish wrong. Stopping Lewd reading his book because his reading it will make Prude unhappy seems undesirable because Prude could just decide not to be unhappy. If that is not the case, and Prude is incapable of not feeling sick at the reading, and it cannot be kept from him, then Prude is as much a consumer of the reading as Lewd, and non-reading is better. This argument is a utilitarian one, provided that I am allowed the rather elastic sense of utility that makes utilitarianism an acceptable doctrine. It provides some strong reasons for ignoring some external effects. Indeed a utilitarian should be prepared to agree that liberties are extremely important, as protection against the personal and other biasses that affect policy and its contact with individuals.

Utilitarianism does not give an instant answer to the question what kind of constitution, bill of rights, or government is optimal. It is first a way of providing optimal answers to questions from an ideal government. On the question of optimal government, some work remains to be done.

Summary

Utility is a way in which the considered preferences of an individual, regarding allocation to his alternative selves, can be described. For the purposes of evaluating outcomes for the individual, it may have to be somewhat modified, so that it need not exactly coincide with his preferences.

In a society of isomorphic individuals, i.e. individuals who are the same with respect to some way of comparing their experiences, the outcomes of economic (or social) policies ought to be evaluated by adding their individual utilities, because everyone ought to agree to have every other individual treated as one of his alternative selves.

Any acceptable method of moral evaluation should agree with utilitarianism at least in the case of a society consisting of isomorphic individuals.

Economic models with isomorphic individuals can provide quite useful pictures approximating the real world. Using such a model, the sum of utilities is a reasonable maximand to use for choosing economic policies to be applied to the real world.

Utilitarianism can be extended to societies with non-isomorphic individuals, but in these cases it is likely to be necessary that some conventional method of compromise among different utility functions be used.

In extreme cases, it may be that there are no grounds for moral choice at all, so that, in such a case as that of population size, there are no grounds for objecting to one size or another, within a wide range.

Utilitarianism should not attempt to answer all questions simply by maximising utility and assuming governments and individuals will meekly play their allotted roles. Using total utility as a criterion, one can go on to examine questions about the optimal information to use in determining economic policies, and the optimal system of economic government by individuals behaving realistically.

It might even be suggested that one could study the optimal economic advice to give, this being in general not the advice that would, if adopted, maximise utility. But that I would resist, believing that economists, like real people, cannot be trusted to give advice unless it is subject to the checks of publishable analysis.

4 Utilitarianism, uncertainty and information

PETER J. HAMMOND

1 Introduction

It is no accident that a large number of the essays in this volume are by economists, since they appear to have made far more use of utilitarianism than have other social scientists. Indeed, the whole study of welfare economics is founded more or less explicitly on utilitarian ideas, even when economists deal only with the idea of Pareto efficiency – when no individual can be made better off without making someone else worse off. In addition, economists appear to have come face to face with a number of challenging issues in applying what amounts to utilitarian techniques to specific economic problems. Examples of such issues are changing tastes, the valuation of life and limb, uncertainty, and incompletely informed individuals. Perhaps one may say that it has almost become one of the hallmarks of a good economist to try to extend the basic utilitarian framework of welfare economics to treat such issues.

In this essay I am going to present an almost entirely verbal and relatively non-technical discussion of the problems which arise in trying to extend utilitarianism to deal with such issues. My concern will be to try to see what questions utilitarianism can be extended to handle sucessfully, and what questions cause great difficulty. Because I am an economist, the ethical issues I shall be discussing will mostly be at least closely related to economic issues, i.e. the problem of allocating scarce resources, and the associated question of the proper distribution of income. Extra difficulties I shall not have considered may well arise in discussing issues which are not purely economic, and it is for the reader to decide how well the utilitarian framework can be extended to treat non-economic issues as well in a similar manner.

Research support from the National Science Foundation under contract number SES-79-24831 is gratefully acknowledged.

In writing this essay, I was much encouraged by Partha Dasgupta and Amartya Sen, and I have also benefited particularly from discussion with Frank Hahn, and James Mirrlees. My thanks to all of these, but without wishing to suggest that they are responsible for or even in agreement with the views expressed here.

2 Static utilitarianism: objectives and constraints

Before tackling challenging issues such as uncertainty and incomplete information, let me review briefly how utilitarianism handles somewhat less challenging issues – at least in welfare economics.

Utilitarianism involves specifying an objective for society which depends on the 'utilities' of the individuals in society. The social objective is usually to maximise a function which economists call the *social welfare function*.[1] This function, as well as each individual's utility function, is defined on a space of 'social states' or, perhaps more precisely, the entire range of possible social outcomes from all sorts of economic and related policy decisions.

In fact, this brings us directly to one of the key principles of welfare economic analysis. The principle is that the social objective – be it utilitarian or not – should always be kept separate from the constraints which one knows will circumscribe the eventual social choice. Thus, no social outcome should be ruled out of consideration as infeasible when we try to specify suitable objectives. For example, the social objective should allow the possibility of bringing about perfect equality of incomes through simple lump-sum redistribution even though one knows perfectly well that eventually the distribution of income will have to satisfy certain incentive constraints if those who are more skilled or more industrious are not to be unduly deterred from working as one would wish. The welfare objective, fully specified, should even enable us to evaluate social outcomes in which everybody is a millionaire at one extreme, or in dire poverty at another. This may seem as though I am merely reiterating the obvious. Yet in due course I shall argue that, when we come to consider more challenging issues such as uncertainty and incomplete information, many common misconceptions have arisen because of a confusion of objectives and constraints.

To return to static utilitarianism, it is now widely recognised that Utilitarian social welfare functions can be constructed provided that one makes the kind of interpersonal comparisons of utility which economists have so long wished to eschew, although, not surprisingly, much

---

[1] Unfortunately, this terminology is somewhat ambiguous. The social welfare function I have in mind here is usually associated with Bergson (1938), who actually calls it, less ambitiously perhaps, the 'Economic Welfare Function'. Arrow (1950, 1951, 1963), however, used the term 'social welfare function' for a rule which determines the social ordering (represented by a Bergson social welfare function, possibly) as a function of individual preference orderings. Later Arrow (1963) came to prefer the term 'constitution'. Current terminology treats Arrow's concept of a constitution (or 'Arrow social welfare function') as a special kind of 'social welfare functional' which maps individual utility functions into social welfare functions – see Sen 1970a, p. 129 and 1977a.

controversy remains over how to make such interpersonal comparisons.[2] There has also been much discussion of what individuals' utility functions are meant to represent – their tastes, their ethical values, or perhaps their interests as seen by whoever is performing the utilitarian analysis. One of the more satisfactory discussions of this last important question – by an economist, at least – is probably that by Broome (1978a). He argues that, for the purpose of utilitarian welfare economics, an individual's utility' should not necessarily correspond to actual choices, as many economists like to assume when they defend the doctrine of 'consumer sovereignty' and when they go on to attribute ethical significance to the fundamental theorems of welfare economics which relate allocations in competitive markets to Pareto efficient and to utilitarian economic allocations.[3] Nor, in case an individual's choices do correspond to preferences, should utility even necessarily correspond to these preferences, unless the preferences are rational. And where an individual's rational preferences include, for example, a certain degree of altruism, or of malice or envy, not even these need correspond to the individual's utility. In fact, for the purposes of utilitarian welfare economics, at least, an individual's utility should correspond to 'choices based on good self-interested reasons'. This seems helpful, although the criterion of 'goodness' here is certainly open to much disagreement, and even the criterion of 'self-interest' contains within it some ambiguities.

Though this question of what constitutes individual utility is crucially important, it is hard to say much more about it, except in the context of some of the challenging issues I propose to face in due course.

3 Rights and liberalism[4]

One outstanding issue I will discuss briefly, though, is the question of rights, both individual rights and group rights. In particular, in a series of papers, Sen (1970b, 1976, 1979a) has pointed out how social choice which accords even with only the rather weak utilitarian criterion of Pareto efficiency can easily conflict with individual rights – e.g. the rights to read a book or not, or for a girl to wear a dress of the colour she prefers.

---

[2] Mirrlees (Chapter 3, above) argues forcefully that the social welfare function should be the (possibly weighted) sum of individual utility functions. This may be correct, but unduly limits the scope of my argument. I want to know whether there is *any* social welfare function which just depends on individual utilities and which represents an appropriate social objective.

[3] Koopmans 1957 is only one of many good presentations of the fundamental efficiency theorems. Some of the more vehement defences of consumer sovereignty can be found in Archibald 1959 and Lerner 1972.

[4] This section is based to some extent on the analysis in Hammond 1981a.

He suggests that one should therefore restrict the scope of the Pareto criterion in particular and of utilitarianism in general. In fact, he suggests that one should construct a social welfare function which respects individual rights in the sense that, where an individual prefers outcome a to outcome b and where he has the right to choose between them, social welfare must be higher in outcome a than it is in outcome b. Buchanan (1976), Nozick (1974) and many other 'libertarians', on the other hand, appear simply to believe that there are some rights – e.g. property rights – which amount to issues over which the government has no legitimate power to choose or to interfere with the individual's own choice. Such rights seem to take the form of constraints on public decision-making. They lead to a restricted or constrained form of utilitarianism in which social welfare is maximised subject to the constraint that nobody's rights are infringed, and each individual chooses what he wants whenever he has a right to do so.

Now there are some rights and some associated preferences which it is simply not possible to respect, either in the Sen sense of constructing a rights-respecting social welfare function, or in the Buchanan and Nozick sense of treating individuals' choices as a constraint. To see this, it suffices to consider an example essentially due to Gibbard (1974). There are two individuals, a conformist and a nonconformist. Then it is clear that there is no way in which one can simultaneously accord a right to the conformist to copy the nonconformist, and a right to the nonconformist to be different from the conformist. Individuals such as the conformist and nonconformist, however, have 'conditional' preferences – preferences which depend on what other individuals choose. One can argue that nobody has a right to the outcome of a conditional preference: nobody has a right to be different, regardless of what other people choose, but only a right to choose a particular outcome they like, such as the colour of the clothes they wear; similarly, nobody has a right to be the same as other people, regardless of what other people choose, but only a right to choose a particular outcome they like. Of course the particular outcomes chosen by individuals may differ, or they may be the same, but that is not the point.

If one grants that rights are to be respected only when individuals have unconditional preferences then all contradictions are avoided. Conversely, if one tries to respect rights even when individuals have conditional preferences, contradictions easily arise. But even when all individuals have unconditional preferences whenever they have rights, there can still be a conflict with the Pareto principle and so with utilitarianism, as Sen pointed out. The conflict of rights with the Pareto principle arises precisely in those cases where an individual's utility depends on other individuals' choices over personal issues where they have rights.

Now, in some cases the conflict arises because of what economists call external effects which may be difficult to correct. For example, one may feel in certain circumstances that a landowner has the right to cut down all the trees on his land in order to grow crops, construct a house or a tennis court or a swimming pool, or whatever. Yet if everybody cuts down all their trees, this may create problems of soil erosion and landslides as well as having adverse effects on the local climate. Then it would be Pareto superior to institute some tree conservation measures in the community as a whole, by taxing any individual landowner for each tree he fells beyond a certain acceptable level which maintains the stock of trees approximately constant. But such a scheme is likely to be expensive to implement and to enforce, and it may still be objected that such a scheme infringes the landowners' property rights. In such a case, therefore, one simply has to recognise that there is an extra constraint on the social welfare maximising choices, arising because conservation measures are not really possible. The chosen social outcome is only Pareto efficient subject to such a constraint: conservation measures would produce a superior outcome but are infeasible. Here the conflict of rights with utilitarianism is resolved simply in the way suggested by Buchanan, Nozick and other proponents of the doctrine of property rights: the social outcome is constrained by the requirement that it must not infringe these rights.

There are other cases, however, such as that originally considered by Sen (1970b), in which the conflict appears to be of a rather different nature. In Sen's example, one individual, the prude, objects to having to read a book which he regards as obscene, and objects even more strongly to a second individual, the lewd, reading it. The lewd, on the other hand, regards the book as worthy literature and, since the prude, in the lewd's view, stands to gain more by reading the book than the lewd himself does, the lewd prefers the prude to read it rather than himself. In this case, if each individual is given the right to read the book or not as he wishes, then only the lewd reads the book, though both would prefer it if only the prude were to read the book. In this example, it is useful to recall Broome's suggestion that utility should correspond to choice based on good self-interested reasons. Now the prude's desire to prevent the lewd reading the book does not seem to derive from especially good self-interested reasons, unless it really is the case that reading the book will encourage the lewd into some dangerous and anti-social behaviour which directly affects the prude. And the lewd's desire to force the prude to read the book, perhaps as part of a 'good liberal education', is also hardly due to good self-interested reasons, unless it really is true that 'educating' the prude in this way has general beneficial effects. Where the lewd will behave dangerously if he reads the book, or where the prude's education really does benefit the lewd, we are back with the kind of external effects I mentioned in the previous paragraph. But if neither of these external effects is present, then the prude's and the lewd's utility functions do not correspond to their expressed preferences because these are not based on good self-interested reasons. In this latter case, then, rights do not conflict with the Pareto principle or with utilitarianism, when individuals' utilities are expressed properly.

The conclusion I draw from this is that utilitarianism, when it is based on proper utility functions, only conflicts with rights when maximising the social welfare function involves correcting certain external effects. Now it may be the case that, in such cases, welfare economists have concentrated unduly on the utilitarian outcome, and have sought to institute public policy programmes to overcome such externalities without sufficient regard for individual rights. If this is so, all it means is that the set of allowable policies and feasible social outcomes may be rather smaller than many economists would like: such rights, which one may perhaps call 'generalised property rights', limit the scope of utilitarianism without really undermining it. But it is also quite possible that the ethical significance of generalised property rights has been greatly exaggerated. Where individuals mistrust governments and political processes, there may be a rational fear of having one's freedom seriously infringed and then individuals may want to stand on their 'rights'. To consider this properly however, we need to bring in uncertainty and incomplete information, as I shall do in due course. With good governments, such fears are groundless, and insistence on 'rights' may often be little more than a selfish ploy to influence the political process unduly. For these reasons, the utilitarian welfare economist's neglect of individual rights is quite understandable in treating purely static economic policy questions with no uncertainty – indeed, one could well argue that it really is the only correct procedure.

4 Uncertainty and expected ex-post social welfare

Up to now I have discussed utilitarian analysis only for the unrealistic special case in which the future outcome is known with certainty. Other challenging issues arise once one recognises that the social outcome is bound to be uncertain.

Since the work of von Neumann and Morgenstern (1944) followed by Savage (1954), Arrow (1971) and others, economists and other decision theorists have recommended a fairly standard technique for treating decisions under uncertainty. In the present context, the space of histories of social outcomes (and, where relevant, of individuals' changing tastes) is expanded into the space of all possible *contingent* histories. Uncertainty, it is assumed, can be described by specifying random events in a given set S of 'states of the world'. A contingent history specifies a (possibly different) history for each possible state of the world. Thus one looks now for a social welfare function which is defined over the whole space of possible contingent histories. The particular contribution of Ramsey (1926) and Savage (1954) was to show that, under certain hypotheses, an individual decision maker – e.g. a utilitarian welfare economist – would ascribe a probability distribution to the states of the world in the set S, and 'von Neumann–Morgenstern' utilities to the possible histories, so that a history would be chosen in order to maximise the mathematical expectation of the 'utility' of the contingent history in each possible state of S. This is often called *subjective expected utility maximisation* because the probabilities are subjective in the sense that they need not conform to any of the standard frequentist or other notions of 'objective' probability. More simply, following Harsanyi, we may simply call it *Bayesian rationality*.

Bayesian rationality has often been criticised, but mostly on the grounds that individuals' actual behaviour is not in accord with it – see, for example, Drèze (1974) and Kahneman and Tversky (1979). The utilitarian welfare economist, of course, is interested in a normative criterion for choice under uncertainty, and then Bayesian rationality or expected utility maximisation becomes much more acceptable. Indeed, without it, one is liable to find oneself facing severe difficulties because the utilitarian's choices are likely to be revised and to become dynamically inconsistent in the sense of Strotz (1956). Without Bayesian rationality, the utilitarian welfare economist might have to anticipate his future choices as events unfold, just as a potential drug addict would be wise to foresee his potential addiction and to avoid taking any harmful drugs to which he is likely to become addicted.[5] Thus, I am going to assume that the utilitarian objective does satisfy Bayesian rationality.

It follows that there has to be a probability distribution over the set S of states of the world. These probabilities may well be entirely subjective, being no more than the utilitarian analyst's best guess, making use of all the information he has. Then there is also a 'von Neumann–Morgenstern' social welfare function. In each state s of the set S, social welfare is taken to be a function of the individual utilities in that state s, which in turn depend on the history in state s. The utilitarian objective is to choose a contingent history in order to maximise the expected value of this von Neumann–Morgenstern social welfare function. The von Neumann–Morgenstern social welfare function is what has come to be called a 'cardinal' welfare function, because only linear transformations preserve the preferences

[5] Cf. Hammond 1976a. For more discussion of this 'dynamic' justification of Bayesian rationality, see Hammond 1981c.

induced by the mathematical expectation of the function. Indeed, the von Neumann–Morgenstern social welfare function incorporates the utilitarian's 'social' attitudes to risk (see, for example, Arrow 1971). One fairly extreme von Neumann–Morgenstern social welfare function would be the 'Rawlsian' one, in which social welfare in every state s is equal to the minimum individual utility, for suitably scaled individual utility functions. This is *not* the same as extreme risk aversion, in which the objective is to maximise social welfare in the worst possible state. Rather, the Rawlsian social welfare function places extreme weight on achieving equality of individual utilities in each state. The precise social attitudes to risk implied by this Rawlsian function depend upon the cardinal scaling of the individual utility functions because the von Neumann–Morgenstern social welfare function is the minimum of these individual utility functions.

5 Utilitarianism ex-ante and ex-post

In the previous section, I claimed that social welfare in each state of the world should be a function of individual utilities in that state. This is the *ex-post* approach to welfare economics under uncertainty, insofar as social welfare in each state is calculated separately as though that state were already known, before the social welfares in all the states are combined into the expected welfare function. Drèze (1970), Starr (1973) and others, following Diamond (1967a, 1967b), have contrasted this to an *ex-ante* approach to welfare economics, which is implicit in Arrow's 1953, 1964, 1971 and Debreu's 1959 efficiency criterion for judging allocations in competitive securities markets. The ex-ante approach treats as each individual's utility the ex-ante expected value of the individual's own von Neumann-Morgenstern utility function. Arrow, Debreu and their many followers have used the ex-ante Pareto efficiency criterion which results naturally from considering these ex-ante utilities for individuals. An *ex-ante social welfare function* is one in which social welfare is a function of individual's ex-ante expected utilities.

The contrast between the ex-ante and the ex-post approaches can be drawn out by considering the distribution of real income in an economy where relative price changes are negligible. Provided that the ex-post welfare function, as a function of ex-post personal distribution of income, has the mathematical properties of being both strictly quasi-concave and symmetric, an optimal distribution of income ex-post involves perfect equality of income in each state of the world. One may call this *ex-post equality*. An ex-ante optimal distribution of income may not be ex-post equal at all, however. Indeed, it can easily happen that no ex-ante Pareto efficient income distribution is ex-post equal.

To see this, let me consider two special examples, each with only two individuals who are relevant. In the first, one individual, Mr A, attaches a higher probability than the other individual, Mrs B, to the event that horse X will win the Grand National. Then, if Mr A places a small bet with Mrs B that the horse X will win, and if the odds are between those implied by the probabilities Mr A and Mrs B attach to this event, both parties have higher expected utilities. Both believe their expected net winnings on the bet are positive and, because the bet is small, this outweighs any worries that arise because of the risks they are taking. Thus an ex-post equal distribution of income is ex-ante Pareto dominated by one in which the individuals undertake this bet and then bring about ex-post inequality. So the ex-post equal distribution cannot be ex-ante Pareto efficient.

The first example above showed, in effect, that any ex-post equal distribution can be ex-ante Pareto dominated unless all individuals have the same subjective probability distribution across the set of all states of the world, because otherwise opportunities for small bets are bound to arise. In the second example below, individuals do have identical subjective probability distributions, but their attitudes to risk differ, and this suffices to allow ex-ante Pareto improvements to any ex-post equal income distribution. In fact, suppose once again that we have two individuals, Mr A and Mrs B, as before. Let us also suppose that Mr A is somewhat risk averse, whereas Mrs B is not risk averse at all and cares only what her expected income is, regardless of its variance (provided only that her income is always enough to subsist on). In such a case, both parties gain whenever any income risk is transferred from risk averse Mr A to risk neutral Mrs B, provided that Mr A pays a (small) insurance premium to avoid risk, and this premium is enough to raise Mrs B's expected income. Thus, an ex-ante Pareto efficient allocation of risk-bearing involves Mr A bearing no risk at all, and having a certain income independent of the state of the world (except, possibly, in a few very bad states where Mrs B has only a subsistence income and Mr A all the rest of the available total income), whereas Mrs B's income absorbs all the risks in total income. Except in the trivial case of a constant total income, such a distribution of income cannot be ex-post equal; indeed, if one starts with an ex-post equal distribution, ex-ante Pareto efficiency requires that Mr A's income be higher than Mrs B's in those states where total income is low, and vice versa when total income is high. The case when Mrs B is risk-neutral is, of course, rather extreme. But even when Mrs B is also risk averse, but is less risk averse than Mr A, one can show that ex-ante Pareto efficiency still requires Mrs B to bear more risk than Mr A.

In fact, as shown by Diamond (1967a), Starr (1973) and others, the contrast or conflict between the ex-ante and ex-post approaches only disappears in a very special case. First, individuals must all share the same subjective probability distribution on the set S of possible states of the world, and this subjective probability distribution must be identical to the probability distribution being used by the utilitarian in calculating the expected value of the ex-post social welfare function.[6] Second, social welfare ex-post must be a weighted sum of the individuals' von Neumann–Morgenstern utility functions, with the weights independent of the state of nature. Then social welfare ex-ante will be the equivalent weighted sum of individuals' ex-ante expected utilities. This is the case of consistency between the two approaches which I shall call the *Vickrey–Harsanyi* case, because Vickrey (1945) and Harsanyi (1955, 1975c) have been especially strong advocates of using such a social welfare function, assuming implicitly that individuals do agree on probabilities.

This contrast between ex-ante and ex-post lies at the heart of the debate in the 1940s and 1950s over whether von Neumann–Morgenstern utilities are equivalent to the utilities that should be used in comparing marginal utilities of income for, say, rich and poor. It is noteworthy that Friedman, the champion of ex-post inequality, where this results from individuals' decisions to bear risks, explicitly rejects this equivalence in Friedman and Savage 1948, 1952. Indeed, Friedman and Savage (1948, p. 283, n. 11), in a claim that they themselves choose to quote in Friedman and Savage 1952 (p. 473), state that 'it is entirely unnecessary to identify the quantity that individuals are to be interpreted as maximizing [i.e. von Neumann–Morgenstern utility] with a quantity that should be given special importance in public policy'. And Arrow, who, as I have remarked before, was the first to analyse the ex-ante Pareto efficiency of the market allocation of risk-bearing, also explicitly disclaims the use of von Neumann–Morgenstern utilities in measuring utility for determining the distribution of income (see Arrow 1963, p. 10). So both deny that there is necessarily consistency between ex-ante and ex-post. Insofar as the argument of section 4 is valid, this implies then that individuals' ex-ante utilities need have no utilitarian ethical significance.

This denial of the necessary ethical significance of individuals' ex-ante utilities may appear somewhat surprising, because the contrast between ex-ante efficiency and ex-post equality would appear to lie right at the heart of the criticisms of equality as a goal of economic policy by Friedman (1962) and others. It is therefore perhaps worth examining Friedman's apparent position in rather more detail, especially as I intend to stick by

---

[6] Strictly speaking, this assumption can be dispensed with, but only at the cost of having the planner or observer attach weights to each individual's utility in each state which are proportional to their subjective probabilities (see Hammond 1981b). Such a weighting scheme seems completely indefensible and so I have chosen to ignore this possibility.

my assertion, based on the previous section, that the ex-post utilitarian approach has to be the right one.

Friedman's defence of ex-post inequality of income would appear to stem from two beliefs (see Friedman 1962, Ch. X). The first is a belief in the right of the individual to undertake risks, and not to see the rewards for successful risk-taking being eroded by redistributive taxation. This, of course, is just a special instance of the rights which I discussed in section 3. Friedman either advocates using a rights-respecting social welfare function, as suggested by Sen, or else believes that the right to take risks should act as a constraint like a property right. A rights-respecting social welfare function would be an ex-ante welfare function, however, and we have already seen how Friedman and Savage have rejected the necessity of consistency between the ex-ante and ex-post approaches. So one is either left with a rights-respecting ex-ante welfare function which is inconsistent with any acceptable ex-post welfare function, and so a likely inconsistency in formulating economic policy over time, or, much more likely, we are forced to suggest that Friedman views the right to take risks as a kind of property right which acts as a constraint on maximising the expected value of the ex-post welfare function.

Viewing the right to take risks as a kind of property right has rather strange implications. It is one thing to claim that a successful capitalist has a right to the proceeds of his risk-taking activities, and even the right to pass these proceeds on to his heirs, as Friedman suggests. It is quite another matter to go on to claim, as one surely must if one is to be consistent, that the failed capitalist has the duty to meet all the consequences of his failure, including discharging all his debts, if he can, and even selling himself and perhaps his heirs too into slavery if necessary. In fact, modern capitalist societies accord the right to failed capitalists of declaring themselves bankrupt, and this in itself undermines the supposed property rights of other capitalists who are more successful, but were unfortunate enough to have made loans to another capitalist who went bankrupt and was unable to discharge his debts.

Thus the right to take risks is inherently limited – at least in an actual economy with incomplete information where it is practically impossible to make sure that nobody ever goes bankrupt. It is possible to argue, I suppose, that the right to take risks should nevertheless be limited only to the extent required to deal with bankruptcy. It is even possible to argue that the only reason for seeking to reduce inequality is to ensure that everybody achieves a certain subsistence income. But then the issue arises of how much income the fortunate should sacrifice in order to meet the debts of the bankrupt or to subsidise the incomes of the poor. And this is an issue that can only be satisfactorily resolved by using an explicit objective function.[7] So the welfare economist really is forced to choose between income distributions, and may as well do so by using the expected value of an ex-post welfare function. Then, if one really wants to respect the property rights of the rich, everybody who receives any kind of subsidy must be right down at some threshold level of poverty. This, however, involves such measures as a means test to determine who is entitled to transfer incomes or to goods such as free medical prescriptions, or even which families are entitled to free schooling for their children, and means tests of this kind to protect the supposed rights of the rich are ethically distasteful to many of us. Thus I do not find it appealing to suppose that there is a kind of property right to take risks.

There is a third reason for accepting ex-post inequality of income which is also hinted at by Friedman (1953). This is that imposing ex-post equality would create adverse incentives for people to work hard, acquire skills, or take risks. Though Kanbur (1979) has recently pointed out that it is not necessarily true that a more risk averse society will display greater equality of income, and so that there may not be the trade-off between risk-taking and equality which Friedman presumed, Kanbur's conclusion depends crucially on there being incentive constraints preventing the attainment of a full ex-post optimum. Thus the trade-off between equality and the incentives to take risk remains. This, however, raises questions concerning incentives which will be taken up later in section 7.

The conclusion of this lengthy discussion, then, is that the ex-post approach to utilitarian welfare economics under uncertainty remains defensible. There is a question over individuals' rights to take risks. These can be accommodated by making ex-post social welfare a state-independent weighted sum of individuals' von Neumann–Morgenstern utility functions, as recommended by Vickrey and Harsanyi, so that the ex-ante and ex-post approaches coincide. It is far from clear, however, that it is ethically necessary to do this, nor that individuals really do have legitimate rights to take more than rather small risks, though, of course, it is socially useful if they undertake risk-bearing activities which happen to be desirable but cannot be fully insured because of the lack of information.

6 Valuing life and limb

In the previous section, the contrast between ex-ante and ex-post was made with reference to the social choice of income distribution. An area

[7] I suppose Friedman and his followers might argue that one should be strictly neutral as regards the distribution of income between those who are not below the poverty line. But even this presupposes a welfare function which is equivalent to total income, for those not below the poverty line. As shown in Roberts 1980a, this is not even consistent with the Pareto principle when there are many goods and individuals' preferences are sufficiently diverse.

where the contrast may appear even starker arises in connection with the social evaluation of life and limb, and questions such as the cost of an accident. These are matters which are obviously far from exclusively economic questions, yet in deciding how much to spend on road safety measures, for example, economic and social consequences become closely linked. And although the utilitarian welfare economist's approach to such questions may seem far from ideal, it is not at all obvious how the approach can be improved upon.

The contrast between ex-ante and ex-post is stark in the case of such choices because, ex-post, one is trading off lives against ordinary economic resources whereas, ex-ante, one is merely trading off *probabilities* of death against economic resources. The latter seems much more comfortable, especially as it seems that individuals do choose to confront small but varying probabilities of death or injury all the time, and may even do so in a way which maximises their ex-ante expected utility. Then, as has been discussed by Drèze (1962), Mishan (1971), and Jones-Lee (1974, 1976, 1980), there is an implicit von Neumann–Morgenstern utility to death or injury. This may be quite consistent with the individual being unwilling to die or even to lose a leg with certainty in exchange for any sum of money, no matter how large, because the utility of being even very poor with both legs can exceed the utility of being extremely rich with only one leg.

The comfort of the ex-ante approach may be more apparent than real, however, for consider the Vickrey–Harsanyi case, in which ex-ante and ex-post coincide. Then, if it is possible to avoid uncertainty altogether but not to avoid some 'accidental' deaths, the social welfare function prescribes that those who have least to gain from living, in terms of von Neumann–Morgenstern utilities, should die, while those who have most to gain should live. This may be right, given that, say, exactly ten people have to die, but it is far from comfortable.

However, I have argued that the ex-ante approach to utilitarianism under uncertainty is only appropriate when it coincides with the ex-post approach, and that this coincidence is actually rather unlikely. Thus I am arguing that one should use the ex-post approach consistently, even in matters of life and death. If this brings us face to face with uncomfortable preferences over who is to die, this may be no bad thing, since such preferences are anyway implicit in the ex-ante approach.

As usual, there remains the issue of whether and how individual attitudes to risk are to be allowed for in the ex-post welfare function, short of making it coincide with an ex-ante welfare function. One might, for example, include ex-ante utility in each individual's ex-post utility function. This does not affect the fundamental principle of ex-post utilitarianism however. There is also the question of whether individuals have the right to avoid unnecessary and, more especially, involuntary risk of death or injury. Of course, any sensible ex-post social welfare function already respects individuals' preferences for less risk of this kind. But whether one wants to go beyond this and impose certain constraints is another matter which has to be judged case by case on merit. Exposing people to risk from uncontrolled guns or drunken drivers seems totally unacceptable; building nuclear power stations, oil refineries, or airports close to settled areas should be avoided if possible but not at all costs.

7 Incomplete information and incentive constraints[8]

After dealing with uncertainty, the next really challenging issues for utilitarian analysis arise when individuals have incomplete information. Complete information is when every individual knows what any other individual knows, and the planner or observer has the same information too. If there really were such complete information, and so if everybody had pooled all their expertise, it might happen that individuals would all share the same subjective probability distribution over the set S of possible states of the world. Of course, it also might not happen. What is almost certain, however, is that if individuals do not have such complete information – if there is incomplete information – then their probability assessments will differ. This is especially clear when some individuals are unsure whether a given state can still occur while others already know it cannot. The term 'incomplete information' arises from Harsanyi (1967–8) and his highly original and profound analysis of such situations.

Were one to adopt the ex-ante approach to utilitarian analysis, the fact that individuals have incomplete information and so differing probability assessments would affect the social objective. What is more, it would do so by counting outcomes for an individual i in all the states of the world which he thinks are still possible, even though some other individual, or even, perhaps, every other individual, knows that some of those states are impossible. In other words, it allows individuals to live in a fool's paradise, if they so choose, and reckons their utility accordingly. Far worse, perhaps, is the consequent tendency to prefer policies which improve paradise for the fool, when more prudent use of all the information the policy-maker has available would dictate otherwise.

With the ex-post approach, however, there is no such problem. What counts in determining probabilities is the planner's or observer's information. The social objective is the expected value of the ex-post von Neumann–Morgenstern social welfare function, based on the planner's or

[8] This section is based on the analysis in Hammond 1981d.

observer's probability assessments. Of course, one wants the planner or observer to be as well informed as possible. Thus, the fact that information is incomplete really has no effect at all on the proper social objective.

This is not to say, of course, that information available to individuals has no effect on the choices recommended by utilitarian analysis. But I claim that information affects the *constraints* which govern those choices, rather than the objectives they are intended to promote. Where there is a single individual – as in a 'Robinson Crusoe' economy – this is fairly clear. Information takes the form of being able to distinguish different states of nature, in that the individual knows either that the true state s belongs to a set S_1, or to a set S_2, or to a set S_3, etc., where $S_1, S_2, S_3, \ldots$ are disjoint sets which together exhaust the set S of all possible states. In other words, $S_1, S_2, S_3, \ldots$ is a partition of S, which we naturally call the *information partition*, while the sets $S_1, S_2, S_3, \ldots$ are *information sets*. The individual can distinguish states in different information sets of his information partition, but cannot distinguish between different states in the same information set. Where the individual cannot tell two states of nature apart, his contingent action must be the same in each state. Thus lack of information prevents the individual from tailoring his action to the true state, as he could if he were perfectly informed. In this sense, information affects the constraints faced by the individual.

In a society or economy with many individuals, the same essential consideration applies, but there are many complications. Initially, it would seem, each individual makes his own decision constrained by his own lack of information and the planner does too. But individuals necessarily interact, through the market, the economic system, the political process, or whatever, and observe one another's behaviour. Then it may even happen that individuals can learn what other individuals know simply by observing each other's behaviour. For example, it seems that in economies of pure exchange, individual traders can sometimes acquire all the information any other trader has simply by observing what prices equate supply and demand for each commodity, as, for instance, in Radner 1979. And, of course, individuals may choose to communicate information more directly and explicitly. Whatever individuals do learn from each other, however, and whatever the planner learns from individuals, the essential point remains. Information serves only to determine policy choices or recommendations by affecting the constraints: it does nothing to affect objectives as such. At least, this is true while one is only considering economic policy with individuals' information fixed; the case where policy affects information will be discussed in the next section.

Other non-essential complications do deserve discussion, however. One is the scope for decentralisation which arises when individuals retain some private information not available to an economic planner. This is discussed in Dasgupta (Chapter 10, below). It is perfectly possible, however, to have the planner consider outcomes which are contingent on what individuals know privately as well as on what the planner himself knows. Another very important complication concerns providing incentives for individuals to reveal private information. In a rather special case, this problem of 'incentive compatibility' has received extensive recent discussion in the economics literature, following Hurwicz's lead especially (Hurwicz 1972, 1973). If an individual realises that revealing the truth will make him worse off than if he concealed it or distorted it in some way the temptation not to reveal the truth is strong. It has now become widely accepted that economists should recognise this problem explicitly and restrict attention to procedures for making social decisions that do not rely on private information unless incentives are provided to encourage individuals to reveal their information truthfully. These are additional constraints on what an economic planner can choose, which we may as well call incentive constraints. Such constraints have been alluded to long ago by such writers as Lerner (1944), Friedman (1953), and Graaff (1957) but only now are their implications being properly explored. In fact, one question at least remains completely undiscussed as far as I know. How much should the planner try to learn from individuals by providing incentives? In other words, to what extent should he trade off constraints imposed by lack of information against constraints imposed by the need to provide incentives for individuals to reveal private information?

To summarise, on the assumption that individuals' information remains exogenous and independent of policy choices, the extent of individuals' information affects only the constraints on the possible social outcomes; the objective remains that of maximising the expected value of the ex-post von Neumann–Morganstern social welfare function, where the appropriate probabilities are based on the planner's own information.

8 Endogenous information

In the previous section I assumed that the policy-maker had no control, direct or indirect, over the information available to individuals. This is clearly an untenable assumption even for an economist concerned only with economic problems, given the importance of the communications industry and of advertising in any modern economy. Yet relaxing it brings us immediately face to face with the sorts of problems which appear to be of most interest to moral philosophers, such as whether to keep promises and whether to tell the truth in all circumstances. We are faced with deciding what people should know, and whether they should be deliberately misled. We are also faced with the possibility that individuals have a right to know the truth: somehow, this right seems to be more appealing than most of the others I have discussed previously.

The issue of what people should know has not been squarely faced by economists as perhaps it should have been. Atkinson (1974) does consider the question of whether it is really worth making a confirmed smoker miserable by informing him of the possible dreadful consequences for his health, but he gives little clue as to how it should be answered.

Here, then, we face the most challenging issue so far. Had we remained with ex-ante utilitarianism, of course, the problem might seem relatively trivial. All that would matter would be individuals' utilities ex-ante, so we would tell them what raises these ex-ante utilities. This, however, would imply that we should try to raise individuals' expectations falsely and, as long as we are believed, should make promises we know we can never keep – the familiar tricks of the trade of most modern candidates for political office. Such scant regard for the truth seems totally indefensible.

The ex-post utilitarian approach also faces difficulties, however. What it suggests is telling individuals not the truth, but whatever serves to relax any incentive constraints which the planner faces in trying to maximise expected ex-post welfare. It is like trying to persuade young children to fall asleep on Christmas Eve by telling them that Santa Claus will not come unless they do fall asleep.

A more appropriate utilitarian criterion might follow Allais' (1947) suggestion of treating the same individual at different times as though he were different individuals. In each state *s*, the ultimate utility of the individual could depend not only on the final outcome, as we have been discussing so far, nor just on the history of the society or economy and of the individual's changing tastes, but also on the history of the individual's ex-ante utilities at each stage, given the information he had. This is actually a perfectly consistent objective which naturally extends that considered in section 4, and also integrates the ex-ante and ex-post approaches to utilitarianism to some extent. What it does not do, however, is establish that individuals should know the truth as far as possible. Instead, it steers a middle course between telling individuals what helps to relax incentive constraints and telling them what they would like to hear ex-ante.

At this point, a rather extreme utilitarian might argue that this is exactly as it should be. Individuals are no more than the pieces in a utilitarian game, to be manipulated for utilitarian ends, though with their best interests in mind. Leaving them misinformed is part of that utilitarian game. But it is here where I must at last part company with such extreme utilitarianism, and recognise that individuals certainly have a right to be fully informed, or at least to acquire as much information as they wish to. It does not follow, however, that utilitarianism cannot handle this possibility. The ultimately utility of the individual now needs to be even more broadly defined, to include what information he had at each stage as a separate and explicit argument, as well as the eventual true state, because ultimate utility depends on whether he was told the truth. One can also insist that the social welfare function respect the right of each individual to know as much of the truth as possible, within certain cost limitations. This, however, need not always be so; somebody who is universally regarded as ugly may prefer not to be told it. Even then, however, the individual can have a right to know as much of the truth as he desires.

9 Conclusion: the limits to utilitarianism?

It might seem like trickery to keep extending the domain of each individual's 'ultimate' utility function further and further until it includes not only the usual social outcome, but also the history of the individual's tastes, expectations, and information. Yet this seems to illustrate what I believe to be a general principle: that utilitarianism can be defined sufficiently broadly to handle any ethical issue, or at least any ethical issue of interest to economists. Applying utilitarianism in this way may well face us with uncomfortable choices, as with issues of life and death. There is also the question of whether property rights should serve as constraints on maximising a utilitarian objective, although I have not yet found any completely convincing instance of a right which cannot be dealt with along utilitarian lines, as considered in section 3. It may be useful to allow 'rights' which decentralise decisions when there is incomplete information, as Dasgupta (Chapter 10, below) has argued, but that is by no means inconsistent with the utilitarian approach. It may also be appropriate to give individuals the right to become informed about certain issues, if they both wish to know and are prepared to pay the (social) cost of providing the relevant information.

What must be admitted is that the ultimate utility functions resulting from such extensions may bear little relation to individual preferences. And, of course, making the interpersonal comparisons necessary to construct a social welfare function is another task for which there is little empirical evidence to help us. Thus, even though it may be possible in principle to apply utilitarian analysis to a very broad range of challenging issues of the kind I have discussed, it is also quite possible that some other approach may be more helpful. That, however, cannot be discussed here.

5   Contractualism and utilitarianism[1]

T. M. SCANLON

Utilitarianism occupies a central place in the moral philosophy of our time. It is not the view which most people hold; certainly there are very few who would claim to be act utilitarians. But for a much wider range of people it is the view towards which they find themselves pressed when they try to give a theoretical account of their moral beliefs. Within moral philosophy it represents a position one must struggle against if one wishes to avoid it. This is so in spite of the fact that the implications of act utilitarianism are wildly at variance with firmly held moral convictions, while rule utilitarianism, the most common alternative formulation, strikes most people as an unstable compromise.

The wide appeal of utilitarianism is due, I think, to philosophical considerations of a more or less sophisticated kind which pull us in a quite different direction than our first order moral beliefs. In particular, utilitarianism derives much of its appeal from alleged difficulties about the foundations of rival views. What a successful alternative to utilitarianism must do, first and foremost, is to sap this source of strength by providing a clear account of the foundations of non-utilitarian moral reasoning. In what follows I will first describe the problem in more detail by setting out the questions which a philosophical account of the foundations of morality must answer. I will then put forward a version of contractualism which, I will argue, offers a better set of responses to these questions than that supplied by straightforward versions of utilitarianism. Finally I will explain why contractualism, as I understand it, does not lead back to some utilitarian formula as its normative outcome.

Contractualism has been proposed as the alternative to utilitarianism before, notably by John Rawls in *A Theory of Justice* (Rawls 1971). Despite the wide discussion which this book has received, however, I think

---

[1] I am greatly indebted to Derek Parfit for patient criticism and enormously helpful discussion of many earlier versions of this paper. Thanks are due also to the many audiences who have heard parts of those versions delivered as lectures and kindly responded with helpful comments. In particular, I am indebted to Marshall Cohen, Ronald Dworkin, Owen Fiss, and Thomas Nagel for valuable criticism.

103

that the appeal of contractualism as a foundational view has been underrated. In particular, it has not been sufficiently appreciated that contractualism offers a particularly plausible account of moral motivation. The version of contractualism that I shall present differs from Rawls' in a number of respects. In particular, it makes no use, or only a different and more limited kind of use, of his notion of choice from behind a veil of ignorance. One result of this difference is to make the contrast between contractualism and utilitarianism stand out more clearly.

I

There is such a subject as moral philosophy for much the same reason that there is such a subject as the philosophy of mathematics. In moral judgements, as in mathematical ones, we have a set of putatively objective beliefs in which we are inclined to invest a certain degree of confidence and importance. Yet on reflection it is not at all obvious what, if anything, these judgements can be about, in virtue of which some can be said to be correct or defensible and others not. This question of subject matter, or the grounds of truth, is the first philosophical question about both morality and mathematics. Second, in both morality and mathematics it seems to be possible to discover the truth simply by thinking or reasoning about it. Experience and observation may be helpful, but observation in the normal sense is not the standard means of discovery in either subject. So, given any positive answer to the first question – any specification of the subject matter or ground of truth in mathematics or morality – we need some compatible epistemology explaining how it is possible to discover the facts about this subject matter through something like the means we seem to use.

Given this similarity in the questions giving rise to moral philosophy and to the philosophy of mathematics, it is not surprising that the answers commonly given fall into similar general types. If we were to interview students in a freshman mathematics course many of them would, I think, declare themselves for some kind of conventionalism. They would hold that mathematics proceeds from definitions and principles that are either arbitrary or instrumentally justified, and that mathematical reasoning consists in perceiving what follows from these definitions and principles. A few others, perhaps, would be realists or platonists according to whom mathematical truths are a special kind of non-empirical fact that we can perceive through some form of intuition. Others might be naturalists who hold that mathematics, properly understood, is just the most abstract empirial science. Finally there are, though perhaps not in an average freshman course, those who hold that there are no mathematical facts in the world 'outside of us', but that the truths of mathematics are objective truths about the mental constructions of which we are capable. Kant held that pure mathematics was a realm of objective mind-dependent truths, and Brouwer's mathematical Intuitionism is another theory of this type (with the important difference that it offers grounds for the warranted assertability of mathematical judgements rather than for their truth in the classical sense). All of these positions have natural correlates in moral philosophy. Intuitionism of the sort espoused by W. D. Ross is perhaps the closest analogue to mathematical platonism, and Kant's theory is the most familiar version of the thesis that morality is a sphere of objective, mind-dependent truths.

All of the views I have mentioned (with some qualification in the case of conventionalism) give positive (i.e. non-sceptical) answers to the first philosophical question about mathematics. Each identifies some objective, or at least intersubjective, ground of truth for mathematical judgements. Outright scepticism and subjective versions of mind-dependence (analogues of emotivism or prescriptivism) are less appealing as philosophies of mathematics than as moral philosophies. This is so in part simply because of the greater degree of intersubjective agreement in mathematical judgement. But it is also due to the difference in the further questions that philosophical accounts of the two fields must answer.

Neither mathematics nor morality can be taken to describe a realm of facts existing in isolation from the rest of reality. Each is supposed to be connected with other things. Mathematical judgements give rise to predictions about those realms to which mathematics is applied. This connection is something that a philosophical account of mathematical truth must explain, but the fact that we can observe and learn from the correctness of such predictions also gives support to our belief in objective mathematical truth. In the case of morality the main connection is, or is generally supposed to be, with the will. Given any candidate for the role of subject matter of morality we must explain why anyone should care about it, and the need to answer this question of motivation has given strong support to subjectivist views.

But what must an adequate philosophical theory of morality say about moral motivation? It need not, I think, show that the moral truth gives anyone who knows it a reason to act which appeals to that person's present desires or to the advancement of his or her interests. I find it entirely intelligible that moral requirement might correctly apply to a person even though that person had no reason of either of these kinds for complying with it. Whether moral requirements give those to whom they apply reasons for compliance of some third kind is a disputed question which I shall set aside. But what an adequate moral philosophy must do, I think, is to make clearer to us the nature of the reasons that morality does provide, at least to those who are concerned with it. A philosophical theory of morality must offer an account of these reasons that is, on the one hand, compatible with its account of moral truth and moral reasoning and, on the other, supported by a plausible analysis of moral experience. A satisfactory moral philosophy will not leave concern with morality as a simple special preference, like a fetish or a special taste, which some people just happen to have. It must make it understandable why moral reasons are ones that people can take seriously, and why they strike those who are moved by them as reasons of a special stringency and inescapability.

There is also a further question whether susceptibility to such reasons is compatible with a person's good or whether it is, as Nietzsche argued, a psychological disaster for the person who has it. If one is to defend morality one must show that it is not disastrous in this way, but I will not pursue this second motivational question here. I mention it only to distinguish it from the first question, which is my present concern.

The task of giving a philosophical explanation of the subject matter of morality differs both from the task of analysing the meaning of moral terms and from that of finding the most coherent formulation of our first order moral beliefs. A maximally coherent ordering of our first order moral beliefs could provide us with a valuable kind of explanation: it would make clear how various, apparently disparate moral notions, precepts and judgements are related to one another, thus indicating to what degree conflicts between them are fundamental and to what degree, on the other hand, they can be resolved or explained away. But philosophical inquiry into the subject matter of morality takes a more external view. It seeks to explain what kind of truths moral truths are by describing them in relation to other things in the world and in relation to our particular concerns. An explanation of how we can come to know the truth about morality must be based on such an external explanation of the kind of things moral truths are rather than on a list of particular moral truths, even a maximally coherent list. This seems to be true as well about explanations of how moral beliefs can give one a reason to act.[2]

Coherence among our first-order moral beliefs – what Rawls has called narrow reflective equilibrium[3] – seems unsatisfying[4] as an account of moral truth or as an account of the basis of justification in ethics just

---

[2] Though here the ties between the nature of morality and its content are more important. It is not clear that an account of the nature of morality which left its content *entirely* open could be the basis for a plausible account of moral motivation.

[3] See Rawls 1974–5, p. 8; and Daniels 1979 pp. 257–8. How closely the process of what I am calling philosophical explanation will coincide with the search for 'wide reflective equilibrium' as this is understood by Rawls and by Daniels is a further question which I cannot take up here.

[4] For expression of this dissatisfaction see Singer 1974 and Brandt 1979, pp. 16–21.

because, taken by itself, a maximally coherent account of our moral beliefs need not provide us with what I have called a philosophical explanation of the subject matter of morality. However internally coherent our moral beliefs may be rendered, the nagging doubt may remain that there is nothing to them at all. They may be merely a set of socially inculcated reactions, mutually consistent perhaps but not judgements of a kind which can properly be said to be correct or incorrect. A philosophical theory of the nature of morality can contribute to our confidence in our first order moral beliefs chiefly by allaying these natural doubts about the subject. Insofar as it includes an account of moral epistemology, such a theory may guide us towards new forms of moral argument, but it need not do this. Moral argument of more or less the kind we have been familiar with may remain as the only form of justification in ethics. But whether or not it leads to revision in our modes of justification, what a good philosophical theory should do is to give us a clearer understanding of what the best forms of moral argument amount to and what kind of truth it is that they can be a way of arriving at. (Much the same can be said, I believe, about the contribution which philosophy of mathematics makes to our confidence in particular mathematical judgements and particular forms of mathematical reasoning.)

Like any thesis about morality, a philosophical account of the subject matter of morality must have some connection with the meaning of moral terms: it must be plausible to claim that the subject matter described is in fact what these terms refer to at least in much of their normal use. But the current meaning of moral terms is the product of many different moral beliefs held by past and present speakers of the language, and this meaning is surely compatible with a variety of moral views and with a variety of views about the nature of morality. After all, moral terms are used to express many different views of these kinds, and people who express these views are not using moral terms incorrectly, even though what some of them say must be mistaken. Like a first-order moral judgement, a philosophical characterisation of the subject matter of morality is a substantive claim about morality, albeit a claim of a different kind.

While a philosophical characterisation of morality makes a kind of claim that differs from a first-order moral judgement, this does not mean that a philosophical theory of morality will be neutral between competing normative doctrines. The adoption of a philosophical thesis about the nature of morality will almost always have some effect on the plausibility of particular moral claims, but philosophical theories of morality vary widely in the extent and directness of their normative implications. At one extreme is intuitionism, understood as the philosophical thesis that morality is concerned with certain non-natural properties. Rightness, for example, is held by Ross[5] to be the property of 'fittingness' or 'moral suitability'. Intuitionism holds that we can identify occurrences of these properties, and that we can recognise as self-evident certain general truths about them, but that they cannot be further analysed or explained in terms of other notions. So understood, intuitionism is in principle compatible with a wide variety of normative positions. One could, for example, be an intuitionistic utilitarian or an intuitionistic believer in moral rights, depending on the general truths about the property of moral rightness which one took to be self-evident.

The other extreme is represented by philosophical utilitarianism. The term 'utilitarianism' is generally used to refer to a family of specific normative doctrines – doctrines which might be held on the basis of a number of different philosophical theses about the nature of morality. In this sense of the term one might, for example, be a utilitarian on intuitionist or on contractualist grounds. But what I will call 'philosophical utilitarianism' is a particular philosophical thesis about the subject matter of morality, namely the thesis that the only fundamental moral facts are facts about individual well-being.[6] I believe that this thesis has a great deal of plausibility for many people, and that, while some people are utilitarians for other reasons, it is the attractiveness of philosophical utilitarianism which accounts for the widespread influence of utilitarian principles.

It seems evident to people that there is such a thing as individuals' being made better or worse off. Such facts have an obvious motivational force; it is quite understandable that people should be moved by them in much the way that they are supposed to be moved by moral considerations. Further, these facts are clearly relevant to morality as we now understand it. Claims about individual well-being are one class of valid starting points for moral argument. But many people find it much harder to see how there could be any other, independent starting points. Substantive moral requirements independent of individual well-being strike people as intuitionist in an objectionable sense. They would represent 'moral facts' of a kind it would be difficult to explain. There is no problem about recognising it as a fact that a certain act is, say, an instance of lying or of promise breaking. And a utilitarian can acknowledge that such facts as these often have (derivative) moral significance: they are morally significant because of their consequences for individual well-being. The problems, and the charge of 'intuitionism', arise when it is claimed that such acts are wrong in a sense that is not reducible to the fact that they decrease individual well-being.

---

[5] Ross 1939 pp. 52–4, 315.

[6] For purposes of this discussion I leave open the important questions of which individuals are to count and how 'well-being' is to be understood. Philosophical utilitarianism will retain the appeal I am concerned with under many different answers to these questions.

How could this independent property of moral wrongness be understood in a way that would give it the kind of importance and motivational force which moral considerations have been taken to have? If one accepts the idea that there are no moral properties having this kind of intrinsic significance, then philosophical utilitarianism may seem to be the only tenable account of morality. And once philosophical utilitarianism is accepted, some form of normative utilitarianism seems to be forced on us as the correct first-order moral theory. Utilitarianism thus has, for many people, something like the status which Hilbert's Formalism and Brouwer's Intuitionism have for their believers. It is a view which seems to be forced on us by the need to give a philosophically defensible account of the subject. But it leaves us with a hard choice: we can either abandon many of our previous first-order beliefs or try to salvage them by showing that they can be obtained as derived truths or explained away as useful and harmless fictions.

It may seem that the appeal of philosophical utilitarianism as I have described it is spurious, since this theory must amount either to a form of intuitionism (differing from others only in that it involves just one appeal to intuition) or else to definitional naturalism of a kind refuted by Moore and others long ago. But I do not think that the doctrine can be disposed of so easily. Philosophical utilitarianism is a philosophical thesis about the nature of morality. As such, it is on a par with intuitionism or with the form of contractualism which I will defend later in this paper. None of these theses need claim to be true as a matter of definition; if one of them is true it does not follow that a person who denies it is misusing the words 'right', 'wrong' and 'ought'. Nor are all these theses forms of intuitionism, if intuitionism is understood as the view that moral facts concern special non-natural properties, which we can apprehend by intuitive insight but which do not need or admit of any further analysis. Both contractualism and philosophical utilitarianism are specifically incompatible with this claim. Like other philosophical theses about the nature of morality (including, I would say, intuitionism itself), contractualism and philosophical utilitarianism are to be appraised on the basis of their success in giving an account of moral belief, moral argument and moral motivation that is compatible with our general beliefs about the world: our beliefs about what kinds of things are in the world, what kinds of observation and reasoning we are capable of, and what kinds of reasons we have for action. A judgement as to which account of the nature of morality (or of mathematics) is most plausible in this general sense is just that: a judgement of overall plausibility. It is not usefully described as an insight into concepts or as a special intuitive insight of some other kind.

If philosophical utilitarianism is accepted then some form of utilitarianism appears to be forced upon us as a normative doctrine, but further argument is required to determine which form we should accept. If all that counts morally is the well-being of individuals, no one of whom is singled out as counting for more than the others, and if all that matters in the case of each individual is the degree to which his or her well-being is affected, then it would seem to follow that the basis of moral appraisal is the goal of maximising the *sum*[7] of individual well-being. Whether this standard is to be applied to the criticism of individual actions, or to the selection of rules or policies, or to the inculcation of habits and dispositions to act is a further question, as is the question of how 'well-being' itself is to be understood. Thus the hypothesis that much of the appeal of utilitarianism as a normative doctrine derives from the attractiveness of philosophical utilitarianism explains how people can be convinced that some form of utilitarianism must be correct while yet being quite uncertain as to which form it is, whether it is 'direct' or 'act' utilitarianism or some form of indirect 'rule' or 'motive' utilitarianism. What these views have in common, despite their differing normative consequences, is the identification of the same class of fundamental moral facts.

II

If what I have said about the appeal of utilitarianism is correct, then what a rival theory must do is to provide an alternative to philosophical utilitarianism as a conception of the subject matter of morality. This is what the theory which I shall call contractualism seeks to do. Even if it succeeds in this, however, and is judged superior to philosophical utilitarianism as an account of the nature of morality, normative utilitarianism will not have been refuted. The possibility will remain that normative utilitarianism can be established on other grounds, for example as the normative outcome of contractualism itself. But one direct and, I think, influential argument for normative utilitarianism will have been set aside.

To give an example of what I mean by contractualism, a contractualist account of the nature of moral wrongness might be stated as follows.

An act is wrong if its performance under the circumstances would be disallowed by any system of rules for the general regulation of behaviour which no one could reasonably reject as a basis for informed, unforced general agreement.

This is intended as a characterisation of the kind of property which moral wrongness is. Like philosophical utilitarianism, it will have normative consequences, but it is not my present purpose to explore these in detail.

[7] 'Average Utilitarianism' is most plausibly arrived at through quite a different form of argument, one more akin to contractualism. I discuss one such argument in section IV below.

As a contractualist account of one moral notion, what I have set out here is only an approximation, which may need to be modified considerably. Here I can offer a few remarks by way of clarification.

The idea of 'informed agreement' is meant to exclude agreement based on superstition or false belief about the consequences of actions, even if these beliefs are ones which it would be reasonable for the person in question to have. The intended force of the qualification 'reasonably', on the other hand, is to exclude rejections that would be unreasonable *given* the aim of finding principles which could be the basis of informed, unforced general agreement. Given this aim, it would be unreasonable, for example, to reject a principle because it imposed a burden on you when every alternative principle would impose much greater burdens on others. I will have more to say about grounds for rejection later in the paper.

The requirement that the hypothetical agreement which is the subject of moral argument be unforced is meant not only to rule out coercion, but also to exclude being forced to accept an agreement by being in a weak bargaining position, for example because others are able to hold out longer and hence to insist on better terms. Moral argument abstracts from such considerations. The only relevant pressure for agreement comes from the desire to find and agree on principles which no one who had this desire could reasonably reject. According to contractualism, moral argument concerns the possibility of agreement among persons who are all moved by this desire, and moved by it to the same degree. But this counter-factual assumption characterises only the agreement with which morality is concerned, not the world to which moral principles are to apply. Those who are concerned with morality look for principles for application to their imperfect world which they could not reasonably reject, and which others in this world, who are not now moved by the desire for agreement, could not reasonably reject should they come to be so moved.[8]

The contractualist account of moral wrongness refers to principles 'which no one could reasonably reject' rather than to principles 'which everyone could reasonably accept' for the following reason.[9] Consider a principle under which some people will suffer severe hardships, and suppose that these hardships are avoidable. That is, there are alternative principles under which no one would have to bear comparable burdens. It might happen, however, that the people on whom these hardships fall are particularly self-sacrificing, and are willing to accept these burdens for the sake of what they see as the greater good of all. We would not say, I think, that it would be unreasonable of them to do this. On the other hand, it

---

[8] Here I am indebted to Gilbert Harman for comments which have helped me to clarify my statement of contractualism.

[9] A point I owe to Derek Parfit.

might not be unreasonable for them to refuse these burdens, and, hence, not unreasonable for someone to reject a principle requiring him to bear them. If this rejection would be reasonable, then the principle imposing these burdens is put in doubt, despite the fact that some particularly self-sacrificing people could (reasonably) accept it. Thus it is the reasonableness of rejecting a principle, rather than the reasonableness of accepting it, on which moral argument turns.

It seems likely that many non-equivalent sets of principles will pass the test of non-rejectability. This is suggested, for example, by the fact that there are many different ways of defining important duties, no one of which is more or less 'rejectable' than the others. There are, for example, many different systems of agreement-making and many different ways of assigning responsibility to care for others. It does not follow, however, that any action allowed by at least one of these sets of principles cannot be morally wrong according to contractualism. If it is important for us to have *some* duty of a given kind (some duty of fidelity to agreements, or some duty of mutual aid) of which there are many morally acceptable forms, then one of these forms needs to be established by convention. In a setting in which one of these forms *is* conventionally established, acts disallowed by it will be wrong in the sense of the definition given. For, given the need for such conventions, one thing that could not be generally agreed to would be a set of principles allowing one to disregard conventionally established (and morally acceptable) definitions of important duties. This dependence on convention introduces a degree of cultural relativity into contractualist morality. In addition, what a person can reasonably reject will depend on the aims and conditions that are important in his life, and these will also depend on the society in which he lives. The definition given above allows for variation of both of these kinds by making the wrongness of an action depend on the circumstances in which it is performed.

The partial statement of contractualism which I have given has the abstract character appropriate in an account of the subject matter of morality. On its face, it involves no specific claim as to which principles could be agreed to or even whether there is a unique set of principles which could be the basis of agreement. One way, though not the only way, for a contractualist to arrive at substantive moral claims would be to give a technical definition of the relevant notion of agreement, e.g. by specifying the conditions under which agreement is to be reached, the parties to this agreement and the criteria of reasonableness to be employed. Different contractualists have done this in different ways. What must be claimed for such a definition is that (under the circumstances in which it is to apply) what it describes is indeed the kind of unforced, reasonable agreement at which moral argument aims. But contractualism can also be understood as an informal description of the subject matter of morality on the basis of which ordinary forms of moral reasoning can be understood and appraised without proceeding via a technical notion of agreement.

Who is to be included in the general agreement to which contractualism refers? The scope of morality is a difficult question of substantive morality, but a philosophical theory of the nature of morality should provide some basis for answering it. What an adequate theory should do is to provide a framework within which what seem to be relevant arguments for and against particular interpretations of the moral boundary can be carried out. It is often thought that contractualism can provide no plausible basis for an answer to this question. Critics charge either that contractualism provides no answer at all, because it must begin with some set of contracting parties taken as given, or that contractualism suggests an answer which is obviously too restrictive, since a contract requires parties who are able to make and keep agreements and who are each able to offer the others some benefit in return for their cooperation. Neither of these objections applies to the version of contractualism that I defending. The general specification of the scope of morality which it implies seems to me to be this: morality applies to a being if the notion of justification to a being of that kind makes sense. What is required in order for this to be the case? Here I can only suggest some necessary conditions. The first is that the being have a good, that is, that there be a clear sense in which things can be said to go better or worse for that being. This gives partial sense to the idea of what it would be reasonable for a trustee to accept on the being's behalf. It would be reasonable for a trustee to accept at least those things that are good, or not bad, for the being in question. Using this idea of trusteeship we can extend the notion of acceptance to apply to beings that are incapable of literally agreeing to anything. But this minimal notion of trusteeship is too weak to provide a basis for morality, according to contractualism. Contractualist morality relies on notions of what it would be reasonable to accept, or reasonable to reject, which are essentially comparative. Whether it would be unreasonable for me to reject a certain principle, given the aim of finding principles which no one with this aim could reasonably reject, depends not only on how much actions allowed by that principle might hurt me in absolute terms but also on how that potential loss compares with other potential losses to others under this principle and alternatives to it. Thus, in order for a being to stand in moral relations with us it is not enough that it have a good, it is also necessary that its good be sufficiently similar to our own to provide a basis for some system of comparability. Only on the basis of such a system can we give the proper kind of sense to the notion of what a trustee could reasonably reject on a being's behalf.

But the range of possible trusteeship is broader than that of morality. One could act as a trustee for a tomato plant, a forest or an ant colony, and such entities are not included in morality. Perhaps this can be explained by appeal to the requirement of comparability: while these entities have a good, it is not comparable to our own in a way that provides a basis for moral argument. Beyond this, however, there is in these cases insufficient foothold for the notion of justification *to* a being. One further minimum requirement for this notion is that the being constitute a point of view; that is, that there be such a thing as what it is like to be that being, such a thing as what the world seems like to it. Without this, we do not stand in a relation to the being that makes even hypothetical justification *to it* appropriate.

On the basis of what I have said so far contractualism can explain why the capacity to feel pain should have seemed to many to count in favour of moral status: a being which has this capacity seems also to satisfy the three conditions I have just mentioned as necessary for the idea of justification to it to make sense. If a being can feel pain, then it constitutes a centre of consciousness to which justification can be addressed. Feeling pain is a clear way in which the being can be worse off; having its pain alleviated a way in which it can be benefited; and these are forms of weal and woe which seem directly comparable to our own.

It is not clear that the three conditions I have listed as necessary are also sufficient for the idea of justification to a being to make sense. Whether they are, and, if they are not, what more may be required, are difficult and disputed questions. Some would restrict the moral sphere to those to whom justifications could in principle be communicated, or to those who can actually agree to something, or to those who have the capacity to understand moral argument. Contractualism as I have stated it does not settle these issues at once. All I claim is that it provides a basis for argument about them which is at least as plausible as that offered by rival accounts of the nature of morality. These proposed restrictions on the scope of morality are naturally understood as debatable claims about the conditions under which the relevant notion of justification makes sense, and the arguments commonly offered for and against them can also be plausibly understood on this basis.

Some other possible restrictions on the scope of morality are more evidently rejectable. Morality might be restricted to those who have the capacity to observe its constraints, or to those who are able to confer some reciprocal benefit on other participants. But it is extremely implausible to suppose that the beings excluded by these requirements fall entirely outside the protection of morality. Contractualism as I have formulated it[10] can explain why this is so: the absence of these capacities alone does nothing to undermine the possibility of justification to a being. What it may do in some cases, however, is to alter the justifications which are relevant. I suggest that whatever importance the capacities for deliberative control and reciprocal benefit may have is as factors altering the duties which beings have and the duties others have towards them, not as conditions whose absence suspends the moral framework altogether.

III

I have so far said little about the normative content of contractualism. For all I have said, the act utilitarian formula might turn out to be a theorem of contractualism. I do not think that this is the case, but my main thesis is that whatever the normative implications of contractualism may be it still has distinctive content as a philosophical thesis about the nature of morality. This content – the difference, for example, between being a utilitarian because the utilitarian formula is the basis of general agreement and being a utilitarian on other grounds – is shown most clearly in the answer that a contractualist gives to the first motivational question.

Philosophical utilitarianism is a plausible view partly because the facts which it identifies as fundamental to morality – facts about individual well-being – have obvious motivational force. Moral facts can motivate us, on this view, because of our sympathetic identification with the good of others. But as we move from philosophical utilitarianism to a specific utilitarian formula as the standard of right action, the form of motivation that utilitarianism appeals to becomes more abstract. If classical utilitarianism is the correct normative doctrine then the natural source of moral motivation will be a tendency to be moved by changes in aggregate well-being, however these may be composed. We must be moved in the same way by an aggregate gain of the same magnitude whether it is obtained by relieving the acute suffering of a few people or by bringing tiny benefits to a vast number, perhaps at the expense of moderate discomfort for a few. This is very different from sympathy of the familiar kind toward

---

[10] On this view (as contrasted with some others in which the notion of a contract is employed) what is fundamental to morality is the desire for reasonable agreement, not the pursuit of mutual advantage. See section V below. It should be clear that this version of contractualism can account for the moral standing of future persons who will be better or worse off as a result of what we do now. It is less clear how it can deal with the problem presented by future people who would not have been born but for actions of ours which also made the conditions in which they live worse. Do such people have reason to reject principles allowing these actions to be performed? This difficult problem, which I cannot explore here, is raised by Derek Parfit in Parfit 1976.

particular individuals, but a utilitarian may argue that this more abstract desire is what natural sympathy becomes when it is corrected by rational reflection. This desire has the same content as sympathy – it is a concern for the good of others – but it is not partial or selective in its choice of objects.

Leaving aside the psychological plausibility of this even-handed sympathy, how good a candidate is it for the role of moral motivation? Certainly sympathy of the usual kind is one of the many motives that can sometimes impel one to do the right thing. It may be the dominant motive, for example, when I run to the aid of a suffering child. But when I feel convinced by Peter Singer's article[11] on famine, and find myself crushed by the recognition of what seems a clear moral requirement, there is something else at work. In addition to the thought of how much good I could do for people in drought-stricken lands, I am overwhelmed by the further, seemingly distinct thought that it would be wrong for me to fail to aid them when I could do so at so little cost to myself. A utilitarian may respond that his account of moral motivation cannot be faulted for not capturing this aspect of moral experience, since it is just a reflection of our non-utilitarian moral upbringing. Moreover, it must be groundless. For what kind of fact could this supposed further fact of moral wrongness be, and how could it give us a further, special reason for acting? The question for contractualism, then, is whether it can provide a satisfactory answer to this challenge.

According to contractualism, the source of motivation that is directly triggered by the belief that an action is wrong is the desire to be able to justify one's actions to others on grounds they could not reasonably[12] reject. I find this an extremely plausible account of moral motivation – a better account of at least my moral experience than the natural utilitarian alternative – and it seems to me to constitute a strong point for the contractualist view. We all might like to be in actual agreement with the people around us, but the desire which contractualism identifies as basic to morality does not lead us simply to conform to the standards accepted by others whatever these may be. The desire to be able to justify one's actions to others on grounds they could not reasonably reject will be satisfied when we know that there is adequate justification for our action even though others in fact refuse to accept it (perhaps because they have no interest in finding principles which we and others could not reasonably reject). Similarly, a person moved by this desire will not be satisfied by the fact that others accept a justification for his action if he regards this justification as spurious.

---

[11] Singer 1972
[12] Reasonably, that is, given the desire to find principles which others similarly motivated could not reasonably reject.

One rough test of whether you regard a justification as sufficient is whether you would accept that justification if you were in another person's position. This connection between the idea of 'changing places' and the motivation which underlies morality explains the frequent occurence of 'Golden Rule' arguments within different systems of morality and in the teachings of various religions. But the thought experiment of changing places is only a rough guide; the fundamental question is what would it be unreasonable to reject as a basis for informed, unforced, general agreement. As Kant observed,[13] our different individual points of view, taken as they are, may in general by simply irreconcilable. 'Judgemental harmony' requires the construction of a genuinely interpersonal form of justification which is nonetheless something that each individual could agree to. From this interpersonal standpoint, a certain amount of how things look from another person's point of view, like a certain amount of how they look from my own, will be counted as bias.

I am not claiming that the desire to be able to justify one's actions to others on grounds they could not reasonably reject is universal or 'natural'. 'Moral education' seems to me plausibly understood as a process of cultivating this desire and shaping it, largely by learning what justifications others are in fact willing to accept, by finding which ones you yourself find acceptable as you confront them from a variety of perspectives, and by appraising your own and others' acceptance or rejection of these justifications in the light of greater experience.

In fact it seems to me that the desire to be able to justify one's actions (and institutions) on grounds one takes to be acceptable is quite strong in most people. People are willing to go to considerable lengths, involving quite heavy sacrifices, in order to avoid admitting the unjustifiability of their actions and institutions. The notorious insufficiency of moral motivation as a way of getting people to do the right thing is not due to simple weakness of the underlying motive, but rather to the fact that it is easily deflected by self-interest and self-deception.

It could reasonably be objected here that the source of motivation I have described is not tied exclusively to the contractualist notion of moral truth. The account of moral motivation which I have offered refers to the idea of a justification which it would be unreasonable to reject, and this idea is potentially broader than the contractualist notion of agreement. For let *M* be some non-contractualist account of moral truth. According to *M*, we may suppose, the wrongness of an action is simply a moral characteristic of that action in virtue of which it ought not to be done. An act which has this characteristic, according to *M*, has it quite independently of any

[13] Kant 1785, section 2, footnote 14.

tendency of informed persons to come to agreement about it. However, since informed persons are presumably in a position to recognise the wrongness of a type of action, it would seem to follow that if an action is wrong then such persons would agree that it is not to be performed. Similarly, if an act is not morally wrong, and there is adequate moral justification to perform it, then there will presumably be a moral justification for it which an informed person would be unreasonable to reject. Thus, even if M, and not contractualism, is the correct account of moral truth, the desire to be able to justify my actions to others on grounds they could not reasonably reject could still serve as a basis for moral motivation.

What this shows is that the appeal of contractualism, like that of utilitarianism, rests in part on a qualified scepticism. A non-contractualist theory of morality can make use of the source of motivation to which contractualism appeals. But a moral argument will trigger this source of motivation only in virtue of being a good justification for acting in a certain way, a justification which others would be unreasonable not to accept. So a non-contractualist theory must claim that there are moral properties which have justificatory force quite independent of their recognition in any ideal agreement. These would represent what John Mackie has called instances of intrinsic 'to-be-doneness' and 'not-to-be-doneness'.[14] Part of contractualism's appeal rests on the view that, as Mackie puts it, it is puzzling how there could be such properties 'in the world'. By contrast, contractualism seeks to explain the justificatory status of moral properties, as well as their motivational force, in terms of the notion of reasonable agreement. In some cases the moral properties are themselves to be understood in terms of this notion. This is so, for example, in the case of the property of moral wrongness, considered above. But there are also right- and wrong-making properties which are themselves independent of the contractualist notion of agreement. I take the property of being an act of killing for the pleasure of doing so to be a wrong-making property of this kind. Such properties are wrong-making because it would be reasonable to reject any set of principles which permitted the acts they characterise. Thus, while there are morally relevant properties 'in the world' which are independent of the contractualist notion of agreement, these do not constitute instances of intrinsic 'to-be-doneness' and 'not-to-be-doneness': their moral relevance – their force in justifications as well as their link with motivation – is to be explained on contractualist grounds.

In particular, contractualism can account for the apparent moral significance of facts about individual well-being, which utilitarianism takes to

[14] Mackie 1977, p. 42.

be fundamental. Individual well-being will be morally significant, according to contractualism, not because it is intrinsically valuable or because
promoting it is self-evidently a right-making characteristic, but simply
because an individual could reasonably reject a form of argument that
gave his well-being no weight. This claim of moral significance is, however, only approximate, since it is a further difficult question exactly how
'well-being' is to be understood and in what ways we are required to take
account of the well-being of others in deciding what to do. It does not
follow from this claim, for example, that a given desire will always and
everywhere have the same weight in determining the rightness of an action
that would promote its satisfaction, a weight proportional to its strength
or 'intensity'. The right-making force of a person's desires is specified by
what might be called a conception of morally legitimate interests. Such a
conception is a product of moral argument; it is not given, as the notion of
individual well-being may be, simply by the idea of what it is rational for
an individual to desire. Not everything for which I have a rational desire
will be something in which others need concede me to have a legitimate
interest which they undertake to weigh in deciding what to do. The range
of things which may be objects of my rational desires is very wide indeed,
and the range of claims which others could not reasonably refuse to
recognise will almost certainly be narrower than this. There will be a
tendency for interests to conform to rational desire – for those conditions
making it rational to desire something also to establish a legitimate interest
in it – but the two will not always coincide.

One effect of contractualism, then, is to break down the sharp distinction, which arguments for utilitarianism appeal to, between the status of
individual well-being and that of other moral notions. A framework of
moral argument is required to define our legitimate interests and to
account for their moral force. This same contractualist framework can
also account for the force of other moral notions such as rights, individual
responsibility and procedural fairness.

IV

It seems unlikely that act utilitarianism will be a theorem of the version of
contractualism which I have described. The positive moral significance of
individual interests is a direct reflection of the contractualist requirement
that actions be defensible to each person on grounds he could not reasonably reject. But it is a long step from here to the conclusion that each
individual must agree to deliberate always from the point of view of
maximum aggregate benefit and to accept justifications appealing to this
consideration alone. It is quite possible that, according to contractualism,

some moral questions may be properly settled by appeal to maximum aggregate well-being, even though this is not the sole or ultimate standard of justification.

What seems less improbable is that contractualism should turn out to coincide with some form of 'two-level' utilitarianism. I cannot fully assess this possibility here. Contractualism does share with these theories the important features that the defense of individual actions must proceed via a defense of principles that would allow those acts. But contractualism differs from *some* forms of two level utilitarianism in an important way. The role of principles in contractualism is fundamental; they do not enter merely as devices for the promotion of acts that are right according to some other standard. Since it does not establish two potentially conflicting forms of moral reasoning, contractualism avoids the instability which often plagues rule utilitarianism.

The fundamental question here, however, is whether the principles to which contractualism leads must be ones whose general adoption (either ideally or under some more realistic conditions) would promote maximum aggregate well-being. It has seemed to many that this must be the case. To indicate why I do not agree I will consider one of the best known arguments for this conclusion and explain why I do not think it is successful. This will also provide an opportunity to examine the relation between the version of contractualism I have advocated here and the version set forth by Rawls.

The argument I will consider, which is familiar from the writings of Harsanyi[15] and others, proceeds via an interpretation of the contractualist notion of acceptance and leads to the principle of maximum average utility. To think of a principle as a candidate for unanimous agreement I must think of it not merely as acceptable to *me* (perhaps in virtue of my particular position, my tastes, etc.) but as acceptable[16] to others as well. To be relevant, my judgement that the principle is acceptable must be impartial. What does this mean? To judge impartially that a principle is acceptable is, one might say, to judge that it is one which you would have reason to accept no matter who you were. That is, and here is the interpretation, to judge that it is a principle which it would be rational to accept if you did not know which person's position you occupied and believed that you had an equal chance of being in any of these positions. ('Being in a person's

---

[15] See Harsanyi 1955, sec. IV. He is there discussing an argument which he presented earlier in Harsanyi 1953.

[16] In discussing Harsanyi and Rawls I will generally follow them in speaking of the acceptability of principles rather than their unrejectability. The difference between these, pointed out above, is important only within the version of contractualism I am presenting; accordingly, I will speak of rejectability only when I am contrasting my own version with theirs.

position' is here understood to mean being in his objective circumstances and evaluating these from the perspective of his tastes and preferences.) But, it is claimed, the principle which it would be rational to prefer under these circumstances – the one which would offer the chooser greatest expected utility – would be that principle under which the average utility of the affected parties would be highest.

This argument might be questioned at a number of points, but what concerns me at present is the interpretation of impartiality. The argument can be broken down into three stages. The first of these is the idea that moral principles must be impartially acceptable. The second is the idea of choosing principles in ignorance of one's position (including one's tastes, preferences, etc.). The third is the idea of rational choice under the assumption that one has an equal chance of occupying anyone's position. Let me leave aside for the moment the move from stage two to stage three, and concentrate on the first step, from stage one to stage two. There is a way of making something like this step which is, I think, quite valid, but it does not yield the conclusion needed by the argument. If I believe that a certain principle, *P*, could not reasonably be rejected as a basis for in- formed, unforced general agreement, then I must believe not only that it is something which it would be reasonable for me to accept but something which it would be reasonable for others to accept as well, insofar as we are all seeking a ground for general agreement. Accordingly, I must believe that I would have reason to accept *P* no matter which social position I were to occupy (though, for reasons mentioned above, I may not believe that I *would* agree to *P* if I were in some of these positions). Now it may be thought that no sense can be attached to the notion of choosing or agreeing to a principle in ignorance of one's social position, especially when this includes ignorance of one's tastes, preferences, etc. But there is at least a minimal sense that might be attached to this notion. If it would be reason- able for everyone to choose or agree to *P*, then my knowledge that I have reason to do so need not depend on my knowledge of my particular pos- ition, tastes, preferences, etc. So, insofar as it makes any sense at all to speak of choosing or agreeing to something in the absence of this knowledge, it could be said that I have reason to choose or agree to those things which everyone has reason to choose or agree to (assuming, again, the aim of finding principles on which all could agree). And indeed, this same reason- ing can carry us through to a version of stage three. For if I judge *P* to be a principle which everyone has reason to agree to, then it could be said that I would have reason to agree to it if I thought that I had an equal chance of being anybody, or indeed, if I assign any other set of probabilities to being one or another of the people in question.

But it is clear that this is not the conclusion at which the original argument aimed. That conclusion concerned what it would be rational for a self-interested person to choose or agree to under the assumption of ignorance or equal probability of being anyone. The conclusion we have reached appeals to a different notion: the idea of what it would be unreasonable for people to reject given that they are seeking a basis for general agreement. The direction of explanation in the two arguments is quite different. The original argument sought to explain the notion of impartial acceptability of an ethical principle by appealing to the notion of rational self-interested choice under special conditions, a notion which appears to be a clearer one. My revised argument explains how a sense might be attached to the idea of choice or agreement in ignorance of one's position given some idea of what it would be unreasonable for someone to reject as a basis for general agreement. This indicates a problem for my version of contractualism: it may be charged with failure to explain the central notion on which it relies. Here I would reply that my version of contractualism does not seek to explain this notion. It only tries to describe it clearly and to show how other features of morality can be understood in terms of it. In particular, it does not try to explain this notion by reducing it to the idea of what would maximise a person's self-interested expectations if he were choosing from a position of ignorance or under the assumption of equal probability of being anyone.

The initial plausibility of the move from stage one to stage two of the original argument rests on a subtle transition from one of these notions to the other. To believe that a principle is morally correct one must believe that it is one which all could reasonably agree to and none could reasonably reject. But my belief that this is the case may often be distorted by a tendency to take its advantage to me more seriously than its possible costs to others. For this reason, the idea of 'putting myself in another's place' is a useful corrective device. The same can be said for the thought experiment of asking what I could agree to in ignorance of my true position. But both of these thought experiments are devices for considering more accurately the question of what *everyone* could reasonably agree to or what no one could reasonably reject. That is, they involve the pattern of reasoning exhibited in my revised form of the three-stage argument, not that of the argument as originally given. The question, what would maximise the expectations of a single self-interested person choosing in ignorance of his true position, is a quite different question. This can be seen by considering the possibility that the distribution with the highest average utility, call it A, might involve extremely low utility levels for some people, levels much lower than the minimum anyone would enjoy under a more equal distribution.

Suppose that A is a principle which it would be rational for a self-interested chooser with an equal chance of being in anyone's position to select. Does it follow that no one could reasonably reject *A*? It seems evident that this does not follow.[17] Suppose that the situation of those who would fare worst under *A*, call them the Losers, is extremely bad, and that there is an alternative to *A*, call it *E*, under which no one's situation would be nearly as bad as this. Prima facie, the losers would seem to have a reasonable ground for complaint against *A*. Their objection may be rebutted, by appeal to the sacrifices that would be imposed on some other individual by the selection of *E* rather than *A*. But the mere fact that *A* yields higher average utility, which might be due to the fact that many people do very slightly better under *A* than under *E* while a very few do much worse, does not settle the matter.

Under contractualism, when we consider a principle our attention is naturally directed first to those who would do worst under it. This is because if anyone has reasonable grounds for objecting to the principle it is *likely* to be them. It does not follow, however, that contractualism always requires us to select the principle under which the expectations of the worse off are highest. The reasonableness of the Losers' objection to *A* is not established simply by the fact that they are worse off under *A* and no-one would be this badly off under *E*. The force of their complaint depends also on the fact that their position under *A* is, in absolute terms, very bad, and would be significantly better under *E*. This complaint must be weighed against those of individuals who would do worse under *E*. The question to be asked is, is it unreasonable for someone to refuse to put up with the Losers' situation under *A* in order that someone else should be able to enjoy the benefits which he would have to give up under *E*? As the supposed situation of the Loser under *A* becomes better, or his gain under *E* smaller in relation to the sacrifices required to produce it, his case is weakened.

One noteworthy feature of contractualist argument as I have presented it so far is that it is non-aggregative: what are compared are individual gains, losses and levels of welfare. How aggregative considerations can enter into contractualist argument is a further question too large to be entered into here.

I have been criticising an argument for Average Utilitarianism that is generally associated with Harsanyi, and my objections to this argument (leaving aside the last remarks about maximin) have an obvious similarity to objections raised by Rawls.[18] But the objections I have raised apply as

---

[17] The discussion which follows has much in common with the contrast between majority principles and unanimity principles drawn by Thomas Nagel in 'Equality', Chapter 8 of Nagel 1979. I am indebted to Nagel's discussion of this idea.

[18] For example, the intuitive argument against utilitarianism on page 14 of Rawls 1971 and his repeated remark that we cannot expect some people to accept lower standards of life for the sake of the higher expectations of others.

well against some features of Rawls' own argument. Rawls accepts the first step of the argument I have described. That is, he believes that the correct principles of justice are those which 'rational persons concerned to advance their interests' would accept under the conditions defined by his Original Position, where they would be ignorant of their own particular talents, their conception of the good, and the social position (or generation) into which they were born. It is the second step of the argument which Rawls rejects, i.e. the claim that it would be rational for persons so situated to choose those principles which would offer them greatest expected utility under the assumption that they have an equal chance of being anyone in the society in question. I believe, however, that a mistake has already been made once the first step is taken.

This can be brought out by considering an ambiguity in the idea of acceptance by persons 'concerned to advance their interests'. On one reading, this is an essential ingredient in contractual argument; on another it is avoidable and, I think, mistaken. On the first reading, the interests in question are simply those of the members of society to whom the principles of justice are to apply (and by whom those principles must ultimately be accepted). The fact that they have interests which may conflict, and which they are concerned to advance, is what gives substance to questions of justice. On the second reading, the concern 'to advance their interests' that is in question is a concern of the parties to Rawls' Original Position, and it is this concern which determines, in the first instance,[19] what principles of justice they will adopt. Unanimous agreement among these parties, each motivated to do as well for himself as he can, is to be achieved by depriving them of any information that could give them reason to choose differently from one another. From behind the veil of ignorance, what offers the best prospects for one will offer the best prospects for all, since no-one can tell what would benefit him in particular. Thus the choice of principles can be made, Rawls says, from the point of view of a single rational individual behind the veil of ignorance.

Whatever rules of rational choice this single individual, concerned to advance his own interests as best he can, is said to employ, this reduction of the problem to the case of a single person's self-interested choice should arouse our suspicion. As I indicated in criticising Harsanyi, it is important to ask whether this single individual is held to accept a principle because he judges that it is one he could not reasonably reject whatever position he turns out to occupy, or whether, on the contrary, it is supposed to be

---

[19] Though they must then check to see that the principles they have chosen will be stable, not produce intolerable strains of commitment, and so on. As I argue below, these further considerations can be interpreted in a way that brings Rawls' theory closer to the version of contractualism presented here.

acceptable to a person in any social position because it would be the rational choice for a single self-interested person behind the veil of ignorance. I have argued above that the argument for average utilitarianism involves a covert transition from the first pattern of reasoning to the second. Rawls' argument also appears to be of this second form; his defence of his two principles of justice relies, at least initially, on claims about what it would be rational for a person, concerned to advance his own interests, to choose behind a veil of ignorance. I would claim, however, that the plausibility of Rawls' arguments favouring his two principles over the principle of average utility is preserved, and in some cases enhanced, when they are interpreted as instances of the first form of contractualist argument.

Some of these arguments are of an informal moral character. I have already mentioned his remark about the unacceptability of imposing lower expectations on some for the sake of the higher expectations of others. More specifically, he says of the parties to the Original Position that they are concerned 'to choose principles the consequences of which they are prepared to live with whatever generation they turn out to belong to'[20] or, presumably, whatever their social position turns out to be. This is a clear statement of the first form of contractualist argument. Somewhat later he remarks, in favour of the two principles, that they 'are those a person would choose for the design of a society in which his enemy is to assign him a place'.[21] Rawls goes on to dismiss this remark, saying that the parties 'should not reason from false premises',[22] but it is worth asking why it seemed a plausible thing to say in the first place. The reason, I take it, is this. In a contractualist argument of the first form, the object of which is to find principles acceptable to each person, assignment by a malevolent opponent is a thought experiment which has a heuristic role like that of a veil of ignorance: it is a way of testing whether one really does judge a principle to be acceptable from all points of view or whether, on the contrary, one is failing to take seriously its effect on people in social positions other than one's own.

But these are all informal remarks, and it is fair to suppose that Rawls' argument, like the argument for average utility, is intended to move from the informal contractualist idea of principles 'acceptable to all' to the idea of rational choice behind a veil of ignorance, an idea which is, he hopes, more precise and more capable of yielding definite results. Let me turn then to his more formal arguments for the choice of the Difference Principle by the parties to the Original Position. Rawls cites three features of the decision faced by parties to the Original Position which, he claims,

[20] Rawls 1971, p. 137.   [21] Rawls 1971, p. 152.   [22] Rawls 1971, p. 153.

make it rational for them to use the maximin rule and, therefore, to select his Difference Principle as a principle of justice. These are (1) the absence of any objective basis for estimating probabilities, (2) the fact that some principles could have consequences for them which 'they could hardly accept' while (3) it is possible for them (by following maximin) to ensure themselves of a minimum prospect, advances above which, in comparison, matter very little.[23] The first of these features is slightly puzzling, and I leave it aside. It seems clear, however, that the other considerations mentioned have at least as much force in an informal contractualist argument about what all could reasonably agree to as they do in determining the rational choice of a single person concerned to advance his interests. They express the strength of the objection that the 'losers' might have to a scheme that maximised average utility at their expense, as compared with the counter-objections that others might have to a more egalitarian arrangement.

In addition to this argument about rational choice, Rawls invokes among 'the main grounds for the two principles' other considerations which, as he says, use the concept of contract to a greater extent.[24] The parties to the Original Position, Rawls says, can agree to principles of justice only if they think that this agreement is one that they will actually be able to live up to. It is, he claims, more plausible to believe this of his two principles than of the principle of average utility, under which the sacrifices demanded ('the strains of commitment') could be much higher. A second, related claim is that the two principles of justice have greater psychological stability than the principle of average utility. It is more plausible to believe, Rawls claims, that in a society in which they were fulfilled people would continue to accept them and to be motivated to act in accordance with them. Continuing acceptance of the principle of average utility, on the other hand, would require an exceptional degree of identification with the good of the whole on the part of those from who sacrifices were demanded.

These remarks can be understood as claims about the 'stability' (in a quite practical sense) of a society founded on Rawls' two principles of justice. But they can also be seen as an attempt to show that a principle arrived at via the second form of contractualist reasoning will also satisfy the requirements of the first form, i.e. that it is something no one could reasonably reject. The question 'Is the acceptance of this principle an agreement you could actually live up to?' is, like the idea of assignment by one's worst enemy, a thought experiment through which we can use our own reactions to test our judgement that certain principles are ones that no

---

[23] Rawls 1971, p. 154.   [24] Rawls 1971, sec. 29, pp. 175ff.

one could reasonably reject. General principles of human psychology can also be invoked to this same end.

Rawls' final argument is that the adoption of his two principles gives public support to the self-respect of individual members of society, and 'give a stronger and more characteristic interpretation of Kant's idea'[25] that people must be treated as ends, not merely as means to the greater collective good. But, whatever difference there may be here between Rawls' two principles of justice and the principle of average utility, there is at least as sharp a contrast between the two patterns of contractualist reasoning distinguished above. The connection with self-respect, and with the Kantian formula, is preserved by the requirement that principles of justice be ones which no member of the society could reasonably reject. This connection is weakened when we shift to the idea of a choice which advances the interests of a single rational individual for whom the various individual lives in a society are just so many different possibilities. This is so whatever decision rule this rational chooser is said to employ. The argument from maximin seems to preserve this connection because it reproduces as a claim about rational choice what is, in slightly different terms, an appealing moral argument.

The 'choice situation' that is fundamental to contractualism as I have described it obtained by beginning with 'mutually disinterested' individuals with full knowledge of their situations and adding to this (not, as is sometimes suggested, benevolence but) a desire on each of their parts to find principles which none could reasonably reject insofar as they too have this desire. Rawls several times considers such an idea in passing.[26] He rejects it in favour of his own idea of mutually disinterested choice from behind a veil of ignorance on the ground that only the latter enables us to reach definite results: 'if in choosing principles we required unanimity even where there is full information, only a few rather obvious cases could be decided'.[27] I believe that this supposed advantage is questionable. Perhaps this is because my expectations for moral argument are more modest than Rawls'. However, as I have argued, almost all of Rawls' own arguments have at least as much force when they are interpreted as arguments within the form of contractualism which I have been proposing. One possible exception is the argument from maximin. If the Difference Principle were taken to be generally applicable to decisions of public policy, then the second form of contractualist reasoning through which it is derived would have more far reaching implications than the looser form of argument by

---

[25] Rawls 1971, p. 183.
[26] E.g. Rawls 1971, pp. 141, 148, although these passages may not clearly distinguish between this alternative and an assumption of benevolence.
[27] Rawls 1971, p. 141.

comparison of losses, which I have employed. But these wider applications of the principle are not always plausible, and I do not think that Rawls intends it to be applied so widely. His intention is that the Difference Principle should be applied only to major inequalities generated by the basic institutions of a society, and this limitation is a reflection of the special conditions under which he holds maximin to be the appropriate basis for rational choice: some choices have outcomes one could hardly accept, while gains above the minimum one can assure one's self matter very little, and so on. It follows, then, that in applying the Difference Principle – in identifying the limits of its applicability – we must fall back on the informal comparison of losses which is central to the form of contractualism I have described.

V

I have described this version of contractualism only in outline. Much more needs to be said to clarify its central notions and to work out its normative implications. I hope that I have said enough to indicate its appeal as a philosophical theory of morality and as an account of moral motivation. I have put forward contractualism as an alternative to utilitarianism, but the characteristic feature of the doctrine can be brought out by contrasting it with a somewhat different view.

It is sometimes said[28] that morality is a device for our mutual protection. According to contractualism, this view is partly true but in an important way incomplete. Our concern to protect our central interests will have an important effect on what we could reasonably agree to. It will thus have an important effect on the content of morality if contractualism is correct. To the degree that this morality is observed, these interests will gain from it. If we had no desire to be able to justify our actions to others on grounds they could reasonably accept, the hope of gaining this protection would give us reason to try to instil this desire in others, perhaps through mass hypnosis or conditioning, even if this also meant acquiring it ourselves. But given that we have this desire already, our concern with morality is less instrumental.

The contrast might be put as follows. On one view, concern with protection is fundamental, and general agreement becomes relevant as a means or a necessary condition for securing this protection. On the other, contractualist view, the desire for protection is an important factor determining the content of morality because it determines what can reasonably be agreed to. But the idea of general agreement does not arise as a means of securing protection. It is, in a more fundamental sense, what morality is about.

[28] In different ways by G. J. Warnock in Warnock 1971, and by J. L. Mackie in Mackie 1977. See also Richard Brandt's remarks on justification in Chapter X of Brandt 1979.

Political   Protection (secure Agreement)

Moral   Agreement (secure + Protection)

6 The diversity of goods

CHARLES TAYLOR

1

What did utilitarianism have going for it? A lot of things undoubtedly: its seeming compatibility with scientific thought; its this-wordly humanist focus, its concern with suffering. But one of the powerful background factors behind much of this appeal was *epistemological*. A utilitarian ethic seemed to be able to fit the canons of rational validation as these were understood in the intellectual culture nourished by the epistemological revolution of the seventeenth century and the scientific outlook which partly sprang from it.

In the utilitarian perspective, one validated an ethical position by hard evidence. You count the consequences for human happiness of one or another course, and you go with the one with the highest favourable total. What counts as human happiness was thought to be something conceptually unproblematic, a scientifically establishable domain of facts like others. One could abandon all the metaphysical or theological factors – commands of God, natural rights, virtues – which made ethical questions scientifically undecidable. Bluntly, we could calculate.

Ultimately, I should like to argue that this is but another example of the baleful effect of the classical epistemological model, common to Cartesians and empiricists, which has had such a distorting effect on the theoretical self-understanding of moderns. This is something which is above all visible in the sciences of man, but I think it has wreaked as great havoc in ethical theory.

The distortive effect comes in that we tend to start formulating our meta-theory of a given domain with an already formed model of valid reasoning, all the more dogmatically held because we are oblivious to the alternatives. This model then makes us quite incapable of seeing how reason does and can really function in the domain, to the degree that it does not fit the model. We cut and chop the reality of, in this case, ethical thought to fit the Procrustean bed of our model of validation. Then, since meta-theory and theory cannot be isolated from one another, the distortive conception begins to shape our ethical thought itself.

129

A parallel process, I should like to argue, has been visible in the sciences of man, with similar stultifying effects on the practice of students of human behaviour. The best, most insightful, practice of history, sociology, psychology is either devalued or misunderstood, and as a consequence we find masses of researchers engaging in what very often turns out to be futile exercises, of no scientific value whatever, sustained only by the institutional inertia of a professionalised discipline. The history of behaviourism stands as a warning of the virtual immortality that can be attained by such institutionalised futility.

In the case of ethics, two patterns of thought have especially benefited from the influence of the underlying model of validation. One is utilitarianism, which as I have just mentioned seemed to offer calculation over verifiable empirical quantities in the place of metaphysical distinctions. The other is various species of formalism. Kant is the originator of one of the most influential variants, without himself having fallen victim, I believe, to the narrowing consequences that usually follow the adoption of a formalism.

Formalisms, like utilitarianism, have the apparent value that they would allow us to ignore the problematic distinctions between different qualities of action or modes of life, which play such a large part in our actual moral decisions, feelings of admiration, remorse, etc., but which are so hard to justify when others controvert them. They offer the hope of deciding ethical questions without having to determine which of a number of rival languages of moral virtue and vice, of the admirable and the contemptible, of unconditional versus conditional obligation, are valid. You could finesse all this, if you could determine the cases where a maxim of action would be unrealisable if everyone adopted it, or where its universal realisation was something you could not possibly desire; or if you could determine what actions you could approve no matter whose standpoint you adopted of those persons affected; or if you could circumscribe the principles that would be adopted by free rational agents in certain paradigm circumstances.

Of course, all these formulae for ethical decision repose on some substantive moral insights; otherwise they would not seem even plausible candidates as models of *ethical* reasoning. Behind these Kant-derived formulae stands one of the most fundamental insights of modern Western civilisation, the universal attribution of moral personality: in fundamental ethical matters, everyone ought to count, and all ought to count in the same way. Within this outlook, one absolute requirement of ethical thinking is that we respect other human agents as subjects of practical reasoning on the same footing as ourselves.

In a sense, this principle is historically parochial. This is not the way the average Greek in ancient times, for instance, looked on his Thracian slave. But, in a sense, it also corresponds to something very deep in human moral reasoning. All moral reasoning is carried on within a community; and it is essential to the very existence of this community that each accord the other interlocutors this status as moral agents. The Greek who may not have accorded it to his Thracian slave most certainly did to his compatriots. That was part and parcel of there being recognised issues of justice between them. What modern civilisation has done, partly under the influence of Stoic natural law and Christianity, has been to lift all the parochial restrictions that surrounded this recognition of moral personality in earlier civilisations.

The modern insight, therefore, flows very naturally from one of the basic preconditions of moral thinking itself, along with the view – overwhelmingly plausible, to us moderns – that there is no defensible distinction to be made in this regard between different classes of human beings. This has become so widespread that even discrimination and domination is in fact justified on universalist grounds. (Even South Africa has an official ideology of *apartheid*, which can allow theoretically for the peoples concerned to be not unequal, but just different.)

So we seem on very safe ground in adopting a decision procedure which can be shown to flow from this principle. Indeed, this seems to be a moral principle of a quite different order from the various contested languages of moral praise, condemnation, aspiration or aversion, which distinguish rival conceptions of virtue and paradigm modes of life. We might even talk ourselves into believing that it is not a moral principle in any substantive contestable sense at all, but some kind of limiting principle of moral reasoning. Thus we might say with Richard Hare, for example, that in applying this kind of decision procedure we are following not moral intuitions, but rather our linguistic intuitions concerning the use of the word 'moral'.

Classical utilitarianism itself incorporated this universal principle in the procedural demand that in calculating the best course, the happiness of each agent count for one, and of no agent for more than one. Here again one of the fundamental issues of modern thought is decided by what looks like a formal principle, and utilitarianism itself got a great deal of its *prima facie* plausibility from the strength of the same principle. If everyone counts as a moral agent, then what they desire and aim at ought to count, and the right course of action should be what satisfies all, or the largest number possible. At least this chain of reasoning can appear plausible.

But clear reasoning ought to demand that we counteract this tendency to slip over our deepest moral convictions unexamined. They look like formal principles only because they are so foundational to the moral thinking of our civilisation. We should strive to formulate the underlying moral insights just as clearly and expressly as we do all others.

When we do so, of course, we shall find that they stand in need of justification like the others. This points us to one of the motives for construing them as formal principles. For those who despair of reason as the arbiter of moral disputes (and the epistemological tradition has tended to induce this despair in many), making the fundamental insights into a formal principle has seemed a way of avoiding a moral scepticism which was both implausible and distasteful.

But, I want to argue, the price of this formalism, as also of the utilitarian reduction, has been a severe distortion of our understanding of our moral thinking. One of the big illusions which grows from either of these reductions is the belief that there is a single consistent domain of the 'moral', that there is one set of considerations, or mode of calculation, which determines what we ought 'morally' to do. The unity of the moral is a question which is conceptually decided from the first on the grounds that moral reasoning just is equivalent to calculating consequences for human happiness, or determining the universal applicability of maxims, or something of the sort.

But once we shake ourselves clear from the formalist illusion, of the utilitarian reduction – and this means resisting the blandishments of their underlying model of rational validation – we can see that the boundaries of the moral are an open question; indeed, the very appropriateness of a single term here can be an issue.

We could easily decide – a view which I would defend – that the universal attribution of moral personality is valid, and lays obligations on us which we cannot ignore; but that there are also other moral ideals and goals – e.g. of less than universal solidarity, or of personal excellence – which cannot be easily coordinated with universalism, and can even enter into conflict with it. To decide *a priori* what the bounds of the moral are is just to obfuscate the question whether and to what degree this is so, and to make it incapable of being coherently stated.

2

I should like to concentrate here on a particular aspect of moral language and moral thinking that gets obscured by the epistemologically-motivated reduction and homogenisation of the 'moral' we find in both utilitarianism and formalism. These are the qualitative distinctions we make between different actions, or feelings, or modes of life, as being in some way morally higher or lower, noble or base, admirable or contemptible. It is these languages of qualitative contrast that get marginalised, or even expunged altogether, by the utilitarian or formalist reductions. I want to argue, in opposition to this, that they are central to our moral thinking and ineradicable from it.

Some examples might help here of such qualitative distinctions which are commonly subscribed to. For some people, personal integrity is a central goal: what matters is that one's life express what one truly senses as important, admirable, noble, desirable. The temptations to be avoided here are those of conformity to established standards which are not really one's own, or of dishonesty with oneself concerning one's own convictions or affinities. The chief threat to integrity is a lack of courage in face of social demands, or in face of what one has been brought up to see as the unthinkable. This is a recognisable type of moral outlook.

We can see a very different type if we look at a Christian model of *agapê*, such as one sees, e.g., with Mother Theresa. The aim here is to associate oneself with, to become in a sense a channel of, God's love for men, which is seen as having the power to heal the divisions among men and take them beyond what they usually recognise as the limits to their love for one another. The obstacles to this are seen as various forms of refusal of God's *agapê*, either through a sense of self-sufficiency, or despair. This outlook understands human moral transformation in terms of images of healing, such as one sees in the New Testament narratives.

A very different, yet historically related, modern view centres around the goal of liberation. This sees the dignity of human beings as consisting in their directing their own lives, in their deciding for themselves the conditions of their own existence, as against falling prey to the domination of others, or to impersonal natural or social mechanisms which they fail to understand, and therefore cannot control or transform. The inner obstacles to this are ignorance, or lack of courage, or falsely self-depreciatory images of the self; but these are connected with external obstacles in many variants of modern liberation theory. This is particularly so of the last: self-depreciating images are seen as inculcated by others who benefit from the structures of domination in which subject groups are encased. Fanon has made this kind of analysis very familiar for the colonial context, and his categories have been transposed to a host of others, especially to that of women's liberation.

Let us look briefly at one other such language, that of rationality, as this is understood, for instance, by utilitarians. We have here the model of a human being who is clairvoyant about his goals, and capable of objectifying and understanding himself and the world which surrounds him. He can get a clear grasp of the mechanisms at work in self and world, and can thus direct his action clear-sightedly and deliberately. To do this he must resist the temptations offered by the various comforting illusions that make the self or the world so much more attractive than they really are in the cold light of science. He must fight off the self-indulgence which consists of giving oneself a picture of the world which is satisfying to one's *amour propre*, or one's sense of drama, or one's craving for meaning, or any of these metaphysical temptations. The rational man has the courage of austerity; he is marked by his ability to adopt an objective stance to things.

I introduce these four examples so as to give some intuitive basis to an otherwise abstract discussion. But I did not have to look far. These moral outlooks are very familiar to us from our own moral reasoning and sensibility, or those of people we know (and sometimes of people we love to hate). I am sure that some of the details of my formulation will jar with just about any reader. But that is not surprising. Formulating these views is a very difficult job. Like all self-interpretive activity, it is open to potentially endless dispute. This is, indeed, part of the reason why these outlooks have fallen under the epistemological cloud and therefore have tended to be excluded from the formalist and utilitarian meta-ethical pictures. But one or some of these, or others like them, underly much of our deciding what to do, our moral admirations, condemnations, contempts, and so on.

Another thing that is evident straight off is how different they are from each other. I mean by that not only that they are based on very different pictures of man, human possibility and the human condition; but that they frequently lead to incompatible prescriptions in our lives – incompatible with each other, and also with the utilitarian calculation which unquestionably plays some part in the moral reasoning of most moderns. (The modern dispute about utilitarianism is not about whether it occupies some of the space of moral reason, but whether it fills the whole space.) It could be doubted whether giving comfort to the dying is the highest util-producing activity possible in contemporary Calcutta. But, from another point of view, the dying are in an extremity that makes calculation irrelevant.

But, nevertheless, many people find themselves drawn by more than one of these views, and are faced with the job of somehow making them compatible in their lives. This is where the question can arise whether all the demands that we might consider moral and which we recognise as valid can be coherently combined. This question naturally raises another one, whether it is really appropriate to talk of a single type of demand called 'moral'. This is the more problematic when we reflect that we all recognise other qualitative distinctions which we would not class right off as moral, or perhaps even on reflection would refuse the title to; for instance, being 'cool', or being macho, or others of this sort. So that the question of drawing a line around the moral becomes a difficult one. And it may even come to appear as an uninteresting verbal one in the last analysis. The really important question may turn out to be how we combine in our lives two or three or four different goals, or virtues, or standards, which we feel we cannot repudiate but which seem to demand incompatible things of us. Which of these we dignify with the term 'moral', or whether we so designate all of them, may end up appearing a mere question of labelling – unless, that is, it confuses us into thinking that there is in principle only one set of goals or standards which can be accorded ultimate significance. In certain contexts, it might help clarity to drop the word, at least provisionally, until we get over the baleful effects of reductive thinking on our meta-ethical views.

3

Before going on to examine further the implications of this for social theory, it will be useful to look more closely at these languages of qualitative contrast. What I am gesturing at with the term 'qualitative contrast' is the sense that one way of acting or living is higher than others, or in other cases that a certain way of living is debased. It is essential to the kind of moral view just exemplified that this kind of contrast be made. Some ways of living and acting have a special status, they stand out above others; while, in certain cases, others are seen as despicable.

This contrast is essential. We should be distorting these views if we tried to construe the difference between higher and lower as a mere difference of degree in the attainment of some common good, as utilitarian theory would have us do. Integrity, charity, liberation, and the like stand out as worthy of pursuit in a special way, incommensurable with other goals we might have, such as the pursuit of wealth, or comfort, or the approval of those who surround us. Indeed, for those who hold to such views of the good, we ought to be ready to sacrifice some of these lesser goods for the higher.

Moreover, the agent's being sensible of this distinction is an essential condition of his realising the good concerned. For our recognising the higher value of integrity, or charity, or rationality, etc., is an essential part of our being rational, charitable, having integrity and so on. True, we recognise such a thing as unconscious virtue, which we ascribe to people who are good but quite without a sense of their superiority over others. This lack of self-congratulation we consider itself to be a virtue, as the deprecatory expression 'holier than thou' implies. But the absence of self-conscious superiority does not mean an absence of sensitivity to the higher goal. The saintly person is not 'holier than thou', but he is necessarily moved by the demands of charity in a special way, moved to recognise that there is something special here; in this particular case, he has a sense of awe before the power of God, or of wonder at the greatness of man as seen by God. And a similar point could be made for the other examples: an essential part of achieving liberation is sensing the greatness of liberated humanity – and consequently being sensible of the degradation of the dominated victim; an essential part of integrity is the recognition that it represents a demand on us of a special type, and so on.

Another way of making this point is to say that motivation enters into the definition of the higher activity or way of being in all these cases. The aspiration to achieve one of these goods is also an aspiration to be motivated in a certain way, or to have certain motivations win out in oneself. This is why we can speak of these aspirations as involving 'second-order' motivations (as I have tried to do elsewhere, following Harry Frankfurt[1]).

We can articulate the contrast or incommensurability involved here in a number of ways. One way of saying it is via the notion of obligation. Ordinary goals, e.g. for wealth or comfort, are goals that a person may have or not. If he does, then there a number of instrumental things that he ought to do – hypothetically, in Kant's sense – to attain them. But if he lacks these goals, no criticism attaches to him for neglecting to pursue them. By contrast, it is in the nature of what I have called a higher goal that it is one we *should* have. Those who lack them are not just free of some additional instrumental obligations which weigh with the rest of us; they are open to censure. For those who subscribe to integrity, the person who cares not a whit for it is morally insensitive, or lacks courage, or is morally coarse. A higher goal is one from which one cannot detach oneself just by expressing a sincere lack of interest, because to recognise something as a higher goal is to recognise it as one that men ought to follow. This is, of course, the distinction that Kant drew between hypothetical and categorical imperatives.

Or rather, I should say that it is a closely related distinction. For Kant the boundary between the categorical and the hypothetical was meant to mark the line between the moral and the non-moral. But there are languages of qualitative contrast which we are quite ready to recognise as non-moral, even bearing in mind the fuzzy boundaries of the domain which this word picks out. We often apply such languages in what we call the aesthetic domain. If I see something especially magnificent in the music of Mozart as against some of his humdrum contemporaries, then I will judge you as insensitive in some way if you rate them on a par. The word 'insensitive' here is a word of depreciation. This is a difference one *should* be sensible of, in my view.

[1] Cf. Taylor 1977; Frankfurt 1971.

Of course, I would not speak of this as a *moral* condemnation, but condemnation it would be nevertheless. I do not react to this difference as I do to differences of taste which correspond to no such incommensurability, e.g. whether you like the symphonies of Bruckner or not.

The criterion for incommensurability I am offering here is therefore not the same as Kant's for the moral. But, as I have already indicated, I do not think that a line can be drawn neatly and unproblematically around the moral. Of course, if someone professes to see no distinction between his concern for the flowers in his garden and that for the lives of refugees faced with starvation, so that he proposes to act in both cases just to the degree that he feels interested at the time, we are rightly alarmed, and take this more seriously than the failure to appreciate Mozart over Boieldieu. We feel more justified in intervening here, and remonstrating with him, even forcing him to act, or subjecting him to some social or other penalty for non-acting. We feel, in other words, that the obligation here is 'categorical' in the stronger sense that licenses our intervention even against his will.

But the boundary here is necessarily fuzzier and very much open to dispute. Whereas the weaker sense of 'categorical' that could apply to the distinction I am drawing above turns on the question whether a declared lack of interest in a certain good simply neutralises it for you, or whether on the contrary, it redounds to your condemnation, shows you up as being blind, or coarse, or insensitive, or cowardly, or brutalised, too self-absorbed, or in some other way subject to censure. This, I would like to argue, is a relatively firm boundary – although the languages in which we draw it, each of us according to his own outlook, are very much in dispute between us – but it does not mark the moral from the non-moral. The languages of qualitative contrast embrace more than the moral.

A second way in which we can articulate this contrast is through the notions of admiration and contempt. People who exhibit higher goods to a signal degree are objects of our admiration; and those who fail are sometimes objects of our contempt. These emotions are bound up with our sense that there are higher and lower goals and activities. I would like to claim that if we did not mark these contrasts, if we did not have a sense of the incommensurably higher, then these emotions would have no place in our lives.

In the end, we can find ourselves experiencing very mitigated admiration for feats which we barely consider worthy of special consideration. I have a sort of admiration, mixed with tolerant amusement, for the person who has just downed 22 pancakes to win the eating contest. But that is because I see some kind of victory over self in the name of something which resembles a self-ideal. He wanted to be first, and he was willing to go to great lengths for it; and that goal at least stands out from that of being an average person, living just like everybody else. It is only because I see the feat in these terms, which are rather a caricature than an example of a higher aspiration, that the feeling of admiration can get even a mitigated grip on this case.

But we also find ourselves admiring people where there is no victory over self, where there is no recognisable achievement in the ordinary sense at all. We can admire people who are very beautiful, or have a striking grace or personal style, even though we may recognise that it is none of their doing. But we do so only because the aura of something higher, some magic quality contrasting with the ordinary and the humdrum, surrounds such people. The reasons why this should be so go very deep into the human psyche and the human form of life, and we find them hard to understand, but a special aura of this kind contributes often to what we call the 'charisma' of public figures (a word which conveys just this sense of a gift from on high, something we have not done for ourselves). Those who consider this kind of aura irrational, who resist the sense of something higher here, are precisely those who refuse their admiration to the 'charismatic', or to 'beautiful people'. Or at least they are those who claim to do so; for sometimes one senses that they are fighting a losing battle with their own feelings on this score.

In this way, admiration and contempt are bound up with our sense of the qualitative contrasts in our lives, of there being modes of life, activities, feeling, qualities, which are incommensurably higher. Where these are moral qualities, we can speak of moral admiration. These emotions provide one of the ways that we articulate this sense of the higher in our lives.

A third way we do so is in the experience we can call very loosely 'awe'. I mentioned above that a sensibility to the higher good is part of its realisation. The sense that a good occupies a special place, that it is higher, is the sense that it somehow commands our respect. This is why there is a dimension of human emotion, which we can all recognise, and which Kant again tried to articulate with his notion of the *Achtung* which we feel before the moral law. Once again, I propose to extend a Kantian analysis beyond the case of the unambiguously moral. Just as our admiration for the virtuosi of some higher goal extends to other contexts than the moral, so our sense of the incommensurable value of the goal does. For this sense, as a term of art translating Kant's *Achtung*, I propose 'awe'.

4

It is this dimension of qualitative contrast in our moral sensibility and thinking that gets short shrift in the utilitarian and formalist reductions.

One of the main points of utilitarianism was to do away with this and reduce all judgements of ethical preference to quantitative form in a single dimension. In a different way, formalisms manage to reduce these contrasts to irrelevance; ethical reasoning can finesse them through a procedure of determining what is right which takes no account of them, or allows them in merely as subjective preferences, and therefore is not called upon to judge their substantive merits.

Now my argument was that a big part of the motivation for both reductions was epistemological; that they seemed to allow for a mode of ethical reasoning which fitted widely held canons of validation. We can now see better why this was so.

It is partly because these languages of contrast are so hard to validate once they come into dispute. If someone does not see that integrity is a goal one should seek, or that liberation is alone consistent with the dignity of man, how do you go about demonstrating this? But this is not the whole story. That argument is difficult in this area does not mean that it is impossible, that there is no such thing as a rationally induced conviction. That so many who have opted for utilitarianism or formalism can jump to this latter conclusion as far as higher goals are concerned is due to two underlying considerations which are rarely spelled out.

The first is that the ethical views couched in languages of contrast seem to differ in contestability from those which underlie utilitarianism and formalism. No-one seems very ready to challenge the view that, other things being equal, it is better that men's desires be fulfilled than that they be frustrated, that they be happy rather than miserable. Counter-utilitarians challenge rather whether the entire range of ethical issues can be put in these terms, whether there are not other goals which can conflict with happiness, whose claims have to be adjudicated together with utility. Again, as we saw, formalistic theories get their plausibility from the fact that they are grounded on certain moral intuitions which are almost unchallenged in modern society, based as they are in certain preconditions of moral discourse itself combined with a thesis about the racial homogeneity of humanity which it is pretty hard to challenge in a scientific, de-parochialised and historically sensitive contemporary culture.

The premisses of these forms of moral reasoning can therefore easily appear to be of a quite different provenance from those that deal with qualitative contrast. Against these latter, we can allow ourselves to slip into ethical scepticism while exempting the former, either on the grounds that they are somehow self-evident, or even that they are not based on ethical insight at all but on something firmer, like the logic of our language.

But, in fact, these claims to firmer foundation are illusory. What is really going on is that some forms of ethical reasoning are being privileged over

others because in our civilisation they come less into dispute or look easier
to defend. This has all the rationality of the drunk in the well-known story
(which the reader may forgive me for repeating) who was looking for his
latch key late one night under a street lamp. A passer-by, trying to be
helpful, asked him where he had dropped it. 'Over there' answered the
drunk, pointing to a dark corner. 'Then why are you looking for it here?'
'Because there's so much more light here', replied the drunk.

In a similar way, we have been manoeuvred into a restrictive definition
of ethics, which takes account of some of the goods we seek, e.g. utility,
and universal respect for moral personality, while excluding others, viz.
the virtues and goals like those mentioned above, largely on the grounds
that the former are subject to less embarrassing dispute.

This may seem a little too dismissive of the traditions of reductive
meta-ethics, because in fact there is a second range of considerations
which have motivated the differential treatment of languages of contrast.
That is that they seem to have no place in a naturalist account of man.

The goal of a naturalist account of man comes in the wake of the
scientific revolution of the seventeenth century. It is the aim of explaining
human beings like other objects in nature. But a part of the practice of the
successful natural science of modern times consists in its eschewing what
we might call subject-related properties. By this I mean properties which
things bear only insofar as they are objects of experience of subjects. The
classical example of these in the seventeenth-century discussion were the
so-called secondary properties, like colour or felt temperature. The aim
was to account for what happens invoking only properties that the things
concerned possessed absolutely, as one might put it (following Bernard
Williams' use in his discussion of a related issue in Williams 1978), properties, that is, which they would possess even if (even when) they are
not experienced.

How can one follow this practice in a science of animate beings, i.e. of
beings who exhibit motivated action? Presumably, one can understand
motivated action in terms of a tendency of the beings concerned to realise
certain consummations in certain conditions. As long as these consummations are characterised absolutely, the demands of a naturalistic science of
animate subjects seem to be met. Hence we get a demand which is widely
recognised as a requirement of materialism in modern times: that we
explain human behaviour in terms of goals whose consummations can be
characterised in physical terms. This is what, e.g., for many Marxists
establishes the claim that their theory is a materialist one: that it identifies
as predominant the aim of getting the means to life (which presumably
could ultimately be defined in physical terms).

But without being taken as far as materialism, the requirement of absoluteness can serve to discredit languages of qualitative contrast. For these designate different possible human activities and modes of life as higher and lower. And these are plainly subject-related notions. In the context of a naturalist explanation, one goal may be identified as more strongly desired than others, e.g. if the subject concerned gave it higher priority. But there is no place for the notion of a higher goal, which in the very logic of the contrast must be distinguishable from the strongest motive – else the term would have no function in moral discourse at all.

For those who cleave to naturalism, the languages of contrast must be suspect. They correspond to nothing in reality, which we may interpret as what we need to invoke in our bottom line explanatory language of human behaviour. They appear therefore to designate purely 'subjective' factors. They express the way we feel, not the way things are. But then this gives a rational basis to ethical scepticism, to the view that there is no rational way of arbitrating between rival outlooks expressed in such languages of contrast. This seems to give a strong intellectual basis to downgrading ethical reasoning, at least that cast in contrastive languages. For those who are impressed by naturalist considerations, but still want to salvage some valid form of ethical reasoning, utilitarianism or formalism seem attractive.[2]

But this ground for scepticism is faulty. It leaves undefended the premiss that our accounts of man should be naturalistic in just this sense. Purging subject-related properties makes a lot of sense in an account of inanimate things. It cannot be taken as *a priori* self-evident that it will be similarly helpful in an account of human beings. We would have to establish *a posteriori* that such an absolute account of human life was possible and illuminating before we could draw conclusions about what is real, or know even how to set up the distinction objective/subjective.

In fact, though there is no place to examine the record here, it does not seem that absolute accounts offer a very plausible avenue. Put in other terms, it may well be that much of human behaviour will be understandable and explicable only in a language which characterises motivation in a fashion which marks qualitative contrasts and which is therefore not morally neutral. In this it will be like what we recognise today as the best example of clairvoyant self-understanding by those who have most conquered their illusions. If a science which describes consummations in exclusively physical terms cannot fill the bill, and if we therefore have to take account of the significances of things for agents, how can we know *a priori* that the best account available of such significances will not require some use of languages of qualitative contrast? It seems to me rather likely that it will.

---

[2] For a naturalist attack on the objectivity of value, see Mackie 1977.

In the absence of some demonstration of the validity of naturalism of this kind, the utilitarian and formalist reductions are clearly arbitrary. For they have little foundation in our ethical sensibility and practice. Even utilitarians and formalists make use of languages of contrast in their lives, decisions, admirations and contempts. One can see that in my fourth example above. 'Rational' as used by most utilitarians is a term in a qualitative contrast; it is the basis of moral admiration and contempt; it is a goal worthy of respect. The fact that it finds no place in their own meta-theory says a lot about the value of this theory.

5

Once we get over the epistemologically-induced reductions of the ethical, the problems of moral reasoning appear in a quite different light. I just have space here to mention some of the consequences for social theory.

An obviously relevant point is that we come to recognise that the ethical is not a homogeneous domain, with a single kind of good, based on a single kind of consideration. We have already noted at least three kinds of consideration which are morally relevant. The first is captured by the notion of utility, that what produces happiness is preferable to its opposite. The second is what I called the universal attribution of moral personality. These can combine to produce modern utilitarianism, as a theory that lays on us the obligation of universal benevolence in the form of the maximisation of general happiness. But the second principle is also the source of moral imperatives that conflict with utilitarianism; and this in notorious ways, e.g. demanding that we put equal distribution before the goal of maximising utility. Then, thirdly, there are the variety of goals that we express in languages of qualitative contrast, which are of course very different from each other.

The goods we recognise as moral, which means at least as laying the most important demands on us, over-riding all lesser ones, are therefore diverse. But the habit of treating the moral as a single domain is not just gratuitous or based on a mere mistake. The domain of ultimately important goods has a sort of prescriptive unity. Each of us has to answer all these demands in the course of a single life, and this means that we have to find some way of assessing their relative validity, or putting them in an order of priority. A single coherent order of goods is rather like an idea of reason in the Kantian sense, something we always try to define without ever managing to achieve it definitively.

The plurality of goods ought to be evident in modern society, if we could set aside the blinkers that our reductive meta-ethics imposes on us. Certainly we reason often about social policies in terms of utility. And we also take into account considerations of just distribution, as also of the rights of individuals, which are grounded on the principle of universal moral personality. But there are also considerations of the contrastive kind which play an important role. For instance, modern Western societies are all citizen republics, or strive to be. Their conception of the good is partly shaped by the tradition of civic humanism. The citizen republic is to be valued not just as a guarantee of general utility, or as a bulwark of rights. It may even endanger these in certain circumstances. We value it also because we generally hold that the form of life in which men govern themselves, and decide their own fate through common deliberation, is higher than one in which they live as subjects of even an enlightened despotism.

But just as the demands of utility and rights may diverge, so those of the citizen republic may conflict with both. For instance, the citizen republic requires a certain sense of community, and what is needed to foster this may go against the demands of maximum utility. Or it may threaten to enter into conflict with some of the rights of minorities. And there is a standing divergence between the demands of international equality and those of democratic self-rule in advanced Western societies. Democratic electorates in these societies will probably never agree to the amount of redistribution consistent with redressing the past wrongs of imperialism, or meeting in full the present requirements of universal human solidarity. Only despotic régimes, like Cuba and the DDR, bleed themselves for the Third World – not necessarily for the best of motives, of course.

It ought to be clear from this that no single-consideration procedure, be it that of utilitarianism, or a theory of justice based on an ideal contract, can do justice to the diversity of goods we have to weigh together in normative political thinking. Such one-factor functions appeal to our epistemological squeamishness which makes us dislike contrastive languages. And they may even have a positive appeal of the same kind insofar as they seem to offer the prospect of exact calculation of policy, through counting utils, or rational choice theory. But this kind of exactness is bogus. In fact, they only have a semblance of validity through leaving out all that they cannot calculate.

The other strong support for single-factor theory comes from the radical side. Radical theories, such as for instance Marxism, offer an answer to the demand for a unified theory – which we saw is a demand we cannot totally repudiate, at least as a goal – by revolutionary doctrines which propose sweeping away the plurality of goods now recognised in the name of one central goal which will subsume what is valuable in all of them. Thus the classless society will allegedly make unnecessary the entrenching of individual rights, or the safeguarding of 'bourgeois' civic spirit. It will provide an unconstrained community, in which the good of each will be the goal of all, and maximum utility a by-product of free collaboration, and so on.

But Marxism at least does not make the error of holding that all the goods we now seek can be reduced to some common coinage. At least it proposes to bring about unity through radical change. In the absence of such change, commensurability cannot be achieved. Indeed, it is of the essence of languages of contrast that they show our goals to be incommensurable.

If this is so, then there is no way of saving single-consideration theory however we try to reformulate it. Some might hope for instance to salvage at least the consequentialism out of utilitarianism: we would give up the narrow view that all that is worth valuing is states of happiness, but we would still try to evaluate different courses of action purely in terms of their consequences, hoping to state everything worth considering in our consequence-descriptions.

But unless the term 'consequentialism' is to be taken so widely as to lose all meaning, it has to contrast with other forms of deliberation, for instance one in which it matters whether I act in a certain way and not just what consequences I bring about. To put it differently, a non-consequentialist deliberation is one which values actions in ways which cannot be understood as a function of the consequences they have. Let us call this valuing actions intrinsically.

The attempt to reconstruct ethical and political thinking in consequentialist terms would in fact be another *a priori* fiat determining the domain of the good on irrelevant grounds. Not as narrow as utilitarianism perhaps, it would still legislate certain goods out of existence. For some languages of contrast involve intrinsic evaluation: the language of integrity, for instance. I have integrity to the degree to which my actions and statements are true expressions of what is really of importance to me. It is their intrinsic character as revelations or expressions that count, not their consequences. And the same objection would hold against a consequentialist social choice function. We may value our society for the way it makes integrity possible in its public life and social relations, or criticise a society for making it impossible. It may also be the case, of course, that we value the integrity for its effects on stability, or republican institutions, or something of the kind. But this cannot be all. It will certainly matter to us intrinsically as well as consequentially.

A consequentialist theory, even one which had gone beyond utilitarianism, would still be a Procrustes bed. It would once again make it impossible for us to get all the facets of our moral and political thinking in focus. And it might induce us to think that we could ignore certain demands because they fail to fit into our favoured mode of calculation. A meta-ethics of this kind stultifies thought.

Our political thinking needs to free itself both from the dead hand of the epistemological tradition, and the utopian monism of radical thought, in order to take account of the real diversity of goods that we recognise.

7 Morality and convention

STUART HAMPSHIRE

1. The philosophical dispute about the objectivity of morals has been four, or more, disputes rolled into one. First, there is the argument about predicates standing for moral qualities: are they to be construed as instrinsic qualities of actions or situations? Secondly, there is the quite different dispute as to whether to attribute a moral quality to a person or to an action is properly to be taken as describing that person or action, or to be taken as another kind of performance, e.g. as expressing an attitude, or as recommending conduct, or both. Thirdly, there is the question of whether two persons expressing disagreement about the answer to a moral problem are properly described as contradicting each other, which is usually interpreted as a question about the conditions of applicability of 'true' and 'false' to moral judgements. Fourthly, there is the related, but different, question of whether there is a respectable procedure, recognised in other contexts, for establishing the acceptability of moral judgements of various kinds, or whether moral judgement is in this respect *sui generis* and for this reason problematic.

These four are some, certainly not all, of the clearly distinguishable questions that are to be found in the literature.

2. There is another essential issue, which was best expressed in the ancient controversy about whether moral discriminations are to be accepted as true or correct, when they are true, in virtue of custom, convention and law (νόμῳ) or whether they are true in virtue of the nature of things (φύσει). By an essential issue I here mean an issue which unavoidably arises for thinking men, independently of any theories in philosophy, when they reflect on the apparent stringency and unavoidability of their more disagreeable duties and obligations, and when they ask themselves where this apparent unavoidability comes from. That there is a clear and unavoidable distinction between moral judgements or beliefs issuing from reason and judgements issuing from sentiment is not evident to someone who has not heard of, or is not convinced by, the philosophies of mind that are built around these psychological terms. No philosophical theories have

to be invoked when a man encounters in experience or in reading the actual variety of moral beliefs and practices, and the overlapping similarities between different moral systems, and then asks himself how these differences and similarities are to be interpreted. Do they represent the kind of difference, and the kind of similarities, that one finds, for instance, in different conventions in dress, in personal ornament, in ideals of feminine elegance, in social manners while eating, in dietary conventions? Or do they represent the kinds of difference and similarity that are found in ideals or norms of physical health and of good food? We are disposed at first sight to think of differences and similarities between the discriminations in the first list as differences and similarities in conventions. We are apt to think of the differences and similarities in the second list – ideals or norms of health and of food – as differences and similarities in the assessment of independently testable and objective norms and therefore as differences in nature. We are apt to think that any variety of judgements about good health, which there may be, is simply evidence that there are a number of false or inaccurate opinions on this subject, because there is a standard of good health which medical science can expound and which rests on clearly demonstrable differences in natural processes: similarly for good food, in the sense of food that nourishes.

These two contrasting lists, and the explanation of the contrast, clearly represent only a first, unanalysed and naive view of the Greek distinction between nature and convention. But it is at least clear that there is an accepted contrast between those norms or ideals which are expected to be highly diverse, and which are not expected, and which are not required, to converge on the one hand, and those norms or ideals which (a) refer to ascertainable natural facts and (b) are more or less constant responses to more or less constant human needs and interests and therefore (c) where there is a well established expectation of convergence.

A clear example of a norm or ideal which is essentially diverse and non-converging is to be found in arrangement of hair in either sex prevailing at different times and in different cultures. First, there is no requirement that forms of arrangement of hair in men and women should converge towards a single norm or ideal, any more than there is a requirement that norms of elegance in dress or other kinds of adornment should converge; I shall argue that there is even a *prima facie* requirement that they diverge and remain various. But there is a requirement that all rational men should arrive at a consensus about what constitutes health, if only because health is an ideal which all normal men in all normal conditions and at all normal times want to pursue. Because bad health causes pain and death, it is natural that men in all places at all times should attach at least some considerable value to good health, and that good health should count as a fundamental and constant need and not only as a contingent interest. But there are no ascertainable natural facts which, taken together with more or less constant human needs or interests, imply that one or other arrangement of hair, or manner of adornment, is the most desirable. Partly for this reason both Plato and Aristotle, wishing to stress the objectivity, and the naturalness, of moral distinctions, dwelt on an analogy between the health of the body and the health of the soul; and health of the soul is naturally expressed in moral virtue and just conduct.

But more has to be said about 'nature' and natural in this context: the traditional idea of moral distinctions as founded in the nature of things implies that there is an underlying structure of moral distinctions, partly concealed by the variety of actual moral beliefs, a structure that is defensible by rational argument and by common observation of human desires and sentiments, when a covering of local prejudices and superstitions has been removed. If the underlying structure of moral distinctions has no supernatural source, it must be recognised by rational inquiry as having its origin in nature and, specifically, in human nature: that is, in constant human needs and interests, and in canons of rational calculation. So in Aristotle: so also, in a contemporary continuation, in Rawls' *A Theory of Justice* (Rawls 1971), which notoriously argues that rational choosers, having taken account of entirely general, non-discriminating facts about human nature, will be led to recognise a certain set of principles, constituting a first framework of just institutions, as being evidently reasonable. The most general non-discriminating facts about normal human needs and interests, with human nature taken as it is, are put together with a model of rationality to derive an idea of the principles of justice. This skeletal idea of justice therefore has a claim to acceptance by all rational men at all times and everywhere, and the claim is independent of the variety of prevailing interests and sentiments which distinguish populations at different times and places from one another: independent that is, of specific cultural factors. *A fortiori* the rationally preferred idea of justice is independent of the variety of interests and sentiments which distinguish individuals from each other.

Rationality; a claim to universal acceptance; naturalness: these three properties of the idea of justice, as typically presented by Rawls, are connected within a single argument. The argument is designed to uncover a core of shared rationality, which is the natural distinguishing mark of the species as a whole, and which is typically revealed by a stripping down procedure. The stripping down removes a supposed overlay, or dressing, of local custom, of distinctive, cultural factors, and removes the moral idiosyncracies of individuals, which have their local explanations and their temporary causes. These local causes, studied by historians and anthropologists, are evidently changeable and transient, as social systems and cultures change and decay. Because the moral prescriptions and claims are to be explained by temporary and local interests the duties and obligations prescribed exist by convention rather than in the nature of the things. No convergence towards universal agreement is claimed for this set of prescriptions, in contrast with the principles of justice.

Claims of justice have always been the preferred examples of moral claims that are to be recognised by reason, and as founded in the nature of things, as not essentially diverse, and as not contingent upon any specific type of social order. Plato could argue that the foundations of ethics are to be found in the nature of things, not in convention or in the arbitrary will of powerful men, partly by representing justice as the principal virtue of an individual and of a social order, as health is of the body.

3. If one contrasts justice as a human good with love and friendship, one expects to find that justice prescribes a comparatively fixed, and also a comparatively specific, set of norms for human conduct. One will expect to find that love and friendship, always good things and no less to be desired, require specifically different types of behaviour, and different relationships, in different social contexts; superficially and pre-theoretically, the specific realisations of love and friendship seem likely not to conform to a fixed and definite norm as the specific realisations of justice are expected to conform to a fixed and definite norm, and to principles that can be formulated. One does not normally speak of principles of love and friendship, as of principles of justice and fairness. We have the idea that the specific forms of love and friendship must vary with the different kinship systems and social roles that prevail in different societies, while the principles of justice do not have varying forms, although the circumstances to which they are applied may differ. So we may think that there is at least a difference of degree between moral claims that prescribe just conduct, which purport to be derived from rationally defensible principles, and moral claims that prescribe conduct that counts as friendly or as a manifestation of love; and that this contrast arises within morality.

One may concede that there are just these differences of degree between virtues that have specific and determinate realisations, and that are everywhere and at all times very similar in their behavioural expressions, and virtues that have realisations differing according to the different conventions and social roles in different societies. But perhaps this is only a difference of degree. To take one example, Aristotle's chapters on justice in the *Nicomachean Ethics* bear about as close a resemblance to a representative modern treatise on justice such as Rawls', as Aristotle's chapters on love and friendship bear to some later treatise on that subject, for example that of Montaigne or Stendhal. Perhaps more strange omissions, and strangeness generally, will strike a contemporary ear when reading Aristotle's account of the moral significance of love and friendship, and the strangeness of tone and detail may be rather less when a contemporary reader considers Aristotle on justice. On the other hand, Aristotle notoriously does not see a contravention of principles of justice in slavery, and was generally much less inclined than modern theorists to count unequal distributions of primary goods as generally unfair. There seems to be a difference in the principles of justice, and perhaps even in the conception of justice, rather than a difference in the situations to which the principles are applied.

4. To notice a disputable difference of degree among and within the recognised virtues in this respect still leaves the more fundamental question: taking different moralities as wholes, are they not all *partly* human artifices, and to be defended by appeals to the imagination, rather than to reason, in the sense in which social manners are partly a human artifice, and to be defended by appeals to the imagination, and in the sense in which works of literature and sculpture and drama are wholly human artifices, and to be assessed by the imagination?

Within this notion of artificiality and artifice a distinction has to be made. Let it be argued that there are some definite and comparatively clear restraints, argumentatively and rationally defensible, upon what conduct, and what social arrangements, can at any time and anywhere be counted as just and fair. With justice the notion of imagination seems out of place, and reason, and reasonable considerations, are alone in place, as in the establishment of rules of law. The setting in which just conduct and just and fair arrangements are distinguished from unjust ones is an argumentative setting, a judicial setting with a verdict in view, and with a contest between rational considerations always a possibility. In so far as artificiality is taken to imply, or is associated with, the imagination and with imaginative invention, the principles of justice must be represented as not artificial, just because they are intended to be principles solely defensible by rational argument. In this respect justice is to be contrasted with love and friendship because the prescriptions that express these virtues may be justified, as manifestations of love and friendship, by appeals to imagination as much as to reason. New forms and varieties of love and friendship are brought into existence and are recognised as new forms, and are recognised even as new kinds of love and friendship. This recognition is not defensible by rational considerations without any appeals to imagination; one has to envisage a particular person or persons in a particular situation and to invent or to recognise a form of behaviour that seems to be right in the peculiar circumstances. There is not the same requirement of convergence just because reasonable argument is less in place in such cases of envisaging the right conduct in the particular circumstances. There is no obvious requirement that everyone at all times should love and be friendly in the same way, or in accordance with fixed principles that can be formulated and defended.

The contrast in respect of artificiality between the rational virtue of justice and the not entirely rational virtue of love or friendship might be explained by distinguishing two kinds of artificiality. The transition from a state of nature, in which men act according to their unmoralised and unsocialised impulses, is usually represented as a rationally intelligible improvement of life chances for all men, wherever they are and at all times. They conclude a contract among themselves, and their descendants, making the same calculation all over again as reasonable men, are ready always to ratify this contract. There is a sense in which the reasonably just social arrangements, and the structure of law and of the constitution, which emerge from the supposed original contract, are artificial; certainly they are constructions of human reason to restrict and control natural forces. But there is the other sense in which just arrangements, being independent of culturally modified preferences and interests, are natural to all men, who are as a species capable of a true appreciation of their own permanent nature, using their reason. Apart from love and friendship, there are other virtues of human association, which for different reasons are non-convergent.

5. In the Greek argument, we are told to contrast the great variety of social customs prevailing in different places and at different times with those fundamental principles of desirable or acceptable human associations which emerge from the ideal social contract. No rational reconstruction or transcendental deduction of these divergent social customs is to be attempted. In Herodotus and Xenophon and elsewhere you are led to expect that social customs will diverge, and that different populations will distinguish themselves, and identify themselves, both in their own minds and in the minds of others, by their customs. Part of the point of the customs resides in their diversity, in the discriminations that they mark. The glory of being Greek emerged in following the social customs, the habits in matters of address and social manners and in conduct generally, which are distinctively Greek; and the glory of being Athenian, or being Spartan, rather than of being just any Greek, resided in following the very different and distinctive customs of these two very discriminating cities. If the word 'glory' seems too high flown and seems an exaggeration in this context, one could say instead that the point of thinking of oneself as

Greek or as Athenian resided in the thought of the distinctiveness of their way of life; and their way of life consisted not only of social customs and habits of address and habits of conduct more generally, but also of distinctive moral codes and principles, with typical prescriptions derived from them. This implies that no convergence to general agreement is required in a justification of these prescriptions.

When one values the customs and morality of one's own society or group as distinctive, one is thinking of them as discriminatory. So far there is no requirement to universalise the prescriptions, implicit or explicit, which govern the customs and values, and to think of the prescriptions as applicable to all men, whatever their condition. Equally the converse is not entailed either; that the customs and peculiar moral prescriptions of a particular group ought to be confined to that group. One could consistently think of one's own moral habits and dispositions as at present existing only among one's own people, say, the Greeks, and at the same time consistently believe that the barbarians ought to adopt Greek moral prescriptions and dispositions and ought to cease to be barbarians. If one looks at the customs from another angle, it does not even follow from the fact that one takes pride in the thought that one's own habits and dispositions are distinctive and different, and that they constitute a definite identity for the group to which one belongs, that one thinks that all men should belong to groups which have distinctive habits and dispositions. None of these strong conclusions is entailed. The recognition of distinctiveness, and the moral endorsement of it, only entail that there are acceptable moral prescriptions which are not to be defended and justified by the kind of rational argument which enters into ideal social contract theory, whether in Plato, Hobbes, Locke, Rousseau or Rawls. The prescriptions have to be defended and justified in a quite different way.

6. In what way? How do these non-convergent moral claims and prescriptions differ in the defence and justification offered for them from those that can be defended and justified by a rational argument, as the principles of justice can be, by the stripping down argument, that is, by the argument that a common requirement of justice, and of the broad principles of justice, would be recognised by all men who abstract from their contingent and divergent interests?

In order to distinguish moral prescriptions from mere custom and social manners, first one should distinguish between dispositions and habits, and accompanying prescriptions, which are taken very seriously and to which importance is attached, and those which are regarded as comparatively trivial and unimportant; and the test is the kind and degree of the feeling of shock and repugnance and disapproval which would normally occur when the custom or habit is not followed; and, secondly, whether this feeling is a reflective one, and survives after it is evaluated, or whether it is merely an immediate reaction to be explained away by personal factors. The strong repugnance and disapproval, which after reflection seems to the subject appropriate to the particular case, would normally be accounted a moral attitude and a moral emotion, resting on a moral judgement of the case; the subject would think of his repugnance and his disapproval as a moral attitude implying a moral judgement: not just a matter of custom and social propriety. His reflection on his attitude, and on the implied judgement, would be an attempt to detach himself from reactions which he thought could not be defended and justified on a clear and calm consideration of the case, but could only be explained by features of his own temperament.

To claim impartiality in judgement, in this sense, is not to claim that the judgement is one that rational men must assent to if they are similarly impartial – which is the claim made for judgements about fundamental principles of justice. A reflective repugnance and moral disapproval, and implied moral judgement, may be concentrated upon a breach of a moral code, say a code of honour, which is an essential element in the way of life of a particular social group, a group that takes pride in this distinction, in precisely the way in which a Welsh nationalist or a Basque nationalist may take pride in speaking and preserving their particular languages, which are also essential elements in their ways of life. They may consistently admit that men of different origins and having different roles may rightly, or at least reasonably, follow quite different and incompatible rules. So far from wishing to generalise the distinctive moral claims to which he is reflectively committed, a man proud of his culture may contrast these moral claims, in virtue of their distinctiveness, with the moral claims of justice and reasonable benevolence, or of concern for happiness, which he specifically counts as universal claims, arising from a shared humanity and an entirely general norm of reasonableness. He may agree that he can easily conceive of alternative rules which are neither more nor less reasonable; for reasonableness is not the prime consideration in this sphere. He will not be disturbed by evidence that in other societies quite different rules or conventions prevail among entirely reasonable men, who would broadly agree with him about the principles of justice and about a necessary concern with happiness.

7. There are good reasons to expect that most men have been, and always will be, ready to acknowledge both kinds of moral claim, the universal and convergent moral claim, and the distinctive moral claim, which is to be defended by direct reference to one actually existing way of life in which it is a necessary element, and to the imagination of particular cases which

arise within this way of life. The good reasons for distinguishing the two are repeatedly foreshadowed in the literature of moral and political philosophy: for example, in Hegel's criticisms of the abstractness of Kant's rational will and moral law, and in Burke's criticisms of the morality of the French Enlightenment. As morality cannot be separated from canons of practical reasoning and of prudence, and from the rational foundations of law and justice on the one side, so it cannot be separated from social manners and custom, and habits of thought and speech, and the distinctive elements of a culture on the other side – at least under known normal conditions, and until humanity is transformed, as both utilitarians and Kantians have wished that it should be, though for quite different reasons. Personal relations between people within families and kinship systems, and in love and friendship; sexual customs and prohibitions; duties and obligations associated with the dead and with ancestors and with death itself; rituals and customs that express social solidarity in different kinds of institution; customs and prohibitions in war: it is a genuinely universal requirement of morality that there should be some rules or customs governing conduct in these areas of strong emotions. The rules and customs observed in these areas, particularly those of sexuality and the family, constitute much of the central core of a way of life, even though they are subject to general principles of social justice and of benevolence. I may for many reasons want my actual way of life, inherited and developed, to be modified or changed, but it is still the starting-point of my morality, the bedrock of my moral dispositions, upon which I must build differently.

More than a pride in distinctiveness and a more definite sense of identity is involved in the acknowledgement of moral claims in the areas mentioned, claims that are not to be adequately defended by a rational calculation of common human necessities; just as any natural language has to satisfy the common requirements of language as such, being a means of communication, so on the other side a language has to develop in history, and over a period of time, its own distinguishing forms and vocabulary, if it is to have any hold on men's imagination and memory. The project of Esperanto, the generally shared and syncretistic language, does not succeed. A language distinguishes a particular people with a particular shared history and with a particular set of of shared associations and with largely unconscious memories, preserved in the metaphors that are imbedded in the vocabulary. So also with some parts of morality: for example, the prohibitions and prescriptions that govern sexual morality and family relationships and the duties of friendship.

8. Rather banal and familiar Aristotelian reasons can be given for these

two faces of morality: the lawlike and rational, the language-like and imaginative: that men are not only rational and calculative in forming and pursuing their ideals and in maintaining rules of conduct, but they are also in the grip of particular and distinguishing memories and of particular and distinguishing local passions; and the Aristotelian word to emphasise is 'particular'. Love and affection are necessarily concentrated on a particular person or a particular place, as a disposition to justice is directed towards a general rule or a repeatable process. A disposition to love and friendship is a central virtue, and it has always been recognised as such, no less than justice and courage. Justice is the disposition to treat all men and women alike in certain respects, in recognition of their common humanity: love and friendship are dispositions to treat men and women very differently, in recognition of their individuality and unrepeated nature. The species is sustained and prolonged by sexual drives and family ties which are necessarily to some degree exclusive and particularised. It is precisely the basic biological phenomena of sex and family relationships, of childhood, youth and age which, being obviously natural, are modified by diverse and distinctive conventions and filtered through various restraints, some morally trivial and some not. Any particular sexual morality is underdetermined by purely rational considerations, which are everywhere valid. Defense and justification will also take the form of pointing to the distinctive and peculiar virtues of one way of life, to its history and to the reciprocal dependence of the elements of this way of life on each other. At all times and in all places there has to be a sexual morality which is recognised; but it does not have to be the same sexual morality with the same restraints and prescription. The rational requirement is the negative one: that the rules and conventions should not cause evident and avoidable unhappiness or offend accepted principles of fairness. These bare requirements plainly underdetermine the full, complex morality of the family and of sexual relationships and of friendship in any man's actual way of life. Justice in respect of property rights and ownership is also underdetermined by the universal requirements of justice, since it in part depends upon local customs; but the rights, if challenged, have to be defended at every level by rational argument. The argument will appeal to principles and to precedents.

One particular sexual morality is an integral and indispensable part of a way of life which actually exists, one among others, and which the judging subject believes ought to be preserved as a valuable way of life, actually realised, not perfect but still valuable. But rational argument is not available below the level of the general requirements of fairness and of utility; and the lower level of specific habits and specific conventions is of binding importance in sexual morality.

The kind of 'must not' that arises within this area of morality can be compared with a linguistic prohibition, e.g. that you must not split an infinitive a particular rule of a particular language, which is not made less binding by the fact that it is not a general rule in language. The grammar and rules of propriety in any particular language may seem arbitrary and artificial when compared with the general logical framework of language, or with some presumed deep structure in all languages. The grammar is arbitrary and in this sense artificial only to the degree that it is not to be explained by the natural needs of communication and of thought alone, but must also be explained supplementarily by reference to a particular history of the language's development; and even this supplementary explanation will almost certainly be incomplete and will fall short, because of the complexity of the relationships involved. As in languages and in social customs, so also everyone recognises that there must be rules and conventions of conduct that deserve to be called moral in certain definite areas, and everyone also recognises that these rules (a) must fit into, and be compatible with, universal, rationally explicable principles of justice and utility analogous to a deep structure in language, and (b) that the strict rules within these limits will be diverse and will seem arbitrary, because they have historically performed the function of distinguishing one social group from all others.

How then does one balance the comparatively conventional moral claims against rationally defensible principles of justice and of utility, the claims of rational morality? The condensed and cryptic answer that men are only half rational carries the implication that our desires and purposes are always permeated by memories and by local attachments and by historical associations, just as they are always permeated by rational calculation; and that this will always be true. There is a rational justification for respecting some set of not unreasonable moral claims of a conventional kind, because some moral prescriptions are necessary in the areas of sexuality and family relationships and friendship and social customs and attitudes to death; and that men are reasonably inclined to respect those prescriptions which have in fact survived and which have a history of respect, unless they find reasons to reject them drawn from moral considerations of the opposing rational type. It evidently does not follow from the fact that a way of life has survived, and that it has some hold over men's sentiments and loyalties, that that way of life, with the moral claims which are a necessary element of it, ought for these reasons to be protected and prolonged; there may well be overriding reasons of a rational kind against these claims – e.g. that they are unfair or that they destroy happiness or freedom.

9. The degree of permeation by local memories and local attachments

varies with different human interests: at its greatest where emotions and passions have an instinctual foundation, as in sexual and family relationship, and less extensive in areas where rational calculation guides passions, as in the morality surrounding property relations and ownership.

Exactly in those areas of experience where natural impulses and emotions are strongest, and where rational control and direction are weak, distinctive and conventional moral prohibitions are naturally in place and naturally respected: and they are respected for reasons largely independent of justice and of the avoidance of harm and the promotion of welfare. To take a familiar example, the proper treatment of the dead, whatever the obligatory treatment may be in any particular society, has always been at the centre of moralities, and failure to bury the dead, or to do whatever is locally accounted necessary, has always been morally shocking. The force of particular moral claims of this type is not to be explained by general principles of justice or of benevolence and welfare. That the dead must be appropriately disposed of, even at a high cost, is a very general requirement, and a mark of humanity; but it is also generally recognised that what is appropriate for one people, and one set of circumstances, is not generally appropriate elsewhere. The fact that there is no general requirement of convergence is not an indication that the moral duty of respect for the dead, and the appropriate custom, is not to be taken seriously. Freud's superb essay 'On Mourning' explains the complementary relation between nature and convention here.

Men are unavoidably born into both a natural order and a cultural order, and sexuality, old age, death, family and friendship are among the natural phenomena which have to be moralised by conventions and customs, within one culture or other, and that means within a very particular and specific set of moral requirements. The one unnatural, and impossible, cry is the consequentialist's: 'Away with convention: anything goes provided that it does not interfere with welfare or with principles of justice.'

To summarise: to the old question of whether moral claims are νόμῳ or φύσει, conventional or in the nature of things, like norms of social propriety or like norms of health, 'both' is my answer. There are two kinds of moral claim – those that, when challenged, are referred to universal needs of human beings and to their reasonable calculations, which should be the same everywhere, and hence to the stripping down argument: and those that, when challenged, are referred to the description of a desired and respected way of life, in which these moral claims have been an element thought essential within that way of life. The first kind of claim represents moral norms as not unlike norms of good health: the second as not unlike social customs. The issue is sharply focussed by the old eight-eenth-century Whig idea of the veil of ignorance: behind the veil is an abstract universal man dressed in neo-classical drapery, as in some Reynolds paintings, to indicate that he belongs to no particular place or time. In the unearthly light of the ideal, classical and timeless scene, reason cannot tell him how he should be married or how he should speak to his children or educate them or fit into his community or give one local loyalty precedence over another. For these purposes some Tory history, as in a Scott novel, has to be told of the complex conventions in which he was brought up and which fix him in a certain time and place and constitute an identity for him, so that certain moral repugnances reasonably seem to him natural to a man in his time and place and in his particular role, given the history, though certainly not natural at all times and places and in all roles.

One could clear away the obscurities of the *nature versus convention* distinction by substituting the distinction between moral claims with a requirement for convergence, for the stripping down argument as a test, such as justice and utility, and the moral claims with no requirement for convergence and with a tendency to distinctiveness or, at least, to a licence for distinctiveness. As Plato implied, half the point of justice and the maximisation of utility is lost if there is no convergence, no universal tendency, towards the cultivation of these virtues, founded on argument: not so for love and friendship and loyalty, which have their point as virtues, even if there is a chaos of different forms and different realisations of them in the world that we know.

8   Social unity and primary goods*

JOHN RAWLS

In this essay I have two aims: first, to elaborate the notion of primary goods, a notion which is part of the conception of justice as fairness presented in my book *A Theory of Justice*;[1] and, second, to explain the connection between the notion of primary goods and a certain conception of the person which leads in turn to a certain conception of social unity. Following a brief preface in section I, the main part of my discussion is in sections II–V. Here I describe how in justice as fairness primary goods enable us to make interpersonal comparisons in the special but fundamental case of political and social justice. I remove certain gaps in the exposition in my book and by emphasizing that the notion of primary goods depends on a certain conception of the person I also remove a serious ambiguity. My thesis is that the problem of interpersonal comparisons in questions of justice goes to the foundations of a conception of justice and depends on the conception of the person and the way in which social unity is to be conceived. In justice as fairness the difficulties in defining these comparisons turn out to be moral and practical. The last three sections, VI–VIII, try to clarify these ideas by contrasting them with an account of interpersonal comparisons in the utilitarian tradition which informs so much of contemporary economic theory when it turns to questions of justice. In this tradition interpersonal comparisons are thought to raise difficulties of another kind, namely, the various problems connected with knowledge of other minds. These difficulties are said to be resolved by finding a sufficiently accurate interpersonal measure (or indicator) of satisfaction, or well-being, founded on psychology and

* An earlier version of parts of this paper was given as one of four lectures at Stanford in May, 1978. It has, however, been much revised. I am grateful to Derek Parfit, Joshua Rabinowitz, A. K. Sen and Steven Strasnick for valuable comments on the first version; and to K. H. Arrow, Gilbert Harman, Thomas Nagel and T. M. Scanlon for their criticisms of a later version. Arnold Davidson and Thomas Pogge have given me helpful suggestions on the final draft. I am particularly indebted to Burton Dreben for extensive discussion and advice. I owe to him the suggestion to focus on the contrast between how liberalism and utilitarianism conceive of social unity.
[1] Rawls 1971. Henceforth referred to as *TJ*.

economic theory. Our question is: What lies at the bottom of this contrast? Why should a Kantian doctrine like justice as fairness view the problem of interpersonal comparisons so differently from the way utilitarianism does?

I

To approach the answer we must first note that one deep division between conceptions of justice is whether they allow for a plurality of different and opposing, and even incommensurable, conceptions of the good, or whether they hold that there is but one conception of the good which is to be recognised by all persons, so far as they are rational. Conceptions of justice which fall on opposite sides of this divide treat the problem of interpersonal comparisons in entirely different ways. Plato and Aristotle, and the Christian tradition as represented by Aquinas and Augustine, fall on the side of the one (rational) good. Indeed, since classical times, the dominant tradition has been that there is but one rational conception of the good. The presupposition of liberalism (as a philosophical doctrine), as represented by Locke, Kant and J. S. Mill,[2] is that there are many conflicting and incommensurable conceptions of the good, each compatible with the full autonomy and rationality of human persons. Liberalism assumes, as a consequence of this presupposition, that it is a natural condition of a free democratic culture that a plurality of conceptions of the good is pursued by its citizens. The classical utilitarians – Bentham, Edgeworth and Sidgwick – appear to accept this liberal presupposition. I believe, however, that this appearance is misleading and arises from the special subjective nature of their view of the rational good. I shall indicate how both classical utilitarianism and a contemporary version of utilitarianism imply a conception of the person which makes this doctrine incompatible with the presupposition that there are many rational conceptions of the good.

As a Kantian view, justice as fairness accepts the liberal presupposition. The consequence is that the unity of society and the allegiance of its citizens to their common institutions rest not on their espousing one rational conception of the good, but on an agreement as to what is just for free and equal moral persons with different and opposing conceptions of the good. This conception of justice is independent of and prior to the notion of goodness in the sense that its principles limit the conceptions of the good which are admissible in a just society. These principles of justice are to be regarded as the public principles for what I shall call 'a well-

---

[2] The choice of these three names, especially Mill's, needs an explanation I cannot provide here. I can only remark that, in my opinion, Mill's view is a form of liberalism and not utilitarianism, given how I use these terms in this paper. Support for this opinion is found in Isaiah Berlin's essay on Mill in Berlin 1969.

ordered society'. In such a society each citizen accepts these principles and each knows that everyone else accepts them as well. Moreover, the basic institutions of society actually satisfy these public principles, and that this is the case is recognised by all citizens for good and sufficient reasons. The role of basic social institutions is to set up a framework within which citizens may further their ends, provided that these ends do not violate the prior and independent principles of justice.

Another feature of a well-ordered society is that there is a public understanding concerning the kinds of claims which it is appropriate for citizens to make when questions of justice arise, and this understanding involves a further understanding as to what can support such claims. These understandings are necessary in order to reach agreement as to how citizens' claims are to be assessed and their relative weight determined. The fulfilment of these claims is accepted as advantageous for citizens and is counted as improving their situation for purposes of justice. An effective public conception of justice presupposes a shared understanding of what is to be recognised as advantageous in this sense. Thus the problem of interpersonal comparisons in justice as fairness becomes: given the different and opposing, and even incommensurable, conceptions of the good in a well-ordered society, how is such a public understanding possible?

The notion of primary goods addresses this moral and practical problem. It rests on the idea, to anticipate a bit, that a *partial* similarity of citizens' conceptions of the good is sufficient for political and social justice. Citizens do not affirm the same rational conception of the good, *complete* in all its essentials and especially its final ends and loyalties. It is enough that citizens view themselves as moved by the two highest-order interests of moral personality (as explained below), and that their particular conceptions of the good, however distinct their final ends and loyalties, require for their advancement roughly the same primary goods, for example the same rights, liberties and opportunites, as well as certain all-purpose means such as income and wealth. Claims to these goods I shall call 'appropriate claims', and their weight in particular questions of justice is determined by the principles of justice.

II

After this preface, let us now turn to the account of primary goods and their role in the two principles of justice that are used in justice as fairness.[3] These two principles are:

1. Each person has an equal right to the most extensive scheme of equal basic liberties compatible with a similar scheme of liberties for all.

[3] For a further discussion, see *TJ*, pp. 60–83. For the most complete statement, see pp. 302–3.

2. Social and economic inequalities are to satisfy two conditions: they must be (a) to the greatest benefit of the least advantaged members of society; and (b) attached to offices and positions open to all under conditions of fair equality of opportunity.

These principles apply to what I shall call the 'basic structure of society', that is, to the way in which the major social institutions fit into one system. These institutions assign fundamental rights and duties, and by working together they influence the division of advantages which arise through social cooperation. The first principle has priority over the second, so that all citizens are assured the equal basic liberties; similarly, part (b) of the second principle has priority over part (a), so that the conditions of fair equality of opportunity are also guaranteed for everyone.

Part (a) of the second principle requires specifications of the notions of advantage and benefit in order that the notion of the benefit of the least advantaged be fully explicit. In their general form these specifications assign weights to certain of the primary goods and citizens' fair shares of these goods are specified by an index which uses these weights. The primary goods may be characterised under five headings as follows:

(a) First, the basic liberties as given by a list, for example: freedom of thought and liberty of conscience; freedom of association; and the freedom defined by the liberty and integrity of the person, as well as by the rule of law; and finally the political liberties;

(b) Second, freedom of movement and choice of occupation against a background of diverse opportunities;

(c) Third, powers and prerogatives of offices and positions of responsibility, particularly those in the main political and economic institutions;

(d) Fourth, income and wealth; and

(e) Finally, the social bases of self-respect.

Given the priority of the first principle over the second, and of part (b) of the second principle over part (a), all citizens in a well-ordered society have the same equal basic liberties and enjoy fair equality of opportunity. The only permissible difference among citizens is their share of the primary goods in (c), (d) and (e). In the general case, then, we require an index of these goods. In this paper, however, I shall, for the most part, take the two principles of justice in what I shall call their 'simplest form': that is, part (a) of the second principle (the 'difference principle') directs that the basic structure be arranged so that the life-time expectations of the least advantaged, estimated in terms of income and wealth, are as great as possible given fixed background institutions that secure the equal basic liberties and establish fair equality of opportunity. This simplest form serves as an example of the use of primary goods to make interpersonal comparisons; it ignores, however, the primary goods under (c) and (e) and hence avoids the problem of defining an index. On the assumption that the question of private property democracy versus democratic socialism involves the weighting of primary goods under (c), (d) and (e), using income and wealth alone in the difference principle presumably cannot resolve this historic question. While I shall sometimes speak of an index of primary goods, in this paper I do not consider the problem of an index for the general case.[4] The simplest form is offered as an example to fix ideas. It suffices for our purpose here, which is to focus on the contrast between justice as fairness and the utilitarian tradition with respect to how the problem of interpersonal comparisons is conceived.

Several further points about primary goods deserve mention. First, primary goods are certain features of institutions or of the situation of citizens in relation to them. Whether the basic structure guarantees equal liberty of conscience, or freedom of thought, is settled by the content of the rights and liberties defined by the institutions of the basic structure and how they are actually interpreted and enforced. We are not required to examine citizens' psychological attitudes nor their comparative levels of well-being; and the relevant features of institutions that decide the question are open to public view. To say this, however, is not to deny that the question may sometimes be hard to answer. And the same is true for whether fair equality of opportunity exists. Again, while measures of income and wealth are not easy to devise, the relative standing of citizens, granted such a measure, is in principle a publicly decidable matter.

Second, the same index of primary goods is to be used to compare everyone's social situation, so that this index defines a public basis of interpersonal comparisons for questions of social justice. Primary goods are not, however, to be used in making comparisons in all situations but only in questions of justice which arise in regard to the basic structure. It is another matter entirely whether primary goods are an appropriate basis in other kinds of cases. The parties in the original position know that an index of primary goods is part of the two principles of justice and therefore part of their agreement when these principles are adopted.

---

[4] Allan Gibbard (Gibbard 1979), by avoiding the problem of constructing an index and considering the one primary good of income, examines what in the text I call the difference principle in its 'simplest form'. Gibbard shows that in this form the difference principle is incompatible with the Pareto principle. I do not believe that this is not a serious problem in view of the balance of reasons for using primary goods as the basis of interpersonal comparisons in questions of justice, and of the subordinate role of the Pareto principle in justice as fairness, particularly in its welfarist interpretation. See also Gibbard's remarks, pp. 280–2.

Third, the least advantaged are defined as those who have the lowest index of primary goods, when their prospects are viewed over a complete life. This definition implies that social mobility is not considered a primary good. Individuals actually born into this group have some likelihood of improving their situation and of belonging to the more favoured; but whatever this likelihood is, it is irrelevant, since the least advantaged are, by definition, those who are born into and who remain in that group throughout their life. The two principles of justice allow for social mobility through the principle of fair equality of opportunity: it is not a primary good to be weighted in the index. (The circumstances that secure equality of opportunity are, of course, part of the scheme of background justice established by the two principles working together.) Finally, it was noted in section I that in a well-ordered society there must be a public understanding as to what claims are appropriate for citizens to make in matters of justice. The fulfilment of appropriate claims specifies what is publicly counted as advantageous and as improving situations of citizens. In the well-ordered society regulated by the two principles of justice appropriate claims are claims to certain primary goods, and the relative weight of such claims is settled by these principles, which include an index of these goods. But on what basis do the primary goods come to be accepted? Or, as we asked in section I, how is a shared understanding of what are appropriate claims possible, in view of citizens' conflicting and incommensurable conceptions of the good?

III

The answer is given by the conception of the person which is fundamental to justice as fairness, together with the practical nature of primary goods. Consider first the conception of the person: since a conception of justice applies to the basic structure of society regarded as a system of social cooperation, we start by assuming that citizens are free and equal moral persons who can contribute to, and honour the constraints of, social cooperation for the mutual benefit of all. Social cooperation is not merely coordinated social activity efficiently organised for some overall collective end. Rather, it presupposes a notion of fair terms of cooperation which all participants may reasonably be expected to accept over the course of a complete life; it also presupposes that participants have different final ends they wish to advance, and that these ends specify each person's good. Justice as fairness regards each person as someone who can and who desires to take part in social cooperation for mutual advantage. Thus in formulating a conception of justice for the basic structure of society, we start by viewing each person as a moral person moved by two highest-order interests, namely, the interests to realise and to exercise the two powers of moral personality. These two powers are the capacity for a sense of right and justice (the capacity to honour fair terms of cooperation), and the capacity to decide upon, to revise and rationally to pursue a conception of the good. Moral persons also have a higher-order (as opposed to a highest-order) interest in advancing their determinate conceptions of the good (defined by certain specific final ends and aspirations) that they have at any given time. In sum, then, this conception of the person give regulative primacy to the two highest-order interests, so that moral persons are said to have both the capacity and the desire to cooperate on fair terms with others for reciprocal advantage; and this implies a regulative desire to conform the pursuit of one's good, as well as the demands one makes on others, to public principles of justice which all can reasonably be expected to accept.[5]

Now in order to find reasonable principles for the basic structure we assume that each citizen is represented by a party in what I have called in *A Theory of Justice* 'the original position'. The parties are to reach an agreement on certain principles of justice, and in doing this they follow the instructions of those they represent. These instructions direct the parties to do the best they can for those they represent subject to the constraints of the original position, such as the restrictions on information, the fact that the parties are symmetrically situated, and so on. Given the set-up of the original position, the assumption is that the parties can best represent citizens as free and equal moral persons by deciding between alternative principles of justice according to how securely these principles provide for all citizens the primary goods. To ground this assumption, an explanation of why it is rational for the parties to assess principles of justice in terms of primary goods is needed:[6]

(i) The basic liberties (freedom of thought and liberty of conscience, etc.) are the background institutions necessary for the development and exercise of the capacity to decide upon and revise, and rationally to pursue, a conception of the good. Similarly, these liberties allow for the development and exercise of the sense of right and justice under political and social conditions that are free.

---

[5] In this section I remove the ambiguity in *TJ* about whether the account of primary goods is a matter for social theory alone, or depends essentially on a conception of the person. In *TJ*, §15, pp. 92ff, where primary goods are first discussed at some length, this question is not discussed. See also pp. 142f, 253, 260, and 433f. I am grateful to Joshua Cohen, Joshua Rabinowitz, T. M. Scanlon, and Michael Teitelman for helpful criticism and clarification on this important point.

[6] A fuller discussion can be found in Buchanan 1975. For a more general account, of which primary goods is a special case, see Scanlon 1975.

(ii) Freedom of movement and free choice of occupation against a background of diverse opportunities are required for the pursuit of final ends as well as to give effect to a decision to revise and change them, if one so desires.

(iii) Powers and prerogatives of offices of responsibility are needed to give scope to various self-governing and social capacities of the self.

(iv) Income and wealth, understood broadly as they must be, are all-purpose means (having an exchange value) for achieving directly or indirectly a wide range of ends, whatever they happen to be.

(v) The social bases of self-respect are those aspects of basic institutions that are normally essential if citizens are to have a lively sense of their own worth as moral persons and to be able to realise their highest-order interests and advance their ends with self-confidence.

These observations must suffice here to show that the parties' reliance on primary goods is rational. To obtain a ranking of these goods, the parties refer to the highest-order interests of citizens as moral persons, and the fact that they do not know citizens' determinate conceptions of the good. The highest-order interests in developing and exercising the two moral powers, along with the normal conditions of human social life, not only single out the primary goods but also specify their relative importance. Thus, the priority of the first principle of justice over the second, and the priority of part (b) of the second principle over part (a), reflects the pre-eminence of and the relation between the highest-order interests in the conception of the person.

Certainly all of this, particularly the last point, which includes the question of the priority of liberty, requires a much fuller discussion than I can provide here. That the primary goods are necessary conditions for realising the powers of moral personality and are all-purpose means for a sufficiently wide range of final ends presupposes various general facts about human wants and abilities, their characteristic phases and requirements of nurture, relations of social interdependence and much else. We need at least a rough account of rational plans of life which shows why they normally have a certain structure and depend upon the primary goods for their formation, revision, and execution. I shall assume that how all this works out is clear enough for our purposes. But note that what are to count as primary goods is not decided by asking what general means are essential for achieving the final ends which a comprehensive empirical or historical survey might show that people usually or normally have in common. There may be few if any such ends; and those there are may not serve the purposes of a conception of justice. The characterisation of primary goods does not rest on such historical or social facts. While the determination of primary goods invokes a knowledge of the general circumstances and requirements of social life, it does so only in the light of a conception of the person given in advance.

We can now complete the answer as to how a public understanding of what is counted advantageous in questions of justice is possible despite citizens' conflicting and incommensurable conceptions of the good. Here we invoke the practical nature of primary goods. By this I mean that we can actually provide a scheme of basic equal liberties which, when made part of the political constitution and instituted in the basic structure of society (as the first subject of justice), ensures for all citizens the development and exercise of their highest-order interests, provided that certain all-purpose means are fairly assured for everyone. Of course, it is neither possible, nor desirable, to enable everyone to advance their final ends no matter what these ends are, for some may desire, for example, the oppression of others as an end in itself. Nevertheless, a sufficiently wide range of ends can be accommodated to secure ways of life fully worthy of human endeavour. That such a framework of social cooperation can be instituted, and is in this sense practically possible, cannot be derived solely from the conception of the person as having two highest-order interests, nor solely from the fact that given the normal structure of rational plans of life certain things, such as the primary goods, can serve as all-purpose means. Both these elements must cohere together into a workable and stable basic structure as a framework of social cooperation over a complete life. That such a scheme can be set up is suggested by social experience, and by our reflecting on the historical development of democratic institutions, and the principles and possibilities of constitutional design.

IV

Since the discussion so far has been quite general, the next two sections elaborate what has been said by turning to several more specific matters. I begin by considering what might seem to be an objection to the use of primary goods in a well-ordered society. It may be said that when we take the two principles of justice in their simplest form, so that income and wealth is the only primary good with which the difference principle is concerned, this principle cannot be reasonable or just. This can be shown, one might argue, by two examples: special medical and health needs, and the variation of preferences between persons.[7] The economist's utility function is designed to cope with cases of this kind; but when the

---

[7] This objection, discussed in this section, was raised by K. J. Arrow in his review, Arrow 1973, pp. 253f.

difference principle relies on income and wealth alone, it clearly fails, the objection continues, to make a reasonable or just allowance for citizens' different needs and preferences.

It is best to make an initial concession in the case of special health and medical needs. I put this difficult problem aside in this paper and assume that all citizens have physical and psychological capacities within a certain normal range. I do this because the first problem of justice concerns the relations between citizens who are normally active and fully cooperating members of society over a complete life. Perhaps the social resources to be devoted to the normal health and medical needs of such citizens can be decided at the legislative stage in the light of existing social conditions and reasonable expectations of the frequency of illness and accident. If a solution can be worked out for this case, then it may be possible to extend it to the hard cases. If it cannot be worked out for this case, the idea of primary goods may have to be abandoned. The point is, however, that a conception of justice need not rest on a few universal principles which apply to all cases. What is required is that from the standpoint of the original position, or some other appropriate stage, the whole family of principles can be combined into a coherent framework of deliberation.[8]

The second example bears on our present purposes. Imagine two persons, one satisfied with a diet of milk, bread and beans, while the other is distraught without expensive wines and exotic dishes. In short one has expensive tastes, the other does not. If the two principles of justice are understood in their simplest form (as I assume here), then we must say, the objection runs, that with equal income both are equally satisfied. But this is plainly not true. At best, citizens' income and wealth is only a rough indicator of their level of satisfaction and even an index could not be very accurate. More important, it will often be too inaccurate to be fair. The reply is that as moral persons citizens have some part in forming and cultivating their final ends and preferences. It is not by itself an objection to the use of primary goods that it does not accommodate those with expensive tastes. One must argue in addition that it is unreasonable, if not unjust, to hold such persons responsible for their preferences and to require them to make out as best they can. But to argue this seems to

---

[8] As the remarks in this paragraph suggest, the weights for the index of primary goods need not be established in the original position once and for all, and in detail, for every well-ordered society. What is to be established initially is the general form of the index and such constraints on the weights as that expressed by the priority of the basic liberties. Further details necessary for practice can be filled in progressively in the stages sketched in *TJ*, §31, as more specific information is made available. When we attempt to deal with the problem of special medical and health needs a different or a more comprehensive notion than that of primary goods (at least as presented in the text) will, I believe, be necessary; for example, Sen's notion of an index which focuses on persons' basic capabilities may prove fruitful for this problem and serve as an essential complement to the use of primary goods. See Sen. 1980, pp. 217–19.

presuppose that citizens' preferences are beyond their control as propensities or cravings which simply happen. Citizens seem to be regarded as passive carriers of desires. The use of primary goods, however, relies on a capacity to assume responsibility for our ends. This capacity is part of the moral power to form, to revise, and rationally to pursue a conception of the good. Thus, in the case we are discussing, it is public knowledge that the principles of justice view citizens as responsible for their ends. In any particular situation, then, those with less expensive tastes have presumably adjusted their likes and dislikes over the course of their lives to the income and wealth they could reasonably expect; and it is regarded as unfair that they now should have less in order to spare others from the consequences of their lack of foresight or self-discipline.

The idea of holding citizens responsible for their ends is plausible, however, only on certain assumptions.[9] First, we must assume that citizens can regulate and revise their ends and preferences in the light of their expectations of primary goods. This assumption is implicit in the powers we attribute to citizens in regarding them as moral persons. But by itself this assumption does not suffice. We must also find workable criteria for interpersonal comparisons which can be publicly and, if possible, easily applied. Thus we try to show, second, how primary goods are connected with the highest-order interests of moral persons in such a way that these goods are indeed feasible public criteria for questions of justice. Finally, the effective use of primary goods assumes also that the conception of the person which lies at the basis of these two assumptions is at least implicitly accepted as an ideal underlying the public principles of justice. Otherwise, citizens would be less willing to accept responsibility in the sense required.

Thus, the share of primary goods that citizens receive is not intended as a measure of their psychological well-being. In relying on primary goods, justice as fairness rejects the idea of comparing and maximising satisfaction in questions of justice. Nor does it try to estimate the extent to which individuals succeed in advancing their ends, or to evaluate the merits of these ends (so long as they are compatible with the principles of justice). While an index of primary goods serves some of the purposes of a utility function, the basic idea is different: primary goods are social background conditions and all-purpose means generally necessary for forming and rationally pursuing a conception of the good. The principles of justice are to ensure to all citizens the equal protection of and access to these conditions, and to provide each with a fair share of the requisite all-purpose means. The upshot is that, once an index of primary goods is made a part

---

[9] This paragraph revises my brief sketch of the presuppositions of the use of primary goods, in Rawls 1975. I believe it now accords with Scanlon's view in 'Preference and Urgency' (Scanlon 1975). I am grateful to Scanlon and Samuel Scheffler for helpful discussion of these points.

of the two principles of justice, the application of these principles with the index permits the characterisation of what are citizens' appropriate claims to social resources. Although the shares that result must fit society's sense of justice on due reflection, this fit need not, of course, be perfect, but only close enough so that a sufficient convergence of opinion in questions of justice is achieved to sustain willing social cooperation. Thus primary goods help to provide a public standard which all may accept.[10] On the other hand, given the circumstances of justice in which citizens have conflicting conceptions of the good, there cannot be any practical agreement on how to compare happiness as defined, say, by success in carrying out plans of life, nor, even less, any practical agreement on how to evaluate the intrinsic value of these plans. Workable criteria for a public understanding of what is to count as advantageous in matters of justice, and hence as rendering some better situated than others in the relevant interpersonal comparisons, must, I believe, be founded on primary goods, or on some similar notion.

V

The preceding account of primary goods shows that their use in making interpersonal comparisons in questions of justice rests on the conception of moral persons and connects with the public conception of justice in a well-ordered society. This conception includes what we may call a social division of responsibility: society, the citizens as a collective body, accepts the responsibility for maintaining the equal basic liberties and fair equality of opportunity, and for providing a fair share of the other primary goods for everyone within this framework, while citizens (as individuals) and associations accept the responsibility for revising and adjusting their ends and aspirations in view of the all-purpose means they can expect, given their present and foreseeable situation. This division of responsibility relies on the capacity of persons to assume responsibility for their ends and to moderate the claims they make on their social institutions in accordance with the use of primary goods. Citizens' claims to liberties, opportunities and all-purpose means are made secure from the unreasonable demands of others.

[10] In the next to last paragraph of 'Preference and Urgency' (Scanlon 1975), Scanlon distinguishes two interpretations of urgency, a naturalist and conventionalist. While I should not want to call the use of primary goods a 'convention', the background doctrine is not naturalistic, as the connection of primary goods with the conception of the person, for example, makes clear. An index of these goods is closer to Scanlon's description of a conventionalist interpretation of urgency, that is, it is 'a construct put together for the purposes of moral argument . . . its usefulness . . . stems from the fact that it represents, under the circumstances, the best available standard of justification that is mutually acceptable to persons whose preferences diverge'.

We arrive, then, at the idea that citizens as free and equal persons are at liberty to take charge of their lives and each is to adapt their conception of the good to their expected fair share of primary goods. The only restrictions on plans of life is that their fulfilment be compatible with the public principles of justice, and claims may be advanced only for certain kinds of things (primary goods) and in ways allowed for by these principles. This implies that strong feelings and zealous aspirations for certain goals do not, as such, give people a claim upon social resources, or a claim to design public institutions so as to achieve these goals. Desires and wants, however intense, are not by themselves reasons in matters of justice. The fact that we have a compelling desire does not argue for the propriety of its satisfaction any more than the strength of a conviction argues for its truth. Combined with an index of primary goods the principles of justice detach reasons of justice not only from the ebb and flow of fluctuating wants and desires but even from long-standing sentiments and commitments. The significance of this is illustrated by religious toleration, which gives no weight to the strength of conviction by which we may oppose the religious beliefs and practices of others.[11]

The principles of justice treat all citizens with respect to their conception of the good as equals. All citizens have the same basic liberties and enjoy fair equality of opportunity; they share in the other primary goods on the principle that some can have more only if they acquire more in ways which

---

[11] The priority of liberty and this detachment of reasons of justice from reasons of preference and desire is related to the Paradox of the Paretian Liberal discovered by A. K. Sen, namely, the incompatibility (given certain standard assumptions) between the Pareto Principle and even a minimal assignment of individual rights. See Sen 1970a, pp. 82–8, 87–8. Many proposed solutions to this incompatibility are surveyed in Sen 1976. The problem is far too complicated to be considered here, except to say that the paradox cannot, I think, arise within justice as fairness because of the priority of liberty and the subordinate scope allowed for reasons of preference. The basic liberties are, in effect, unalienable and therefore can neither be waived nor limited by any agreements made by citizens, nor overridden by shared collective preferences. These liberties are not on the same plane as these considerations. In this respect the view of justice as fairness resembles the way Robert Nozick treats the paradox, Nozick 1974, pp. 164–6. However, the rights which Nozick takes as fundamental are different from the equal basic liberties included in the principles of justice, and his account of the basis of rights is distinct from that of the equal basic liberties in justice as fairness. Thus, these liberties are not, I think, inalienable in Nozick's view, whereas in justice as fairness any undertakings to waive or to infringe them are *void ab initio*; citizens' desires in this respect have no legal force and should not affect these rights. Nor should the desires of however many others to deny or limit a person's equal basic liberties have any weight. Preferences which would have this effect, never, so to speak, enter into the social calculus. In this way the principles of justice give force to the agreement of the parties in the original position, an agreement framed to secure their highest-order interests. Both the agreements and preferences of citizens in society are counted as hierarchically subordinate to these interests, and this is the ground of the priority of liberty. Of course, none of this rules out that justice as fairness may have its own paradoxes.

improve the situation of those who have less. Moreover, all conceptions of the good (consistent with justice) are regarded as equally worthy, not in the sense that there is an agreed public measure of intrinsic value or satisfaction with respect to which all these conceptions come out equal, but in the sense that they are not evaluated at all from a social standpoint. The role of the conception of the person in the explanation and derivation of the two principles of justice allows us to say that these principles define a just scheme of social cooperation in which citizens are regarded as free and equal moral persons.

It remains to conclude with a few remarks on the notion of appropriate claims in questions of justice. Note first that, by relying on primary goods, justice as fairness asserts that for questions of justice only certain kinds of considerations are relevant. The reason is that we make interpersonal comparisons in many different contexts and for many different purposes; each context has its relevant considerations according to the appropriate ends in view. On birthdays we give things that we know are wanted, or that will please, to express affection; our gifts are chosen in the light of intimate knowledge and shared experiences. But doctors are expected to assess the situations of their patients, and teachers to judge their students, on an entirely different basis and from the standpoint of a distinct conception of their role. Thus doctors consider their patients' medical needs, what is required to restore them to good health and how urgent their treatment is; whereas desert, in the sense of conscientious effort to learn, may be thought relevant by teachers in deciding how best to guide and encourage their students. Thus the relevant considerations depend on how a case is understood.

Now of the three kinds of considerations just mentioned (those involving desires, needs and deserts) the idea of restricting appropriate claims to claims to primary goods is analogous to taking certain needs alone as relevant in questions of justice. The explanation is that primary goods are things generally required, or needed, by citizens as free and equal moral persons who seek to advance (admissible and determinate) conceptions of the good. It is the conception of citizens as such persons, and as normal cooperating members of society over a complete life, which determines what they require. Since the notion of need is always relative to some conception of persons, and of their role and status, the requirements, or needs, of citizens as free and equal moral persons are different from the needs of patients and students. And needs are different from desires, wishes and likings. Citizens' needs are objective in a way that desires are not; that is, they express requirements of persons with certain highest-order interests who have a certain social role and status. If these requirements are not met, persons cannot maintain their role or status, or achieve their essential aims. A citizen's claim that something is a need can be denied when it is not a requirement. Thus, in regarding the members of society as free and equal moral persons, we ascribe to them certain requirements, or needs, which, given the nature of these requirements and the form of rational plans of life, explain how primary goods can be used to define appropriate claims in questions of justice. In effect, the conception of the person and the notion of primary goods simply characterise a special kind of need for a conception of justice. Needs in any other sense, along with desires and aspirations, play no role.

It might seem, however, that if restricting appropriate claims to primary goods is analogous to taking certain needs alone as relevant, then justice must require distribution according to these needs. And since one might also think that the requirements of citizens as free and equal moral persons are equal, why is not an equal share of *all* primary goods the sole principle of justice? I cannot argue this question here and shall only comment that, although the parties in the original position know that the persons they represent require primary goods, it does not follow that it is rational for the parties as their representatives to agree to such a strict principle of equality. The two principles of justice regulate social and economic inequalities in the basic structure so that these inequalities work over time to the greatest benefit of the least advantaged citizens. These principles express a more rational agreement. They also express a kind of equality, since they take an equal division of primary goods as the benchmark of comparison.[12]

VI

In his monograph, *Justice et Équité*, Kolm observes that interpersonal comparisons in questions of justice rest on some kind of identity of preferences. The necessary identity, he says, can be achieved in two ways.[13] The first way is to restrict the preferences considered to those few things which all members of society are presumed to want more of, or, more generally, to preferences described by an index such that everyone is presumed to want a larger share of the bundle of things this index measures. The reliance on primary goods is an example of the first way. The

[12] To see this, refer to *TJ*, p. 76, Figure 6. Note that the maximin point on the OP curve, which is the point identified as just by the difference principle, is the point on the Pareto-efficient frontier closest to equality, as represented by the 45° line. The points to the right of the maximum on the part of the curve sloping downwards to the right define this efficient frontier. Of course, this figure presupposes a two-class economy and serves only to illustrate an idea. A fuller and more instructive figure and explanation is found in Phelps, 1973, pp. 333–5.

[13] See Kolm 1972, pp. 28–9.

second way of arriving at an identity of preferences Kolm explains as follows:[14]

Fondamentalement, tous les individus ont les mêmes besoins, les mêmes goûts, les mêmes désirs. Cette assertion demande sans doute une explication.

Si deux personnes ont des préférences qui semblent différer, il y a une raison à cela, il y a quelque chose qui les rend différentes l'une de l'autre. Mettons ce 'quelque chose' dans *l'objet des préférences* que nous considérons, en le retirant, donc, des *paramètres* qui déterminent la structure de ces préférences. Les préférences ainsi définies de ces deux personnes sont nécessairement identiques.

Kolm adds:

Pour n'importe quelle société, on peut réaliser la même opération: mettre dans *l'objet* des préférences tout ce qui causerait des différences entre celles des divers membres. Une préférence ainsi obtenue, identique pour tous les membres de cette société, s'appelle une *préférences fondamentale* de ceux-ci. C'est une propriété décrivant les goûts et besoins de l'"individu représentatif" de cette société.

Si cette société est l'ensemble de tous les êtres humains, ce que saisit fondamentalement cette préférence commune est 'la nature humaine'.

What Kolm calls a 'fundamental preference' of the society in question, I shall call a 'shared highest-order preference'. Kolm's account of justice and equity bases interpersonal comparisons on this notion.

In order to illustrate how interpersonal comparisons may be regarded as based on this notion of a shared highest-order preference, I shall sketch how these comparisons might be made in a well-ordered society regulated by what I shall call the 'principle of co-ordinal utilitarianism'. In such

---

[14] *Ibid.*, pp. 79–80. I understand this passage as follows:

'At bottom, all individuals have the same tastes, the same desires. Without doubt, this assertion requires explanation.

'If two persons have preferences which appear to differ, there is a reason for this, there is something which makes them different from each other. Let us place this "something" within *the object of the preferences* which we are considering, thereby removing it from the parameters which determine the structure of these preferences. The preferences of these two persons defined in this way are necessarily identical.

'We may carry out this operation in the case of any society: namely, the operation of placing in the object of preferences everything which would cause differences between the preferences of different members of society. An identical preference of all members of this society obtained in this way is called a "fundamental preference" of the members of this society. It is a property which describes the tastes and needs of the "representative individual" of this society.

'If this society includes all human beings, then that which discerns this common preference is at bottom "human nature".'

On page 29 Kolm remarks that the operation of placing the causes of the differences between preferences in the object of preferences is 'tautological'. We can always carry out this formal manoeuver. Kolm attributes the notion of what he calls a 'preference fondamentale' to J. C. Harsanyi (1955, pp. 309–21). He also refers to Tinbergen, (1957, pp. 490–503). In Harsanyi, see also section V, pp. 316–21; in Tinbergen, section VII, pp. 498–503.

a society the notion of what is publicly advantageous must be revised to accord with this principle. The contrast between a well-ordered society regulated by the two principles of justice and a well-ordered society regulated by co-ordinal utilitarianism will bring out the division between this view and justice as fairness, a division founded on the way in which social unity is conceived. I believe that much the same division obtains between justice as fairness and classical utilitarianism as well, since this division arises from the divergence of doctrine concerning the one rational good.[15] In explaining co-ordinal utilitarianism I shall follow Arrow's formulation of it, which incorporates Kolm's notion of a shared highest-order preference. It should be noted, however, as I discuss below (in section VII), co-ordinal utilitarianism is not a view which Arrow accepts.

Co-ordinal utilitarianism is defined as follows.[16] It holds essentially the same conception of the good as classical utilitarianism, and therefore the one rational good is the satisfaction of desire or preferences, or, more generally, the satisfaction of the most rational ordering of desires and preferences. Co-ordinal utilitarianism differs from the classical doctrine by rejecting cardinal interpersonal comparisons of satisfaction and relying solely on ordinal, or, more accurately, on co-ordinal comparisons between the levels of satisfaction, or well-being, of different persons. This means that while we can ascertain whether two persons are equally well-off, or whether one is better off than the other, the differences between levels of satisfaction cannot be given a meaningful numerical measure. These levels can only be ordered as greater or less. Interpersonal comparisons are co-ordinal in the sense that judgements comparing the levels of well-being of different persons are unaffected whenever the numbers assigned to these levels (numbers which are significant only in showing the order of levels) are transformed by the same monotone (always increasing) function. (Expressed another way, the same monotone function may be applied to everyone's utility function without changing any of the interpersonal comparisons.) Given this understanding of interpersonal comparisons, the

---

[15] This fact implies that to interpret the difference principle as the principle of maximin utility (the principle to maximise the well-being of the least advantaged persons) is a serious misunderstanding from a philosophical standpoint. However, this need not affect the application of the difference principle to economic or social choice theory, provided an index of primary goods, or preferences for these goods, may be presumed to have the formal or other properties these applications require.

[16] In this paragraph I adapt the account of co-ordinal utility presented by K. J. Arrow in Arrow 1977. Arrow's concern is to discuss the so-called leximin theorem proved independently by Peter Hammond and Steven Strasnick in 1974 (Hammond 1976b; Strasnick 1976). I assume for simplicity that co-ordinal utility is consistent with a principle to maximise utility thus defined. For our purposes here, what is crucial is the conception of the good.

principle of justice in the corresponding well-ordered society is the principle to maximise co-ordinal utility.

I now sketch how in this well-ordered society citizens may be thought of as making the interpersonal comparisons required for questions of justice. Following Arrow, we imagine that citizens' judgements can be represented as follows. We assume that everything that might plausibly affect someone's overall satisfaction is represented by a vector v. Split this vector into two component vectors, x and y. The vector y includes entries for all features of the person that might affect interpersonal comparisons: natural endowments and abilities, capacities to make various discriminations and realised skills, along with final ends, desires and preferences, and all other elements that affect our good. (We must exclude, however, those aspects of persons which specify their sense of right and justice and their moral feelings generally, since in a utilitarian doctrine the good is prior to and independent of the right, which is defined as maximising the good.[17]) The vector x is a list of things which describes a person's circumstances and includes not only goods, real property and tangible assets of all kinds, but also the social aspects of someone's situation, for example a person's rights, liberties and opportunities. In general, goods and social features are transferable or interchangeable, whereas abilities and endowments, desires and attitudes, and so on, are not; but nothing depends on this distinction being always clear or sharp. The idea is that the entries in the vector y characterise the person: these bases of comparison can be changed or altered over time but not in the usual sense transferred or interchanged. With this rough division between the two kinds of bases of comparison, we assume that there is a function which matches all citizens' judgements in making interpersonal comparisons, and written as follows:

$$w = u(x,y)$$

where the x,y have the indicated sense. We can think of u as a utility function and w as well-being in the broad sense of overall satisfaction, taking into account the person's total situation.[18]

[17] I believe that this exclusion accords with Arrow's intentions. See his account in a longer version of Arrow 1977 (Arrow 1978a, section 2).

[18] Arrow remarks that a similar notion to the one I have followed in this paragraph is found in Suppes (1966), and in S. C. Kolm (1972). I believe, however, that the notion Suppes uses is not the same as the one Arrow presents in two crucial respects: first, Suppes expressly excludes personal attributes from the domain of the function u (p. 295); second, he recognises the difficulty of developing an account of justice founded solely on preferences. He says: 'I think it may be rightly objected that the intuitive success of the theory depends upon these individual preference rankings themselves satisfying certain criteria of justice. To admit this objection is not to accede to a charge of circularity, for moral principles of justice, logically independent of the theory developed here, can be consistently introduced

Following Arrow's suggestion, let us suppose that citizens could make these judgements by an extension of sympathetic identification.[19] We can certainly, in a limited way at least, imagine ourselves in another person's situation and answer the question whether it is better (in our judgement) to be ourselves in our situation than to be the other in that person's situation. Thus, if we are wealthy and others impoverished, it seems easy to reach the judgement that it is better for one of the poor to receive the marginal dollar than one of us. Any entry in the vectors x,y may affect the value w of u. Thus the function u, which matches citizens' judgements, extends (or generalises) the notion of sympathetic identification so that it covers all relevant aspects of a person's total situation. (Of course, the fact that u applies to each citizen and fits everyone's judgements does not mean that all have the same well-being, since citizens have different features y, and hold different goods x.)

We can visualise the generalisation of sympathetic identification in the following way.[20] We suppose that the choices persons and associations make are determined by two elements: their preference ordering and the alternatives available (the feasible set). Preference orderings are thought to belong to the agent in question and to be given in advance, and hence to be relatively stable from one choice situation to another. Thus a preference ordering specifies choices over indefinitely many possible situations, most of which may be purely hypothetical. The feasible set simply defines on any given occasion which alternatives are on hand. Thus, those who are sick, or relatively less wealthy, or less educated than others, may be said to prefer being healthy, or more wealthy, or better educated, even when there is no prospect of their being so. They may have illnesses with no known means of cure, or be situated so that their becoming more wealthy or better educated is out of the question. We also often know what we would prefer if some of our final ends and needs were different, and certain among our endowments and abilities were altered in various ways. The function u generalises the idea involved in these judgements; it covers all possible choices, even those that comprehend at once all features of a person's situation which may affect satisfaction.

as constraints on individual preference rankings' (pp. 303–4). Both of these points accord with the account I have given of primary goods and the priority of justice, and, as we shall see, sharply distinguish Suppes's presentation of interpersonal comparisons from Arrow's. On the other hand, Kolm's view is analogous to the one Arrow discusses. To see the resemblance, refer to the quotation from Kolm and think of the vector y as representing the fact that we have put into the object of preferences those things about persons that appear to cause a difference in their preferences. By this formal manoeuver, we have removed, or withdrawn, these things from the parameters that determine the structure of preferences. If we carry this process to the limit, we get, as Kolm says, a theory of human nature.

[19] Here I follow Arrow's account in Arrow 1963, pp. 114–15.
[20] Here I somewhat elaborate Arrow's remarks in Arrow 1977, p. 222.

Now, as I have said, in any well-ordered society there is a shared understanding among citizens as to what is publicly advantageous in questions of justice, and hence an understanding of what is to be counted as making citizens better off when these questions are at issue. Characteristic of utilitarianism is the conception of the good as satisfaction of desire or preferences. The function u, then, as this conception of the good requires, is fully comprehensive: it takes into account everything that may affect someone's well-being, and thus it represents a person's good. It is not restricted to a limited list of objective features of citizens' circumstances, as exemplified by primary goods.[21]

But if the function u is to represent interpersonal comparisons of citizens in a well-ordered society in which the public principle of justice is to maximise co-ordinal utility (as defined by u), the function must match each citizen's judgements as to what is publicly advantageous. This means that u must satisfy two conditions: first, each citizen can rank all possible vectors with components x,y and all these rankings agree. Second, for any two persons, if person 1 with goods x_1 and features y_1 has a higher index w than person 2 with goods x_2 and features y_2 (that is, if $u(x_1,y_1) > u(x_2,y_2)$), then *all* citizens, including persons 1 and 2, regard the overall situation of the first person as more advantageous than the overall situation of the second. Everyone shares a common notion of the advantageous as applied to a person's *overall* situation, since the component vectors x,y cover everything that is taken to affect well-being. Thus for fixed y, all citizens try to maximise u by varying x; and, for fixed x, all try to maximise u by varying y (that is, by changing their desires, realised abilities, traits of character, and so, to the extent that this is possible). In the above comparison between persons 1 and 2, everyone (including 1 and 2) would rather be in 1's overall situation than 2's; and in this sense each would rather be person 1 complete with 1's final ends and traits of character.

In view of these two features of the function u, I shall call it, modifying Kolm's term, a 'shared highest-order preference function'. It matches what

---

[21] To clarify this contrast, we can write the function which represents interpersonal comparisons in questions of justice made by citizens in the well-ordered society of justice as fairness as: $g = f(x_i, \bar{p})$. Here g is the index of primary goods (a real number), f is the function that determines the value of g for individual i, and x_i is the vector of primary goods held or enjoyed by individual i. The vector y, which in $w = u(x,y)$ includes entries for all features of the person which may affect satisfaction, is here replaced by a constant vector $\bar{p}$ which has entries only for the characteristics of free and equal moral persons presumed to be fully cooperating members of society over a complete life. This vector is constant since all citizens are taken to possess these features to the minimum sufficient degree. Thus the same function holds for all citizens and interpersonal comparisons are made accordingly. The difference between the functions f and u expresses the fact that in justice as fairness individuals' different final ends and desires, and their greater or less capacities for satisfaction, play no role in determining the justice of the basic structure. They do not enter into $\bar{p}$.

is, in effect, a highest-order preference common to all citizens on the basis of which they think it rational for them to adjust and revise their final ends and desires, and to modify their traits of character and to reshape their realised abilities, so as to achieve a total personal situation ranked higher in the ordering defined by u. In this well-ordered society, what makes interpersonal comparisons possible in questions of justice, as well as public understanding of what is advantageous, is the shared highest-order preference represented by the function u. It is this shared highest-ordered preference which sustains the social unity of a well-ordered society governed by the principle of co-ordinal utility. Citizens agree on the one rational good and in turn believe it is right and just for society to advance this good as far as possible.

VII

The notion of a shared highest-order preference function is plainly incompatible with the conception of a well-ordered society in justice as fairness. For in the circumstances of justice citizens' conceptions of the good are not only said to be opposed but to be incommensurable. These conceptions are incommensurable because persons are regarded as moved not only by the two highest-order interests in developing and exercising their moral powers, but also by a determinate conception of the good, that is, a conception defined by certain definite final ends and aspirations, and by particular attachments and loyalties, and the like. Citizens must assess the overall situations of others and different ways of life from their *own* standpoint, as defined by the content of the final ends and particular loyalties, of their own conception of the good. In the well-ordered society of justice as fairness, therefore, a shared highest-order preference on the basis of which shared evaluation of persons' overall situations can be made does not exist. Thus, imagine a society divided into two parts, the members of which affirm different and opposing ways of life. In order to avoid complications I assume that these ways of life are compatible with the principles of justice, and hence can be advanced without violating these principles.[22] One part of society affirms certain aesthetic values and attitudes of contemplation toward nature, together with the virtues of gentleness and the beneficient stewardship of natural things. The other group affirms the values of self-discipline and enjoys the risks and excitement of adventure achieved in competition and rivalry with others. I assume that those in one group appear to regard the way of life of the other with distaste and aversion, if not contempt. These conceptions of the good are

---

[22] These complications are not by any means trivial but I cannot discuss them here. For what I have in mind, see *TJ*, pp. 30–2, 449–51.

incommensurable because their final ends and aspirations are so diverse, their specific content so different, that no common basis for judgement can be found. There is not, as in a well-ordered utilitarian society, a shared highest-order preference function in the light of which everyone's total situation can be ordered. Thus, in the imagined society, social unity is secured by an allegiance to certain public principles of justice, if indeed it can be secured at all. Social unity has a more or less firm foundation depending upon how far the conceptions of the good which actually exist cohere with and lend support to the public conception of justice. However, this last point leads to the important question of the stability of a conception of justice which I cannot pursue here. Instead, I shall comment further on the notion of a shared highest-order preference function.

Arrow, whose formulation I have used to express this notion, believes it to have unsettling implications. He writes:[23]

reducing the individual to a specified list of qualities [the entries falling under y] is denying his individuality in a deep sense. In a way that I cannot articulate well and am none too sure about defending, the autonomy of individuals, an element of incommensurability among people, seems denied by the possibility of interpersonal comparisons. No doubt it is some such feeling as this that has made me so reluctant to shift from pure ordinalism, despite my desire to seek a basis for a theory of justice.

While I agree that it is somehow erroneous to reduce the individual to a list of qualities, the grounds for dismay seem clearer if we note certain features of persons as members of a utilitarian well-ordered society. Thus, first, the notion of a shared highest-order preference implies that such persons have no determinate conception of the good to which they are committed, but regard the various desires and capacities of the self as features to be adjusted in the quest for the highest possible place in the *public* ranking defined by the function *u*. Thus it is natural for Arrow to say that the *individuality* of persons is denied. All their conceptions of the good are publicly commensurable via a shared highest-order preference as to what is desirable; and so in this important respect the distinctiveness of persons is lost. Neither persons nor associations have arrived at or fashioned a conception of the good and of how to lead a life which is peculiarly theirs.[24]

This loss of individuality suggests that the notion of a shared highest-order preference defines persons as what we may call 'bare persons'.[25]

---

[23] Arrow 1977, pp. 222–3.
[24] The importance of this is stressed by Mill in *On Liberty* (Mill 1974), especially in Chapter III (paras 3–6).
[25] This name was suggested to me by John Bennett.

Such persons are ready to consider any new convictions and aims, and even to abandon attachments and loyalties, when doing this promises a life with greater overall satisfaction, or well-being, as specified by a public ranking. The notion of a bare person implicit in the notion of shared highest-order preference represents the dissolution of the person as leading a life expressive of character and of devotion to specific final ends and adopted (or affirmed) values which define the distinctive points of view associated with different (and incommensurable) conceptions of the good. I believe that this conception of the person is psychologically intelligible only if one accepts, as Sidgwick did, a hedonist account of the good as the basis of an account of the rational judgements of individuals. Given the hedonistic picture of how such judgements might be formed, we can at least describe in words how rational persons are to proceed when they generalise the procedure of sympathetic identification in order to make the necessary interpersonal comparisons. Thus, they are to ask themselves: which total situation would yield the greatest net balance of satisfaction understood as some recognisable agreeable feeling. I shall not pursue these matters here, since the notion of shared highest-order preference and of a bare person suffice to illustrate the contrast between utilitarianism and justice as fairness.[26]

In his remarks Arrow appears not to distinguish between the loss of autonomy of individuals and the loss of their individuality. Individuality is indeed one sense of autonomy. But in a Kantian view autonomy has a further sense as part of the conception of persons as free and equal moral persons. In justice as fairness this notion is represented in the original position and therefore this notion is used in accounting for the content of the principles of justice and in explaining how these principles can be justified to citizens of a well-ordered society in which this conception of the person is affirmed. Co-ordinal utilitarianism (and utilitarianism generally) starts by regarding persons in terms of their capacities for satisfaction. It then interprets the problem of justice as how to allocate the means of satisfaction so as to produce the greatest sum of well-being. This notion fits nicely with the deep-rooted view of economic theory which sees it as the study of how to allocate scarce resources for the most efficient advancement of given ends. Of course, all this is familiar. What is less obvious is that in such a doctrine the notion of autonomy in the sense involved in the conception of free and equal moral persons has no part in the derivation of the content of the utilitarian principle of justice. One reason for formulating the conception of the original position in justice as fairness is to model the role of the conception of

---

[26] In *TJ*, §§83–84 I have tried to indicate how hedonism arises from the idea of a completely general first-person procedure of rational choice.

persons as free and equal in determining the principles of justice as visibly as possible.[27]

We may view the subjective nature of the utilitarian conception of the good as a way of adapting the notion of the one rational good to the institutional requirements of a modern secular and pluralistic democratic society. The citizens of such a society pursue many different and opposed final ends, and the constitutional liberties protect the existence of diverse ways of life. The utilitarian might argue, therefore, that the public conception of the one rational good to be advanced by basic institutions cannot be understood as a *determinate* conception with definite ends and aspirations. For example, if the one good were perfectionist, so that society arranged its basic institutions in order best to advance a public interpretation of the values of truth, beauty and human excellence, there is no reason to expect these institutions to be democratic. This is even more obvious when the one good is a conception of religious salvation. In a democratic society, then, the one good must be conceived as subjective, as the satisfaction of desire or preferences.

Now suppose that democratic political and social institutions are believed to maximise this subjective good under existing social conditions; and suppose also that these conditions are believed to be more or less stable and unlikely to change much in the near future. Then it might seem that the principle to maximise this subjective conception of the one rational good is a suitable principle of justice for a democratic society. A Kantian view cannot accept this adaptation of the one rational good for reasons evident from what has already been said. First, the subjective view of the one rational good rests on the notion of a bare person; and thus the self is not regarded as having any antecedent moral structure in accordance with a conception of the person as part of a conception of justice. Second, since utilitarianism starts from an independent and prior conception of the good, no restrictions founded on right and justice are imposed on the ends through which satisfaction is to be achieved. All restrictions on ends arise only from what is necessary in the design of institutions if they are to realise the greatest good under given circumstances. But it is easy enough to describe realistic social situations in which the pattern of a people's desire and preferences are such that the greatest satisfaction would not be achieved by securing the basic equal liberties. Hence these liberties are most secure when the possibility is recognised of many determinate conceptions of the good each constrained by the principles of justice. We do best to start from a notion of social unity which rests on a public conception of justice if we want to establish

[27] For a further discussion of the role of the notion of autonomy in justice as fairness, see Rawls 1980, the first lecture entitled 'Rational and Full Autonomy', especially pp. 522–33.

a firm foundation for democratic institutions. Of course, neither of these considerations shows that utilitarianism is false or incoherent; they only trace out the consequences of this view. I should also add that the idea (in justice as fairness) of many admissible conceptions of the good does not imply scepticism in assessing these conceptions from the standpoint of persons in society. For they can be assessed by rational principles given someone's interests, abilities and situation, and persons (and those who advise them) regard some ways of life more worthy of pursuit than others even though these evaluations have no effect on citizens' claims to basic liberties and other primary goods.

VIII

I have tried to show how the problem of interpersonal comparisons connects with the basic notions of a conception of justice by contrasting the notion of primary goods in justice as fairness with the notion of a shared highest-order preference function in co-ordinal utilitarianism. This contrast brings out the different philosophical backgrounds of these two ways of making interpersonal comparisons, and explains how they are related to different conceptions of the person and of social unity. Since justice as fairness accepts the liberal presupposition of many different and irreconcilable conceptions of the good, it takes a shared conception of justice as the starting point. The public recognition of this conception secures the ties of social unity rather than a public recognition of one rational good. With this starting point, the priority of the equal basic liberties allows for the normal condition of a democratic society, namely, the affirmation by its citizens of a plurality of distinct conceptions of the good. Guided by the conception of justice, together with its conception of the person and of social cooperation, we select a practical and limited list of things (the primary goods) which free and equal moral persons, who are to engage in social cooperation over a complete life, can accept as what they in general need as citizens in a just society. This list provides a basis for interpersonal comparisons compatible with autonomy. It also allows for individuality in the form of a plurality of conceptions of the good (within the limits of justice) between which citizens are at liberty to choose.

In justice as fairness the members of society are conceived in the first instance as moral persons who can cooperate together for mutual advantage, and not simply as rational individuals who have aims and desires they seek to satisfy. The notion of cooperation has, as I have said, two elements: a notion of fair terms of cooperation which all participants may reasonably be expected to accept, and a notion of each participant's rational advantage, or good. When the notion of cooperation, which is distinct from the notion of socially coordinated activity for certain ends, is applied to the basic structure of society, it is natural to take the two moral powers as the essential features of human beings. We then say that the two highest-order interests are the two main forms of moral motivation for the purposes of developing the content of the first principles of justice. Thus citizens in the well-ordered society of justice as fairness have both the capacity and the regulative desire to cooperate on fair terms with others for reciprocal advantage over a complete life. This in turn implies the desire on the part of individuals and groups to advance their good in ways which can be explained and justified by reasons which all can and do accept as free and equal moral persons. The public recognition of these principles is consistent with everyone's status as such as person, whatever one's social position.

This emphasis on the notion of cooperation brings out that, in the overall moral conception to which justice as fairness belongs, the conceptions of justice and of the good have distinct though complementary roles. Justice is prior to the good in the sense that it limits the admissible conceptions of the good, so that those conceptions the pursuit of which violate the principles of justice are ruled out absolutely: the claims to pursue inadmissible conceptions have no weight at all. On the other hand, just institutions would have no point unless citizens had conceptions of the good they strove to realise and these conceptions defined ways of life fully worthy of human endeavour. Hence a conception of justice must allow sufficient scope for admissible conceptions to meet this requirement. The moral conception as a whole is most likely to be stable if, among the admissible conceptions of the good, those which gain the widest support are ones which cohere with and sustain the conception of justice, for example by a certain compatibility between the ends and values of the prevalent conceptions of the good and the virtues required by justice. These brief remarks set out some of the differences from the utilitarian view, which takes the (subjective) good as the independent and prior notion and the right is defined as maximising this good and therefore as subordinate to it.

To an economist concerned with social justice and public policy an index of primary goods may seem merely *ad hoc* patchwork not amenable to theory. It is for this reason that I have tried to explain the philosophical background of such an index. For the economist's reaction is partly right: an index of primary goods does not belong to theory in the economist's sense. It belongs instead to a conception of justice which falls under the liberal alternative to the tradition of the one rational good. Thus the problem is not how to specify an accurate measure of some psychological or other attribute available only to science. Rather, it is a moral and practical problem. The use of primary goods is not a makeshift which better theory can replace, but a reasonable social practice which we try to design so as to achieve the workable agreement required for effective and willing social cooperation among citizens whose understanding of social unity rests on a conception of justice. Economic theory is plainly indispensable in determining the more definite features of the practice of making interpersonal comparisons in the circumstances of a particular society. What is essential is to understand the problem against the appropriate philosophical background.

9 On some difficulties of the utilitarian economist

FRANK HAHN

0 Introduction

The economic theory of public policy is relentlessly utilitarian: policies are ranked by their utility consequences. In the context of that theory, I want to discuss three matters: (a) is it reasonable to insist that the utilities of agents depend only on the consequences of public actions? (b) how are we to evaluate actions designed to change the utility function of agents? and (c) how are we to treat the fact that the consequences of actions are uncertain? This of course leaves a good many other questions which it would be interesting to discuss.

Before I consider these problems, a general point seems worth making. The utilitarian stance of Welfare Economics has proved very powerful in the following sense: it has given precise arguments why one policy under precisely stated conditions was to be preferred to all others available. In this way, it has made discussion of policy possible. Even to a non-utilitarian, these Welfare Economics arguments will be relevant and important. But it is difficult to see how they could be decisive. This is so for at least two reasons. The utilitarian requires a cardinalisation of the utility functions of agents and interpersonal comparability of utilities. This cardinalisation cannot be derived from the preferences of agents over social states unless the agents are essentially alike[1] and also utilitarians. Moreover, no one has ever attempted to derive such a cardinalisation in practice. Hence different utilitarians with different cardinalisations can come to different policy conclusions. The disagreement between them will turn on their social preferences and it is not clear that it is resolvable. The contribution of Welfare Economics will have been to lay bare what the disagreement is really about.

The second reason why the Welfare Economics conclusions may not be decisive is simpler: reasonable and serious persons may not be utilitarians. I can argue that the utilities of individuals are relevant to my social choice without considering them to be decisive. For instance I may, like Rawls,

---

[1] See the contribution of J. Mirrlees (Chapter 3, above).

have a lexicographic ordering of social states in which liberty ranks first and utilities second. This may be too extreme and the utilitarian may be able to persuade me of this: 'are you willing to trade any amount of human misery for a little extra liberty?' But I can certainly argue as follows. A social state for me is not fully described if I am only given the utilities of agents in that state. I also need to know the liberty enjoyed by them. It follows that my ranking of social states which differ in the amount of liberty cannot be of the form of the social welfare function whose arguments are only the utilities of individuals. If the utilitarian asks why I should care about liberty over and above what is already recorded in the utility functions I can answer that, for me, liberty is an intrinsic good just as for him utilities are intrinsic goods.

The general point then is this: it seems plain that utility consequences of social actions are highly relevant to the evaluation of such actions. But there is, in general, no unique way in which these consequences can be aggregated and even if there were such a unique way, it seems simply wrong to assert that these consequences are the only relevant criteria for evaluating social actions.

1 Policies and consequences

The domain of the utility function of the individual is of considerable importance to the utilitarian exercise. For instance it matters whether I care only about goods allocated to myself or about the allocation of goods to everyone. If for instance we are all envious, then the utilitarian calculus had better record it.[2] This is well understood. But there is a subtler difficulty with the domain which is rarely mentioned and never considered by the welfare economist: my utility may not only depend on what I (or others) get but on the manner in which I get it. That is my utility may not only depend on the consequences of policy but on the policy itself.

Suppose I chose to work eight hours a day for five days a week at the current wage and at the current prices of goods. Suppose next that I wake up one morning and find that the government has passed a law forcing me to work at my existing job at the existing wage for five days a week. Prices are still the same. All that has happened is that I am now by law obliged to do what I had freely chosen to do before. Nonetheless, I claim that it is reasonable for me to feel a great deal worse off than I did before the law was passed.

---

[2] Martin Hollis has suggested to me that the utilitarian might wish to count only the utilities of 'normal' or 'reasonable' people. But this, on reflection, seems to open a pandora's box. Children and madmen are easy, but what about smokers? In my case envy is neither abnormal nor unreasonable.

An obvious reason for this might be that I consider that circumstances and my tastes may change and that I will now be bound by the extra legal constraint. This, however, would already be fully accounted for in the utilitarian reckoning of consequences. For the utilitarian would be interested in my expected utility. So let us suppose that I know that my circumstances and tastes will not change. Nonetheless the situation – the social state – has changed. What I chose I am now ordered to do. I may reasonably object to being ordered to work at a particular job, even though I would freely have chosen to work there anyway, because I object to, get disutility from, the fact of being ordered in my work choice at all. The knowledge that, if my utility function were different from what in fact it is I would be constrained by that order, may make me consider the order as unjust.

Or consider a dangerous military mission. In one situation five men volunteer. In another the same five men are ordered to undertake it. It seems to me plausible to suppose that the utility consequences to the five men are different in the two situations.

Or lastly, suppose that I give a certain amount to a particular charity. The government decides to tax me to that amount and gives it to the same charity. Am I indifferent between these two situations? Before the tax, I had the possibility of acting otherwise than I did even though I chose not to, after the tax the possibility is gone. But even if one attaches no probability of wishing to avail oneself of a possibility, its loss by restricting one's potential freedom may be felt as a loss of utility.

Let us be a little more precise. Let P be a public policy and let $C_i(P)$ be the allocation of goods to agent i under this policy. Amongst 'goods' include leisure. The welfare economist now writes i's utility function as $U_i(C_i(P))$ or, more rarely, as $U_i(C_1(P)) \ldots C_i(P) \ldots C_n(P))$ when there are n agents. Hence P affects utilities only via its consumption consequences. My examples suggest that we should plausibly write the utility function as $U_i(P,C_i(P))$ or as $U_i(P,C_1(P) \ldots C_n(P))$. In other words the domain of the utility function is the Cartesian product of the goods and policy spaces.

This proposal does not depart from the consequentialism of utilitarianism. We are still only interested in the utility consequences of policies. But the policies themselves, separately from their consequences for the allocation of goods, are carriers of utility (or disutility). The proposal is not the same as one which would count amongst the consequences of an action the action itself – consequences of an action are utilities. Nor is it a proposal to ascribe intrinsic value to actions. Since no-one can hold that the rightness of an action is quite independent of its consequences, the person who holds actions as intrinsically valuable would have a welfare function (moral choice function) of the form $W(a, U_1 \ldots U_n)$ where a stands for action and

U_i for utility of the ith agent. He would thus, contrary to the utilitarian, be willing to trade utilities against 'rightness' of action. However, all that I have proposed is a traditional welfare function $W(U_1 \dots U_n)$ where, however, each U_i depends on the action taken.

The validity of my argument depends on the facts. If, as I believe, the facts support it, then the consequences to the utilitarian welfare economists are fairly serious. Suppose, for instance, that people dislike divulging their income to tax officials. They consider it a violation to their rights to privacy. Having to divulge is a source of disutility (quite separate from that occasioned by having to fill in forms). Then some very old welfare arguments about optimal taxation are at risk. Indeed, once one allows policies into the domain of preferences, almost any welfare proposition proposed by economists may fail to stand up.

In all of this, the welfare economist and indeed many utilitarians seem to have been excessively narrow when thinking of the domain of preferences. They may well be correct in resisting an argument which, for instance, suggests a trade off between the integrity of an action and utilities. But they may be wrong in ignoring the integrity of an action as a source of utility. The condemned men in Bernard Williams' example (1973) may prefer to die rather than have one of their number chosen for death at random. They may not only value their lives but the circumstances which let them live. In the same way, one may derive utility from rights. As I have already argued, I may value the right to property even if I give all of it away to socially approved causes. Just so, a slave may value the right to liberty even though when freed he will in the circumstances find it optimal to live in the material conditions of his slavery. Indeed introspection suggests that violation of what one considers one's right is a rather potent source of disutility – indeed more so than quite large reductions in one's income.

The utilitarian has no business in prescribing the domain of preferences. Welfare economists, for good reasons, have always, however, taken this domain as very narrow: essentially the commodity space. The good reason is tractability. But this may well mean that their prescriptions are not, on a utilitarian valuation, optimal.

2 Changing preferences

It seems clear that we have preferences over preferences. This for instance is shown when we say that A has a better character than B. It also seems clear that social and economic conditions and policies can affect preferences. It is true that we know rather little about this process in practice. But, for the sake of this argument, let us suppose that it is well understood. Then policies have consequences which include their effects on preferences. How then does a utilitarian proceed in choosing policies? How does a utilitarian deal with preferences over preferences?

Let us note straightaway that the manner in which policy becomes an argument of an agent's utility function is now quite different from that of the previous section. There the agent had preferences over policies. Here the argument indicates that preferences over outcomes may be affected by policy. Thus suppose e is the amount spent on the education of a given agent, b the number of books bought by him, and c his consumption of other things. Write the utility function of this agent as $U(e,b,c)$. The entry of e need not denote a direct valuation of education but rather that for different values of e his preference between b and c is different. Of course education may be valued directly as well.

As another example, take the optimum distribution of income. The traditional, utilitarian argument goes as follows. One compares the sum total of utilities for different distributions assuming that utilities depend on income, effort and ability. The optimum distribution of income maximises this sum subject to the constraints (a) that one cannot distribute more than is produced and (b) the information needed for the policy is included in the information available to the maximiser. On the other hand there are many, e.g. Marxists, who consider that the distribution of income and wealth can have profound effects on preferences. For instance with greater equality commodities may come to be valued less relative to the quality of one's work. This may be incorrect but the utilitarian economist should have a way of proceeding if it is not.

But we must make sure that we are considering a genuine change in preferences and here the domain of preferences is again important. For instance it may well be that this domain includes one's relative position in the income distribution. When that position changes, one's willingness to forgo goods for working more conscientiously may also change but that can occur without a change in preference. The latter involves a change in the ranking of at least some elements of the domain. For instance in this case if propaganda, say of a religious kind by claiming that God had fore-ordained the given inequality, changes preferences between goods and conscientious work at the same income distribution, then a change in preferences is involved. In any case much that looks like a preference change may not be one. But preferences can be changed and I am concerned with that.

The natural way for the utilitarian to proceed in these cases is to invoke preferences over preferences, or if one likes, preferences over alternative selves. Behind and beyond the ordinary utility function there lurks a super-utility function. I may choose to be hypnotised to change my taste for cigarettes, I may vote socialist because I believe that under socialism I would be less greedy, I may expose myself to religious propaganda to make me more satisfied with my lot. In all of these cases, I prefer to be someone else and I need instruments to effect the transformation. In any event, I may have a ranking over these alternative selves and the ranking may admit of a numerical representation – a super-utility function. (However, note that I can only be one of these alternative selves at a time.) The utilitarian can now carry out his utilitarian arithmetic with these super-utility functions. In doing so, he will have to take account of the manner in which any policy is instrumental in picking one of the alternative selves for each agent. For instance, take education expenditure. To increase it, say, reduces what is available for consumption. Suppose education is not intrinsically valued by anyone. However, a number of agents can now attain a utility function of the educated, which they prefer. A perfectly straightforward calculation now emerges involving the loss in super-utilities from less consumption and the gain in super-utilities from achieving a preferred identity. The utilitarian seems to be home and dry.

But this is an illusion. Certainly the proposed route has the obvious flaw that one may be wrong in the evaluation of alternative selves – if I have always been aggressive I may not really know what it is like to be meek – if I learn to read I cannot be certain what it will do to my preferences between watching T.V. and reading. However, these arguments are taken up in the next section in a different context and for the moment I am ready to assume that there are no mistakes. The objection that I have to the utilitarian's method of changing preferences, as I have sketched it, is that he has substituted one unchanging preference for a changing one and that it is not at all obvious that that can be done. But even if it can be done it can only be the case contingently – the move could be empirically impossible. If so the utilitarian would have to proceed differently than I have suggested.

The point is quite simple: Why should preferences over preferences be immune to change through policies? In one society one might prefer the preferences of a soldier (fighting over sitting at home) to those of a scholar. In another it might be the other way round. It is not extravagant to suppose that institutions have some influence over our preferences over types. There seems no compelling reason to suppose that there is a 'real' and ultimate preference system over a large enough domain which is immutable under economic (and social) change. I do not wish to imply that an individual's preferences can be molded by policy in any old way. This is much more than the argument requires. All that is needed is that policy should have some effect on preferences including that over preferences.

Of course the notion of having preferences over alternative selves in the way in which I have used it is not straightforward either. If I would prefer to prefer one apple to two cigarettes to the other way round, then why do I not do so? In fact do I not straightforwardly prefer one apple to two cigarettes? One answer, deriving from weakness of will, is that in my actions I behave as if I had the less preferred preferences. Moreover, were I to act according to the preferred preferences I would, as I now am, feel less satisfaction. There does not seem to be a contradiction in this claim. 'Oh God make me chaste, but not yet.' Nonetheless there are some difficulties here recently studied in an interesting book by Elster (1979) and I leave the matter there.

Now it does not follow from the above argument that the utilitarian welfare economist is in insuperable difficulties in every application of his craft. As an example consider the case studied by Dixit and Norman (1978). Let there be two goods one of which is advertised and monopolised while the other is not. Let $U(a,x,y)$ be a utility function, the same for all agents where a denotes the amount of advertising, x the quantity of the advertised (and monopolised) good consumed and y the amount of the unadvertised (competitive) good consumed. Notice again that the fact that a is an argument of U does not denote that advertising is intrinsically valued but rather that preferences depend on the amount of advertising. Assume that there are n identical consumers who chose (x,y) in their budget to maximise their utility. Now suppose that without any regulation by the government the profit maximising monopolist would choose an advertising level of a^* and that the price of the monopolised good in terms of the non-monopolised one would be p^*. Since demand depends on (p^*,a^*) we can work out the total utility of households at the preferences induced by a^*. Let the government order a (small) reduction in advertising to $a < a^*$. The price will now change to p and we can once again work out the total utility of households but now at the a-induced preferences.

What Dixit and Norman show is that whether we take a^*-induced preferences or a-induced preferences the total utility achieved at (p,a) exceeds that achieved at (p^*,a^*). In that sense then an unregulated economy spends too much on advertising. That is households with a^*-induced preferences *and* households with a-induced preferences are better off when they can consume the bundle provided at (p,a) than when they consume that provided at (p^*,a^*). On the other hand it should be noticed that there is here a careful avoidance of a comparison of the a-induced welfare function with the a^*-induced welfare function. That is, there is no comparison of welfare between households with a^*-induced preferences and households with a-induced preferences.

Even so, for a very wide class of cases, the Dixit trick will not work: we will get different answers when we use preferences induced by the change of policy, from those that we get when we use unchanged preferences.

For instance, it is pretty clear that this will be so in the case of changes in preferences induced by income redistribution. In general then the utilitarian will need a ranking of preferences.

So one comes back to postulating a large enough domain and preferences over that domain which are immutable. In much of the recent literature, this is done by an appeal to the initial pre-social position where individuals have to consider all the preferences which they might have and all the social arrangements which there might be. As a *Gedankenexperiment* this procedure has something to recommend it. But only if it can be performed by at least the thoughtful and the intelligent. Also conclusions here are not to be had without the aid of some non-obvious axioms (see Hammond 1976b). In any case the notion of a pre-social preference system (over a domain which includes preferences) is not uncontroversial nor even perhaps meaningful.

But, for my present purposes, I need not attempt to make a case for or against this move. It suffices to note that the utilitarian welfare economist has no chance whatsoever of discovering what these pre-social preferences are, let alone of scaling them. If for instance he is asked how many resources it would be good to invest in creating 'educated tastes' he will have to consult his own perferences over preferences and scale accordingly. For we would not be surprised to find that the preference for educated tastes are different for the educated and the uneducated. This would simply confirm that here the preference over preferences is not independent of this policy (the investment in education). Any claim that one could dig down to primeval, pre-social preferences here is pure cant. On the other hand, the welfare economists' procedure should not be dismissed. By his habits of precision and by his formulation of an explicit welfare function, he makes argument possible.

I have not yet mentioned the technical device which is sometimes available to sidestep problems of changing tastes. Suppose we replace the utility function $U(e,b,c)$ (p. 191, above), by $V(eb,c)$. The meaning would be this. Agents have essentially the same utility function and the consequence of more education is simply to make books more efficient generators of utility. It is as if the educated man with one book is as 'well off' as the uneducated is with ten. An education policy will thus not be essentially different from a policy which provides more of any good: it simply provides books more effectively or more books in efficiency units. In particular, in these units, preferences are not affected by the policy. By a simple re-definition we have converted what looks like a difference in preferences between the educated and the less educated into a difference in quantities of a good.

Of course the example is far-fetched. There is also a plausible argument that, for a certain range at least, we should write $V(b/e,c)$ on the grounds that more education requires more books to leave one as satisfied as before. (This might prove awkward for the education minded utilitarian.) Nonetheless, there are situations where this technical trick is appropriate. They are all cases where policy leaves preferences essentially unchanged. But not all policies do that.

3 Uncertain consequences

If the consequences of actions are uncertain then so are their utility consequences. On certain assumptions, an agent's preference over uncertain outcomes of actions can be represented by his expected utility of these outcomes. Thus suppose there are two outcomes of a given action which are possible and that the agent has probability λ that the outcome will be x and probability $(1 - \lambda)$ that it will be y. Then the utility of this lottery is $\lambda U(x) + (1 - \lambda)U(y)$. The probability λ is a numerical representation of the agent's beliefs which themselves depend on his past experience. This representation can, under particular axioms, be jointly derived from preferences and beliefs (Savage 1954). For sense the utility function must be cardinal: i.e. invariant under transformation of scale and origin. However, for utilitarian purposes when we want to compare expected utilities we cannot just take the route proposed by Von Neumann and Morgenstern (1944), by which cardinalisation is achieved from the agents' preferences over lotteries. As usual, we shall need to find a cardinalisation suitable for interpersonal comparisons of utility.

Assuming this has been done the utilitarian may now rank outcomes by the expected utilities of agents – perhaps by their sum. In doing so, we must recall that the probabilities of agents for the same event may differ. This may be due to differences in information and in practice also to differences in abilities to learn from information. This way of ranking outcomes is often called the *ex ante* social welfare function.

But there plausibly is an alternative *ex post* ranking possible. For instance we may take the sum of utilities in each state, multiply it by the 'social probability' of this state and add over states. The beliefs of the agents may not be given any weight in this ranking.

An interesting technical question is under what conditions these two rankings are equivalent. An account of this is given in a fine paper by Hammond (1980) to which the interested reader is referred. What emerges is that the attempt to make these two criteria consistent can lead to somewhat implausible results. For instance the utilitarian's willingness to trade output (efficiency) for distributional improvements may depend on agents' attitudes to risk. But there is no reason why this willingness should depend on attitudes to risk. A full account requires more technicalities than would here be appropriate.

What weight should the utilitarian give to the beliefs of agents? In simple cases the answer seems simple: if an agent gives positive probability to an impossible event or if in certain cases his probability distribution diverges from a well established frequency or if he makes mistakes in probability calculus, e.g. in compounding, then perhaps we would be justified in ignoring his beliefs. Careful thought will convince one that even that is not obvious but let us assume it is correct. However, ignoring his beliefs is not an invitation to ignore his utility. If we are to take account of it, then we shall have to replace the 'faulty' probabilities of this agent by others. Which others? In the frequency case or in the case of mistaken calculations, this is not difficult. But if he is more simply wrong without there being any known right probability distribution it seems that the utilitarian welfare economist must simply replace the agent's with his own beliefs.

Now if each agent knew the probability distribution of every other, possibly better informed, agent and if he knew that these agents were expert at Bayesian inference then one can show that agents would have similar probability distributions. But the hypothesis of this result is far fetched and whatever arguments might be addressed in favour of essentially similar utility functions there do not seem any convincing ones in favour of essentially similar beliefs. Even the thoughtful agent would have to observe far more than he could observe, apart from being a good deal better at calculation than the best computer.

The question then is whether the utilitarian should not use his own beliefs in ranking outcomes even when the different beliefs of other agents are not straightforwardly mistaken. The expected utility of an agent is the presently (*ex ante*) calculated utility consequence. It may be quite different not only from the actual consequence (that is the nature of uncertainty), but also from what the utilitarian policy maker calculates the utility lottery to be. He cannot show that the agent's beliefs are mistaken but they are not his. It seems to me that there is a case that he should be interested in the utility consequences as he calculates them and that means that he would rank outcomes by an *ex post* welfare function using his own probabilities. For this calculation is his best estimate of the lottery of actual utility consequences and it is not immediately clear why he should use what for him is not the best estimate.

There are of course objections to this line of argument. To ignore the beliefs of agents means ignoring their expected utility over outcomes and thus one sort of utility consequence of policy. There may be an objection on the grounds that one cannot be confident in one's beliefs as represented by a subjective probability distribution although I think that this objection turns into difficulties with an axiomatic foundation of probability.

It may be that in some way the *ex post* route is judged to be authoritarian although it would not be straightforward to translate this objection into utilitarian terms. Lastly on the lines of my previous discussion one may hold that those whose beliefs are ignored in policy formulation thereby experience a direct utility loss.

Certainly these are real objections. In fact economists have mainly opted for the *ex ante* approach if for no other reason than that it preserves some fundamental results from the certainty case for the situation with uncertainty. But when there is not equivalence with the *ex post* approach it also leads to difficulties. For instance it would always be an improvement to induce people to be more optimistic even when optimism is not justified by the state of affairs. More importantly, in the economic context, the just allocation of goods between people in any realised state would depend on their beliefs concerning its occurrence before it came about. This has no immediate moral appeal. Indeed if this is recognised one may want to change one's policy after the event and that is only another way of saying that the two approaches may be inconsistent. Moreover, as I have already noted, the attempt to impose consistency leads to other difficulties and restricts the class of social welfare functions rather arbitrarily: e.g. to those that are linear in the expected utilities of agents.

There are thus objections to both approaches and there seems no generally acceptable way of making them equivalent. One must conclude that there is an essential ambiguity in the proposal to judge actions by their (uncertain) utility consequences.

The discussion so far has been concerned with the uncertainty of states. But in practice there is also another source of uncertainty, namely that the preferences and beliefs of other agents are at best imperfectly known to any one agent or to the policy maker. For instance in the *ex ante* approach the policy maker would have to calculate his expectation of the expected utilities of agents. There is here another source of potential disagreement between two utilitarian policy makers; one is the cardinalisation they adopt for known preferences, the other is now their beliefs over the beliefs and preferences of others. While this last disagreement might in principle be resolvable by the facts it cannot actually be so resolved. Utilitarians need not agree.

The ambiguity of consequentialism and the other difficulties which I have discussed we have to live with and I do not believe that they in themselves contribute an argument in favour of some other approach. For one cannot easily think of any moral calculations which completely disregard consequences so that when these are, for instance, uncertain similar problems would arise.[3] Rather what emerges is that utilitarianism does not lead to a unique ranking of actions partly because there seems no higher principle which can decide between the *ex post* and the *ex ante* approach and partly because the ranking of the actions will not be independent of the person doing the ranking.

[3] There are of course other objections to a consequentialist calculus which are held to arise even if there are no difficulties and ambiguities in reckoning consequences.

10 Utilitarianism, information and rights

PARTHA DASGUPTA

1 Distributive justice and individual rights

'Social justice,' writes Hayek, 'can be given a meaning only in a directed or "command" economy (such as an army) in which individuals are ordered what to do . . . Indeed . . . no free action of the individuals could produce results satisfying any principle of distributive justice' (Hayek 1976, p. 69). Such an unequivocal position is no doubt rare. But the claim that the demands of distributive justice conflict with individual rights – in particular, the right to decision-making – is one that has often been made.

An individual right (such as the right to be treated with the same respect and concern as anyone else) may be defended on the ground that it is an end in itself. Alternatively, it may be defended on the ground that it is *instrumental* in realising certain desirable ends (e.g. in arguing for the right to private property, because, under certain circumstances, it sustains an efficient allocation of resources). Admittedly, the distinction between these two types of defences is not always sharp. For example, even if a right is regarded as an end, the end may still require justification. Presumably, the justification will be based on the human interests it serves and promotes – for example, by an appeal to the Kantian notion of the autonomy of the individual, or from straightforward utilitarian considerations. In this paper I shall be concerned with *economic decentralisation*, and, therefore, with the right that individuals may be thought to possess to certain private regions of decision-making – an aspect of 'protected spheres', as Professor Hayek would call them. I shall ask whether the claims of distributive justice require a systematic violation of rights to individual decision-making, and I shall argue that they do not, that the exercise of rights to *certain* regions of decision-making is *instrumental* in promoting the attainment of distributive justice. The argument is founded on the observation that much information in any society is only privately known; indeed, that no single individual or decision-making unit can

While writing this essay I have gained much from discussions with Ronald Dworkin and Julian Le Grand. This version was completed during a stay at Princeton University which was supported by a grant from the U.S. National Science Foundation.

199

feasibly known the sum-total of all information. From this observation it is possible to argue that the goal of distributive justice is best served in an environment where individuals are encouraged to exploit some of their private information; or, in other words, that except for certain very extreme circumstances some form of decentralisation in decision-making is desirable. In particular, this implies that a pure command system is almost never an optimal mode of organisation even from the point of view of distributive justice, let alone from the vantage point of the innate rights that individuals may possess to private decision-making.

For my purposes here I shall be thinking of society as a cooperative venture among individuals for mutual advantage, and shall take it that some form of centralised authority is required for coordinating the activities of the members of society. To be sure, classical criteria of social welfare, such as utilitarianism, require for their furtherance a central authority whose activities far exceed the provision of the limited number of public services, such as the enforcement of contracts, and the protection of persons or groups against force, theft and fraud that delineate the activities of the minimal state. The claims of distributive justice would, as a minimum, require that this central authority be engaged in addition with the task of redistributing purchasing power among individuals via taxes and subsidies.

It has been argued by Nozick (1974) that the imposition of such taxes and subsidies violates the inalienable rights that individuals have to the *actual* goods and services they are historically entitled to. In this paper I shall not concern myself with the question of whether the arguments leading to such a view are compelling.[1] In any case, it has long been noted by political philosophers that the claims of distributive justice – such as those emanating from utilitarianism – can readily conflict with certain rights that individuals are entitled to. Indeed, Sen (1970a, 1976) has recently noted that certain minimal demands of 'liberty' may conflict with even so weak a welfare criterion as the one embodied in the Pareto ranking. Such conflicts do not pose any analytical difficulties. For example, if it is granted that individuals possess innate rights – such as a well-defined region of private decision-making – which considerations of distributive justice, let alone 'progress' or efficiency, must not override, then an observance of these rights must be viewed as constraints that must not be violated in the execution of policies that result in the maximisation of the chosen criterion of social welfare.[2] Now, it is an observation of the

---

[1] For extended discussions of this, see e.g. Arrow 1977 and Dasgupta 1980.

[2] In what follows I shall suppose that the central authority is concerned with the maximisation of a criterion of social welfare which includes, among other things, a conception of distributive justice. For illustrative purposes I shall often suppose this criterion to be classical utilitarianism.

utmost banality that if these constraints are 'biting' constraints in the maximisation exercise, then the maximum social welfare that can be achieved in the presence of these constraints is less than the level which could have been achieved had these constraints not been imposed. Indeed, one can even calculate the cost – in terms of forgone social welfare – that the imposition of such constraints leads to. These are familiar matters: that not all rights are typically viewed with equal urgency, that individual rights often clash with one another and that they in turn conflict with other social goals.[3] Ultimately what one seeks is an ordering of social states. I take it that when one talks of a social state one includes in its characterisation not only the production and distribution of goods and services – 'end states' in the sense of Nozick – but also the actions that people choose, those they are entitled to choose, what treatment they are entitled to expect from others, and so on. I recognise that a committed utilitarian will make the claim that if such an extended notion of social states matters to people then it will have found expression in their utility functions. But I take it also that it will be agreed by many that this device misses much of the point raised by non-utilitarian political philosophers in recent years. If political philosophy is much concerned with the characterisation of social states and the arguments that are relevant in seeking an ordering among them, welfare economic theory is much concerned with the design of economic environments that are conducive to the realisation of those social states that are judged desirable in the light of this ordering. Admittedly, in some extreme cases – as in the philosophy of Nozick – this role of welfare economic theory is vanishingly small. Granted that a decision has to be reached on the *degree* of protection which the minimal state is expected to provide, a matter which is hardly touched on in Nozick's work; it must nevertheless be granted that the end of personal rights, as Nozick sees them, dictates that the only economic organisation which is justified is one that is born under the benign indifference of the minimal state. But this is an extreme position, and most political philosophies allow for a certain scope in the design of economic organisations that best serve the purpose at hand. Thus, for example, in his celebrated work Rawls (1971) expresses the opinion that whether the requirements of social justice are best met in a private property system or under a socialist regime cannot be judged in advance, so long as market institutions are relied upon in each. And he says 'A . . . significant advantage of a market system is that, given the required background institutions, it is consistent with equal

---

[3] When goals conflict one is forced to entertain the idea of tradeoffs among them. The 'social weights' attached to these goals typically will depend on the extent to which the goals are realised. At an extreme are lexicographically ordered goals, such as the two principles of justice in Rawls' system.

liberties and fair equality of opportunity . . . a system of markets decentralises the exercise of economic power . . . It is necessary, then, to recognise that market institutions are common to both private-property and socialist regimes . . . which of these systems and the many intermediate forms most fully answers to the requirements of justice cannot . . . be determined in advance' (Rawls 1971, pp. 272–4).

In this paper I shall approach matters from a different end and suppose that social welfare depends only on individual welfares and that individual welfares depend solely on the allocation of goods and services. Furthermore, for expositional ease, I shall take it that individual welfares are based on preferences that are entirely *personal*, in the sense that an individual's welfare depends only on the goods and services assigned to him.[4] I shall suppose that the state is concerned with the maximisation of a criterion of social welfare subject to whatever technological and informational constraints there may be.[5] Often, for illustrative purposes, I shall take it that the criterion of social welfare is utilitarianism, or the sum of individual utilities (or welfare). It will be noted that in this formulation no account is taken of individual rights, except the right to have one's welfare included in the social ranking of economic states. The question I want to ask is whether economic decentralisation, or the assignment of rights to certain regions of individual decision-making, is instrumental in implementing the optimal allocation of goods and services in the light of the chosen criterion of social welfare. This is discussed in the next two sections.

2 The fundamental theorem of welfare economics

If welfare economic theory has not usually emphasised the right on the

---

[4] As the reader will note, I am borrowing Dworkin's terminology in distinguishing *personal* from *external* preferences (see Dworkin 1977, pp. 234 and 275). Actually, unless strong assumptions are made on individual preferences, it is not possible to isolate an individual's personal preferences from his external ones, in that in general a person's preference over his own consumption of wine and beer will depend on the goods consumed by others. For my purpose this does not matter, because much of what I have to say can accommodate the inclusion of external preferences, provided that they are allowed to be counted in the social calculus.

[5] I shall also abstract from uncertainties in the state of the world – e.g. about tomorrow's weather condition – as well as an individual's uncertainties about his own future preferences. Furthermore, I am abstracting from time here and, therefore, the idea that for any state of nature a person may know that his preferences will change in a predictable way as time passes. Each of these issues can be accommodated in the discussion that follows. But not without further thought and care. Rawls (1971, Chapter 9) presents a deep analysis of the concept of 'self' and, in Chapter 8, pp. 416–24, discusses the idea of deliberative rationality. This latter discussion includes an account of what economists call intertemporally consistent preferences on the part of an individual (see Strotz 1956). Both this last and the distinction between ex-ante and ex-post social welfare functions in the face of uncertainty are discussed by Hammond (Chapter 4, above).

part of individuals to certain areas of personal decision-making, it is because in many of the circumstances that have been explored there is, in fact, no necessary conflict between this and the claims of distributive justice. For consider the example of an economy in which individuals possess an initial endowment of goods and services.[6] Suppose that the state knows the utility (or welfare) function and the initial endowment of each and every individual in society. Then it is a theorem in welfare economics that, provided that the utility functions satisfy certain technical conditions, the *full* optimum allocation of goods and services (i.e. the optimum in the light of the chosen criterion of social welfare constrained only by the total initial endowment of goods and services in the economy) can be realised by way of the following scheme. The scheme consists in the state simultaneously announcing a set of prices, one for each and every commodity and service; rearranging the initial endowments of individuals by imposing lump-sum taxes and subsidies; and allowing individuals to trade at these prices. The rule for trading is precisely what one would expect: the market value of the final consumption bundle each person chooses must not exceed the income allotted to him by the state via the lump-sum taxes (or subsidies). A formal way of stating this is to say that, provided that the utility functions satisfy certain conditions, the full optimum is a competitive equilibrium allocation of goods and services associated with an appropriate distribution of initial endowments among the members of society.[7]

I want to make three observations about this theorem. First, the structure of the economic organisation described by the theorem has the formal characteristics of a *game*; which is to say that each and every individual, as well as the state, is empowered to *choose* from a personalised set of actions, and in addition there is a publicly known rule which translates the chosen actions of all players (including the state) into a final allocation of goods and services. To be precise, the state wishes to maximise the criterion of social welfare and is empowered to impose lump-sum taxes and subsidies on individuals and to choose prices at which individuals then trade. And each individual is empowered to choose his most preferred bundle of goods and services subject to the constraint that the market

---

[6] For simplicity of exposition I shall suppose that it is a pure exchange economy; that is, there is no production. This is not at all crucial in what follows. One can also allow for the passage of time in the model I am describing. For a good account of what follows with the inclusion of features I am abstracting from here, see Malinvaud 1972.

[7] This result, often called the Fundamental Theorem of Welfare Economics, has been much discussed both in the economics and political philosophy literature, and formed the basis of the socialist pricing debate (see Lerner 1944 and Hayek 1948). For a technical presentation of the theorem, see e.g. Malinvaud 1972. Meade 1964 and Rawls 1971, section 42, provide excellent discussions of it.

value of his final consumption bundle does not exceed the income he has been allotted via the tax system. The theorem says that the (equilibrium) outcome of this game is the optimal allocation of goods and service.[8] Second, contrary to what is on occasion thought, it is simply not true that in order to sustain the full welfare optimum the state, in the economy we are discussing, must prohibit persons from engaging in mutually beneficial trade among themselves.[9] The point is that the commodity prices are so chosen and the lump-sum redistribution of assets is so arranged by the state that the outcome of the subsequent market transactions postulated by the Fundamental Theorem leaves no scope for further mutually beneficial trade among persons.[10]

Third, it will have been noted that in the economy under study a person is characterised by his preferences (or utility function) and his initial endowment of goods and services, and it has been supposed that the state knows each person's characteristics. Thus, in fact, the lump-sum taxes and subsidies required to attain the welfare optimum are person-specific. Thus, while the competitive process is an anonymous one, in the sense that all individuals trade at the same set of prices, the redistributive taxes and subsidies are not. This last should come as no surprise. Since the state knows individual characteristics, it behoves the state to make use of its knowledge for the sake of social welfare. Persons who are needy will have subsidies given to them, obtained via taxes from those who are not.

Now it may be remarked that if the state in fact knows as much as the Fundamental Theorem of Welfare Economics invites it to know, it can rather readily enforce the full optimum directly, by expropriating the initial endowments of individuals and then distributing the (welfare) optimum allocation. This would be a *command* system and the question arises whether there is much to choose between these two allocative mechanisms for attaining the welfare optimum. It may be pointed out that

[8] This leads to the question of whether there are other games, and therefore other economic systems, with this same outcome. The answer is 'yes'. For a discussion of this in a different context, see Mas-Colell 1978. It should be noted that the Fundamental Theorem envisages the game to be played in two moves. The state makes the first move by announcing prices and imposing transfers. Individuals then make the second move by engaging in transactions. The planning models to be discussed in the next section will also have this 'two-moves' structure.

[9] See Nozick 1974, pp. 161–3, in which the dilemma confronting Wilt Chamberlain and his admirers is based on the contrary supposition.

[10] Formally, what I am referring to here is the fact that in the economy under study a competitive equilibrium outcome is not merely efficient in the sense of Pareto, but is also in the *core*; that is, subsequent to the imposition of the appropriate lump-sum taxes and subsidies, *no* sub-group can, by restricting trade to its members, do better than what it attains at the welfare optimum. For a formal definition of the core and the result I am stating here, see Malinvaud 1972. Nozick 1974, Chapter 10, has a good discussion of the concept.

the set of 'messages' the state must transmit under the command mode of planning will far exceed the set of messages it must transmit under the price mechanism.[11] But let us suppose that messages can be costlessly transmitted and received. Is there then much to choose between these two special mechanisms as devices for sustaining the full optimum? It may be argued that the freedom enjoyed by individuals under the price mechanism envisaged in the Fundamental Theorem is illusory – that, after all, the state knows precisely what will be chosen by each, and, indeed, that it has so chosen the commodity prices and income transfers that each individual will eventually choose precisely what the state wants it to choose in the light of the social optimum. This argument, plausible at first blush, is not really satisfactory. For the fact that the state knows what an individual will in fact choose does not mean that the individual could not have chosen otherwise. Indeed, the individual will know that the state knows what he will choose. But this in itself is clearly not a good reason for the individuals to think that he is not exercising choice.

3 Differential information and economic decentralisation

The Fundamental Theorem of Welfare Economics states that under certain circumstances a full welfare optimum can be attained through a decentralised mechanism. But it was also noted that under these circumstances the welfare optimum can be attained via a complete command system as well. As an instrument for sustaining the welfare optimum each mode would appear to be equally effective. But, then, the operational appeal of the Fundamental Theorem is also minimal. The information that the state is assumed to possess is awesome in amount. For our example it is assumed to know the preferences and endowments of each and every member of society. These observations alone suggest that individual rights to certain private decisions may not only be a moral imperative, but may at once be a necessity prompted by the fact that the state possesses incomplete information.

One supposes that there are certain pieces of information that are known (or which will be known) only by the individuals in question; that is they are costly (or in the extreme, impossible) to monitor publicly. These *private* pieces of information presumably include (i) an individual's personal characteristics (e.g. his preferences and personal endowments); that

---

[11] If there are m persons and l goods and services then, roughly speaking, the state needs to transmit $(m + l)$ messages (m income transfers and l prices) under the decentralised scheme, and ml messages (l quantities of goods to each individual) under the command system. If m and l are large then obviously ml is greatly in excess of $m + l$.

is, what kind of person he *is*, (ii) the actions that he takes (e.g. how hard he works at a given task); that is, what he *does*, and (iii) localised pieces of information about the state of the world – or certain aspects of specialised technological possibilities.[12] One supposes as well that there are certain pieces of information that are publicly known or which *can* be publicly observed at relatively little cost. These may be precise pieces of information (e.g. the amount of pollution emitted by a firm) or they may be statistical information (e.g. the age distribution in a given society at a given moment of time). Thus we are invited to consider organisations in which the outcome (i.e. an allocation of goods and services) is a function of private decisions that are based on private information and public decisions that are based on publicly known information. And we are invited to choose among them on the basis of their outcomes as measured by the chosen criterion of social welfare.[13]

This is a difficult task, and it had been neglected until quite recently – the choice among social organisations when the individuals and the state entertain different information structures. But it may first be asked why the state does not require of individuals to make their private information available to it – the point being that if it were to collect all the private information it could implement the full optimum. There are at least two answers to this question and quite clearly both are valid in the world we know. The first is that if an individual knows how the answers will be translated into social action he may have an incentive to lie with a view to tilting the social outcome more towards his favour than the full optimum would allow. The second is that even if all individuals are morally committed to the chosen criterion of social welfare and are truly prepared to act always with a view to maximising this common criterion, the costs of communication – i.e. the costs in transmitting such messages – may be too high.[14] This second answer, which provided the motivation for the Marschak–Radner theory of teams is of great importance precisely because it alerts us to the fact that even if all individuals act on the basis of a common goal there is still the need for private decision-making – so as to exploit private information. In particular, the construct tells us that a command system – one in which the final allocation is a function solely of *public*

---

[12] In the insurance literature the terms *adverse selection* and *moral hazard* are used to characterise the problems raised by the first and second categories of private information, respectively.

[13] The basic idea, therefore, is the same as the one discussed in the previous section. Myerson 1980 and Laffont and Maskin 1981 have presented a unified formulation of a general planning problem in which each of the three categories of private information mentioned above is present.

[14] There is a third answer of course, which has to do with the right that people may be thought to have to 'privacy'. Since I am concerned here with the *instrumental* role of decentralised decision-making, I naturally ignore this answer.

information – is almost never optimal (see e.g. Weitzman 1978 and Dasgupta, Hammond and Maskin 1980).

It is, however, the first answer which has prompted an enormous theoretical literature during the past few years.[15] For, one is led directly to a consideration of designing *incentive* schemes with a view to maximising the chosen criterion of social welfare. It is clear enough in advance that it may not be possible in general to design social organisations that will yield the full optimum as an (equilibrium) outcome.[16] Usually the best that can be achieved is what economists clumsily call a 'second-best' outcome. I shall illustrate the general problem and the point I wish to make by means of a strikingly simple example due to Mirrlees (1971).

Consider an artisan economy where individuals possess innate abilities for transforming leisure into a single consumption good, which I shall call income. To be precise, I shall suppose that if a person has an innate ability (or productivity) level of n, where n is a positive number, then, if he works l hours at this productivity level, the amount of the consumption good he can produce is nl. A person's utility depends only on his own leisure time and his own disposable income and it increases with both leisure and disposable income. Thus preferences are personal. In fact I shall suppose that individual utility functions are identical. But while individuals have identical utility functions, they are not of identical ability. Thus individuals can be grouped by productivity types. The number of persons of ability n is $N(n)$, by assumption. For the same number of hours worked a more able person obviously *can* produce more income. In what follows I shall take it that even though a person cannot pretend and demonstrate an ability level *greater* than his innate one, he can work at any *lower* ability level, were he to choose to do so.[17]

I want first to look at the *laissez-faire* outcome in this economy, or, to put it more accurately, the outcome under the minimal state. Notice first that since leisure cannot be transferred from one person to another, there is no scope for trade in this economy. For what can a person offer to another of a higher ability in return for the fruits of his higher productivity? Likewise, there is no scope for exchange between persons of the same productivity. Thus, it is clear that under the minimal state each person will work on his own, at his innate ability level, having chosen his income–

---

[15] The question of incentive compatible resource allocation mechanisms, an issue pioneered by Hurwicz (1972) has been much discussed in recent years. Laffont 1979 contains a rich sample of essays on the subject. See Dasgupta, Hammond and Maskin 1979 for a classification of different social organisations designed to implement welfare optima.

[16] The full optimum here is the same as the full optimum of the previous section; i.e. that which is based on the *true* underlying preferences and endowments of individuals.

[17] Since by hypothesis a person's utility depends only on his leisure time and disposable income I am assuming that there is no pride in being recognised as an able person.

leisure mix so as to maximise his utility. Since people, by hypothesis, have identical utility functions, it will come as no surprise that the more able will realise a higher utility level. The distribution of utility levels, as a function of the ability level, n, is depicted in the figure below. I need hardly add that this distribution of realised utilities is efficient in the sense of Pareto.

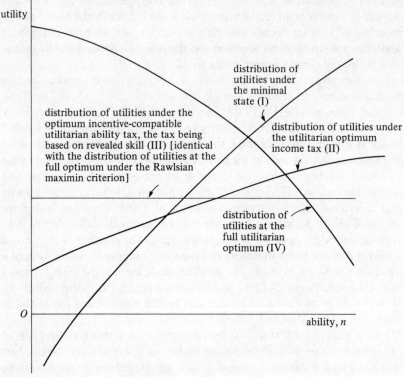

Figure 1. If $u_n(x)$ denotes the utility level of person of ability n in scheme x, and if $W(x)$ $(=\sum_n N(n)u_n(x))$ is the *sum* of utilities in scheme x, then $W(IV) > W(III) > W(II) > W(I)$.

I want to compare this outcome with the outcome that would be reached if the state were to intervene with a view to maximising a criterion of social welfare. But the point that I wish to emphasise is that the best outcome that can be achieved depends on the information that each of the participants in the economy possesses (or can obtain). By hypothesis each person knows his own utility function and his own innate ability. Thus by varying the amount of information at the disposal of the state I shall be able to trace the extent to which maximum attainable social welfare can in fact be varied. To bring this out sharply I shall assume that this society is wedded to the philosophy of Sidgwick, so that the criterion of social welfare is the sum of utilities. It is this sum which the state seeks to maximise.

In what follows I shall assume throughout that the state knows the common utility function and that it knows how many persons there are of each ability type. Furthermore, I shall assume that the government can monitor a person's income costlessly. I want first to look at the full utilitarian optimum – the outcome which can be achieved if the state knows each person's innate ability level as well.[18] Now, it transpires that for a large class of individual utility functions (and, therefore, individual preferences), the full utilitarian optimum is characterised by persons of *higher* innate ability attaining *lower* utility levels.[19] The distribution of utilities at the full utilitarian optimum is also depicted in Figure 1. Quite obviously, this distribution of utilities is also efficient in the sense of Pareto.

The most striking thing about this result is the complete reversal of the *ordering* of utilities from the one under the minimal state. Under the minimal state the more able attain higher utility levels. Under the utilitarian state they attain lower utility levels. Utilitarianism seeks to maximise the *sum* of utilities. The result I am describing says that in order to maximise this sum the really able ought to work much longer hours – so as to help raise the amount of income that is produced in the economy – to such an extent that they emerge with lower utility levels. The point is that the greater income so generated is used to subsidise the less able. The really able will no doubt be worse off under a utilitarian state than under the minimal state – they work a good deal harder. But the less able will be better off, so much so that the sum of utilities will be greater.[20]

How is this utilitarian optimum to be implemented? Since the state, by assumption, knows the innate ability of each person, and can monitor a person's income, one route is for the state to require of people to produce stipulated amounts of income which the state collects and then proceeds to distribute. Since the state can calculate precisely how long each person ought to work and how much each ought to consume at the full utilitarian

---

[18] Notice that it is possible for the state to know how many persons there are of each ability type without its being able to distinguish between persons and, therefore, not being able to say who is of what type. It is this distinction which I shall exploit subsequently.

[19] See Mirrlees 1974 and Allingham 1975 for conditions on individual preferences for which this is true. The conditions are in fact fairly innocuous.

[20] I am emphasising these stark features precisely because there *is* a sense in which the more able are 'made' to work for the less able under the utilitarian state – a crystalline example of a policy odious to Nozick. A committed utilitarian will, of course, not care. If this is what utilitarianism dictates, he will say, so be it.

optimum, it can enforce these commands. Another option is for the state to impose a tax on each person based solely on his ability, and for individuals to choose their number of working hours. The optimal ability tax schedule will, of course, be a tax on the more able and subsidy on the less able. This is a decentralised mechanism, an application of the Fundamental Theorem of Welfare Economics, where a person is allowed to choose his activity – here the number of hours he works – in the face of the optimal ability tax (or subsidy) imposed on him. The key point is that in the face of the optimal tax (or subsidy) a person, in the light of his own interests, will in fact choose precisely that number of working hours which the utilitarian optimum requires of him. I contrasted these two modes of implementation in the previous section.

Now let us relax our assumptions and suppose that the state does not know who is of what type. In fact, suppose that the state cannot monitor the number of hours a person chooses to work, but can only monitor a person's income. Thus the state cannot tell merely by observing a person's income whether the person is of 'high' ability and has chosen a 'high' leisure level or whether he is of 'low' ability and has worked long hours.[21] But now one can see that the full utilitarian optimum cannot be achieved. For example, the state clearly cannot achieve it by asking people to announce their innate abilities. At the full utilitarian optimum the more able are worse off than the less able. Since individuals know that their answers will be used to implement the full optimum, high-ability people will have a strong incentive to announce and act as though they are of low ability, so as to be eligible for state subsidies! What is equally important, the state will know that there are such incentive problems. I want to consider the case where any form of communication between the state and the individuals, other than the enforcement of taxes, is prohibitively costly. Quite clearly the state must impose its tax only on what it can monitor. Since the state can only observe a person's income the only policy it can pursue is to impose an income tax schedule. It is helpful to think of this as a game, in which income tax schedules are the state's strategies, and the choice of leisure (and therefore the number of working hours) is individual choice.[22] Moreover, the state chooses the income tax schedule with a view to maximising the sum of utilities, knowing the manner in which persons of any given type will respond. It can be shown that if the state imposes the optimum income tax schedule each person will be better

---

[21] The example therefore contains both the problems of adverse selection and moral hazard referred to in 12, p. 206.

[22] Since a person can work at an ability level less than his innate one this too is up to a point a choice for the individual. But, as we shall see, persons will in fact wish to choose to work at their innate ability levels when the optimal income tax schedule is imposed.

off than anyone who is less able than himself, and therefore each will indeed work at his innate ability level. This outcome is depicted in Figure 1. The least able earn very little on their own and, under the tax schedule, receive an income subsidy (a negative income tax). This is financed by income taxes collected from the able who choose to earn a good deal. The sum of utilities achieved under the optimum income tax schedule is, of course, less than the sum of utilities at the full optimum. But it is the best outcome (from the utilitarian point of view) that can be realised, given the limited information that the government possesses, and given that we have ruled out as prohibitively costly any form of communication between the government and the citizens other than the filing of income tax returns and the imposition of taxes.

Three points bear emphasis. First, we have seen that although a utilitarian government would ideally like to impose an ability tax – i.e. a person-specific tax – it is unable to do so because it does not know who is of what type. By contrast, the optimal income tax is 'anonymous': the tax is levied (or subsidy paid) on the income earned. Two people, under such a schedule, are liable to the same tax (or subsidy) provided they earn the same income.[23] It does not matter if they are of different types. The state, by hypothesis, cannot distinguish them anyway. People *choose* their income in the face of the tax schedule, by choosing the number of hours they work. In this sense all are treated equally. They are treated unequally if they *reveal* themselves to be different, in the sense of earning different incomes. But the choice is there.

Second, this mode of decentralisation – the one associated with the use of the optimum income tax – is a necessity prompted by the limited information at the disposal of the government. It is not solely a moral requirement. There is no command system which can achieve the outcome resulting from the imposition of the optimal income tax. Given the limited information that the government has been taken to possess all command modes of planning will result in lower social welfare.

Now, the imposition of the optimum income tax introduces what economists call a 'distortion' into the economy. The resulting allocation of utilities (scheme II in Figure 1; see also Table 1) is not Pareto efficient:

---

[23] It is not difficult to produce models in which the optimum income tax schedule has a random component; that is, the schedule may say, to give an example, that if a person earns £10,000 a year he is liable to an income tax of £2,000 with probability ¼ and £3,000 with probability ¾. In this case, of course, two people earning the same income will not necessarily pay the same tax. That is, *ex-post*, the principle of horizontal equity is violated here, but not *ex-ante*. See Stiglitz 1976 and Maskin 1981 for a discussion of optimal random taxation. In the text I am assuming that the optimum income tax does not have a random component.

Table 1. Summary of outcomes possible for a utilitarian government. In all cases it is assumed that government knows the (identical) utility function, and the number of persons in each skill (ability) category. Person of ability n can choose labour time l and output y satisfying the relation $y \leqslant nl$. U_n denotes the utility level of person with intrinsic skill, or ability, level n.

Variables government can observe	Type of optimum	Optimum tax/subsidy based on	Distribution of utilities
y, n	full optimum (Pareto efficient)	true skill (ability), n	for all n and n' with $n > n'$, $U^n > U^n$. (scheme IV in diagram)
y	second-best (informationally constrained Pareto efficient)	income, y	$U^n > U^{n'}$ for all n and n' satisfying $n > n'$ (scheme II in diagram)
y, l	second-best and Pareto efficient (identical to full-optimum for Rawlsian government)	'revealed' ability (or skill) y/l	$U^n = U^{n'}$ for all n,n' (scheme III in diagram)

that is, it is possible to imagine technologically feasible alternative allocations of leisure and consumption across persons that result in higher utility to all. This brings me to the third point, namely, that, while indeed there are such *technologically* feasible allocations, because of the limited information at the disposal of the government and because of the incentives problem, such allocations cannot be implemented. That is to say, such allocations are not *informationally* feasible. This implies that the imposition of the optimum tax schedule results in what one might call an 'informationally constrained' Pareto efficient allocation. That this is so can be easily confirmed. For, given the limited information at the disposal of the government, if there were an informationally feasible alternative allocation that made all better off, it would lead to a higher sum of utility levels; in which case the income tax schedule being considered would not be the (utilitarian) optimum income tax schedule!

I come now to the final case I wish to consider; one where the government can observe not only a person's income, but also the number of hours he works. But I continue to assume that the government does not know who is of what intrinsic ability (or skill). As the reader will recognise, this case eschews the moral hazard problem but retains the adverse selection feature. This is what makes the problem interesting. It is clear that a utilitarian government will in this case be able to achieve more than it can with the optimal income tax, but typically will still not be able to achieve the *full* utilitarian optimum, since people can pretend and act as though they are of lower ability than they actually are. As we noted earlier, the point is that a person of skill level, say $\bar{n}$, can, if he works for l hours, produce output y given by $y = \bar{n}l$. But, should he choose to do so, he can also work below par at any ability level n less than $\bar{n}$ and produce output equal to nl. The government can, by assumption, monitor only y and l. Thus it cannot catch a person working below par if the person finds it in his interest to do so. Dasgupta and Hammond (1980) and Mirrlees (1981) have shown that the best that a utilitarian government can guarantee to be achieved under this information structure is the *maximum uniform* distribution of utilities that is technologically feasible; (scheme III in the diagram.)[24] The second of the emphasised adjectives characterising this second-best utilitarian optimum says that all individuals attain the same utility level, and the first implies that the allocation is Pareto efficient in the full sense of the term.[25] But these two characteristics suggest at once that *this* second-best utilitarian optimum is in fact the *full* optimum for a government wedded to Professor Rawls' Difference Principle. This is indeed so. That is to say, in the economy we are discussing a Rawlsian government loses nothing if it cannot observe a person's intrinsic ability but can instead observe the number of hours he works. A utilitarian government does lose something: it has to switch from scheme IV to scheme III in the diagram. It is in this sense that unlike the Utilitarian Principle the Difference Principle is 'incentive-compatible'.[26]

4 Professor Hayek on progress and freedom

Utilitarianism is a consequentialist philosophy, and in the previous two sections I have consciously defined consequences in a very narrow manner

[24] The tax–subsidy scheme which enables this second-best optimum to be realised in a decentralised manner is discussed in Dasgupta and Hammond 1980. The tax/subsidy on a person is based on the ability level the person chooses to display; that is, on the value of y/l the government observes in his case. Quite obviously, this allocation cannot be implemented by a command system.

[25] Since all attain the same utility level a person gains nothing by working below par. Admittedly he loses nothing either. But we make the innocuous assumption that a person will always choose to work at his intrinsic ability level if he loses nothing by doing so. Thus at this second-best optimum the government can infer the true skill of each person by observing his chosen y and l. But it cannot, obviously, make use of this inference to establish the full-optimum!

[26] Maskin (1980) has recently demonstrated this last claim in a wider class of economic models than the one I have been analysing in this section.

– the allocation of goods and services and, by implication, the allocation of utilities. In this essay I have also, consciously, looked at the instrumental role of individual discretion – or the liberty to make certain decisions. I have not taken into account the innate rights that persons may possess to such freedom. I have tried to argue that, contrary to Hayek's view, certain forms of individual discretion are not only not inconsistent with the goals of distributive justice, they must be encouraged if one were to promote distributive justice. I wish now to argue that despite his well-known libertarian views Hayek is very much a consequentialist, and that the value he attaches to individualism in general, and unbridled market forces in particular, is entirely instrumental in origin, and that he is loath to explain why it is instrumental in promoting the goal that he seeks.

Hayek's individualism springs from the fact that a good deal of information in a society is not publicly known. For he observes that, 'practically every individual has some advantage over all others because he possesses unique information of which beneficial use might be made, but of which use can be made only if the decisions depending on it are left to him or are made with his active cooperation' (Hayek 1945, pp. 521–3). If Nozick talks of voluntary transfers and leaves the matter at that, Hayek continually extols the virtues of the spontaneous play of market forces, and in particular the price mechanism. For in his classic essay on the use of knowledge in society he says, 'We must look at the price system as . . . a mechanism for communicating information if we want to understand its real function . . . The most significant fact about this system is the economy of knowledge with which it operates, or how little the individual participants need to know in order to be able to take the right action. In abbreviated form, by a kind of symbol, only the most essential information is passed on and passed on only to those concerned. It is more than a metaphor to describe the price system as a . . . system of telecommunications which enables individual producers to watch merely the movement of a few pointers' (Hayek 1945, pp. 526–7).

It can immediately be argued that the fact that much information is private is not on its own sufficient to warrant the unfettered play of market forces to be judged the best possible resource allocation mechanism. If in pointing to the privacy of information all that Hayek intends to assert is that a government ought not to pretend that it knows more than it actually does, or that a social organisation ought to encourage individuals to exploit some of their private information, the point is obviously well taken. But, of course, Hayek intends to assert a great deal more than just that. The problem is that the only alternative to the unfettered play of market forces that Hayek is really willing to consider is an institution in which the government decides everything. For he says at one point, 'The concentration of all decisions in the hands of authority itself produces a state of affairs in which what structure society still possesses is imposed upon it by government and in which the individuals have become interchangeable units with no other definite or durable relations to one another than those determined by the all-comprehensive organisation' (Hayek 1948, p. 27). Faced with this as the only alternative it is no wonder that the market mechanism wins hands down. But as the examples I discussed earlier suggested, there are other mechanisms which acknowledge the privacy of a great deal of knowledge and whose outcomes are superior – in the light of the chosen criterion of welfare – to that of the market mechanism. One should note also that the maximisation of a given criterion of social justice does not entail that the state would not wish to rely on prices as an essential ingredient in the mechanism which is chosen.

Hayek would have us believe that the demands of social justice necessitate a fully command system. In this, I have tried to argue, he is wrong. He rejects the claims of distributive justice because he thinks they conflict with individual liberty. But his defence of individual liberty would appear to be based on instrumental considerations. For, in his influential treatise, *The Constitution of Liberty*, Hayek makes clear that the end that he seeks, and what in his mind a spontaneous market process will achieve, is *progress*; and, he says, 'progress [is] a process of formation and modification of human intellect, a process of adaptation and learning in which not only the possibilities known to us but also our values and desires continually change' (Hayek 1960, p. 40); and furthermore that, 'The changes to which . . . people must submit are part of the cost of progress, an illustration of the fact that not only the mass of men but, strictly speaking, every human being is led by the growth of civilisation into a path that is not his own choosing' (Hayek 1960, p. 50).

What is disturbing is not so much the fact that Hayek in his treatise ultimately produces no argument for the supposition that unbridled market forces are the right ones for generating progress, but rather the belief he holds that he has no obligation to provide us with an argument. His escape route is complete; he does not pretend to understand the market mechanism and warns all not to try. For in an earlier article he says that '[true individualism] is a product of an acute consciousness of the limitations of the individual mind which induces an attitude of humility towards the impersonal and anonymous social processes by which individuals help to create things greater than they know' (Hayek 1948, p. 8). Is there any prescription other than that we ought to be humble before this mystical force – the spontaneous process of the market mechanism? There is, for Professor Hayek talks of 'the necessity, in any complex society in which the effects of anyone's action reach far beyond his possible range of vision, of the individual *submitting to the anonymous and seemingly irrational forces of society*' (Hayek 1948, p. 24, emphasis mine). If one asks 'why', Professor Hayek has a ready answer, one which I alluded to earlier. For he says, 'Man in a complex society can have no choice but between adjusting himself to what to him must seem the blind forces of the social process and obeying the orders of a superior' (Hayek 1948, p. 24).

Such an anti-rational view, disagreeable though it may be to many, is still not the most disturbing feature of Hayek's philosophy. Ultimately, it seems to me, what is most disturbing is the degree of authoritarianism that he would appear to be willing to tolerate for the sake of his conception of progress. Indeed, Hayek appears to be willing to renounce individual liberty if that were to be found *useful* to society. For he says, 'the case for individual freedom rests chiefly on the recognition of the inevitable ignorance of all of us concerning a great many of the factors on which the achievement of our ends and welfare depends. If there were omniscient men, if we could know not only all that effects the attainment of our present wishes but also our future wants and desires, there would be little case for liberty . . . what is important is not what freedom I personally like to exercise but what freedom some person may need in order to do things beneficial for society' (Hayek 1960, pp. 29, 32); and, furthermore, '*if the result of individual liberty did not demonstrate that some manners of living are more successful than others, much of the case for it would vanish*' (Hayek 1960, p. 85, emphasis mine).

Some of Hayek's views are so astonishing that it is hard to believe that he takes them seriously. For example, he seems to think that just as we cannot talk of the 'justice' or 'injustice' of a drought (a blind act of nature), we cannot use the adjective 'just' or 'unjust' on the allocation arising from the free-play of market forces. No one, after all, has *consciously* willed such an allocation.[27] Quite apart from the fact that this last would be the case in any social organisation in which the outcome depends on the actions chosen by everyone, and that 'chosen' by Mother Nature, whether to leave society to the mercies of the free-play of market forces is itself a social decision. But while he is convinced that the question as to whether the distribution of incomes resulting from the competitive process is just has no meaning, he certainly approves of whatever distribution results – for the process, in his mind, is fair. If in the unconscious pursuit of progress the economy is littered with the debris of the unsuccessful and the offspring of the unsuccessful, it would not seem to matter. The successful few are 'the first sign of a new way of living begun by the advance guard' (Hayek 1960, p. 130). Is there a reward scheme he favours? There is, for at

[27] See Hayek 1960, p. 99 and 1976, pp. 62–96.

one point he says, 'The fact is, of course, that we do not wish people to earn a maximum of merit but to achieve a maximum of usefulness at a minimum of pain and sacrifice and therefore a minimum of merit' (Hayek, 1960, p. 96). Comment is superfluous.

5 Authority and individual discretion

All social organisations operate under a mixed system of commands and individual discretion. Even in a hierarchical structure of authority, such as a firm, each member is allowed a certain amount of discretion. As has been emphasised by Simon (1957) even an employment contract has built within it the agreement that the employer will expect obedience from the employee for certain forms of command, such as the assignment of tasks. But in all cases the employee too can exercise a certain amount of discretion – in the manner in which he undertakes these tasks. In this essay I have tried to emphasise that a central reason why such discretion is desirable from the point of view of the goals of an organisation is the differences in the information that its members possess. When the goals of every member of the organisation coincide there is an advantage in allowing for individual discretion, as the work of Marschak and Radner (1972) implies. This remains true when the goals differ, as the discussion in section 3 makes clear. Furthermore, there is a case for individual discretion simply because an individual's genuine productivity may be weakened if he is under command – a possibility I have ignored in the formal account of sections 2 and 3. It can be argued that an employee, in signing an employment contract – and therefore committing himself to obeying certain commands – does so voluntarily. But his alternative options may be severely limited in an economy with a large dispersion of income and wealth. When the state subsidises one member with the tax collected from another, then, other things remaining the same, the set of options of the first is increased and that of the second is decreased. There is a transference of rights from one to the other. Admittedly, it can be argued, as recently by Nozick (1974), that such redistribution of purchasing power violates individual rights to the actual goods and services that they are historically entitled to. In this essay I have not attempted to evaluate this argument. Instead, I have approached the problem from a different end and have ignored rights, excepting for the right to have one's own welfare given weight in the social calculus. The arguments developed in this essay imply that certain forms of individual discretion – that is, empowering individuals to choose from certain sets of actions – is instrumental in promoting the end of social-welfare. To be sure, there are special circumstances, such as during an emergency, when it will be found *useful* to rely on a command system, such as the rationing of goods during a war or a famine. But even here it will often be better, from the point of view of social welfare, to allow individuals, should they wish, to engage in trade with their rations. And the reason here is the same as the one explored in section 3 – the fact that not all private information is publicly known.

All this is not to say that the claims of distributive justice cannot conflict with individual rights. They can, and an enormous literature, both in political philosophy and economics, bears witness to this. But not all rights are equally compelling. In any case, I have not attempted to discuss precisely which rights are instrumental in promoting distributive justice in an economy with dispersed information. They will clearly vary from case to case. My aim has been to argue that a pure command system, narrowly defined, is not the optimum mode of organisation even from the point of view of distributive justice.

11 Sour grapes – utilitarianism and the genesis of wants[1]

JON ELSTER

I want to discuss a problem that is thrown up by all varieties of utilitarianism: act and rule utilitarianism, average and aggregate, cardinal and ordinal.[2] It is this: why should individual want satisfaction be the criterion of justice and social choice when individual wants themselves may be shaped by a process that preempts the choice? And, in particular, why should the choice between feasible options only take account of individual preferences if people tend to adjust their aspirations to their possibilities? For the utilitarian, there would be no welfare loss if the fox were excluded from consumption of the grapes, since he thought them sour anyway. But of course the cause of his holding the grapes to be sour was his conviction that he would be excluded from consumption of them, and then it is difficult to justify the allocation by reference to his preferences.

I shall refer to the phenomenon of sour grapes as *adaptive preference formation* (or adaptive preference change, as the case may be). Preferences shaped by this process I shall call adaptive preferences.[3] The analysis of this mechanism and of its relevance for ethics will proceed in three steps. Section I is an attempt to circumscribe the phenomenon from the outside, by comparing it with some other mechanisms to which it is closely related and with which it is easily confused. Section II is an analysis of the fine

---

[1] Earlier drafts of this paper were read at the universities of Oslo, Oxford and East Anglia, resulting in major improvement and changes. I am also grateful for valuable and invaluable comments by G. A. Cohen, Robert Goodin, Martin Hollis, John Roemer, Amartya Sen, Arthur Stinchcombe and Bernard Williams.

[2] In fact, the problem is relevant for all want-regarding theories of ethics and justice. John Rawls' theory might seem to escape the difficulty, because it relies on primary goods rather than on utility or preferences. But in fact even his theory needs preference in order to compare undominated bundles of primary goods, and then the problem of sour grapes could easily arise.

[3] The term 'adaptive utility' is used by Cyert and DeGroot (1975), but in a sense more related to what I here call endogenous preference change due to learning. These authors also use the term to refer to what should rather be called 'strategic utility', which is the phenomenon that expected future changes in utility due to learning can be incorporated in, and make a difference for, present decisions. I do not know of any discussions in the economic literature of adaptive preferences in the sense of the term used here, but some insight can be drawn from the economic analysis of Buddhist character planning in Kolm 1979.

grain of adaptive preferences, and proposes some criteria by which they may be distinguished from other preferences. And section III is a discussion of the substantive and methodological implications of adaptive preference formation for utilitarianism, ethics and justice.

I

I shall compare adaptive preference formation to one mechanism that in a sense is its direct opposite; and then to five mechanisms that either have similar causes or bring about similar effects. The purpose of this conceptual mapping is to prepare for the discussion in section III of the exact relevance of adaptive preferences for ethics.

The opposite phenomenon of sour grapes is clearly that of 'forbidden fruit is sweet', which I shall call counteradaptive preference formation.[4] If when I live in Paris I prefer living in London over living in Paris, but prefer Paris over London when in London, then my wants are shaped by my feasible set, as in adaptive preference formation, but in exactly the opposite way. The question then is whether, in the theory of social choice, we should discount wants that have been shaped by counteradaptive preference formation. If someone wants to taste the forbidden fruit simply because it is forbidden, should we count it as a welfare loss that he is excluded from it? And would it be a welfare gain to give him access, if this would make him lose his taste for it? An ordinal-utilitarian theory of social choice offers no answers to these questions. This indeterminacy in itself points to an inadequacy in that theory, although we shall see in section III that counteradaptive preferences are less troublesome for ethics than adaptive ones, because they do not generate any conflict between autonomy and welfare.

Adaptive preference formation is now to be distinguished, firstly, from preference change through learning and experience. Consider the example of job preferences. Imperfect regional mobility sometimes leads to dual labour markets, e.g. to income in agriculture being systematically lower than in industry. Such income gaps may reflect the agricultural labourer's preference for being his own master, or for certain commodities that are cheaper in the countryside than in the city. The labourer may prefer to stay in the countryside rather than move to the city, even if the demand for agricultural goods is too small to enable him to earn the same monetary income as a factory worker. What are the welfare implications of this state of affairs? The standard answer is that a transfer of the labourer to the city

---

[4] For the record, it may well be adaptive in some larger sense to have counteradaptive preferences, because of the incentive effects created by a moving target.

implies a loss in welfare for him and, *ceteris paribus*, for society. Consider, however, an argument proposed by Amartya Sen:

Preferences about one's way of life and location are typically the result of one's past experience and an initial reluctance to move does not imply a perpetual dislike. The distinction has some bearing on the welfare aspects of employment policy, since the importance that one wishes to attach to the wage gap as a reflection of the labourer's preferences would tend to depend on the extent to which tastes are expected to vary as a consequence of the movement itself.[5]

On a natural reading of this passage, it seems to sanction the transfer if the *ex post* evaluation of city life makes it preferable to the countryside life that was more highly valued *ex ante*. We then need to ask, however, about the exact nature of the induced change in preferences. Two possibilities come to mind. One is that the transfer would imply learning and experience, another that it is due to habituation and resignation (adaptive preference change). On the first explanation the process is irreversible, or at least it cannot be reversed simply by a reverse transfer to the countryside. (It may, of course, be reversed by learning even more about the alternatives.) The second explanation does, however, permit a reversal of the preference change. I do not imply that irreversibility is a sufficient reason for concluding that preference change is due to learning more about the alternatives: preference change due to addiction also is irreversible in some cases. Nor is it exactly a necessary condition, for it is easy to think of ways in which preference change due to learning may be reversed, and not only through more learning. But, in the present context, irreversibility is the salient feature that permits us to distinguish between these two mechanisms of induced preference change: the reversal to the initial situation does not by itself bring about a reversal of the preferences.

Explanations in terms of learning can be fitted into an extended utilitarian framework, in which situations are evaluated according to *informed* preferences rather than just the given preferences. One should attach more weight to the preferences of someone who knows both sides of the question than to someone who has only experienced one of the alternatives. These informed preferences are, of course, those of the individuals concerned, not of some superior body. They are informed in the sense of being grounded in experience, not in the sense (briefly mentioned in section III) of being grounded in meta-preferences. They differ from given preferences at most in their stability and irreversibility. Informed preferences could be implemented in social choice by a systematic policy of experimentation that gave individuals an opportunity to learn about new alternatives without definite commitment. This no doubt would leave the persons

[5] Sen 1975, pp. 43–54.

involved with more information, but also with less character.[6] If individuals were reared every second year in the countryside, their eventual choice would be better informed, but they would have less substance as persons.

Be this as it may, it is clear that explanations in terms of habituation and resignation cannot even be fitted into this extended utilitarianism. If preferences are reversibly linked *to* situations, then preferences *over* pairs of situations appear in a very different light. If an initial preference for city life could be reversed by extended exposure to the countryside and *vice versa*, then Sen's argument (in my reading of it) implies that we do not have to bother with preferences at all. And this is not an extension of utilitarianism, but its breakdown. At least this holds for ordinal utilitarianism.[7] Cardinal utilitarianism, in its classical version, is perfectly capable of handling the problem, by comparing the total want satisfaction of countryside life with countryside preferences to city life with city preferences. But, as further argued in section III, cardinal utilitarianism then has to face other and even more serious problems.

Adaptive preference formation can be distinguished, secondly, from precommitment, by which I mean the deliberate restriction of the feasible set.[8] If my preferred alternative in the feasible set coincides with my preferred alternative in a larger set of possible alternatives, this may indeed be due to adaptive preference change, but it may also happen because I have deliberately shaped the feasible set so as to exclude certain possible choices. Some people marry for this reason, i.e. they want to create a barrier to prevent them from leaving each other for whimsical reasons. Other people abstain from marriage because they want to be certain that their love for each other is not due to adaptive preference formation. It does not seem possible to ensure both that people stay together for the right reasons, and that they do not leave each other for the wrong reasons. If one deliberately restricts the feasible set, one also runs the risk that the preferences that initially were the reason for the restriction ultimately come to be shaped by it, in the sense that they would have changed had they not been so restricted.

Another example that shows the need for this distinction is the desire for submission to authority. As brilliantly argued by Paul Veyne[9] in his study of authority relations in Classical Antiquity, the mechanism of sour grapes may easily lead the subjects to glorify their rulers, but this is then an

[6] This observation owes much to Williams 1976a.
[7] I am grateful to G. A. Cohen for pointing out to me the crucial difference between ordinal and cardinal utilitarianism in this respect.
[8] Elster 1979, Ch. II has an extended analysis of this notion, with many examples.
[9] Veyne 1976. For an exposition and interpretation of Veyne's view, see Elster 1980.

ideology induced by and posterior to the actual submission, not a masochistic desire that generates and justifies it. As in the preceding example, we need to distinguish between preferences being the cause of a restricted feasible set, and their being an effect of the set. The oppressed may spontaneously invent an ideology justifying their oppression, but this is not to say that they have invented the oppression itself.

Adaptive preferences, thirdly, differ from the deliberate manipulation of wants by other people. If one only wants what little one can get, one's preferences are perhaps induced by other people in whose interests it is to keep one content with little:

A may exercise power over B by getting him to do what he does not want to do, but he also exercises power over him by influencing, shaping or determining his very wants. Indeed, is it not the supreme exercise of power to get another or others to have the desires you want them to have – that is, to ensure their compliance by controlling their thoughts and desires? One does not have to go to the lengths of talking about Brave New World, or the world of B. F. Skinner, to see this: thought control takes many less total and more mundane forms, through the control of information, through the mass media and through the processes of socialisation.[10]

There is an ambiguity in this passage, for does it propose a purposive or a functional explanation of wants? Do the rulers really have the power to induce deliberately certain beliefs and desires in their subjects? Or does the passage only mean that certain desires and beliefs have consequences that are good for the rulers? And if the latter, do these consequences explain their causes? As argued by Veyne, the purposive explanation is implausible.[11] The rulers no doubt by their behaviour are able to induce in their subjects certain beliefs and values that serve the rulers' interest, but only on the condition that they do not deliberately try to achieve this goal. From the rulers' point of view, the inner states of the subjects belong to the category of *states that are essentially byproducts*.[12] The functional explanation hinted at in the reference to 'processes of socialisation' is no more plausible. True, adaptive preference formation may have consequences that are beneficial to the rulers, but these do not explain how the preferences came to be held. On the contrary, the very idea of adaptation points to a different explanation. It is good for the rulers that the subjects be content with little, but what explains it is that it is good for the subjects. Frustration with the actual state of affairs would be dangerous for the

---

[10] Lukes 1974, p. 23.
[11] Veyne 1976, passim.
[12] Farber 1976 has a brief discussion of a similar notion, 'willing what cannot be willed'. He restricts the idea, however, to the inducement of certain states (belief, sleep, happiness) in oneself, whereas it can also be applied to paradoxical attempts to induce by command certain states (love, spontaneity, disobedience) in others. For the latter, see the works of the Palo Alto psychiatrists, e.g. Watzlawick 1978.

rulers, but also psychologically intolerable to the ruled, and the latter fact is what explains the adaptive preferences. How it explains them is brought out by the next distinction.

Adaptive preference formation, fourthly, differs from deliberate character planning. It is a causal process taking place 'behind my back', not the intentional shaping of desires advocated by the Stoic, buddhist or spinozistic philosophies, by psychological theories of self-control or the economic theory of 'egonomics'.[13] The psychological state of wanting to do a great many things that you cannot possibly achieve is very hard to live with. If the escape from this tension takes place by some causal mechanism, such as Festinger's 'reduction of cognitive dissonance',[14] we may speak of adaptive preference change. The process then is regulated by something like a drive, not by a conscious want or desire. If, by contrast, I perceive that I am frustrated and understand why, I may deliberately set out to change my wants so as to be able to fulfil a larger part of them. I then act on a second-order desire, not on a drive. To bring home the reality of the distinction between drives and second-order wants, consider counter-adaptive preferences. No one could choose to have such preferences, and so they can only be explained by some kind of perverse drive of which it can be said, metaphorically speaking, that it has the person rather than the other way around.

The difference between adaptive preference formation and deliberate character planning may show up not only in the process, but in the end result as well. One difference is that I may, in principle at least, intentionally shape my wants so as to coincide exactly with (or differ optimally from) my possibilities, whereas adaptive preference formation tends to overshoot, resulting in excessive rather than in proper meekness.[15] Another is that adaptive preference change usually takes the form of downgrading the inaccessible options ('sour grapes'), whereas deliberate character planning has the goal of upgrading the accessible ones.[16] In a less than perfect marriage, I may adapt either by stressing the defects of the wise and beautiful women who rejected me, or by cultivating the good points of the one who finally accepted me. But in the general case adaptive preferences and character planning can be distinguished only by looking into the actual process of want formation.

Lastly, adaptive preference formation should be distinguished from wishful thinking and rationalisation, which are mechanisms that reduce frustration and dissonance by shaping the perception of the situation

[13] Schelling 1978.
[14] Festinger 1957; 1964.
[15] Veyne 1976, pp. 312–13.
[16] Kolm 1979.

rather than the evaluation of it. The two may sometimes be hard to tell from each other. In the French version of the fable of the sour grapes, the fox is deluded in his perception of the grapes: they are too green. (And similarly for counteradaptive preferences, as in 'The grass is always greener on the other side of the fence'.) But in many cases the phenomena are clearly distinct. If I do not get the promotion I have coveted, then I may rationalise defeat either by saying that 'my superiors fear my ability' (misperception of the situation) or 'the top job is not worth having anyway' (misformation of preferences). Or again I may change my life style so as to benefit from the leisure permitted by the less prestigious job (character planning).

Just as one cannot tell from the preferences alone whether they have been shaped by adaptation, so one cannot always tell from the beliefs alone whether they arise from wishful thinking. A belief may stem from wishful thinking, and yet be not only coherent, but true and even well-founded, if the good reason I have for holding it is not what makes me hold it. I may believe myself about to be promoted, and have good reasons for that belief, and yet the belief may stem from wishful thinking so that I would have held it even had I not had those reasons. This shows that wishful thinking, like adaptive preference formation, is a causal rather than an intentional phenomenon. Self-deception, if there is such a thing, has an intentional component in that I know the truth of what I am trying to hide from sight. But if what I believe out of wishful thinking is also what I have reason to believe, there can be no such duality. Wishful thinking, it seems to me, is best defined as a drive towards what I want to believe, not as a flight from what I do not want to believe.[17]

In the short run the result of wishful thinking and of adaptive preference change is the same, viz. reduction of dissonance and frustration. In the long run, however, the two mechanisms may work in opposite directions, as in the following important case. This is the classical finding from *The American Soldier* that there was a positive correlation between possibilities of promotion and level of frustration over the promotion system.[18] In the services in which the promotion chances were good, there was also more frustration over promotion chances. In Robert Merton's words, this paradoxical finding had its explanation in that a 'generally high rate of mobility induced excessive hopes and expectations among members of the group so that each is more likely to experience a sense of frustration in his present position and disaffection with the chances for promotion'.[19] Other explanations have also been proposed that make the frustration depend on

[17] I elaborate on these slightly cryptic remarks in Elster (forthcoming).
[18] Stouffer 1949.
[19] Merton 1957, Ch. VIII.

rational rather than excessive expectations.[20] We might also envisage, however, a quite different explanation in terms of sour grapes: frustration occurs when promotion becomes sufficiently frequent, and is decided on sufficiently universalistic grounds, that there occurs what we may call a release from adaptive preferences. On either hypothesis, increased objective possibilities for well-being bring about decreased subjective well-being, be it through the creation of excessive expectations or by the inducement of a new level of wants. The relevant difference between the two mechanisms for ethics is the following. Giving the utilitarian the best possible case, one may argue that frustration due to wishful thinking should be dismissed as irrational and irrelevant. But on the standard utilitarian argument, it is hardly possible to dismiss in the same manner frustration due to more ambitious wants. If we are to do so, we must somehow be able to evaluate wants, but this brings us outside the standard theory.

To recapitulate, then, adaptive preference formation has five distinctive features that enable us to locate it on the map of the mind. It differs from learning in that it is reversible; from precommitment in that it is an effect and not a cause of a restricted feasible set; from manipulation in that it is endogenous; from character planning in that it is causal; and from wishful thinking in that it concerns the evaluation rather than the perception of the situation. These phenomena are all related to adaptive preference formation, through their causes (reduction of dissonance) or their effects (adjustment of wants to possibilities). They also differ importantly from adaptive preferences, notably in their relevance for ethics. Some of these differences have been briefly noted in the course of the discussion; they form a main topic of section III below.

II

From the external characterisation of adaptive preferences, I now turn to the internal structure of that phenomenon. I shall take an oblique route to the goal, beginning with a discussion of the relation between adaptive preference formation and freedom. In fact, both welfare and freedom, as well as power, have been defined in terms of getting or doing what one most prefers. It is well known, but not particularly relevant in the present context, that the attempt to define power in terms of getting what you want comes up against the problem of adaptive preferences.[21] It is equally

---

[20] Boudon 1977, Ch. V.

[21] Goldman 1972, following Robert Dahl, calls this the problem of the *chameleon*. Observe that adaptive preferences do not detract from power, as they do from welfare and freedom. If you have the power to bring about what you want, it is irrelevant whether your wants are shaped by the anticipation of what would have been brought about anyway. There is nothing shadowy or insubstantial about preemptive power.

well known, and more to the point, that adaptive preferences also create problems for the attempt to define freedom as the freedom to do what you want.

We need to assume that we have acquired some notion of what it means to be *free to do* something. This is not a simple question. It raises problems about the relation between formal freedom and real ability; between the distributive and the collective senses of mass freedom; between internal and external, positive and negative, man-made and natural, deliberate and accidental obstacles to freedom. I cannot even begin to discuss these issues here, and so I shall have to take for granted a rough notion of what freedom to act in a certain way means. But not all freedom is freedom to do something; there is also freedom *tout court*, being a free man. Freedom in this sense clearly in some way turns upon the things one is free to do – but how?

We may distinguish two extreme answers to this question. One is that freedom consists in being free to do what one wants to do. This view is sometimes imputed to the Stoics and to Spinoza, with dubious justification. In a well-known passage Isaiah Berlin argues against this notion of freedom: 'If degrees of freedom were a function of the satisfaction of desires, I could increase freedom as effectively by eliminating desires as by satisfying them; I could render men (including myself) free by conditioning them into losing the original desire which I have decided not to satisfy.'[22] And this, in his view, is unacceptable. Berlin is not led by this consideration into the opposite extreme, which is that freedom is simply a function of the number and importance of the things one is free to do, but his view is fairly close to this extreme.[23] The possibility of adaptive preferences leads him into downgrading the importance of actual wants, and to stress the freedom to do things that I might come to want even if I do not actually desire them now.

There is, however, an ambiguity in Berlin's argument. 'Conditioning men' into losing the desires that cannot be satisfied is a form of manipulation, which means that the ensuing want structure is not a fully *autonomous* one. And I completely agree that full (or optimal) satisfaction of a non-autonomous set of wants is not a good criterion of freedom. And the same holds for the adjustment of aspirations to possibilities that takes place behind my back, through adaptive preference formation. But there is a third possibility, that of autonomous character formation. If I consciously shape myself so as only to want what I can get, I can attain full satisfaction of an autonomous want structure, and this can with more justification be called freedom, in the Stoic or spinozistic sense. Being a free

[22] Berlin 1969, pp. xxxviii–xl.
[23] See Berlin 1969, p. 130 n for an exposition of his view.

man is to be free to do all the things that one autonomously wants to do. This definition is less restrictive than Berlin's (and certainly less restrictive than the extreme view to which he is closest), but more restrictive than the extreme Berlin is attacking, that being free is to be free to do the things one wants, regardless of the genesis of the wants.

If this definition of freedom is to be of real value, we need a definition or a criterion for autonomous wants. This I cannot provide. I can enumerate a large number of mechanisms that shape our wants in a non-autonomus way, but I cannot say with any confidence whatsoever that the wants that are not shaped in any of these ways are *ipso facto* autonomous. And so it seems that for practical purposes we must fall back on a definition similar to Berlin's. But I think we can do better than this. We can exclude operationally at least one kind of non-autonomous wants, viz. adaptive preferences, by requiring freedom to do otherwise. If I want to do x, and am free to do x, and free not to do x, then my want cannot be shaped by necessity. (At least this holds for the sense of 'being free to do x' in which it implies 'knowing that one is free to do x'. If this implication is rejected, knowledge of the freedom must be added as an extra premiss.) The want may be shaped by all other kinds of disreputable psychic mechanisms, but at least it is not the result of adaptive preference formation. And so we may conclude that, other things being equal, one's freedom is a function of the number and the importance of the things that one (i) wants to do, (ii) is free to do and (iii) is free not to do.

An alternative proof that my want to do x is not shaped by the lack of alternatives would be that I am not free to do x. It would be absurd to say that my freedom increases with the number of things that I want to do, but am not free to do, but there is a core of truth in this paradoxical statement. If there are many things that I want to do, but am unfree to do, then this indicates that my want structure is not in general shaped by adaptive preference formation, and this would also include the things that I want to do and am free to do, but not free not to do. And this in turn implies that the things I want to do and am free to do, but not free not to do, should after all count in my total freedom, since there is a reason for believing the want to be an autonomous or at least non-adaptive one. The reason is weaker than the one provided by the freedom to do otherwise, but it still is a reason of a sort. Given two persons with exactly the same things which they both want to do and are free to do, then (*ceteris paribus*) the one is freer (or more likely to be free) who is free not to do them; also (*ceteris paribus*) the one is freer (or more likely to be free) who wants to do more things that he is not free to do.

These two criteria do not immediately carry over from freedom to welfare. The objects of welfare differ from the objects of freedom in that, for some of them at least, it makes little sense to speak of not being free to abstain from them. It makes good sense to say that freedom of worship is enhanced by the freedom not to worship, but hardly to say that the welfare derived from a certain consumption bundle is enhanced by the option of not consuming that bundle, since one always has that option. Nevertheless it remains true that (i) the larger the feasible set and (ii) the more your wants go beyond it, the smaller the probability that your wants are shaped by it. Or to put it the other way around: a small feasible set more easily leads to adaptive preferences, and even with a large feasible set one may suspect adaptive preferences if the best element in the feasible set is also the globally best element.

On the other hand, even if the best element in the feasible set is also globally best, preferences may be autonomous, viz. if they are shaped by deliberate character formation. The question then becomes whether we can have evidence about this beyond the (usually unavailable) direct evidence about the actual process of want formation. Quite tentatively, I suggest the following *condition of autonomy for preferences*:

If S_1 and S_2 are two feasible sets, with induced preference structures R_1 and R_2, then for no x or y (in the global set) should it be the case that xP_1y and yP_2x.

This condition allows preferences to collapse into indifference, and indifference to expand into preference, but excludes a complete reversal of preferences. Graphically, when the fox turns away from the grapes, his preference for raspberry over strawberry should not be reversed. The condition permits changes both in intra-set and inter-set rankings. Assume x,y in S_1 and u, v in S_2. Then xP_1u and xI_2u could be explained as a deliberate upgrading of the elements in the new feasible set. Similarly xP_1y and xI_1y could be explained by the fact that there is no need to make fine distinctions among the alternatives that are now inaccessible. And uI_1v and uP_2v could be explained by the need to make such distinctions among the elements that now have become available. By contrast, xP_1u and uP_1x would indicate an upgrading of the new elements (or a down-grading of the old) beyond what is called for. (Recall here the observation that adaptive preferences tend to overshoot.) Similarly xP_1y and yP_2x (or uP_1v and vP_2u) are blatantly irrational phenomena, for there is no reason why adjustment to the new set should reverse the internal ranking in the old.

For a conjectural example of preference change violating this autonomy condition, I might prefer (in my state as a free civilian) to be a free civilian rather than a concentration camp prisoner, and to be a camp prisoner rather than a camp guard. Once inside the camp, however, I might come to prefer being a guard over being a free civilian, with life as a prisoner ranked bottom. In other words, when the feasible set is (x,y,z), I prefer x

over y and y over z, but when the feasible set is (y,z) I prefer z over x and x over y. In both cases the best element in the feasible set is also globally best, not in itself a sign of non-autonomy. But in addition the restriction of the feasible set brings about a reversal of strong preferences, violating the condition. If the restricted set had induced indifference between x and y, both being preferred to z, this would have been evidence of a truly Stoic mastery of self. For another example, consider the labourer who after a transfer to the city comes to reverse his ranking of the various modes of farming, preferring now the more mechanised forms that he previously ranked bottom. Thirdly, observe that modernisation does not merely imply that new occupations are interpolated at various places in the prestige hierarchy, but that a permutation of the old occupations takes place as well.

When a person with adaptive preferences experiences a change in the feasible set, one of two things may happen: readaptation to the new set, or release from adaptation altogether. Proof of the latter would be if the globally best element were no longer found in the feasible set. And even if the feasible best remained the global best, release from adaptation might be conjectured if no reversal of strong preferences took place. Readaptation was illustrated in the city–countryside example, whereas release from adaptation is exemplified below in the example of the Industrial Revolution. In this example the release is diagnosed through the first criterion, that the global best is outside the feasible set. The second criterion (no strong reversal of preferences) presumably would not find widespread application, because of the relative rarity of conscious character planning.

A final remark may be in order. It is perhaps more common, or more natural, to think of preferences as induced by the actual state than by the feasible set. I believe, however, that the distinction is only a conceptual one. Consider again the city–countryside example. To live in the city may be considered globally as a state which (when in the city) I prefer over the countryside, considered as another global state. With a more fine-grained description of the states, however, it is clear that there are many modes of farming, all accessible to me when in the countryside, and many modes of city life that I can choose when I live in the city. Adaptive preferences then imply that according to my city preferences my globally best alternative is some variety of city life, but there may well be some varieties of countryside life that I prefer to some city lives. But in a useful shorthand we may disregard this and simply speak of states as inducing preferences, as will be done in the example developed below.

III

To discuss the relevance of adaptive preferences for utilitarian theory, I shall take up the question whether the Industrial Revolution in Britain was a good or a bad thing. In the debate among historians over this question,[24] two issues have been raised and sometimes confused. First, what happened to the welfare level of the British population between 1750 and 1850? Secondly, could industrialisation have taken place in a less harsh way than it actually did? Focussing here on the first issue, what kind of evidence would be relevant? Clearly the historians are justified in singling out the real wage, mortality, morbidity and employment as main variables: their average values, dispersion across the population and fluctuations over time. But if we are really concerned with the question of welfare, then we should also ask about the level of wants and aspirations. If the Industrial Revolution made wants rise faster than the capacity for satisfying them, should we then say that the Pessimist interpretation was correct and that there was a fall in the standard of living? Or, following the non-Pessimist[25] interpretation, should we say that an increased capacity for want satisfaction implies a rise in the standard of living? Or, following Engels,[26] should we say that, even if there was a fall in the material standard of living, the Industrial Revolution should be welcomed because it brought the masses out of their apathetic vegetation and so raised their dignity?

The problem is analogous to the one of *The American Soldier*, and as in that example there is also the possibility that frustration (if such there was) stemmed from excessive expectations and not from rising aspirations. If that proved to be the case, the utilitarian might not want to condemn the Industrial Revolution. He could say, perhaps, that insatisfaction derived from irrational beliefs should not count when we add up the sum total of utility. If we require preferences to be informed, then surely it is reasonable also to require beliefs to be well-grounded? But I do not think the utilitarian could say the same about frustration derived from more ambitious wants, and if this proved to be the main source of insatisfaction he could be led into a wholesale rejection of the Industrial Revolution. I assume in the immediate sequel that there was indeed some frustration due to a new level of wants, and try to spell out what this implies for utilitarianism. Later on I return to the problem of excessive expectations.

Imagine that we are initially in pre-industrial state x, with induced

---

[24] Elster 1978a, pp. 196 ff. has further references to this debate.
[25] As argued in Elster 1978a, the terms 'optimism' vs. 'pessimism' are misleading. The issue of pessimism vs non-pessimism is the factual one discussed here, and the question of optimism vs non-optimism the counterfactual one of alternative and better ways of industrialisation.
[26] Engels 1975, pp. 308–9.

utility functions $u_1 \ldots u_n$. We may think of these as either ordinal and non-comparable (i.e. as shorthand for continuous preferences) or as fully comparable in the classical cardinal sense. I shall refer to the two cases as the ordinal and the cardinal ones, but the reader should keep in mind that the crucial difference is that the latter permit one, as the former do not, to speak unambiguously of the sum total of utility. Assume now that industrialisation takes place, so that we move to state y, with induced utility functions $v_1 \ldots v_n$. In addition there is a possible state z, representing a society in which more people enjoy the benefits of industrialisation, or all people enjoy more benefits. Given the utility functions, we assume some kind of utilitarian device for arriving at the social choice. In the ordinal case, this must be some kind of social choice function; in the cardinal case we say that one should choose that state which realises the greatest sum total of utility. We then make the following assumptions about the utility functions $u_1 \ldots u_n$:

Ordinal case: According to the pre-industrial utility functions, x should be the social choice in (x,y,z)
Cardinal case: According to the pre-industrial utility functions, the sum total of utility is larger in x than it would be in either y or z.

We then stipulate the following for the utility functions $v_1 \ldots v_n$:

Ordinal case: According to the industrial utility functions, the social choice mechanism ranks z over y and y over x.
Cardinal case: According to the industrial utility functions, there is a larger sum of utility in z than in y, and a larger sum in y than in x.

And finally I add for the

Cardinal case: The sum total of utility in x under the pre-industrial utility functions is greater than the sum total of utility in y under the industrial utility functions.

This means that before industrialisation, in both the ordinal and the cardinal case, the individuals live in the best of all possible worlds. After industrialisation, this is no longer true, as the social choice would now be an even more industrialised world. Nevertheless the industrialised state is socially preferred over the pre-industrial one, even though (assuming the cardinal case) people are in fact worse off than they used to be. The intuitive meaning is that for everybody z is better than y on some objective dimension (actual or expected income) and y better than x; indeed y is sufficiently much better than x to create a new level of desires, and z sufficiently much better than y to engender a level of frustration that actually makes people (cardinally) worse off in y than they were in x, although, to repeat, the social choice in y is y rather than x. 'We were happier before we got these fancy new things, although now we would be miserable without them.' Clearly the story is not an implausible one.

What in this case should the utilitarian recommend? The ordinal utilitarian has, I believe, no grounds for any recommendation at all. State x is socially better than y according to the x-preferences, and y better than x according to the y-preferences, and no more can be said. The cardinal utilitarian, however, would unambiguously have to recommend x over y on the stated assumptions. But this, I submit, is unacceptable. It cannot be true that the smallest loss in welfare always counts for more than the largest increase in autonomy. There must be cases in which the autonomy of wants overrides the satisfaction of wants. And the release from adaptive preferences has exactly these consequences in the case that we have described; inducement of frustration and creation of autonomous persons. We do not want to solve social problems by issuing vast doses of tranquillisers, nor do we want people to tranquillise themselves through adaptive preference change. Engels may have overestimated the mindless bliss of pre-industrial society and underrated the mindless misery, but this does not detract from his observation that 'this existence, cosily romantic as it was, was nevertheless not worthy of human beings'.[27]

I am not basing my argument on the idea that frustration in itself may be a good thing. I believe this to be true, in that happiness requires an element of consummation and an element of expectation that reinforce each other in some complicated way. 'To be without some of the things you want is an indispensable part of happiness.'[28] But a utilitarian would then be happy to plan for optimal frustration. I am saying that even more-than-optimal frustration may be a good thing if it is an indispensable part of autonomy. Nor am I arguing that the search for ever larger amounts of material goods is the best life for man. There certainly comes a point beyond which the frustrating search for material welfare no longer represents a liberation from adaptive preferences, but rather an enslavement to addictive preferences. But I do argue that this point is not reached in the early stages of industrialisation. Only the falsely sophisticated would argue that to strive for increased welfare was non-autonomous from its very inception.

I should now explain exactly how this example provides an objection to utilitarian theory. Generally speaking, a theory of justice or of social choice should satisfy two criteria (among others). Firstly, it should be a guide to action, in the sense that it should enable us to make effective choices in most important situations. If in a given case the theory tells us that two or more alternatives are equally and maximally good, then this

[27] Engels 1975, p. 309.
[28] Bertrand Russell, quoted after Kenny 1965–6.

should have a substantive meaning and not simply be an artifact of the theory. The latter is true, for example, of the Pareto principle that x is socially better than y if and only if one person strictly prefers x and y and no one strictly prefers y over x, whereas society is 'indifferent' between x and y if some person strictly prefers x over y and some other person strictly prefers y over x. Even though this principle formally establishes a ranking, it is hopelessly inadequate as a guide to action. A theory should not tell us that some alternatives are non-comparable, nor try to overcome this problem by stipulating that society is indifferent between all non-comparable alternatives.

Secondly, we must require of a theory of justice that it does not strongly violate our ethical intuitions in particular cases. If a theory suggests that people should take tranquillisers when the Coase theorem requires them to,[29] then we *know* that it is a bad theory. True, the proper role of such intuitions is not well understood. If they are culturally relative, one hardly sees why they should be relevant for a non-relative theory of justice. And if they are culturally invariant, one suspects that they might have a biological foundation,[30] which would if anything make them even less relevant for ethics. Perhaps one could hope that persons starting from different intuitions might converge towards a unique reflective equilibrium,[31] which would then represent man as a rational rather than a culturally or biologically determined being. Such problems notwithstanding, I do not see how a theory of justice can dispense with intuitions altogether.

My argument against utilitarianism then is that it fails on both counts. Ordinal utilitarianism in some cases fails to produce a decision, and cardinal utilitarianism sometimes generates bad decisions. The indecisiveness or ordinal utilitarianism is due, as in other cases, to the paucity of information about the preferences. Cardinal utilitarianism allows for more information, and therefore ensures solutions to the decision problem. But even cardinalism allows too little information. Satisfaction induced by resignation may be indistinguishable on the hedonometer from satisfaction of autonomous wants, but I have argued that we should distinguish between them on other grounds.

The distinctions elaborated in section I may now be brought to bear on these issues. The reason why counteradaptive preferences are less problematic for ethics than adaptive ones is that release from counteradaptive preferences simultaneously improves autonomy and welfare. When I no longer possess (or no longer am possessed by) the perverse drive for novelty and change, the non-satisfaction of non-autonomous wants may

---

[29] As suggested by Nozick 1974, p. 76 n.
[30] As suggested by Rawls 1971, p. 503.
[31] Rawls 1971 is at the origin of this notion.

turn into the satisfaction of autonomous ones. The destructive character of counteradaptive preferences is well illustrated in an example due to von Weiszäcker.[32] Here a person obsessed by the quest for novelty is bled to death by a series of stepwise changes, each of which is perceived as an improvement in terms of the preferences induced by the preceding step. Clearly, to be released from this obsession is both a good thing in itself and has good consequences for welfare. Release from adaptive preferences, however, may be good on the autonomy dimension while bad on the welfare dimension.

Similar remarks apply to character planning, which may improve welfare without loss of autonomy. I am not arguing that character planning is *ipso facto* autonomous, for surely there are non-autonomous second-order wants, e.g. being addicted to will-power.[33] But I do not believe these cases to be centrally important, and in any case I am here talking about *changes* in the degree of autonomy. Character planning may improve welfare compared both to the initial problematic situation and to the alternative solution, which is adaptive preference change. First, recall that character planning tends to upgrade the possible, which cardinally speaking is better than a downgrading of the impossible. Both solutions reduce frustration, but character planning leaves one cardinally better off. Secondly, observe that the strategy of character planning is fully compatible with the idea that for happiness we need to have wants somewhat (but not too much) beyond our means. True, this notion is incompatible with the Buddhist version of character planning that sees in frustration *only* a source of misery.[34] But I believe that this is bad psychology, and that Leibniz was right in that 'l'inquiétude est essentielle à la félicité des créatures'.[35] And this means that character planning should go for optimal frustration, which makes you better off than in the initial state (with more-than-optimal frustration) and also better off than with adaptive preferences, which tend to limit aspirations to, or even below, the level of possibilities, resulting in a less-than-optimal level of frustration.

Endogenous preference change by learning not only creates no problems for ethics, but is positively required by it. If trying out something you believed you would not like makes you decide that you like it after all, then

---

[32] von Weiszäcker 1971; also Elster 1978a, p. 78, who gives as an illustration the sequence (1/2,3/2), (3/4,1/2), (1/4,3/4), (3/8,1/4) . . . in which each bundle is seen as an improvement over the preceding one because it implies an increase in the smallest component. A very conservative person, conversely, might reject each change in the opposite direction because it implies a reduction in the largest component. Such conservatism is akin to adaptive preference change, since it implies that you systematically upgrade what is most abundantly available (or downgrade the relatively unavailable).

[33] Elster 1979, p. 40.

[34] See Kolm 1979.

[35] Leibniz 1875–90, vol. V, p. 175.

the latter preferences should be made into the basis for social choice, and social choice would not be adequate without such a basis. This is, of course, subject to the qualifications mentioned above: the new preferences should not be reversible simply by making the preferred object inaccessible, and the need for knowledge may be overridden by the need for substance of character. Nor does precommitment create any difficulties. If the wants are prior to and actually shape the feasible set, then the coincidence of aspirations and possibilities is in no way disturbing. As to the deliberate (exogenous) manipulation of wants, it can be condemned out of hand on grounds of autonomy, and possibly on grounds of welfare as well.

Hard problems remain, however, concerning the relation between misperception of the situation and misformation of the preferences. Consider again the alternative interpretation of the Industrial Revolution, in terms of excessive anticipations rather than of rising aspirations. From the work of Tocqueville, Merton and Veyne, it would appear that below a certain threshold of actual mobility, expected mobility is irrationally low, in fact zero. Above this threshold, expected mobility becomes irrationally high, close to unity. And so, in society with little actual mobility, preferences may adapt to the perceived rather than to the actual situation, a contributing factor to what I have called overshooting or over-adaptation. Similarly, once a society has passed the mobility threshold, irrational expectations are generated, with a corresponding high level of wants. The intensity of the desire for improvement grows with the belief in its probability, and the belief in turn through wishful thinking feeds on the desire.

This view, if correct, implies that one cannot sort out in any simple way the frustration due to irrational expectations from the one due to a new level of aspirations. Let us imagine, however, that there was no tendency to wishful thinking. Then the actual and the expected rates of mobility would coincide (or at least not differ systematically), and the rational expectation would then generate a specific intensity of desire or aspiration level, with a corresponding level of frustration. The utilitarian might then want to argue that in this counterfactual state with rational expectations there would not be generated so much frustration as to make people actually worse off after the improvement in their objective situation. I am not certain that this is a relevant counterargument, for should one's acceptance of utilitarian theory turn upon empirical issues of this kind? And in any case I am not sure that the counterfactual statement is in fact true. Even when one knows that there is only a modest probability that one will get ahead, it may be sufficient to induce a state of acute dissatisfaction. But I have less than perfect confidence in both of these replies to the utilitarian counterargument, and so there is a gap in my argument. I leave it to the reader to assess for himself the importance of the difficulty.

The criticism I have directed against utilitarian theory is, essentially, that it takes account of wants only as they are *given*, subject at most to a clause about the need for learning about the alternatives. My objection has been what one might call 'backward-looking', arguing the need for an analysis of the *genesis* of wants. Before I spell out some methodological implications of this objection, I would like to point out that the assumption of given wants may also be questioned from two other directions, which for mnemonic purposes I shall call 'upward-looking' and 'forward-looking' respectively.

The language of directions suggests that preferences may be viewed along two dimensions. One is the temporal dimension: the formation and change of preferences. The other is a hierarchical dimension: the ranking of preferences according to higher-order preferences. If, in addition to information about the first-order preferences of individuals, we have information about their higher-order preferences, we may be able to get out of some of the paradoxes of social choice theory. This approach has been pioneered by Amartya Sen.[36] For some purposes this 'upward-looking' correction of preferences may be useful, but it can hardly serve as a general panacea.

Preferences, however, may also be corrected in a more substantial manner. Instead of looking at politics as the *aggregation* of given preferences, one may argue that the essence of politics is the *transformation* of preferences through public and rational discussion. This 'forward-looking' approach has been pioneered by Jürgen Habermas in numerous recent works. On his view, the multifarious individual preferences are not a final authority, but only idiosyncratic wants that must be shaped and purged in public discussion about the public good. In principle this debate is to go on until unanimity has been achieved, which implies that in a rationally organised society there will be no problem of social choice as currently conceived. Not optimal compromise, but unanimous agreement is the goal of politics. The obvious objection is that unanimity may take a long time to achieve, and in the meantime decisions must be made – and how can we then avoid some kind of aggregation procedure? In addition the unanimity, even if sincere, could easily be spurious in the sense of deriving from conformity rather than from rational conviction. There is no need to assume force or manipulation as the source of conformity, for there is good psychological evidence that a discordant minority will fall into line simply to reduce dissonance.[37] Habermas assumes crucially that in the absence of force rationality will prevail, but this is hardly borne out by the facts. I have argued that the containment of wants within the limits

[36] Sen 1974; 1977b.
[37] Asch 1956.

of the possible should make us suspicious about their autonomy, and similarly I believe that unanimity of preferences warrants some doubts about their authenticity. This implies, at the very least, that the forward-looking approach must be supplemented by the backward-looking scrutiny. The end result of unanimity does not in itself ensure rationality, for we must also ascertain that agreement is reached in an acceptable way.

The backward-looking approach in all cases involves an inquiry into the history of the actual preferences. One should note, however, that there are other ways of taking historical information into account. Thus we may make present decisions a function of present and past preferences, rather than of present preferences together with their past history. The rationale for using sequences of preferences as input to the social choice process could only be that they would somehow capture the relevant historical aspects of present preferences, and this they might well do. Persons tending to have adaptive preferences might be detected if they exhibit systematic variation of preferences with changing feasible sets. But the correlation would at best be a crude one, since the tendency towards adaptive preferences need not be a constant feature of a person's character.

The backward-looking principle is one of *moral hysteresis*.[38] Since information about the present may be insufficient to guide moral and political choice in the present, we may have to acquire information about the past as well. In Robert Nozick's terminology, I have been engaged in a polemic against end-state principles in ethical theory.[39] In Nozick's own substantive theory of justice, we need information about the historical sequence of transfers in order to determine what is a just distribution in the present. In Marxist theories of justice we also need to go beyond present ownership of capital goods, in order to determine whether it is justified by past labour.[40] And Aristotle argued that in order to blame or condone actions in the present, it is not enough to know whether the person was free to do otherwise in the present: we also need to know whether there was freedom of choice at some earlier stage.[41] In the present article, I have raised a more elusive problem, the historical dimension of wants and preferences. Adaptive preference formation is relevant for ethics, and it is not always reflected in the preferences themselves, and so it follows that ethics needs history.[42]

[38] Elster 1976 has a discussion of the more well-known notion of causal hysteresis.
[39] Nozick 1974, pp. 153 ff.
[40] Elster 1978b,c.
[41] *Nicomachean Ethics*, 1114a.
[42] This conclusion parallels the conclusion of my forthcoming essay on 'Belief, bias and ideology': 'Since epistemology deals with the rationality of beliefs, and since the rationality of a belief can neither be read off it straight away nor be assessed by comparing the belief with the evidence, we must conclude that epistemology needs history.'

12   Liberty and welfare

ISAAC LEVI

According to A. K. Sen, liberalism (or 'libertarianism' as he now prefers to call it[1]) permits each individual in society 'the freedom to determine at least one social choice, for example having his own walls pink rather than white, other things remaining the same for him and the rest of society'.[2]

Sen contends that the value involving individual liberty illustrated by this example imposes a constraint on social welfare functions – i.e. rules which specify a ranking of social states with respect to whether they serve the general welfare better or worse given information about the preferences of individual members of society for these social states or their welfare levels in these social states. This constraint 'represents a value involving individual liberty that many people would subscribe to' regardless of whether it captures all aspects of the presystematic usage of the terms 'liberalism' or 'libertarianism'.[3]

Sen's condition L asserts that each citizen ought to have his preference ranking of at least one pair of social states determine the social ranking of the same pair of states with respect to welfare.[4]

P. Bernholz pointed out that libertarians do not concede individuals rights to determine the social ranking of social states but to determine aspects of social states.[5] P. Gärdenfors has recently combined Bernholz's observation with R. Nozick's suggestion that granting rights to individuals cedes to them the ability to constrain the domain of social choice to a given class of social states.[6]

In his interesting discussion of Nozick's idea, Sen points to an ambiguity in the interpretation of a social ordering. He suggests that a social ordering can be construed 'to be purely a mechanism for choice' or as 'reflecting a view of social welfare'.[7]

[1] Sen 1976, p. 218.
[2] Sen 1970b, p. 153.
[3] loc.cit., n1.
[4] loc. cit.
[5] Bernholz 1974, pp. 100–1.
[6] Gärdenfors 1978; and Nozick 1974, pp. 165–6.
[7] Sen 1976, pp. 229–31.

In the following discussion, I shall distinguish between a mechanism for social choice, a standard for social value and a view of social welfare.

Mechanisms for social choice are to be understood to be institutionally sanctioned procedures for selecting social states. Liberalism or libertarianism is a doctrine recommending the imposition of constraints on social choice mechanisms. Instead of having social states selected by some special panel, rights holders make choices concerning *aspects* of social states over which they hold socially sanctioned rights in accordance with their personal preferences. Through their choices, these aspects of the social state are determined. Either the result is the determination of the total social state (in all relevant respects) or something is left for a governmental agency or agencies to determine. To simplify the discussion, I shall suppose that under a libertarian social choice mechanism the social state is totally determined by the decisions of the rights holders over the domains to which they hold rights.

In debating the merits of different social choice mechanisms, we should consider the social states selected by the use of these mechanisms relative to different contexts of social choice where the sets of feasible options or social states vary. Presumably it is a mark in favour of a choice mechanism when it chooses states which are best among those available when best options exist and it is a mark against the mechanism when it chooses inferior states when best options exist.

To make assessments of this sort requires some standard of social value which evaluates social states with respect to whether they are better or worse. Such a standard need not provide a complete ordering of the states in any feasible set. It need not guarantee that there be at least one best option in a feasible set. Nor need it be assumed that such a standard must rank social states as better or worse according to how well they promote social welfare. A view of social welfare may be endorsed as a standard of social value. Whoever does so may be called a *social-welfarist*.

Views of social welfare are representable by social welfare functions which by definition do completely order social states with respect to social welfare as a function of the preferences or welfares of the individual members of society. Different views of social welfare correspond to different types of constraint on social welfare functions. Of course, one can entertain a view of social welfare without being prepared to advocate its use as a standard of social value to be employed in assessing the admissibility of feasible options in contexts of social choice. But such views of social welfare play no clear role in policy making. To be a social-welfarist (of one of the many varieties entertainable) one should be ready to appraise the admissibility of options in problems of social choice using a social welfare function as a standard of social value and, to this extent, to appraise the legitimacy of social choice mechanisms.[8]

Non-social-welfarists may be divided into two categories. Some non-social-welfarists commit themselves in advance to a non-social-welfarist standard of social value and appraise choice mechanisms in terms of how well they promote the values licensed by the standard. If the 'fit' is poor, they will propose tinkering with the choice mechanism rather than the standard of value.

Other non-social-welfarists proceed in the opposite manner. If the fit is poor, they will leave the choice mechanism intact and revise the standard of social value.

Of course, non-social-welfarists might fail to belong strictly in either category but, when the fit between choice mechanism and standard of social value breaks down too badly may, depending on the type of breakdown, tamper with one or the other or with both. My own inclination is to favour a view of this sort.

In any case, Nozick, Gärdenfors and recently F. Schick[9] have argued

---

[8] Social-welfarism should be distinguished from what Sen has called 'welfarism'.

Both welfarism and social–welfarism are 'outcome moralities'. Moreover, welfarism according to Sen requires a standard of value representable by a social welfare function. Hence, welfarism is a species of social-welfarism in my sense.

But there are types of social-welfarism which are not welfaristic in Sen's sense. Anyone who endorses a standard of social value representable by a Social Welfare function is a social-welfarist. Sen imposes additional constraints on the social welfare function. In section 8 of 'On Weights and Measures: Informational Constraints on Social Welfare Analysis', Sen 1977a, Sen requires that a welfarist social welfare function obey strong neutrality. In 'Utilitarianism and Welfarism', Sen 1979b, p. 468, he requires conformity with the Pareto principle as well. In this last cited paper, Sen contrasts welfarism with weak paretianism which endorses social welfare functions obeying the weak Pareto principle. He acknowledges that weak paretianism belongs in the same family of views as welfarism, it can violate strong neutrality and, hence, may fail to be welfarist in the strict sense (or one of the two strict senses) employed by Sen.

My 'social-welfarism' is intended as a generic term covering Sen's welfarism as well as weak paretianism.

I contend that a standard of value appraising the goodness of states has ramifications for the appraisal of feasible options as admissible or inadmissible. I have just tried to indicate briefly what I think some of these ramifications are. They fall short of what Sen calls a 'consequentialist' view (Sen 1979b, p. 464).

[9] Schick's statements (Schick 1980) are quite explicit on this point. He contends that liberals (i.e. libertarians) focus on the distribution of goods rather than on the maximisation of welfare, where goods are understood to endow their possessors with control over some aspects of the social state. He points out that a ranking of alternative distributions of goods so construed is not to be confused with a social welfare ranking. Social welfare functions and the rankings they induce are not excluded from consideration (although the purpose they serve in the formation of policy remains obscure). However, Schick explicitly denies that liberals rank distributions of goods in terms of their efficiency in promoting welfare and concludes that one can consistently impose the Pareto principle P on social welfare functions and over the entire domain of social states while remaining a liberal. This is so because constraints on social welfare functions have no bearing on the evaluation of the justness and fairness of alternative distributions of goods. (Cont.)

that application of a social choice mechanism should not be evaluated in terms of its efficacy in promoting social welfare. So they are clearly non-social-welfarists. But their views seem stronger than that. They insist that the rights of individuals are somehow fundamental in the appraisal of choice mechanisms. I conjecture that they endorse variants of non-social-welfarist libertarianism which require modification of the standard of social value when its fit with libertarian choice mechanisms turns out to be poor. Whatever the precise views of these authors might be, however, I shall consider anyone who endorses such a position a *rugged libertarian*.

It is important to keep in mind that libertarianism (whether rugged, social-welfaristic or of some non-social-welfaristic alternative to rugged libertarianism) is distinguished by the constraints it advocates for mechanisms of social choice. On the assumption that ideally such a mechanism should select states which are admissible relative to some standard for social valuation, a libertarian view of the social choice mechanism has ramifications for the standard of social valuation to be adopted; but unless libertarianism is combined with social welfarism, libertarianism imposes no constraints on social welfare functions.[10]

Sen does not characterise libertarianism as imposing constraints on the social choice mechanism. His condition L is understood as a constraint on social welfare functions; and he correctly establishes the incompatibility of condition L with the weak Pareto principle.

A logomachy over the correct use of 'libertarianism' would be futile. But it seems fairly noncontroversial that under normal circumstances a person

I think this way of formulating the matter is somewhat less misleading than the Gärden-fors–Nozick approach according to which the social welfare function is defined on those states which remain after rights holders have exercised their rights and excluded others. I doubt whether any issue of substance is involved.

It should also be mentioned that those rugged libertarians I have identified seem to reject any evaluation of a system of rights by reference to the efficiency of the system in promoting the goodness of social states in any other sense of goodness than one which takes the endowment with rights as a measure of goodness.

[10] Some liberals or libertarians who are by no means social-welfaristic in their conception of the goodness of social states have clearly been opposed to rugged libertarianism. This was clearly true of John Dewey in the 1930s and 1940s who attacked those defenders of property rights who did so in the name of freedom. Dewey thought that the systems of property rights being defended were not effective in maximising more 'liberty' for individuals. It is clear that Dewey did not mean, by liberty for individuals, legally sanctioned rights but a character attribute which individuals may or may not lack – a capacity to realise one's 'potentialities'. Nor did he mean welfare in the sense in which Sen and I are using that term. But like social-welfarists and in opposition to rugged libertarians he was concerned to pick and choose among systems of institutionalised rights in terms of how well they promoted good social consequences. I think it is to be regretted that the recent discussion has tended to polarise around the opposition between social-welfarist libertarians and rugged libertarians. Other forms of libertarianism are worth examining. I do not, of course, think that any of the authors I have mentioned would disagree. (See Dewey 1946, especially Chapters 9 and 10.)

should have the right to sleep on his back or on his belly. What is noncontroversial in this claim is that no institutional procedures be adopted which prevent anyone from sleeping as they choose and that sanctions be adopted prohibiting others from interfering with such choice. Thus, what is noncontroversial is a view of mechanisms for social choice and not a view of social welfare. Hence, Sen may call his condition L a libertarian principle if he likes; but that does not establish that L represents 'a value involving individual liberty' of the sort illustrated by the fairly noncontroversial view that a person should have a right to sleep on his back or his belly as he chooses.

On the other hand, Sen's thesis is not refuted either. The question to be settled is whether a commitment to a libertarian mechanism for social choice presupposes a version of L as a constraint on social welfare functions. If the answer is in the affirmative, Sen's condition L represents 'a value involving individual liberty' even if one is a libertarian in the sense in which libertarianism imposes constraints on mechanisms for social choice.

We have already seen that libertarianism does have ramifications for standards of social value. On the other hand, unless the standard of social value adopted is social-welfaristic, libertarianism has no implications for social welfare functions. Rugged libertarians are not committed in virtue of their libertarianism to any particular view of social welfare and, hence, are not committed to condition L.

On the other hand, it is at least entertainable that a commitment to social-welfarist libertarianism incurs a commitment to condition L as a constraint on social welfare functions used as standards of social value. If so, Sen's arguments will have established that a welfarist libertarian cannot endorse a social welfare function as a standard of social value conforming to the weak Pareto principle P and the condition of unrestricted domain U.

Social-welfarist libertarianism does not entail a commitment to L. Moreover, the constraints which are entailed are compatible with principle P and, counter to what Bernholz suggests, with U as well.[11]

Social-welfarist libertarianism does presuppose, however, that the preferences of rights holders over *disjunctions* of social states are related to social preference over social states in certain ways. But these constraints may be met by restricting the beliefs rights holders have about the behaviour of other rights holders and not their preferences over social states.

If these observations are sound, it is perfectly possible to be a paretian, social-welfarist libertarian. This possibility does not derive from any flaw in Sen's proof that commitment to his condition L cannot be consistently

[11] Bernholz 1974, p. 100.

embraced along with commitment to conditions U and P on social welfare functions. It is based on the fact that condition L is not a necessary presupposition of social-welfarist libertarianism and that the presuppositions which are necessary do not preclude satisfaction of conditions U and P.

Bernholz and Gärdenfors have both correctly emphasised that if agent X possesses a right, the right concerns some aspect of social states.[12] The social choice mechanism does not secure for X the power to determine social states but only some aspect of such states. When X exercises his right, he does not choose a social state but chooses one of several alternative determinations of an aspect of social states.[13]

Thus, if X has the right to choose the colour of his walls, he is not entitled by his choice of a colour for his walls to determine the complete social state (including, for example, the colour of Y's walls).

This applies, of course, to the rights granted agents as part of the social choice mechanism.

In response to Bernholz on his point, Sen alleges that his remarks 'would seem to be based on a misunderstanding of the type of space on which these preferences are to be formulated. Given the rest of the world Ω, Jack's choice over the "measure" of sleeping on his back and that of sleeping on his belly *is* a choice over two "social states".'[14]

It is true that if Jack knew the condition Ω of the rest of the world or social state, his choice of sleeping on his back over sleeping on his belly (or vice versa) would be a choice of one social state over another. But when Jack makes his decision, the 'rest of the world Ω' is not given to him. What Jack chooses to be true is that the social state be described correctly by 'Jack sleeps on his back and (either Ω_1 or Ω_2 or . . . or Ω_n)' over the state described by 'Jack sleeps on his belly and (either Ω_1 or Ω_2 or . . . or Ω_n).' It is true that when Jack makes his decision and when all other rights holders

---

[12] Bernholz 1974, pp. 100 ff. and Gärdenfors 1978.

[13] Gärdenfors makes a distinction between exercising a right and failing to do so. X may fail to exercise his right to have his walls painted white by not deciding at all – e.g. by letting the colour be decided by some agency or by a lottery. I find it preferable to say that X did make a choice and did exercise his right by choosing to have the colour selected by an agency or lottery. On the view I favour, a right is characterised as a legally or socially sanctioned set of options from which the agent is free (legally or socially) to choose at least one and is constrained to choose at most one. Other circumstances beyond legal or social control may cut down the space of options further. The right need not be characterised by actually listing the set of options but may be described in some more general way (such as having the right to decide the colour of one's walls). But any choice with regard to the issue is an exercise of the right. This mode of representation may not conform to common legal or political categories; but I do not see that it prejudices any issues critical to the present discussion. I suspect it would simplify the formal articulation of the issues as compared with the proposals made by Gärdenfors. But I do not undertake such formalisation here.

[14] Sen 1976, p. 228.

make their decisions and when the other institutional agencies make whatever residual decisions are required, a social state may be fully determined. But the decisions of other rights holders and of the other social agencies are not given to Jack (at least not necessarily). What he chooses to be true in exercising his rights is that a disjunction of social states be true without choosing true that one of the disjuncts be true.

To illustrate, let us use Sen's well-known example. a and b each have the right to read or not to read *Lady Chatterley's Lover*. The following matrix gives the utility payoffs to the two parties in each of the four possible social states:

	Rb	$-Rb$
Ra	(1,4)	(3,3)
$-Ra$	(2,2)	(4,1)

a has the right to choose Ra or $-Ra$. But choosing Ra (i.e. choosing that Ra be true) is equivalent to choosing $Ra\&Rb$ or $Ra\&-Rb$. It is choosing that a disjunction of social states be true but not that one particular social state be true. The same applies *mutatis mutandis* to a's other option.

To be sure, if a knew that Rb obtains, his choosing that Ra be true would be equivalent to his choosing that $Ra\&Rb$. But even if it is true that Rb, if a does not know this, a's decision is not that $Ra\&Rb$ be true but that $Ra\&Rb$ or $Ra\&-Rb$ be true.

That is to say, this is so if we are thinking of choice in the sense in which choice is the outcome of deliberation where the agent adopts an option he judges admissible with respect to his preferences.

Thus, if a does not know b's decision, his decision whether to read or not to read the book will be based on his preference over the pair of options represented by the two disjunctions of social states cited above. His preferences over any pair of social states will be relevant only insofar as that preference determines or contributes to determining his preference over the pair of disjunctions of social states. It is a's preference over the disjunctions which ought to control his choices. Since the same thing obtains for b, it is apparent that whether or not the net effect of choices made by a and b is an optimal social choice of a social state depends upon how the preferences of rights holders over appropriate pairs of disjunctions of social states relate to social preferences of social states. The decisiveness of a's preferences over the pair $Ra\&Rb,-Ra\&Rb$ or the pair $Ra\&-Rb,-Ra\&-Rb$ for the social ranking has nothing to do with this.

Thus, suppose the social ranking is $Ra\&-Rb,Ra\&Rb,-Ra\&Rb,$ $-Ra\&-Rb$. The Pareto principle P is satisfied. a prefers $-Ra\&Rb$ to $Ra\&Rb$. But social preferences is in the opposite direction. a prefers

$-Ra\&Rb$ to $Ra\&-Rb$. Again society prefers the opposite. a's preference over the appropriate pairs of social states is not decisive for society.

Does this mean that a lacks the rights to decide whether to read or not to read the book in accordance with a's preferences for these two options? Not at all. Is it possible that a's preferences for the two options available to him can induce him to choose in a manner which does not prevent a socially optimal choice of a social state? Clearly if a prefers to read the book rather than not, his choice will not prevent a socially optimal social state from being selected.

What needs to be shown now is that a's preferences for disjunctions of states (and b's preferences for disjunctions) can be so constrained that the socially optimal state is selected by their choosing in accordance with their preferences within the framework of rights and that this can be done without imposing any constraint ruling out possible congeries of individual preference profiles for social states in violation of condition U or modifying the Pareto condition P on social welfare functions. Constraints may be necessary on preferences over disjunctions of social states. That is obvious. But such constraints ought not to be construed as restrictions on preferences over social states.

Bernholz has correctly observed that decision problems like those faced by a and by b are decision problems under uncertainty.[15] If the numbers assigned his values represent cardinal utilities unique up to a positive linear transformation and, if conditional on his reading *Lady Chatterley's Lover* he has numerically definite probability assignments for Rb and $-Rb$ and corresponding assignments conditional on his not reading the book, expected utilities can be computed for a's two options and his preferences determined accordingly.

Notice that even if the utility function for the social states representing a's preferences remains fixed, a's preferences for the two options open to him in virtue of his rights can be modified by changes in his probability judgements (which I shall call his *credal state*) unless each disjunct in one disjunction is preferred over every disjunct in the other – a condition not met in our example. In our example, a's preferences for the social states are such that $-Ra$ dominates Ra relative to the two states Rb and $-Rb$ but does not superdominate it.[16] Hence, by assigning a probability near 1 to $-Rb$ conditional on a's choosing to read the book and a probability near 1 to Rb conditional on a's choosing not to read the book, a can be in a credal state where he prefers reading to not reading – in the sense of preference which should dictate his choice when exercising his rights.

This observation does not depend upon the assumption that preferences

[15] Bernholz 1974, p. 101.
[16] This terminology is due to E. McLennan.

are represented by a utility function unique up to a positive linear transformation and probabilities by a unique probability function. I have suggested elsewhere that an agent's preferences may be represented by a set of utility functions and his credal state by a set of probability functions.[17] Both sets should be nonempty but the former need not be restricted to positive linear transformations of a given utility function and the latter need not be a unit set.

An option among the set feasible for the agent is *E-admissible* if and only if it ranks highest in expected utility relative to one permissible utility function in the set of utility functions representing the agent's preferences and to a probability function in the set representing the credal state. Ignoring some special complications, the agent's choice of an option should be restricted to maximin (or, perhaps better, leximin) solutions from among the E-admissible options.

In our example, if a's credal state is sufficiently indeterminate, both options will be E-admissible. He should then choose not to read because that is the maximin solution even though he does not rank that option preferable with respect to expected utility. If b's credal state is similarly indeterminate, he will choose to read not because it is preferable to not reading but because it bears the superior security level.

When the credal states of the two rights holders are of this kind, the social state chosen will, prisoner's-dilemma-like, be Pareto dominated by another social state. Although the exercise of rights leads neither to violation of condition U nor of condition P on social welfare functions, the choice mechanism based on the grant of rights to a and b fails to lead to the maximisation of welfare.

Social-welfarists will find such situations unpleasant and seek remedies. But they need not restrict the rights of a and b, modify the social welfare function, violate P, or prohibit a and b from ranking the social states the way they do.

It is enough to seek to promote conditions under which a and b will have credal states such that, given their individual preferences for the social states, will lead to preferences over disjunctions of social states that will induce the determination of a social state which is optimal with respect to welfare. Thus, a should be persuaded to assign near certainty to b's choosing not to read conditional on a's reading and near certainty to b's choosing to read conditional on a's not reading. Under these circumstances, a acquires a sharp preference for reading over not reading. Similar adjustments in b's credal state secures that b prefers not reading to reading leading to a welfare maximising solution.

[17] Levi 1974, pp. 391–418. A more articulate version appears in Levi 1980.

Making such adjustments requires no violation of conditions U or P on social welfare functions. It requires no modification of the rights built into the mechanism for social choice. It does require an alteration in the climate of trust, and ability of individuals to communicate with one another and to negotiate cooperative solutions.[18]

Situations can arise where a rights holder prefers one option over all others granted by his right and no modification of his credal state can induce a legitimate modification of his preferences over the options (which are disjunctions of social states). This can happen when one option superdominates all others. That is to say, the rights holder prefers any social state which is a disjunct in that option to every social state which is a disjunct in a rival option.

Social-welfarist libertarians must, in such cases, restrict the social welfare function to one which assigns maximum welfare to at least one social state which is a disjunct in the option which is superdominating for the rights holder (or at least ensure that no other option bears greater social welfare).

This is the only sense in which the preferences of a rights holder over social states constrains the social ranking for a social-welfarist libertarian. This constraint is far weaker than Sen's L or L'.

It is not news that libertarians, whether they are welfarists or, like John Dewey, prize liberty because it promotes some other sort of good, often insist that liberties be integrated in an organisation of institutions in such a way 'that men's "ultimate" values – their consciences, their sense of meaning of life, their personal dignity – do not become elements of public conflict'.[19] If they are social-welfarists, they would also promote institutional arrangements providing for negotiation over conflicting values (whether 'ultimate' or not) so that welfare may be promoted without depriving anyone of their rights.

It is not always possible to ensure social and institutional arrangement which will induce rights holders to adjust their beliefs so that it is rational for them to exercise their rights in a cooperative manner. And sometimes doing so will conflict with requirements of intellectual integrity. We may be reluctant to persuade rights holders to adjust their credal states in ways which run counter to common sense or the best scientific evidence available solely for the sake of promoting welfare maximising solutions to social decision problems through the exercise of rights.

[18] Libertarians who, like Dewey, are neither rugged nor welfaristic libertarians may be prepared to modify individual preferences in order to induce behaviour in rights holders conducive to maximising whatever it is they regard as good where these preferences are over social states. The point I am now making, however, is that such manoeuvers are not necessary in the case of welfarist libertarians in the narrow sense and may not be for other sorts of libertarians either.

[19] Frankel 1958, p. 83.

Any libertarian who contends that a given system of liberties is justifiably integrated into a social choice mechanism because it leads to or tends to lead to social states maximising some sort of good – whether it is social welfare or something else – runs the risk that economic, social and other relevant conditions may not be conducive to the use of such a choice mechanism. Such libertarians (whether social welfarist or not) may have to reconsider the system of rights they defend. Under these circumstances, only radical forms of rugged libertarianism advocated by those ready to modify the standard of social value in order to save the choice mechanism and the system of liberties it embodies may oppose advocates of radical reform of the choice mechanism without discomfort.

But social-welfarists are not precluded on any logical or conceptual grounds from endorsing libertarianism while remaining loyal to paretianism and the condition of unrestricted domain. Whatever difficulties social-welfarism may face, they must be sought elsewhere.

13 Under which descriptions?

FREDERIC SCHICK

The modern utilitarian has turned his back on his hedonist sources. His theory now takes in more than it did, and many of the old objections fail. But the current post-hedonism faces problems of its own. There is at least one central question it has no way of handling.

I will here speak of utilitarianism in its act-focussed form and will begin by assuming that its ethics is consequentialist. This is true of most versions of it, though (we shall see) not of all. The utilitarian, as this has him, holds two theses about right conduct. The first is that, wherever a person must act in one way or another, he should take some option whose consequences are at least as good as those of any alternative. The second thesis is that the better-or-worseness of the consequences is measured by the sums of the utilities people set on them.

The wording of the second thesis reflects the modern turn. None of the classical utilitarians spoke of utilities as *being set*. Utilities were to be *enjoyed* or *pursued*, for utility was simply pleasure or (for Bentham) 'that property in any object whereby it tends to produce . . . pleasure'. The line of analysis more common today interprets utility in terms of preference – a person's total utility function numerically maps out his preference ranking. Preferences can be of any sort: I can prefer my having more pleasure to my having less, or prefer more pleasure for others to more pleasure for me, or prefer one thing to another where neither offers pleasure to anyone. So my setting a greater utility on x than on y does not mean that x yields me more pleasure than y does.

The first of the utilitarian's theses directs us to look to the consequences. What are we asked to consider here? Suppose, for a start, that an action's consequences are its causal effects. Those of an option to act in some way are then the effects of so acting, or (cutting corners) the effects of that option. On this reading, the utilitarian holds that a person should always take some option whose effects have at least as great a utility-sum as the effects of any other option.

An agent's doing this or that may have effects that are unknown to him. This must make for uneasiness, for why consider effects the agent did not know would follow? Perhaps we might back off a step and confine an option's consequences to the effects the agent foresees. This would not do either: sometimes having failed to foresee is an excuse but often it isn't. The issue hinges on what the agent *could have* seen in advance, on what he could have foreseen in the light of his information. In the utilitarian's thinking, the consequences are the effects the agent could have foreseen, given what he knew.[1]

Two sorts of utilitarianism ought to be distinguished, a prospective analysis and a retrospective one. The first is an agentival affair, the second is God's at the Final Judgement. The first has to do with what it seems from the agent's position that the consequences will (or would) be, the second with what, looking backward, one could know that they were (or would have been). I am here concerned with the prospective analysis only. Thus the 'could haves' in the last paragraph are not those that come out in hindsight. Again, what the agent could have noted is what was predictable on the basis of his information, or perhaps (a different concept) on the basis of that available to him.

Let me restate utilitarianism for the prospective utilitarian's purposes – let me draw out the way I put it above. Both of the theses call for expansion. The first now is that, wherever a person must act in one way or another, he should take some option whose *foreseeable causal effects* are at least as good as those of any alternative, what is foreseeable being a matter of what this person has sufficient grounds for believing. The second thesis is that the better-or-worseness of these foreseeable effects is measured by the utilities *the agent has sufficient grounds for believing* people set on them. For brevity and familiarity's sake, I will keep to the initial wordings. But I will take them to be expressing these more specific ideas.

Either way of putting the theses obliges us to notice another point. The consequences of an option need not come about. The effects the agent should think would follow need not actually follow, and besides only one of the options of an issue is ever taken – the others leave no mark. The utilitarian speaks nonetheless of considering the consequence of all of the options, of weighing them against each other. Thus he speaks of the *consequences* in an extended sense, and also of *effects* and of *events* and *situations*. He allows these concepts to cover non-occurrent as well as occurrent states. I will do the same.

So much for laying the ground. Let me now bring out a difficulty. The utilitarian analyst ranks the consequences in terms of the utilities people set on them – this is true enough, but it misses a basic point. The utilitarian

---

[1] This does not take us beyond the case of certainty of foresight. The introduction of probabilities makes for some complications, but nothing of substance here must go.

is not focussed on the consequences in themselves. Consequences *per se* cannot be ranked in utility terms, for effects *per se* cannot be so ranked. Effects are events or situations, and people can't be said to value events or situations *per se*.

Our senses relate to the world directly, and a rose by any other name must smell the same. If people valued events *per se*, it could not matter how an event were labelled either. But valuation does not respect the self-identity of events. Perhaps Jimmy Carter was the first man from Georgia to have read all the works of Kierkegaard. The election of Carter then was the same event as the election of the first Georgian who had read all those books. Still, some people did not know this and valued the prospect of Carter's election differently than they did that of any heavy reader's. Likewise, the utility that you assign to the prospect of your winning the local lottery is not the same as the utility you assign to that of the last ticket sold's being drawn, and this though (without your knowing it) you bought that last ticket yourself and the event of your winning is thus the same as that of its being drawn.

Nothing about the facts is dependent on how we describe them. What we say about the result of an election cannot affect who won. Not so with how we value what happens: how much we care about someone's winning does depend on how we see him. That is, the utility we assign to something depends on how we understand it. The values we set do not focus on events or situations in their natural fullness but on the way we represent them, or, better, they focus on events or situations so represented. In this sense, they have to do with the prospects we have of these matters, with how we propose them to ourselves. I shall say (meaning just this) that they focus on propositions.

My point here is nothing new. It is an application of the principle of the intensionality of the mental. This says that what we believe or want or favour is always some proposition or other, that what we take for reflecting upon are not small bits of possible reality but various aspects of them, or, rather, these bits of reality considered under these aspects. The bearing of this idea on beliefs has been very intensively studied. For some reason, its bearing on values has had no attention.

Why should the utilitarian be uneasy? In looking to the consequences, he considers the values that people set on them. Intensionality thus directs him not to the effects in all their fullness, or to those the agent could have foreseen. It directs him to these events under certain descriptions of them: it has him look to the propositions expressing these events. This in itself is not troublesome.

Two points however must be noted. The first is that events do not have unique propositions corresponding to them. Not only can we label people or objects very differently (as President Carter or as the first president who had read his Kierkegaard), but the entire event can be construed in ways that bring out different aspects. (The defeat of Carter as President was also the victory of Reagan.) A proposition is a representation, and any event can be variously represented. It expresses a state of affairs but is only one of many expressions of it.

This is not troublesome either. The trouble stems from the second fact that people sometimes set different values on the different propositions expressing an event. That is, two propositions expressing an event may be differently valued by the same people. They can be differently valued only where these people don't know that they express the same event, but often people don't know this, or at least some people don't. So if we look to the consequences and sum up the utilities we see are set on them, we may wind up making judgements that differ depending on what propositions we pick: we may know of certain propositions that they are co-expressive, but some of the other people may not know it. This means that the injunction to look to the consequences is open-ended. To which of the many propositions expressing the consequences should we attend? Which of the many descriptions of the effects should be relevant for us? Here is a question to which the utilitarian has no adequate answer.

The question is one for the modern sort of utilitarian only, only for the utilitarian who interprets utilities in terms of preferences. Bentham and Mill took a simpler position: utility was pleasure or what it was that produced it. Intensionality kept out of this, for kicks are kicks, however we get them. Events give whatever pleasure they give however they are understood. So the question of proper descriptions never came up for these authors.[2]

Their current non-hedonist followers cannot avoid the question. Utilities, for them, are metricised preferences, and preferences focus on aspects of events. These new thinkers must find a way of saying which of the aspects of the consequences should be studied. Which descriptions of the consequences ought to figure in a utility summation? But is there really a difficulty? Why not defer to the agent? The proper reports of the consequences then are those that express what the agent sees in them. Let me call this way with the question the *agent-relativist* line and a utilitarian who follows it an agent-relativising utilitarian.

What the agent sees is here assumed to appear in a single proposition. This makes for a problem right off, for a person often acknowledges many propositions about an event. Should some one of these be identified as the

---

[2] Mill in fact opened the door to it. He defined one pleasure as *higher* than another where all people who had experience of both *preferred* the first to the second. But he did not develop this.

one that expresses what he sees in it – or, rather, is some one of them uniquely proper for agent-relativising? Is the proposition that should be considered their either–or disjunction, the weakest proposition to which the agent is committed? Is it the conjunction of them, the strongest such proposition? Or is it some proposition of intermediate strength? Different answers provide for different utility-sums, and so for different utilitarian judgements. But which is the answer we want?

There is also a second problem independent of the first. However he identifies what someone sees, the agent-relativist works out the course his theory prescribes for an agent when it is geared to the propositions reporting the consequences as this person sees them. The trouble is that the agent may fail him. The method keeps to what is foreseen, but the consequences may stretch beyond. The consequences of an agent's options are the effects that are foreseeable by him, whether or not he foresees them. Whether they are foreseen or not, they enter the analysis only via descriptions, and where the agent does not foresee them one cannot turn to him to determine which descriptions to use. Nothing at all is seen by the agent in effects he does not foresee. So there are no propositions expressing what he sees in them.

Consider the British and French appeasement of Germany in the 1930s. A utilitarian may be convinced that the appeasers were shortsighted. They knew enough to tell which way the wind was blowing. What they were doing led to disaster, and this effect was foreseeable by them. He would then judge their conduct in terms of the utilities people set on this consequence. But, again, under what description? We typically report the disaster by saying that Europe was engulfed in a war. But why is that the way to describe it? Why not say instead that the peace arranged at Versailles collapsed – most people cared much less about this. (Most people didn't know that the war undid that particular peace.) We cannot hope here to pass the buck by agent-relativising. The politicians did not see what would follow under any description.

The project of taking the agent's view fails where the agent does not see what he should. Could we provide against this by allowing for thought experiments? Suppose we proposed to describe the consequences that are foreseeable but not foreseen by the agent in the way he would have viewed them had he foreseen them. There is little promise here. Foreseeing too is a mental state and so it too is intensional. No one can foresee an event except under this description or that. The experiment thus reduces to asking: if the agent had foreseen the consequences under some description, what description would that have been? In most cases, there is no answer. He might have foreseen them in any number of ways.

This may suggest still another analysis. Foreseeability itself is intentional. It has to do with what about the future a person's information implies, and only propositions figure in implications. One of two propositions expressing an event may be implied by the information and the other not: what is foreseeable under one description need not be foreseeable under another. Could we now propose to describe the consequences not foreseen by an agent in terms of the descriptions under which they are foreseeable for him? Not without raising a problem very like one that stopped us some paragraphs back. An event is often foreseeable under each of several descriptions. Does one of these descriptions have priority over the others? Is the disjunction of them all the proper description for utility assessment? Is the proper description their conjunction instead? Again we are brought to a halt.

Perhaps we could turn in some other direction. Could we somehow relativise to the people whom the agent's actions would affect? Or perhaps to some neutral party – the Pope, or the President, or the Dalai Lama? This would not provide against the problem of unforeseen effects, for these people too need not foresee all that the agent could have foreseen. Besides, it would be arbitrary. We would now be judging the agent in terms of the perspective of some others, and this even where we do not think that the agent should have shared this perspective. But what if we think that he should have shared it? What if this perspective is the right one to take? In that case, no more would be needed. A reference to the right-minded others would be redundant. Here a new door opens for us. Let me briefly consider this very different approach to the problem.

This new approach starts out by proposing that judgement is a two-step affair and that the comparison of utility-sums is only step number two. The step that precedes finds the propositions whose utilities should be summed. The suggestion is that methodology is itself a sort of morals and that the procedure at this first step is very like that at the second.

At the earlier step we ask which propositions best express the effects. How are the consequences best described? For the utilitarian, this means one of two things. It either comes down to asking whether the total benefit would be greater if the agent (assumed a utilitarian) always considered the consequences under these descriptions or under those. Or it comes down to asking whether the total benefit would be greater if all people always considered the consequences in this way or that. (The rule-utilitarianism here is brought in for the preliminaries only; the main event remains the evaluation of the consequences of particular actions.)

This line does not advance us at all. Our question only reproduces itself. How is the general benefit in the prior analysis to be computed? The utilitarian's course is clear: he must attend to the consequences of the agent's (or everyone's) always using descriptions of this or of other sorts.

So the question arises for him how these new consequences should be described. He stands at the top of a bottomless structure of questions here. Any position he takes on any issue of proper descriptions gets whatever support is has from his position on the next deeper such issue.

Let me call this second answer to our question the *tortoising* answer, after the theory that the earth rests on the back of a giant tortoise, the tortoise stands on the back of another, that one on the back of still another, etc. A tortoising answer to any question presupposes an answer to one just like it – there are tortoises all the way down. Of course we can simply refuse to dig further. We can say we have gone deep enough: the proper descriptions are those we are using, and that is where it ends. But if we will pound the table after the seventh tortoising, why not pound at the first?

Or why not just drop the whole thing and start over? All of this discussion derives from the utilitarian's looking to the consequences. Could he free himself of the problem by renouncing consequentialism? Suppose he keeps to this, that a person should always take some option that is at least as good as any other, and that the worth of his options is measured by the sums of the utilities people set on them. The consequences do not enter here, or enter only indirectly. Options can be described in ways that refer to certain of their effects, but the options themselves are different from the events that follow from them. And the option-restricted analysis is distinct from the consequentialist one, for often people set different utilities on an option of causing something and on what this option, if taken, would cause. (Think of our different reactions to a person's dying and to his being killed.)

The second analysis is distinct from the first, and yet the problem is still with us. What would I do if I had to betray either my friend or my country – E. M. Forster considered this question. Someone more patriotically minded would complain that Forster put it badly: his question should have been whether or not he would betray his country. A third person might hold that he should have asked whether or not he would betray his friend. Does it matter which way this is put? It matters to a utilitarian of the nonconsequentialist sort. For he must look to how people feel about the actions an agent might take, and people may set different values on different propositions that report the same actions. How he describes what the agent might do determines which utilities he will sum up. And so it may determine what conduct he will endorse.

Forster's predicament was hypothetical. Consider the real problem some years ago of the distribution of artificial kidneys. There were then far fewer devices than kidney patients who needed them. Who was to get this scarce equipment? Different countries had different policies. In Britain the rule was to provide the kidneys to those most likely to benefit from them. Poor medical risks were excluded, and sometimes also people unlikely to stick to the diet that was part of the treatment. This ruled out the old and the young and (it is said) those who did physical labour. In effect, it reserved the kidneys for the middle aged and the well-to-do.

Were the British acting rightly? Doubtless many people thought so. Others disagreed. Professor Giovanetti of Pisa, on whose diet the policy rested, held that such a programme 'would violate all humane principles'.[3] He was not in favour of reserving the kidneys for people less likely to benefit from them. His point was that it was wrong to think in terms of long-run improvement here. The policy he favoured – the official Italian policy – was to treat all the sick alike, to give the kidneys to all who needed them on a first-come first-served basis.

Suppose we called in the utilitarian. Which policy would he endorse? The British took a stand on whether to go by the likelihood of recovery or not. If our consultant worked out the sums of the utilities people set on the options so described, he might side with the British. If he computed the utility-sums for the equality-versus-nonequality descriptions, he might side with the Italians instead. Coming down one way or the other would call for deciding how to describe the options. Should the extent to which they promised to promote recovery be reported? Or should their evenhandedness or lack of it? (Or did both the British and the Italians attend to half the scene only; or was there more yet that should have been mentioned?)

How should we describe the options? Unlike our question about consequences, this one has been around for some time. Rule-utilitarians have been aware that they must handle it somehow, for there are countless rules that cover any given action, one for every possible way of describing it. Kantians have worried about this for the very same reason. I see no promise in any of the several rule-utilitarian proposals, neither in their own context nor in their application here. They all involve attending to the consequences of some adherence to rules, and so they take us back to the problem of consequences we hoped to evade.[4] Nor again is there any point to the tortoising idea, to finding the proper descriptions in a prior utilitarian step. This again only raises questions of the same sort as the ones it proposes to answer.

How about agent-relativising in this new connection? This was Kant's way out. What Kant required to be willable into a law was the *maxim* of an

---

[3] Quoted in Calabresi and Bobbitt 1978, p. 185. My report of the kidney case is taken from this book.
[4] For the rule-utilitarian analysis of the question, see Singer 1961, pp. 71–90; and Lyons 1965, pp. 52–61.

action, the agent's self-direction to it under the view he himself had of it. The agent may see his options in several ways at once, and so the question arises again which of his views of them should be followed. Also, we know that the agent's lead does not always go the whole distance. Where some consequences of an agent's options were foreseeable but not foreseen by the agent, the agent had no view of these we could follow in summing utilities. But this cannot worry the utilitarian who has renounced consequentialism.

Still, a similar problem comes up regarding the actions that are at issue. The non-consequentialist utilitarian says that a person should always take some option that is at least as good as any other. In this he is not speaking of what this person thinks he might do but of what he has grounds for thinking – not of the opportunities the agent sees but of those he *could* see, given what he knows. Where the agent is blind to certain courses open to him, he has no view of these that could determine their proper descriptions. So we cannot tell which valuations of these options should be counted and so cannot tell which option is best. Again the agent's lead must fail us.[5]

Dropping consequentialism does not dispose of our problem but only redirects it. The question was how to construe the effects. Now it is how to construe the actions. No better sorts of answers suggest themselves here – there is still only relativism and tortoising. The first falls short where people do not see all the courses that are open, or see them in several ways. The second proposes an analysis that calls for another just like it. The non-consequentialist utilitarian is no better off than the consequentialist.

Those on the sidelines ought not to gloat: they may be in trouble too. Our problem arises for any theory that judges conduct by the values people set on the consequences of agent's options. It also arises for any theory that considers people's valuations of the options directly. In technical terms, it arises for any theory that proposes a social welfare function (or functional) on either the consequences or the options. This includes utilitarian theories and maximinning theories and all sorts of variants of them. It includes theories that call for attending only to people in this or that group. It even includes certain egoist theories, those that direct people to take the option whose consequences are the best for them (or again, more simply, the option that itself is best).

Indeed a parallel problem comes up outside the precincts of ethics. Some years ago, Nelson Goodman raised what he called 'The New Riddle of Induction'.[6] Suppose that one hundred marbles, all of them blue, are

---

[5] This does not affect Kant, who speaks of perceived options only. For Kant on the problem of descriptions, see Nell 1975.
[6] See Goodman 1973.

drawn from an urn; the next to be drawn will very likely be blue. All the drawn marbles are also *bleen,* a bleen marble being one that is either drawn before January 1 and is blue or drawn after and is green. Parity of reasoning implies that the next marble will very likely be bleen, but this says that if it is drawn after January 1 it is likely to be green and *so not* likely to be blue. Formally identical inferences from evidence described in different ways yield incompatible judgements. We avoid the contradiction by rejecting the bleen-descriptions. But where is our warrant for this? What makes these descriptions improper?

Our problem of descriptions is very like Goodman's. We too find different descriptions of events supporting incompatible judgements. There is only this distinction. The descriptions improper for inferential judgement wear their impropriety on their sleeves. The predicates 'is bleen' and 'is grue' are odd – no issue there. It remains for us to say wherein their oddity consists. In moral judgement, the case is less clear. Neither the British nor the Italian statements of the kidney options used suspect jargon. Nor is there anything special about either of our descriptions of the start of the Second World War. We here face not only the problem of how to define the propriety of descriptions but also the often more pressing problem of saying which descriptions are proper.

14 What's the use of going to school? The problem of education in utilitarianism and rights theories

AMY GUTMANN

Education seems to present special difficulties for all liberal theories.[1] Utilitarians and those whom I shall call 'rights theorists', i.e. those who give priority to the equal right of all to civil and political freedom, agree on one point about the education of children: at least in principle they both are committed to providing an education that is neutral among substantive conceptions of the good life.[2] Yet we probably will never be able to educate children without prejudicing their future choice of particular ways of life. One might argue, therefore, that education creates the same problem for any form of liberalism. That argument is incorrect. Although rights theorists also must take consequences into account, they can provide a more consistently liberal solution to the problem of education for several reasons, which I shall summarise here and elaborate below. Freedom provides a better standard than happiness by which to determine what and how to teach children. In addition, one can derive some essential features of a liberal educational programme from the standard of freedom that cannot be derived from that of happiness. That educational programme will be neutral towards many, though not all, ways of life and concrete enough to guide educators. In addition, unlike utilitarianism, rights theorists can respond cogently to the conservative claim that education must perpetuate particular societal values and prepare children for necessary social functions.

1 Education for happiness

Utilitarians pay a high price for assuming that happiness must be subjectively defined by each individual, an assumption that frees them of the

---

[1] For the definition of liberalism upon which this essay relies, see Dworkin 1978, p. 127.
[2] For recent examples of rights theories, see Rawls 1971; Dworkin 1978; Fried 1978; and Donagan 1977. Nozick's theory in Nozick 1974 is also a rights theory, but it is hard to imagine how a state based only upon the right not to be interfered with can provide for the education of children.

need to defend an objective conception of the good. How is society to prepare children for the pursuit of their own, self-defined happiness? Children cannot themselves determine the particular ends of education, nor is maximising their present happiness a reasonable utilitarian standard for education, if only because the rest of their life is likely to be much longer than their childhood. Yet what will make children happy in the future is largely indeterminate. To make matters more complicated still, education itself significantly shapes how children will define their happiness once they become adults. To guide the education of children, utilitarians need to find a standard that is not tied to a particular conception of the good life and that is not derived from the circular argument that if they become happy adults their prior education must have been good. Thus, the major problems that utilitarians face in determining the purpose of educational institutions are prior to the problem of aggregating happiness, for which utilitarians have been amply criticised by rights theorists.[3] These problems can be best illustrated by looking more closely at the foundations of Benthamite utilitarianism and at Bentham's specific recommendations for educating children.

Benthamite utilitarianism takes the preferences of individuals as a given and regards attempts to maximise satisfaction of those preferences as 'good'. 'Pushpin is as good as poetry', so long as the satisfaction a person derives from each is equal and each contributes equally to the happiness of others. As J. J. C. Smart points out, the latter condition will almost certainly mean in practice that poetry will be a better activity than pushpin, because poetry will add to the happiness of others more than pushpin will.[4] Even critics of utilitarianism recognise that happiness, broadly interpreted, is a minimally controversial good in that it accommodates almost all conceptions of the good life.[5] Very few people want to lead an *un*happy or *un*satisfying life.[6] Utilitarianism maintains a neutral position among conceptions of the good life, asking people only to recognise the equal claims of all others to lead a happy life as they define it.

Of course, that request may entail a sizable amount of self-sacrifice since, at least in theory, the greatest happiness principle can override one person's claim to happiness by its recognition of the validity of many claims with which it comes in conflict. However, rights theories

[3] For criticisms of the aggregative aspect of utilitarianism, see Rawls 1971, pp. 187–92; Williams 1973, pp. 82–118, 135–50; and Dworkin 1977, pp. 231–8, 272–8.

[4] See J. J. C. Smart in Smart and Williams 1973, p. 24.

[5] See, for example, Williams 1972, p. 91.

[6] This assessment of utilitarianism is independent of one's understanding of the meaning of happiness so long as happiness is understood as a subjectively-defined state of individuals. The same problems arise whether happiness is what individuals deliberately approve or what gives them pleasure.

must also have to establish some priority in such cases. The neutrality principle, combined with the Benthamite view that happiness is a subjectively defined state, requires that every person's capacity for happiness be considered equal. This equality assumption and the law of diminishing marginal utility all but guarantee that utilitarianism will demand no greater sacrifice of individuals for the general good than will most rights theories, which also make provisions for overriding an individual's right in extreme situations.[7]

Utilitarians must reject a few common solutions to the problem of education. They cannot avoid the task of specifying standards that ought to guide the education of children simply by allocating decision-making authority to some paternalistic agent. According to utilitarian reasoning, neither parents nor the state have a natural right to determine the education of children. Children are neither the property of their parents nor mere creatures of the state.[8] Utilitarians are correct on this score: even if we must ultimately allocate rights of control over education, the exercise of those rights ought to be contingent upon the fulfilment of duties to educate properly. Therefore, the definition of educational standards should be prior to the allocation of paternalistic authority.[9]

A strict utilitarian must also reject John Stuart Mill's suggestion that education be guided by the perfectionist ideal of maximising development of the particular capacities of each individual. Mill claims that what constitutes maximum development of character is decided by reference to happiness as the standard, and that therefore perfectionism (as he understands it) is consistently utilitarian. Mill provides two standards by which he claims perfectionism is rendered compatible with happiness. Both are inadequate. His first standard of happiness – 'the comparatively humble sense of pleasure and freedom from pain' – does not necessarily lead to a perfectionist ideal: playing pushpin is probably more pleasurable, at least in the comparatively humble sense of the word, than writing poetry. And his second – that life which 'human beings with highly developed faculties can care to have' – is extremely problematic from a utilitarian or any other liberal perspective, because it smuggles in a particular conception of the good life under the guise of a universally acceptable choice criterion of pleasure.[10] So, although perfectionism would save utilitarianism from the problem of finding some standard of happiness external to children's

---

[7] For a recent description of the convergence of consequentialist and rights theories, see Barry 1979, pp. 629–35.

[8] Compare Fried 1978, p. 152. See also Justice McReynold's decision in *Pierce v. Society of Sisters*, 268 U.S. 535.

[9] I make a more thorough argument for this position in Gutmann 1980.

[10] See Mill 1950, p. 358.

preferences, it would do so only by sacrificing utilitarianism's neutrality with regard to conceptions of the good life.

Utilitarians could dodge the problem entirely by educating children so as to maximise the happiness of adults. Since the future preferences of children are unknown while those of adults are known and relatively stable over time, this might be a 'safe' utilitarian strategy. But it is also an intuitively unappealing course, which would again raise in the educational context the general aggregation problem of utilitarianism. The intuitively plausible rationale for discounting the present preferences of children is to help them realise greater happiness in the future, not to sacrifice their happiness entirely to that of their elders. What if 'educating' children to be garbage collectors would maximise the happiness of adults? Although children seem to wallow in dirt (as Fourier noted), no sane utilitarian has ever advocated such a policy, which could hardly be called educational. Even on utilitarian standards, it would be shortsighted to educate children for the happiness of adults. Since children will outlive adults, their education then will cease to have any point.

Education, according to James Mill, ought to render each individual's mind, 'as much as possible, an instrument of happiness, *first* to himself, and next to other beings'.[11] Utilitarians cannot consistently claim that education ought first be concerned with a child's own happiness because such an education is a child's right or because that is the intrinsic nature of the educational good. But they can plausibly claim that most *educated* persons will be better judges and hence better 'instruments' of their own happiness then they will be of others' happiness. The classic utilitarian plan for education, *Crestomathia*, therefore focusses upon education as a means of rendering each child's mind an instrument of his or her own happiness. (Bentham argued that girls as well as boys be admitted to Crestomathia.) As the neologism implies, education ought to 'conduce to useful learning'.[12]

Useful for what? Happiness is surely too indefinite an end (as utilitarians themselves admit) to guide an educational programme. Bentham therefore listed secondary ends, which he assumed were constitutive of every child's future happiness. Education ought to supply children with the means to (1) avoiding 'inordinate sensuality (and its mischievous consequences)', (2) securing profit-yielding employment, (3) securing admission into 'good company' from which the previous advantage could also be obtained, (4) avoiding ennui and the 'pain of mental vacuity', and (5) gaining a 'proportionable share of general respect'.[13]

[11] Burston 1969, p. 41. Emphasis added.
[12] See Jeremy Bentham, *Chrestomathia* in Bentham 1843, Vol. 8, p. 8.
[13] *Ibid.*, pp. 8–10.

Surveying Bentham's list, we discover that each secondary end is problematic. Either it is not clearly derivable from happiness as an ultimate end, not sufficiently neutral among conceptions of the good life, or as indeterminate an educational goal as happiness itself.

If *inordinate* sensuality is defined as the amount that proves counterproductive to the pursuit of long-term happiness, then utilitarians can of course consistently teach children to control their inordinate sensual desires. Otherwise, the goal of avoiding sensuality is not clearly consistent with utilitarian principles. One suspects that Bentham has conveniently yielded to prevailing moral opinion that sensuality is a bad thing.

Securing profit-yielding employment and admission into good company is no more consistent with the greatest happiness principle. Surely, many types of employment that are not often profit-yielding – artistic vocations, for example – can be pleasure yielding, perhaps even more so than jobs in business. But if a child has no independent source of income, then income-producing employment is likely to be essential to living a minimally happy life. Once one accepts the prevailing economic reality – that only independently wealthy children can afford to be educated to pursue non-income producing vocations – then Bentham's educational goal seems to follow. Similarly, if admission into good company provides a ticket to gainful employment, then from a utilitarian perspective an education that enables children to enter into good company may be sufficiently neutral among conceptions of the good life.

Yet the results of this reasoning are incongruous with liberalism. A theory that on principle is neutral among a wide range of ways of life turns out to be partial to those particular ways that happen to produce steady income and social approval. Furthermore, those people who will determine that partiality will not be the same people who will be subject to its consequences. Utilitarianism thus appears to be in this sense illiberal and to have conservative consequences when applied to education: children are to be educated so that they can fit into society as it exists. Whether this is a fatal criticism of utilitarianism from a liberal perspective will depend upon whether any liberal theory can better cope with this educational dilemma.

The goals of avoiding ennui and gaining the respect of others are sufficiently neutral among conceptions of the good life and can be derived from the summa bonum of happiness.[14] However, neither is more

---

[14] One could specify some plausible conditions of achieving *self*-respect through education such that they conflict with other ways of educating children to find happiness. If certain methods of education undermine self-respect by subjecting children to unquestionable and inaccessible authority and by continually ranking children in a hierarchy of intellectual merit, then this secondary goal is not as innocuous as Bentham's educational plan suggests. In fact, the monotorial method of education endorsed by Bentham and the panopticonal design of Crestomathia (wherein the schoolmaster could observe all classes without being

determinate than happiness. Indeed, it would be hard to conceive of a more nebulous educational goal than avoiding the 'pain of mental vacuity'.

II Education for freedom

Rights theorists face a problem analogous to that of utilitarians, since children cannot plausibly be granted freedoms equal to those of adults and education necessitates a curtailment of freedom. As Russell noted in a lecture on J. S. Mill, 'There is one sphere in which the advocate of liberty is confronted with peculiar difficulties: I mean the sphere of education.'[15] Does freedom provide a better standard than happiness by which to determine what and how to teach children? Can one derive from the standard of freedom an educational programme that remains neutral among conceptions of the good life?

Some of Bentham's secondary goals for education are more compatible with an education designed to prepare children for freedom than with one designed for happiness. By preparing every child through education for profit-yielding employment, we are providing children with the background conditions for free choice in a society that attaches a price to most valued goods. And if admission to good company facilitates access to many valued goods, then education directed at securing such access will also increase a child's future freedom. In fact, these secondary goals seem more reasonably connected to the end of future freedom than to that of future happiness. By all accounts, children of the Old Order Amish who are denied secondary schooling by their parents, and are therefore trained for only a very narrow range of vocations, grow up to be as happy as, and probably more secure than, their more educated peers.[16] But, by their parents' own admission and intent, their lesser education makes them less free to choose among ways of life. Utilitarians have traditionally denied that 'he that increaseth knowledge increaseth sorrow', but they have offered little or no specific evidence to support their counterclaim that the question of whether people should have more or less education 'is merely the question, whether they should have more or less of misery, when happiness might be given in its stead'.[17] A consistent utilitarian could, of course, deny the need for education in cases like those of the Amish. But it

---

seen) might be challenged on these non-utilitarian grounds – even if a Crestomathic education would produce the happiest of people. 'Call them soldiers, call them monks, call them machines, so long as they be [or, in the case of education, become] happy ones, I shall not care' is not a response open to anyone who takes self-respect to be a demanding criterion of distributive justice, and its development a goal of education.

[15] Russell 1955, p. 56.
[16] See Hostetler and Huntington 1971; Erickson 1969, pp. 15–59.
[17] James Mill in Burston 1969, p. 105.

is hard to find a consistent utilitarian because most are unwilling to abandon their commitment to educating children in order to pursue the goal of maximising happiness.[18]

But suppose utilitarians did remain faithful to the principle of happiness, and in the case of the Amish children defer to their parents' opposition to secondary education. Utilitarians will then face the problem of neutrality. Amish children did not themselves choose to pursue the traditional Amish way of life; their parents have no right to determine how their children will live when they grow up. Then, why should utilitarians defer to the preferences of the adult Amish in denying an education to their children? Once having been raised in an Amish family, Amish children may well be happier, and thus be better off by utilitarian standards, without any secondary education. Therefore utilitarians seem bound to defer to the wishes of Amish parents. Yet in so doing, they forsake any commitment to educating children for their own choice among ways of life.

So the problem of neutrality now reappears on another level. Amish parents raise their children so as to prevent them from finding happiness outside of the Amish way of life. If happiness is subjectively determined, utilitarians committed to maximising social happiness cannot be content to permit any group to shelter their children from influences that permit a wide range of choice among ways of life that might lead to happiness. Yet so long as all forms of education predispose children toward certain ways of finding happiness and away from others, utilitarians must choose the forms that are most likely to produce happy people. The more serious problem specific to utilitarianism is that it lacks any means of comparing the level of satisfaction gained from radically different ways of life.

John Stuart Mill's choice criterion of pleasure can be viewed as an attempt to solve this problem of incommensurability, but it begs the issue from a utilitarian perspective.[19] Socrates cannot possibly know what it is like to be as happy as a fool. And once we are educated and exposed to worldly influences, we are effectively deprived of the possibility of experiencing the satisfactions of the Amish way of life. That we then choose not to become Amish is immaterial to the question of which is a better way of life on utilitarian grounds.

Dewey's educational criterion shares the same problem as Mill's choice criterion of pleasure. A utilitarian cannot recommend as the standard for what 'the community [must] want for all of its children' what 'the best and

---

[18] Those who do defend the position of the Amish parents do so on grounds of religious freedom. See Justice Burger's opinion for the majority in *State of Wisconsin v. Yoder* 406 U.S. 205. I have examined and criticised this position in Gutmann 1980.

[19] See Mill 1962, Ch. 2, para. 6.

wisest parent wants for his own child'.[20] Only actual preferences or actual satisfactions can count on utilitarian grounds. Dewey's standard appears equally suspect on grounds of free choice. A liberal cannot assume that the best education is that which a particular group of people want to provide for their children. At the very least, liberals must provide criteria for what a good education is or else tell us why a particular group has the right to determine educational standards for the whole community.

III The social boundaries of freedom

The issue of education puts the conflict between utilitarians and rights theorists in a different light than it is usually seen. Defenses of education in both schools of thought are consequentialist; neither invokes the claim that compulsory education is a good in itself or that the pursuit of knowledge can be justified by its own internally generated principles.[21] But the nature of the consequentialist reasoning differs significantly. Utilitarians must judge the subjective outcome of being educated relative to that of remaining uneducated. Rights theorists need only determine whether education expands or contracts the opportunities children will have for rational choice in the future. This objective criterion is easier to apply in practice because it does not depend upon a difficult counter-factual assessment of future states of mind: how much happier or sadder would they have been were they uneducated? Nor does it succumb to the circularity of Mill's choice criterion of pleasure.

But the task of rights theorists still is not easy. They have to determine how to select among the possible courses of education that which will maximally expand each child's future civil and political freedom. An education directed at maximising future choice cannot be neutral among all ways of life. Even if Bentham's curriculum was unduly restrictive (he opposed teaching music in schools because it would make too much noise),[22] there is no way of educating children to choose impartially between becoming a farmer in an Amish community and becoming a jazz musician. Any curriculum that is secular and imparts scientific knowledge will make the choice of some religious ways of life much more difficult than would a religious education. In addition, the methods of teaching – reliance upon competition or cooperation, upon rewards or punishment – also predispose children towards particular private and political choices in the future.

Education for freedom, then, must operate within some boundaries in

---

[20] Dewey 1943, p. 7.
[21] Compare Hirst 1972, pp. 391–414.
[22] See *Chrestomathia* (Bentham 1843), p. 40.

any case. The question becomes: which boundaries are most justifiable? Freedom itself seems to provide a standard if one counts the possibilities left open by each educational programme and chooses the one that leaves open the most (reasonable) options. But notice that his standard depends on the nature of the society to which it is applied. What one counts as reasonable options will be determined in part by the social context within which children will have to make their future choices. Were we living in seventeenth-century America, a religious education would provide children with more opportunities for choice among ways of life than would a secular education. An education that employs cooperative methods of learning would prepare children for more occupations in Maoist China than would the competitive educational methods used in most schools in the United States. Interpreted in this way, the freedom standard also has a conservative bias: it permits partiality – reflected both in educational content and methods – towards those conceptions of the good life that are most commonly pursued and that are income-producing within any given society.[23] Once again, this non-neutrality cannot itself be justified by reference to the choices children have made or will make, once educated, to pursue these established ways of life.

We might ask, therefore, whether a more conservative theory provides a better prescription for the content of education. Unlike utilitarians and rights theorists, Durkheim explicitly defends the idea that education should have a conservative function. He criticises both the utilitarian view that education ought to be a means toward individual happiness and the idea (which he gathers from Kant) that education ought to be a means towards individual perfection. Because happiness is a subjective state, Durkheim argues, it leaves the end of education to individual fancy and hence undetermined. Perfectionism ignores the demands that the division of labour places upon modern education for specialised training. More generally, Durkheim maintains that the educational philosophies of political theorists are all misguided: 'they assume that there is an ideal, perfect education, which applies to all men indiscriminately; and it is this education, universal and unique, that the theorist tries to define'. In place of an ideal education, Durkheim argues for an education that is the product of the common life of a society and therefore expresses the educational needs of that society. 'Of what use is it to imagine a kind of education that would be fatal for the society that put it into practice?'[24]

Even if an education 'fatal for the society that put it into practice' is an idle – and perhaps dangerous – fancy, Durkheim's recommendation does

[23] I mean 'conservative' in the strict sense of that which is intended to preserve the values of any society, even one that is liberal or Marxist.
[24] Durkheim 1956, p. 64.

not immediately follow. Why should education perpetuate the particular roles demanded by the collective life of each particular society? Durkheim himself makes the transition from 'is' to 'ought' without explicit argument. He seems to assume that because education serves this integrative function in most societies, it ought to do so. But there is something to be said for Durkheim's conclusion. In advanced industrial societies, educational institutions are well-equipped to perpetuate common and unifying beliefs. Aside from the family, schools and television are the only institutions that come into prolonged contact with the younger generation of citizens. As long as family life is to remain a private realm – valued in part for its diversity and immunity from intervention – then schools and television are the only plausible socialising institutions that can be effectively regulated (even if not fully controlled) by a liberal or illiberal state. This functional importance does not of course justify a conservative use of education, but it does suggest that if a society's values are worth preserving the educational system may be an essential instrument.

Must rights theorists oppose this socialising function of schools as a form of tyranny of the majority over the individual? Durkheim denies that socialisation (through education) is tyranny. Education gives children what is uniquely human and moral: control over their inclinations, a socially determined morality and a language that enables them to communicate that morality to their peers. Socialisation into a liberal democratic society entails more than mere discipline and the acquisition of language. The state also has a legitimate interest in educating children to respect reason, science, and the 'ideas and sentiments which are at the base of democratic morality'.[25] Now, one might dispute the importance of the particular objects of respect that Durkheim has chosen (e.g. respect for science), but the challenge that his argument poses for liberalism would remain the same. At least in its early stages, education is not primarily a liberating institution but a constraining one; the constraints are justified by the needs of society for cohesion; and children are 'humanized' (which for Durkheim means socialised) by those constraints. According to Durkheim, this same rationale of social cohesion also accounts for specialisation of education at higher levels, because 'without a certain diversity all cooperation would be impossible; education assures the persistence of this necessary diversity by being itself diversified and specialised'.[26] Insofar as children themselves are the beneficiaries, rights theorists must also embrace the socialising function of schools.

But Durkheim's challenge to liberalism is only partially successful.

[25] *Ibid.*, p. 81.
[26] *Ibid.*, p. 70. More accurately: without a certain diversity, *some* important kinds of cooperation would be impossible.

Rights theories can account for the constraints education places upon the thoughts of children and for the fact that those constraints are – and ought to be – relative to the society in which children are raised. Rights theorists must also justify those constraints by taking into account the interests of children in becoming social beings and, more specifically, in becoming citizens of the society in which they are born. But for rights theorists, social cohesion is a virtue only in a society in which membership is a benefit, rather than a burden, i.e. in a society in which children will become citizens with the full range of civil and political liberties, and not be mere subjects of the state. Even if elementary education must discipline children, the ultimate purpose of education on a rights theory will be to equip every child with the intellectual means to choose a way of life compatible with the equal freedom of others.

Social cohesion is a prerequisite for this freedom, but such cohesion can be achieved through many different educational and non-educational methods, some of which are inimical to freedom. Rights theorists must choose those methods that are most consistent with maximising the future freedom of children. Durkheim and rights theorists converge in their reasoning so long as the state provides the context within which individual freedom is best protected.[27] But they part company in their understanding of how diversity should be accomplished within a democratic state. If social cohesion and economic welfare are the only rationales for educational specialisation, then tracking children into particular specialised vocational programmes would be justified so long as the number of children in each track was sufficient to meet future social needs and the tracks were divided according to ability. Rights theory, however, also demands that education provide (as far as possible given the diversity of natural talents) an equal educational opportunity for every child. This demand is based upon the value of maximising each child's freedom to choose a way of life consistent with the like freedom of all others.[28] The requirements of the division of labour, therefore, are only to be met by specialised education after children are given sufficient opportunity to discover how they wish to specialise within the range of options that their natural capacities permit.

Were the only justifiable function of education from the standpoint of freedom to maximise choice among readily available ways of life, then rights theory would rest upon a conservative educational foundation very similar to that which Durkheim recommends and upon which (I have argued) Benthamite utilitarianism must rest. But there is a justifiable and

[27] This means, however, that outside of the context of a liberal state, the positions of Durkheim and of rights theorists will conflict.
[28] See, e.g., Rawls 1971, pp. 101, 107.

essential function of education that goes beyond preparing children for becoming law-abiding citizens, for pursuing happiness or for choosing vocations. Education ought also to provide children with the ability to conceive of and evaluate ways of life, and the political systems appropriate to them, other than those found within their own society or within any existing society. This educational goal is often based upon the view that knowledge should be pursued for its own sake, that is, for the sake of developing the intellect and its logical and imaginative capacities. Our lives are in fact often altered by knowledge of ways of life and types of polities not readily available for us to choose. We may become more critical of political participation and representation in our own society with the knowledge of how much more extensive political participation would be in Rousseau's ideal society. Utilitarians could teach *The Social Contract* as a means of convincing children that Rousseau's theory is utopian or as a means of introducing children to impractical literature that might occupy their leisure time as adults. But neither rationale is very compelling. Knowledge of Rousseau and of Greek literature is surely not necessary to ensure social cohesion and is very unlikely to make children happier or more satisfied with their lives or even more productive and hence more useful to people in the future. However, education in literature, history, anthropology, and political philosophy (for example) does provide a type of freedom — freedom to think beyond the established forms of private and political life. Such knowledge is necessary in order both to appreciate fully and to criticise the political systems and the choice among ways of life we have inherited. One might therefore conclude that this knowledge is a prerequisite for being a good democratic citizen, but this is not the sort of knowledge upon which any existing democratic government is likely to depend for its (mere) survival.

IV   The content of education: vocational or theoretical?

Utilitarianism is commonly recommended over rights theories on the grounds that it supplies one standard, the common currency of happiness, by which all goods can be ranked.[29] By contrast, rights theorists lack a single standard and therefore must devise priority rules for ranking freedoms and goods that come into conflict with each other. This necessity arises once again in the case of education. Educating children to be capable of finding profit-yielding employment in their society places very different demands upon schooling than does the goal of educating children to think beyond the established forms of life and thereby freeing them 'from the tyranny of

---

[29] For a critique of this characteristic of utilitarianism, see Williams 1972, pp. 92 ff.

the present'.[30] The advocate of liberty can embrace both goals in his theory. But, without some priority rule, the theory will be inadequate to determining educational practice in a non-ideal society. The imperfections in our economic and political institutions as well as scarcity of time and resources demand that we choose between an education instrumental to finding employment and what is commonly called a liberal education.[31]

The job of equipping children for profit-yielding employment seems to place very specific demands upon schools: that they teach technical skills to future technicians, secretarial skills to future secretaries, teaching skills to future teachers, etc. But even Bentham did not give priority to teaching more practical subjects because they prepared people for specific occupations, but because he believed that applied sciences (for example) were easier to learn than pure science. Only if one believed that children were destined for particular vocations and that educators could discern their predestinations would the goal of vocational training be this simple to implement educationally. Otherwise, elementary, secondary and perhaps even higher education must be broad enough to allow children themselves to determine their future vocational plans. If equality of opportunity includes the right to choose and not only the right to be selected on grounds of merit, then even the liberal goal of vocational preparation demands an education sufficiently extensive to expose children to many types of intellectual skills, or skills and knowledge general enough to be useful in many professions.

At the elementary school level, however, the requirements of vocational training probably do not conflict with the requirements of a 'liberal education': the three 'Rs' are no doubt a prerequisite to all desirable vocations and not only to understanding *Macbeth* and *The Origin of Species*. But as children graduate to higher levels, the requirements of a vocational and a liberal education are likely to diverge more. A curriculum designed to sharpen the critical and imaginative capacities of the mind will place more emphasis on literature and political philosophy than one designed to prepare students for choosing among available careers, given the job structure of our society.

The criterion of neutrality itself does not help us choose between a more theoretical and more applied curriculum. Neither is neutral among ways of life. A more theoretical curriculum is more likely to encourage children to seek intellectual vocations, while a more practical curriculum will discourage children from pursuing the life of the mind. Ideally, we would want schooling equally to serve the functions of expanding the intellectual

[30] See Postman 1979, p. 37.
[31] Alternatively, one might call the latter a 'general' education. See the Report of the Harvard Committee, *General Education in a Free Society*, Cambridge, Mass., 1945, and Hirst 1972.

imagination and of preparing all children for a socially useful and desirable profession, at least until children reach the age when they can choose a vocation or a form of education for themselves. But in the practice of our non-ideal society, most children will not be exposed to enough education to accomplish both tasks before they reach the age of consent. So, rights theorists face a common liberal dilemma of having to choose between two incomplete and not totally compatible goods.

The resolution of this dilemma, if there is one, does not depend upon a determination of which function is more important: expanding the minds or the job opportunities of children. Arguments claiming saliency for the life of the mind cannot succeed on liberal grounds. And a rights theorist cannot accept Durkheim's claim that, beyond teaching the basic principles upon which social unity depends, teaching specialised job-related skills is the most important role of schooling. Specialisation may be necessary for the survival of industrial societies, but it does not follow that it is therefore a more important function of education in a liberal society than a broader, more general education. But if we cannot rank the two educational goals by their intrinsic importance, we must be able to decide which educational end schools can most effectively serve and which end is less likely to be better served by another social institution.

Although Americans have had a tendency to view education as a panacea for all social ills, surely we should not be surprised to discover that schooling in itself is not an effective means to equalising economic opportunity. No kind of education – vocational or liberal – can overcome the effects of intentional discrimination on racial or class grounds. That there is as much inequality among adults with the same level of schooling as there is among the general population could be attributable to discrimination, to the ineffectiveness of our present methods (or content) of education, or to the unmeasured, or unmeasurable, difference in talents and skills among those with the same amount of schooling.[32]

However, even if schools by themselves cannot equalise economic opportunity, they still may have a necessary role in achieving such a desirable egalitarian purpose. Perhaps more vocational education for less-advantaged children would provide them with more job opportunities than they now have. But when we argue for equalising economic opportunity, we are not arguing simply that all children should be prepared for *some* job, but that all should be given an education that prepares them for choosing a satisfying job that is not wasteful of their talents. This is one reason why even if a highly-specialised education is a pre-condition for certain occupations, it should be chosen by, rather than imposed upon,

[32] See Jencks 1972, p. 218; and Duncan 1967, pp. 85–103.

children. But this criterion of choice suggests that a highly-specialised education ought only to follow a more general education since children of five and ten are very different in their capacity to choose than adolescents of sixteen or young people of twenty. At least, this should be the case unless something is *very* wrong with education, from a liberal point of view. Accepting this premise, we will begin education by teaching those arts, skills and knowledge most essential to all future choice; reading, writing and arithmetic are most clearly among such arts. Later, we will give students greater, and increasingly greater, freedom to determine their own programmes of education because they become better equipped to make choices as they mature, and also because they need exercise in making choice. This line of argument suggests that specialised, vocational education may have a place in liberal schooling, but that it must follow a broader, less specialised education and must be the object of genuine choice by students capable of choice, and not a substitute for a broader education or part of a mandated curriculum.

Suppose that specialised, vocational education could be effective in equalising economic opportunity. In general, schools are likely to be less efficient (and probably also less successful, once we take problems of motivation into account) providers of such education than are employers who use on-the-job training. Educators themselves know very little about the details of non-academic jobs, and on-the-job success depends upon attendance to those details. Now more than ever, vocational education within schools is bound to lag behind job specifications, as the demands of the division of labour change in ways unforeseeable by educational institutions. Educators are unlikely to be aware of the different skills that are required for what are nominally the same jobs, another fact which suggests that vocational schooling will be less effective and less efficient than on-the-job training.

I have granted that even the best education of which we are capable will not be neutral towards all conceptions of the good life. Yet the neutrality ideal still requires that liberals seek to provide an education that maximises choice among ways of life. This ideal demands recognition of the fact that more ways of life are possible than now are pursued and that collective action is often necessary to actualise some possible – but unrealised – ways of life. Collective action is greatly facilitated if people are aware of remote as well as actual possibilities, as they are more likely to be if they are taught anthropology, history, philosophy and literature, and if they are capable of thinking abstractly about polities, economies and other social institutions.[33]

---

[33] I am grateful to Stanley Kelley, Jr for bringing this argument and the argument on pp. 274–5 to my attention.

There is also another positive, more political reason to choose a theoretical above a vocational education. The legitimacy (as distinguished from the justice) of liberal democracies is generally based upon a theory of the consent of citizens to democratic rule. Yet most citizens of liberal democracies have no real choice but to obey the government of the society in which they were born, raised and educated. Although they have no real option to leave, they might at least not be required to accept their state uncritically. That option is a real one only if they are intellectually exposed to alternative political systems and ways of life more common within other political systems. Schools are uniquely equipped to supply children with the knowledge and intellectual skills necessary to appreciate alternative political philosophies and ways of life.[34] An education designed to facilitate this exposure will be closer to a traditional liberal education than to a vocational education, although a liberal can reject the metaphysical baggage that supported the classical idea of a liberal education: that the mind can come 'to know the essential nature of things and can apprehend what is ultimately real and immutable' and that the attainment of knowledge therefore is in itself the realisation of the good life.[35]

The advocate of liberty, like the utilitarian, supports a liberal education for consequentialist reasons: it is useful in preparing children to choose among – or at least to evaluate – alternative ways of private and political life. But since the advocate of liberty is committed to providing equal educational opportunity for all children rather than to maximising the total store of freedom, he need not compare how much freedom could be gained by suppressing the education opportunities of one group to increase the opportunities of another. The consequentialism of rights theorists therefore has form and content that are both distinct from that of utilitarians. The right to education can be constrained only by another child's equal right, and educational rights must be justified by reference to future freedom, not happiness.

Liberals can accept Durkheim's claim that the content of education ought to be determined by the social context within which schools operate. The educational requirements for maximising the future freedom of children surely will vary with societies. A liberal education suitable to contemporary social conditions will not replicate a classical liberal education in which the study of Greek and Latin were primary require-

---

[34] Of course, this is not to say that American and British schools have yet to succeed in achieving this goal, but their failure can more plausibly be attributed to lack of will, rather than to lack of power. Even radical critics acknowledge the unique capacity of schools to expose students to critical political philosophies and alternative ways of life. See, e.g., Bowles and Gintis 1977, pp. 5, 270 ff. See also Jennings 1980, p. 336; Hyman, Wright and Reed 1975; and Hyman and Wright 1979.

[35] Hirst 1972, p. 392.

ments. But education ought not to serve only to maintain the present state of social and political organisation. If the present state of social and political organisation can survive an education that develops critical intellectual faculties, then education will serve an integrative as well as a critical function. If not, then a liberal education will serve to prepare children 'for a possibly improved condition of man in the future'.[36] Whether any existing society is capable of fully providing this sort of liberal education is another question. I have tried here to demonstrate that unlike utilitarians, rights theorists can consistently advocate the use of schools in a liberal democratic society as critical, rather than simply as conserving, social institutions.[37]

[36] Kant 1803 (1960 edn, p. 14).
[37] I am indebted to Michael W. Doyle, Stanley Kelley, Jr and Dennis Thompson for many helpful comments on an earlier draft.

Bibliography

Allais, M., 1947, *Economie et Interêt*, Paris: Imprimerie Nationale.

Allingham, M., 1975, 'Towards an Ability Tax', *Journal of Public Economics*, 4, pp. 361–76.

Anscombe, F. J. and Aumann, R. J., 1963,'A Definition of Subjective Probability', *Annals of Mathematical Statistics*, 34, pp. 199–205.

Anscombe, G. E. M., 1958, 'Modern Moral Philosophy', *Philosophy*, 33, pp. 1–19.

Archibald, G. C., 1959, 'Welfare Economics, Ethics and Essentialism', *Economica*, 26, pp. 316–27.

Arrow, K. J., 1950, 'A Difficulty in the Concept of Social Welfare', *Journal of Political Economy*, 58, pp. 328–46.

1951, *Social Choice and Individual Values*, John Wiley and Yale University Press. Second edition, 1963.

1953, 'Le rôle des valeurs boursières pour la repartition la meilleure des risques', *Econometrie*, 11, pp. 41–8. Translated as Arrow 1964.

1963, See Arrow 1951.

1964, 'The Rôle of Securities in the Optimal Allocation of Risk-Bearing', *Review of Economic Studies*, 31, pp. 91–6.

1971, *Essays in the Theory of Risk Bearing*, Amsterdam: North-Holland Publishing Co.

1973, 'Some Ordinalist-Utilitarian Notes on Rawls' Theory of Justice', *Journal of Philosophy*, 70, no. 9, pp. 245–63.

1974, *The Limits of Organization*, New York: W. W. Norton and Company.

1977, 'Extended Sympathy and the Possibility of Social Choice', *American Economic Review*, Supplementary issue of the Proceedings, pp. 219–25.

1978a, 'Extended Sympathy and the Possibility of Social Choice', *Philosophia*, 7, Sec. 2, pp. 223–37. This is a longer version of Arrow 1977.

1978b, 'Nozick's Entitlement Theory of Justice', *Philosophia*, 7, pp. 265–9.

Asch, S., 1956, 'Studies of Independence and Conformity. I. A Minority of One Against a Unanimous Majority', *Psychological Monographs: General and Applied*, 70, no. 9.

d'Aspremont, C. and Gevers, L., 1977, 'Equity and the Informational Basis of Collective Choice', *Review of Economic Studies*, 44, pp. 199–209.

Atkinson, A. B., 1974, 'Smoking and the Economics of Government Intervention' in *The Economics of Health and Medical Care*, edited by M. Perlman pp. 428–41, ch. 21, London: Macmillan.

279

Barry, B., 1973, *The Liberal Theory of Justice*, Oxford: Oxford University Press.
    1979, 'And Who Is My Neighbor?', *The Yale Law Journal*, 88, pp. 629–35.
Basu, K., 1979, *Revealed Preference of Government*, Cambridge: Cambridge University Press.
Bentham, Jeremy, 1843, *The Works of Jeremy Bentham*, edited by John Bowring, vol. 8, *Chrestomathia*, Edinburgh: William Tait.
    1948, *An Introduction to the Principle of Morals and Legislation*, Oxford: Blackwell.
Bergson, A., 1938, 'A Reformulation of Certain Aspects of Welfare Economics', *Quarterly Journal of Economics*, 52, pp. 310–34.
Berlin, Isaiah, 1969, *Four Essays on Liberty*, Oxford: Oxford University Press.
Bernholz, P., 1974, 'Is a Paretian Liberal Really Impossible?', *Public Choice*, 20, pp. 99–107.
Boudon, R., 1977, *Effets Pervers et Ordre Social*, Paris: Presses Universitaires de France.
Bowles, Samuel and Gintis, Herbert, 1977, *Schooling in Capitalist America*, New York: Basic Books.
Brandt, R. B., 1955, 'The Definition of An "Ideal Observer" Theory in Ethics', *Philosophy and Phenomenological Research*, 15, pp. 407–13; 422–3. This paper constitutes a discussion of R. Firth's essay in vol. 12 of the same journal (see Firth 1952). Also included is a reply by Firth, and some further comments by Brandt.
    1959, *Ethical Theory*, Englewood Cliffs, N.J.: Prentice-Hall Inc.
    1963, 'Towards a Credible Form of Utilitarianism', *Morality and the Language of Conduct*, edited by H.-N. Castaneda and G. Nakhnikian. Detroit.
    1979, *A Theory of the Good and the Right*, Oxford: Oxford University Press.
Broome, J. A., 1978a, 'Choice and Value in Economics', *Oxford Economic Papers*, 30, pp. 313–33.
    1978b, 'Trying to Value a Life', *Journal of Public Economics*, 9, pp. 91–100.
Buchanan, Allen, 1975, 'Revisability and Rational Choice', *Canadian Journal of Philosophy*, 3, pp. 395–408.
Buchanan, J. M., 1976, 'The Justice of Natural Liberty', *Journal of Legal Studies*, 5, pp. 1–16.
Buchanan, J. M. and Tullock, G., 1962, *The Calculus of Consent*, Ann Arbor, University of Michigan Press.
Burston, W. H. (ed.), 1969, *James Mill on Education*, Cambridge: Cambridge University Press.
Calabresi, G. and Bobbitt, P., 1978, *Tragic Choices*, New York: Norton.
Cohen, G. A., 1977, 'Robert Nozick and Wilt Chamberlain: How Patterns Preserve Liberty', *Erkenntnis*, 11, pp. 5–23.
Cyert, R. M. and DeGroot, M. H., 1975, 'Adaptive Utility', in *Adaptive Economic Models*, edited by R. H. Day and T. Groves, New York: Academic Press.
Daniels, Norman, 1979, 'Wide Reflective Equilibrium and Theory Acceptance in Ethics', *Journal of Philosophy*, 76, pp. 256–82.
Dasgupta, P., 1980, 'Decentralization and Rights', *Economica*, 47, no. 186, pp. 107–24.
Dasgupta, P. and Hammond, P., 1980, 'Fully Progressive Taxation', *Journal of Public Economics*, 13, pp. 141–54.

Dasgupta, P., Hammond, P. and Maskin, E., 1979, 'The Implementation of Social Choice Rules: Some General Results on Incentive Compatability', *Review of Economic Studies*, 46, no. 2, pp. 185–216.

1980, 'A Note on Imperfect Information and Optimal Pollution Control', *Review of Economic Studies*, 47, pp. 857–60.

Deaton, A. S. and Muellbauer, J., 1980, *Economics and Consumer Behaviour*, Cambridge: Cambridge University Press.

Debreu, G., 1959, *Theory of Value*, New York: John Wiley.

Deschamps R. and Gevers, L., 1978, 'Leximin and Utilitarian Rules: A Joint Characterisation', *Journal of Economic Theory*, 17, pp. 143–63.

Dewey, John, 1943, *The School and Society*, Chicago: University of Chicago Press.

1946, *The Problems of Men*, New York: Philosophical Library.

Diamond, P. A., 1967a, 'Cardinal Welfare, Individualistic Ethics, and Interpersonal Comparisons of Utility: A Comment', *Journal of Political Economy*, 75, pp. 765–6.

1967b, 'The Role of a Stock Market in a General Equilibrium Model with Technological Uncertainty', *American Economic Review*, 57, pp. 759–76.

Dixit, A. and Norman, V., 1978, 'Advertising and Welfare', *Bell Journal of Economics*, 9, pp. 1–17.

Donagan, Alan, 1977, *The Theory of Morality*, Chicago: University of Chicago Press.

Drèze, J. H., 1962, 'L'utilité sociale d'une vie humaine', *Revue Française de Recherche Operationelle*, pp. 93–118.

1970, 'Market Allocation Under Uncertainty', *European Economic Review*, 2, pp. 133–65.

1974, 'Axiomatic Theories of Choice, Cardinal Utility and Subjective Probability: A Review', in *Allocation under Uncertainty: Equilibrium and Optimality*, edited by J. H. Drèze, London: Macmillan, ch. 1, pp. 3–23.

Duncan, Otis Dudley, 1967, 'Discrimination Against Negroes', *Annals of the American Academy of Political and Social Science*, 371, pp. 85–103.

Durkheim, Emile, 1956, *Education and Sociology*, translated by Sherwood Fox, New York: The Free Press.

Dworkin, Ronald, 1977, *Taking Rights Seriously*, Cambridge, Mass.: also London: Duckworth, 1977. A new impression (corrected) with an appendix came out in 1978, Duckworth.

1978, 'Liberalism', in *Public and Private Morality*, edited by Stuart Hampshire, Cambridge: Cambridge University Press.

1981, 'What is Equality? Part One: Equality and Welfare', *Journal of Philosophy*.

Edgeworth, F. Y., 1881, *Mathematical Psychics – An Essay on the Application of Mathematics to the Moral Sciences*, London: Kegan Paul.

Elster, J., 1976, 'A Note on Hysteresis in the Social Sciences', *Synthèse*, 33, pp. 371–91.

1978a, *Logic and Society*, London: Wiley.

1978b, 'Exploring Exploitation', *Journal of Peace Research*, 15, pp. 3–17.

1978c, 'The Labour Theory of Value', *Marxist Perspectives*, 1, no. 3, pp. 70–101.

1979, *Ulysses and the Sirens*, Cambridge: Cambridge University Press.

1980, 'Un historien devant l'irrationel; Lecture de Paul Veyne', *Social Science Information*, 19, pp. 773–803.

(forthcoming), 'Belief, Bias and Ideology', in *Rationality and Relativism*, edited by M. Hollis and S. Lukes, Oxford: Blackwell.

Engels, F., 1975, *The Condition of the Working Class in England*, in Marx and Engels, *Collected Works*, vol. 4, London: Lawrence and Wishart.

Erickson, Donald A., 1969, 'Showdown at an Amish Schoolhouse: A Description and Analysis of the Iowa Controversy', in *Public Controls for Nonpublic Schools*, edited by Donald A. Erickson, Chicago: The University of Chicago Press, pp. 15–59.

Farber, L., 1976, *Lying, Despair, Jealousy, Envy, Sex, Suicide, Drugs and the Good Life*, New York: Basic Books.

Farrell, M. J., 1976, 'Liberalism in the Theory of Social Choice', *Review of Economic Studies*, 43, pp. 3–10.

Festinger, L., 1957, *A Theory of Cognitive Dissonance*, Stanford: Stanford University Press.

1964, *Conflict, Decision and Dissonance*, Stanford: Stanford University Press.

Firth, Roderick, 1952, 'Ethical Absolutism and the Ideal Observer', *Philosophy and Phenomenological Research*, 12, pp. 317–45. See also vol. 15 (pp. 414–21) of this journal for Firth's reply to R. B. Brandt's subsequent discussion of this paper (Brandt 1955).

Fishburn, P. C., 1973, *The Theory of Social Choice*, Princeton: University Press.

Fisher, I., 1927, 'A Statistical Method for Measuring Marginal Utility', in *Economic Essays in Honor of J. B. Clark*, New York.

Frankel, C., 1958, *The Case for Modern Man*, Boston: Beacon Press. .

Frankfurt, Harry, 1971, 'Freedom of the Will and the Concept of a Person', *Journal of Philosophy*, 67, no. 1, pp. 5–20.

Fried, Charles, 1978, *Right and Wrong*, Cambridge, Mass.: Harvard University Press.

Friedman, M., 1953, 'Choice, Chance and the Personal Distribution of Income', *Journal of Political Economy*, 61, pp. 277–99.

1962, *Capitalism and Freedom*, Chicago: University of Chicago Press.

Friedman, M. and Savage, L. J., 1948, 'The Utility Analysis of Choices Involving Risk', *Journal of Political Economy*, 56, pp. 279–304.

Friedman, M. and Savage L. J., 1952, 'The Expected Utility Hypothesis and Measurement of Utility', *Journal of Political Economy*, 60, pp. 463–74.

Gärdenfors, P., 1978, 'Rights, Games and Social Choice' (mimeo.).

Gaertner W., and Krüger, L., 1981, 'Self-supporting Preferences and Individual Rights: The Possibility of Paretian Liberalism', *Economica*, 48, pp. 17–28.

Gibbard, A., 1974, 'A Pareto Consistent Libertarian Claim', *Journal of Economic Theory*, 7, pp. 399–410.

1979, 'Disparate Goods and Rawls' Difference Principle: A Social Choice Theoretic Treatment', *Theory and Decision*, 11, pp. 267–88.

Goldman, A., 1972, 'Toward a Theory of Social Power', *Philosophical Studies*, 23, pp. 221–68.

Goodman, Nelson, 1973, *Fact, Fiction, and Forecast*, 3rd edition, Indianapolis: Hackett.

Gorman, W. M., 1968, 'The Structure of Utility Functions', *Review of Economic Studies*, 35, pp. 367–90.

Gottinger, H. W. and Leinfellner, W. (eds.), 1978, *Decision Theory and Social Ethics: Issues in Social Choice*, Dordrecht: Reidel.

Graaff, J. de V., 1957, *Theoretical Welfare Economics*, Cambridge: Cambridge University Press.

Gutmann, Amy, 1980, 'Children, Paternalism and Education; A Liberal Argument', *Philosophy and Public Affairs*, 9, no. 4, pp. 338–58.

Hahn, F. and Hollis, M.(eds.), 1979, *Philosophy and Economic Theory*, Oxford: Oxford University Press. There is a substantial Introduction by the editors.

Hammond, P. J., 1976a, 'Changing Tastes and Coherent Dynamic Choice', *Review of Economic Studies*, 43, pp. 159–73.

1976b, 'Equity, Arrow's Conditions and Rawls' Difference Principle', *Econometrica* 44, pp. 793–800. Reprinted in Hahn and Hollis 1979.

1980, 'Some Uncomfortable Options in Welfare Economics Under Uncertainty', Stanford University mimeo.

1981a, 'Liberalism, Independent Rights and the Pareto Principle', in *Logic, Methodology and the Philosophy of Science*, edited by L. J. Cohen, J. T'os, H. Pfeiffer and K. –P. Podewski, Amsterdam: North-Holland, vol. VI, chapter 45, pp. 221–34.

1981b, 'Ex-Post Optimality as a Consistent Objective for Collective Choice Under Uncertainty', Economics Technical Report, Institute for Mathematical Studies in the Social Sciences, Stanford University.

1981c, 'Consistent Dynamic Choice Under Uncertainty and Bayesian Rationality', Economics Technical Report, Institute for Mathematical Studies in the Social Sciences, Stanford University.

1981d, 'On Welfare Economics with Incomplete Information and the Social Value of Public Information', Economics Technical Report, Institute for Mathematical Studies in the Social Sciences, Stanford University.

Hare, R. M., 1952, *The Language of Morals*, Oxford: Oxford University Press.

1963, *Freedom and Reason*, Oxford: Oxford University Press.

1971, *Practical Inferences*, London: Macmillan.

1972a, *Applications of Moral Philosophy*, London: Macmillan.

1972b, 'Rules of War and Moral Reasoning', *Philosophy and Public Affairs*, 1, pp. 166–81.

1972c, *Essays on the Moral Concepts*, London: Macmillan.

1972d, *Essays on Philosophical Method*, London: Macmillan.

1972/3, 'Principles', *Proceedings of the Aristotelian Society*, 73 pp. 1–18.

1973a, 'Language and Moral Education', in *New Essays in the Philosophy of Education*, edited by G. Langford and D. J. O'Connor, London: Routledge & Kegan Paul.

1973b, 'Critical Study – Rawls' Theory of Justice', *Philosophical Quarterly*, 23, pp. 144–55; 241–52.

1974, 'Some Confusions about Subjectivity', Lindley Lecture, University of Kansas.

1975a, 'Abortion and the Golden Rule', *Philosophy and Public Affairs*, 4, pp. 201–22.

1975b, 'Contrasting Methods of Environmental Planning', in *Nature and Conduct*, edited by R. S. Peters, London: Macmillan, pp. 281–97.

1976, 'Political Obligation', in *Social Ends and Political Means*, edited by T. Honderich, London: Routledge & Kegan Paul, pp. 1–12.

Harrod, R. F., 1936, 'Utilitarianism Revised', *Mind*, 45, pp. 137–56.

Harsanyi, John C., 1953, 'Cardinal Utility in Welfare Economics and in the Theory of Risk-Taking', *Journal of Political Economy*, 61, pp. 434–5. Reprinted in Harsanyi 1976.

1955, 'Cardinal Welfare, Individualistic Ethics, and Interpersonal Comparisons of Utility', *Journal of Political Economy*, 63, pp. 309–21. Reprinted in Harsanyi 1976.

1958, 'Ethics in Terms of Hypothetical Imperatives', *Mind*, 67, pp. 305–16. Reprinted in Harsanyi 1976.

1967/8, 'Games with Incomplete Information Played by "Bayesian" Players', *Management Science*, 14, pp. 159–82; 320–34; 486–502.

1975a, 'Can the Maximin Principle Serve as a Basis for Morality? A Critique of John Rawls' Theory', *American Political Science Review*, 69, pp. 594–606. Reprinted in Harsanyi 1976.

1975b, 'The Tracing Procedure: A Bayesian Approach to Defining a Solution for *n*-Person Noncooperative Games', *International Journal of Game Theory*, 4, pp. 61–94.

1975c, 'Nonlinear Social Welfare Functions: Do Welfare Economists Have a Special Exemption From Bayesian Rationality?', *Theory and Decision*, 6, pp. 311–32. Reprinted in Harsanyi 1976.

1976, *Essays in Ethics, Social Behaviour, and Scientific Explanation*, Dordrecht: Reidel.

1977, 'Rule Utilitarianism and Decision Theory', *Erkenntnis*, 11, pp. 25–53.

Hart, H. L. A., 1979, 'Between Utility and Rights', 79 *Columbia Law Review*, pp. 828–46.

Haslett, D. W., 1974, *Moral Rightness*, The Hague: Martinus Nijhoff.

Hayek, F. von, 1945, 'The Use of Knowledge in Society', *American Economic Review*, 35, pp. 519–30.

1948, *Individualism and Economic Order*, Indiana: Gateway Edition.

1960, *The Constitution of Liberty*, London: Routledge & Kegan Paul.

1976, *The Mirage of Social Justice: Law, Legislation Liberty*, vol. 2, London: Routledge & Kegan Paul.

Hirschman, A. O., 1982, *Shifting Involvements*, Princeton: Princeton University Press, chapter 4.

Hirst, P. H., 1972, 'Liberal Education and the Nature of Knowledge', in *Education and the Development of Reason*, edited by R. F. Dearden, P. H. Hirst and R. S. Peters, London: Routledge & Kegan Paul, pp. 391–414.

Hostetler, J. A. and Huntington G. E., 1971, *Children in Amish Society: Socialisation and Community Education*, New York: Holt, Rinehart and Winston.

Hurwicz, L., 1972, 'On Informationally Decentralized Systems', in *Decision and Organization*, edited by C. B. McGuire and R. Radner, Amsterdam: North-Holland, ch. 14, pp. 297–336. Also in *Studies in Resource Allocation Processes*, pp. 425–59, edited by K. J. Arrow and L. Hurwicz, Cambridge: Cambridge University Press, 1977.

1973, 'The Design of Mechanisms for Resource Allocation', *American Economic Review* (Papers and Proceedings), 63, pp. 1–30.

Hyman, Herbert H. and Wright, Charles R. 1979, *Education's Lasting Influence on Values*, Chicago: University of Chicago Press.

Hyman, Herbert H., Wright, Charles R. and Reed, John Shelton, 1975, *The Enduring Effect of Education*, Chicago: The University of Chicago Press.

Jeffery, R. C., 1965, *The Logic of Decision*, New York: McGraw-Hill.

1974, 'Preference among Preferences', *Journal of Philosophy*, 71, pp. 377–91.

Jencks, Christopher (with M. Smith; H. Acland; M.–J. Bane; D. Cohen; H. Gintis; B. Heyns; S. Michelson), 1972 *Inequality: A Reassessment of the Effect of Family and Schooling in America*, New York: Basic Books. Also published London: Allen Lane, 1973; Peregrine Books, 1975.

Jennings, M. Kent, 1980, 'Comment on Richard Merelman's "Democratic Politics and the Culture of American Education" ', *American Political Science Review*, 74, pp. 333–8.

Jones-Lee, M. W., 1974, 'The Value of Changes in the Probability of Death or Injury', *Journal of Political Economy*, 82, pp. 835–49.

1976, *The Value of Life: An Economic Analysis*, London: Martin Robertson. Also published Chicago: University of Chicago Press.

1980, 'Human Capital, Risk Aversion, and the Value of Life', in *Contemporary Economic Analysis*, edited by D. A. Currie and W. Peters, London: Croom-Helm. vol. 2, ch. 10, pp. 285–321.

Kahneman, D. and Tversky, A., 1979, 'Prospect Theory: An Analysis of Decision Under Risk', *Econometrica*, 47, pp. 263–91.

Kanbur, S. M., 1979, 'Of Risk Taking and the Personal Distribution of Income', *Journal of Political Economy*, 87, pp. 769–97.

Kant, Immanuel, 1785, *Grundlegung zur Metaphysik der Sitten*, translated by H. J. Paton as *The Moral Law*, London: Hutchinson, 1948.

1803, *Pädogogik*, translated as *On Education*, Ann Arbor, Michigan, 1960.

Kelly, J. S., 1978, *Arrow Impossibility Theorems*, New York: Academic Press.

Kenny, A., 1965/6, 'Happiness', *Proceedings of the Aristotelian Society*, N.S. 66, pp. 93–102.

Kolm, S. C., 1969, 'The Optimum Production of Social Justice', in *Public Economics*, edited by J. Margolis and H. Guitton, London: Macmillan.

1972, *Justice et Équité*, Paris: Editions du centre national de la recherche scientifique.

1979, 'La philosophie bouddhiste et les "hommes economiques" ', *Social Science Information*, 18, pp. 489–588.

Koopmans, T. C., 1957, *Three Essays on the State of Economic Science*, New York: McGraw-Hill.

Körner, S., 1976, *Experience and Conduct*, Cambridge: Cambridge University Press.

Laffont, J. J. (ed.), 1979, *Aggregation and Revelation of Preferences*, Amsterdam: North-Holland Publishing Co.

Laffont, J. J. and Maskin, E., 1981, 'The Theory of Incentives: An Overview', mimeo., University of Cambridge.

Leibniz, G. W. F., 1875–90, *Die Philosophische Schriften*, 7 vols, edited by C. I. Gerhardt, Berlin; Weidmannsche Buchhandlung.

Lerner, A. P., 1944, *The Economics of Control*, London and New York: Macmillan.

1972, 'The Economics and Politics of Consumer Sovereignty', *American Economic Review* (Papers and Proceedings), 62, pp. 258–66.

Levi, I., 1974, 'On Indeterminate Probabilities', *Journal of Philosophy*, 71, pp. 391–418.

1980, *The Enterprise of Knowledge*, Cambridge, Mass.: MIT Press.

Lewis, C. I., 1946, *An Analysis of Knowledge and Valuation*, La Salle, Ill.: The Open Court Publishing Company.

Little, I. M. D., 1950, *A Critique of Welfare Economics*, Oxford: Oxford University Press.

Lukes, S., 1974, *Power. A Radical View*, London: Macmillan.

Lyons, David, 1965, *Forms and Limits of Utilitarianism*, Oxford: Oxford University Press.

Mackie, J. L., 1977, *Ethics: Inventing Right and Wrong*, Harmondsworth: Pelican.

1978, 'Can there be a Right-based Moral Theory?', *Midwest Studies in Philosophy*, 3.

Malinvaud, E., 1972, *Microeconomic Theory*, Amsterdam: North-Holland.

Marschak, J. and Radner, R., 1972, *Economic Theory of Teams*, New Haven: Yale University Press.

Mas-Colell, A., 1978, 'An Axiomatic Approach to the Efficiency of Non-cooperative Equilibrium in Economics with a Continuum of Traders', IMSSS Technical Report No. 274, Stanford University.

Maskin, E., 1978, 'A Theorem on Utilitarianism', *Review of Economic Studies*, 45, pp. 93–6.

1980, 'On First-Best Taxation', in *Limits of Redistribution*, edited by W. R. C. Lecomber.

1981, 'Randomization in the Principal-Agent Problem', mimeo, Cambridge University.

Meade, J. E., 1964, *Efficiency, Equality and the Ownership of Property*, London: George Allen & Unwin.

Merton, R. K., 1957, *Social Theory and Social Structure*, Glencoe, Ill.: Free Press.

Mill, John Stuart, 1950, *Philosophy of Scientific Method*, a selection of Mill's writings, edited by E. Nagel, New York: Hafner.

1962, *Utilitarianism* (1861), London: Collins.

1974, *On Liberty* (1859), Harmondsworth: Pelican Classics.

Mirrlees, J. A., 1971, 'An Exploration in the Theory of Optimum Income Taxation', *Review of Economic Studies*, 38, pp. 175–208.

1974, 'Notes on Welfare Economics, Information and Uncertainty', in *Essays on Economic Behaviour under Uncertainty*, edited by M. S. Balch, D. McFadden and S. Y. Wu, Amsterdam: North-Holland.

1981, 'The Theory of Optimal Taxation', in *Handbook of Mathematical Economics*, edited by K. J. Arrow and M. Intriligator, Amsterdam: North-Holland.

Mishan, E. J., 1971, 'Evaluation of Life and Limb: A Theoretical Approach', *Journal of Political Economy*, 79, pp. 687–705.

Moore, G. E., 1903, *Principia Ethica*, Cambridge: Cambridge University Press.

Mueller, D. C., 1979, *Public Choice*, Cambridge: Cambridge University Press.

Myerson, R., 1980, 'Optimal Coordination Mechanisms in Principal-Agent Problems', mimeo, Kellog Graduate School of Management, Northwestern University.

Nagel, Thomas, 1979, *Mortal Questions*, Cambridge: Cambridge University Press.

Nell, Onora [Onora O'Neill], 1975, *Acting on Principle: an essay on Kantian ethics*, New York: Columbia.

Nelson, Leonard, 1917–32, *Vorlesungen über die Grundlagen der Ethik*, 3 vols, Leipzig: Veit.

Ng, Y.-K., 1975, 'Bentham or Bergson? Finite Sensibility, Utility Functions, and Social Welfare Functions', *Revue of Economic Studies*, 42, pp. 545–69.

Nozick, R., 1974, *Anarchy, State and Utopia*, New York: Basic Books;Oxford: 1978, *Strategy and Group Choice*, Amsterdam: North-Holland.

Parfit, D., 1973, 'Later Selves and Moral Principles', in *Philosophy and Personal Relations*, edited by A. Montefiore, London: Routledge & Kegan Paul.

1976, 'On Doing the Best for Our Children', in *Ethics and Population*, edited by M. Bayles, Cambridge, Mass.: Schenkman Publishing Company Inc., pp. 100–15.

Pattanaik, P. K., 1968, 'Risk, Impersonality and the Social Welfare Function', *Journal of Political Economy*, 76, pp. 1152–69. Also appears in *Economic Justice*, edited by E. Phelps, London: Penguin, 1973.

1971, *Voting and Collective Choice*, Cambridge: Cambridge University Press.

1978, Strategy and Group Choice, Amsterdam: North-Holland.

Phelps, E. S., 1973, 'Taxation of Wage Income for Economic Justice', *Quarterly Journal of Economics*, 87, pp. 332–54.

Piaget, Jean, 1962, *The Moral Judgement of the Child*, New York: Collier.

Plott, C. R., 1976, 'Axiomatic Social Choice Theory: an Overview and Interpretation', *American Journal of Political Science*, 20, pp. 511–96.

Postman, Neil, 1979, *Teaching as a Conserving Activity*, New York.

Radner, R., 1979, 'Rational Expectations Equilibrium: Generic Existence and the Information Revealed by Prices', *Econometrica*, 47, pp. 655–78.

Radner, R. and Marschak, J., 1954, 'Note on Some Proposed Decision Criteria', in *Decision Processes*, New York: Wiley, pp. 61–8.

Ramsey, F. P., 1926, 'Truth and Probability', in *The Foundations of Mathematics and Other Logical Essays*, edited by R. Braithwaite, London: Kegan Paul, 1931, pp. 156–98.

Rawls, John, 1955, 'Two Concepts of Rules', *Philosophical Review*, 64, pp. 3–32.

1957, 'Justice as Fairness', *Journal of Philosophy*, 54, pp. 653–62.

1958, 'Justice as Fairness', *Philosophical Review*, 67, pp. 164–94.

1971, *A Theory of Justice*, Cambridge, Mass.: Harvard University Press. Also published by Oxford University Press, 1972.

1974–5, 'The Independence of Moral Theory', *Proceedings and Addresses of the American Philosophical Association 47*.

1975, 'A Kantian Conception of Equality', *The Cambridge Review*, 96, no. 2225 (February), pp. 94–9.

1980, 'Kantian Constructivism in Moral Theory', *The Journal of Philosophy*, 77, no. 9, pp. 515–72.

Richards, D. A. J., 1971, *A Theory of Reasons for Action*, Oxford: Oxford University Press.

Roberts, K. W. S., 1980a, 'Price Independent Welfare Prescriptions', *Journal of Public Economics*, 13, pp. 277–97.

1980b, 'Interpersonal Comparability and Social Choice Theory', *Review of Economic Studies*, 47.

Ross, Sir W. D., 1930, *The Right and the Good*, Oxford: Oxford University Press.

1939, *Foundations of Ethics*, Oxford: Oxford University Press.

Rowley, C. K. and Peacock, A. T., 1975, *Welfare Economics: a Liberal Restatement*, London: Martin Robertson.

Runciman, W. G., 1966, *Relative Deprivation and Social Justice*, London: Routledge & Kegan Paul.

Russell, Bertrand, 1955, *John Stuart Mill*, Oxford: Oxford University Press.

Samuelson, P. A., 1937, 'A Note on Measurement of Utility', *Review of Economic Studies*, 4, pp. 155–61.

1938, 'A Note on the Pure Theory of Consumers' Behaviour', *Economica*, N.S. 5, pp. 61–71. See also the addendum on pp. 353–4 of same volume.

Savage, L. J., 1954, *The Foundations of Statistics*, New York: John Wiley. Second revised edition – Dover, 1972.

Scanlon, T. M., 1975, 'Preference and Urgency', *Journal of Philosophy*, 72, pp. 665–9.

Schelling, T. S., 1978, 'Economics, or the Art of Self-Management', *American Economic Review*, 68, Papers and Proceedings, pp. 290–4.

Schick, F., 1969, 'Arrow's Proof and the Logic of Preference', *Journal of Philosophy*, 66, pp. 127–44.

1980. 'Welfare, Rights and Fairness', in *Science, Belief and Behavior: Essays in honour of R. B. Braithwaite*, pp. 203–16, edited by D. H. Mellor, Cambridge: Cambridge University Press.

Sen, A. K., 1970a, *Collective Choice and Social Welfare*, San Francisco: Holden Day. Also London: Oliver and Boyd, 1970.

1970b, 'The Impossibility of a Paretian Liberal', *Journal of Political Economy*, 78, pp. 152–7.

1973, *On Economic Inequality*, Oxford: Oxford University Press.

1974, 'Choice, Orderings and Morality', in *Practical Reason*, edited by S. Körner, Oxford: Blackwell.

1975, *Employment, Technology and Development*, Oxford: Oxford University Press.

1976, 'Liberty, Unanimity and Rights', *Economica*, 43, pp. 217–46.

1977a, 'On Weights and Measures: Informational Constraints in Social Welfare Analysis', *Econometrica*, 45, pp. 1539–72.

1977b, 'Rational Fools: a Critique of the Behavioural Foundations of Economic Theory', *Philosophy and Public Affairs*, 6, pp. 317–44.

1979a, 'Personal Utilities and Public Judgements: Or What's Wrong with Welfare Economics', *Economic Journal*, 89, pp. 537–58.

1979b, 'Utilitarianism and Welfarism', *Journal of Philosophy*, 76, no. 9, pp. 463–89.

1979c, 'Informational Analysis of Moral Principles', in *Rational Action: Studies* in *Philosophy and the Social Sciences*, edited by R. Harrison, Cambridge: Cambridge University Press, pp. 115–32.

1980, 'Equality of What?', in *Tanner Lectures on Human Values*, I, edited by S. McMurrin, Cambridge: Cambridge University Press.

1981, 'Plural Utility', *Proceedings of the Aristotelian Society*, 81.

1982, 'Rights and Agency', *Philosophy and Public Affairs*, 11.

Sharp, Lynda, 'Forms and Criticisms of Utilitarianism', thesis, deposited in the Bodleian Library at Oxford.

Sidgwick, Henry, 1962, *Methods of Ethics*, 7th edition (reissue), London: Macmillan.

Simon, H., 1957, *Models of Man*, New York: John Wiley & Sons.

1960, *The New Science of Management Decision*, New York: Harper & Brothers.

Singer, Marcus George, 1961, *Generalization in Ethics*, New York: Knopf.

Singer, Peter, 1972, 'Famine, Affluence and Morality', *Philosophy and Public Affairs*, 1, pp. 229–43.

1974, 'Sidgwick and Reflective Equilibrium', *The Monist*, 58, pp. 490–517.

Smart, J. J. C., 1961, *An Outline of a System of Utilitarian Ethics*, Melbourne: Melbourne University Press. Also in Smart and Williams 1973.

Smart, J. J. C. and B. A. O. Williams, 1973, *Utilitarianism: For and Against*, Cambridge: Cambridge University Press.

Smith, Adam, 1976, *Theory of Moral Sentiments*, Clifton, N.J.: Kelley.

Starr, R. M., 1973, 'Optimal Production and Allocation Under Uncertainty', *Quarterly Journal of Economics*, 87, pp. 81–95.

Stiglitz, J. E., 1976, 'Utilitarianism and Horizontal Equity: the Case for Random Taxation', IMSSS Technical Report No. 214, Stanford University.

Stouffer, S. (with E. A. Suchman, L. C. De Vinney, S. Star and R. M. Williams Jr), 1949, *The American Soldier*, Princeton: Princeton University Press.

Strasnick, S., 1976, 'Social Choice Theory and the Derivation of Rawls' Difference Principle', *Journal of Philosophy*, 73, pp. 85–99.

1978, 'Extended Sympathy Comparisons and the Basis of Social Choice Theory', *Theory and Decision*, 10, pp. 311–28.

Strotz, R. H., 1956, 'Myopia and Inconsistency in Dynamic Utility Maximization', *Review of Economic Studies*, 23, pp. 165–80.

Suppes, Patrick, 1966, 'Formal Models of Grading Principles', *Synthèse*, 16, pp. 284–306.

Suzumura, K., 1978, 'on the Consistency of Libertarian Claims', *Review of Economic Studies*, 45, pp. 329–42.

Taylor, Charles, 1977, 'What is Human Agency?', in *The Self: Psychological and Philosophical Issues*, edited by T. Mischel, Oxford: Blackwell.

Thomson, Judith J., 1976, 'Self-defence and Rights', *The Lindley Lecture*, University of Kansas.

Tinbergen, Jan, 1957, 'Welfare Economics and Income Distribution', *American Economic Review*, Papers and Proceedings, 47 (May), pp. 490–503.

Varian, H. R., 1974, 'Equity, Envy and Efficiency', *Journal of Economic Theory*, 9, pp. 63–91.

Veyne, P., 1976, *Le Pain et le Cirque*, Paris: Seuil.

Vickrey, W. S., 1945, 'Measuring Marginal Utility by Reactions to Risk', *Econometrica*, 13, pp. 319–33.

   1960, 'Utility, Strategy, and Social Decision Rules', *Quarterly Journal of Economics*, 74, pp. 507–35.

Von Neumann, J. and Morgenstern, O., 1944, *Theory of Games and Economic Behaviour*, Princeton: Princeton University Press; 3rd edition – 1953.

Von Weiszäcker, C. C., 1971, 'Notes on Endogenous Change of Taste', *Journal of Economic Theory*, 3, pp. 345–72.

Warnock, G. J., 1971, *The Object of Morality*, London: Methuen & Co.

Watzlawick, P., 1978, *The Language of Change*, New York: Basic Books.

Weiss, L., 1976, 'The Desirability of Cheating Incentives and Randomness in the Optimal Income Tax', *Journal of Political Economy*, 84, pp. 1343–52.

Weitzman, M., 1978, 'Optimal Rewards for Economic Regulation', *American Economic Review*, 68, pp. 683–91.

Williams, B. A. O., 1972, *Morality: An Introduction to Ethics*, New York: Harper & Row. Also published: Harmondsworth: Pelican Books, 1973; Cambridge: Cambridge University Press, 1976.

   1973, 'A Critique of Utilitarianism', in Smart and Williams 1973.

   1976a, 'Persons, Character and Morality', in *The Identities of Persons*, edited by A. Rorty, Berkeley: University of California Press, pp. 197–216. Reprinted in Williams 1981.

   1976b, 'Utilitarianism and Moral Self-Indulgence', in *Contemporary British Philosophy*, Series 4, edited by H. D. Lewis, London: Allen and Unwin, pp. 306–21. Reprinted in Williams 1981.

   1978, *Descartes – The Project of Pure Enquiry*, Harmondsworth: Pelican.

   1981, *Moral Luck*, Cambridge: Cambridge University Press.

Wollheim, R., 1973, 'John Stuart Mill and the Limits of State Action', *Social Research*, 40, pp. 1–30.